2006 Edition
Tourism Market Trends

Americas

D1404608

World Tourism Organization
Capitán Haya 42, 28020 Madrid, Spain
Tel: (+34) 915678100; Fax: (+34) 915713733
E-mail: omt@unwto.org
Web: www.unwto.org

Copyright © 2007 World Tourism Organization
Calle Capitán Haya, 42
28020 Madrid, Spain

Tourism Market Trends: Americas
ISBN-13: 978-92-844-1215-0

Published and printed by the World Tourism Organization, Madrid, Spain
First printing in July 2007
All rights reserved

World Tourism Organization
Calle Capitán Haya, 42
28020 Madrid, Spain
Tel.: (+34) 915 678 100
Fax: (+34) 915 713 733
Website: www.unwto.org
Email: omt@unwto.org

Foreword

This report has been prepared by the World Tourism Organization's (UNWTO's) Market Trends, Trade and Competitiveness Section. Chapters I and II, Highlights and Quantitative Analysis of Tourism Performance, were drafted by members of The Travel Business Partnership, led by UNWTO Consultant Nancy Cockerell. UNWTO's Regional Representation for the Americas also made a valuable contribution, as did the organization's Panel of Experts from the Americas, which monitors tourism trends and developments on a regular basis for the three times yearly *UNWTO World Tourism Barometer*.

Except where otherwise indicated, the data presented was gathered by the UNWTO Secretariat from the official institutions of the respective countries and territories. Quantitative data has been supplied by National Tourism Administrations (NTAs), National Tourism Organizations (NTOs), statistical offices, national banks and international organizations.

UNWTO wishes to express its sincere gratitude to all those who have participated in the elaboration of this report for their valuable cooperation, in particular to the organizations and individuals involved from the different countries and territories. It welcomes the active involvement of all countries, as well as their comments and suggestions on the design and contents of this series.

Explanation of symbols and conventions used

*	=	provisional figure or data
..	=	figure or data not (yet) available
0	=	rounded figure where the original figure is lower than 0.5 (-0 when rounding a negative figure)
0.0	=	rounded figure where the original figure is lower than 0.05 (-0.0 when rounding a negative figure)

|	=	change of series
(000)	=	thousand
mn	=	million (1,000,000)
bn	=	billion (1,000,000,000)

Due to rounding, some totals may not correspond exactly with the sum of the separate figures.

Table of Contents

The *Tourism Market Trends, 2006 Edition* series

Tourism Market Trends is one of UNWTO's regular series of reports, the objective of which is to present international tourism trends worldwide, as well as in each region, subregion and individual destination country. The full series, which was launched in 2001, comprises six volumes. The first, *World Overview & Tourism Topics*, provides an overview of global tourism trends, and the five regional volumes highlight international tourism trends in each of the UNWTO world regions – Africa, the Americas, Asia and the Pacific, Europe and the Middle East (including North Africa).

Some changes have been made to the structure of the *Tourism Market Trends* series. Each regional volume now includes the following:

- Section I, Highlights, provides a summary of key trends and developments in tourism in the region, stressing the main factors influencing trends in 2005.

- Section II, Quantitative Analysis of Tourism Performance, includes a more in-depth assessment of trends in the region and its subregions, in terms of international tourist arrivals and international tourism receipts, as well as a breakdown of inbound tourism by region of origin, transport mode and purpose of visit. Statistical trends in outbound tourism are also presented, including data on international tourism expenditure, volume of trips abroad and outbound flows by region of origin/destination.

- Section III, Statistical Trends by Destination Country, comprises detailed statistical results for the individual countries and/or territories of the region. For each country the following information is included (to the extent that data is available):

    - A summary table including the following data series:

        - International arrivals: different categories of inbound tourism;
        - Tourism accommodation: room capacity and number of nights (for inbound and domestic tourism);
        - Trips abroad (outbound tourism);
        - International tourism receipts and expenditure;
        - Various economic and general indicators.

    - Detailed tables on arrivals and nights broken down by country of origin/source market.

- Each of the six volumes concludes with an annex comprising detailed tables containing the latest yearly data on international tourist arrivals and international tourism receipts (in US dollars and in euros) for all countries worldwide for which data is available. Information is also provided on methodologies, concepts and definitions, as well as on sources of the data and other information.

Care should be taken in interpreting the data presented in these reports. In particular, the following should be noted:

- In accordance with the nature of the data provided by the countries and territories, the focus is on inbound tourism. Outbound tourism trends are largely derived from the same inbound-oriented data except for countries that monitor outbound departures.

- The main focus of the analysis, and corresponding tables, is on medium-term rather than on short-term trends and developments. For short-term trends, please refer to the *UNWTO World Tourism Barometer*, which is published three times a year (in January,

June and October). Each issue contains three regular sections: an overview of short-term tourism data from destination and generating countries and air transport; the results of the latest survey among the UNWTO Panel of Tourism Experts, providing an evaluation of and prospects for short-term tourism performance; and selected economic data relevant for tourism. (For further information, refer to the annex or to UNWTO's website at <www.unwto.org/facts/menu.html>).

- The reports generally reflect the data collected by the UNWTO Secretariat for the current edition. However, data is often still provisional and may be updated or revised by the reporting countries at a later stage without further notice. When making references to the data contained in the reports, it is therefore advisable to ensure that the statistics quoted are the most up to date available

- For the world and (sub)regional aggregates (totals, subtotals), estimates are included to make allowance for those countries and territories that do not yet have final full-year data, or which have estimated full-year results. The data presented for the individual countries, however, reflects what has been reported for each country and does not include estimates made by the UNWTO Secretariat.

- The UNWTO Secretariat is aware of the limitations of tourism data. Despite considerable progress made in recent years, statistics are rarely uniform since definitions and data collection methodologies tend to differ from one country to another. This means that the international comparability of statistical data still leaves a lot to be desired.

I

Highlights: Americas

I Highlights: Americas
Summary of Key Trends and Developments

I.1 The Americas in the Context of World Tourism

Terrorism, natural disasters, health scares, oil price rises, exchange rate fluctuations and economic and political uncertainties – these were just some of the issues facing the tourism industry in 2005. Yet international tourist arrivals worldwide beat all expectations, reaching 802 million and, at the same time, achieving an all-time record. The estimated increase reflects a staggering 40 million additional arrivals – of which more than 16 million in Europe, 11 million in Asia and the Pacific, 7.5 million in the Americas, 3 million in Africa and 2 million in the Middle East.

The 2005 total of 802 million arrivals represents an increase of more than 5% worldwide – a consolidation of the bumper growth achieved in 2004 (+10%). Although world tourism growth was much more moderate in 2005, it was still more than one percentage point above the long-term average annual growth rate of 4%.

Results by region show that Europe recorded the weakest growth in percentage terms (+4%) although, as already stated, this translated into a higher volume of arrivals. Africa registered the strongest arrivals growth (+9%), ahead of Asia and the Pacific (+8%), the Middle East (+6%) and the Americas (+6%).

Worldwide, international tourism receipts totalled some US$ 676 billion in 2005, up US$ 47 billion in absolute terms. Most regions and subregions shared in the increase. Europe gained an additional US$ 20 billion, raising receipts to just US$ 349 billion – 52% of the world total. The Americas improved results by US$ 12 billion to US$ 145 billion – a 21% share – and Asia and the Pacific added US$ 11 billion, taking the regional total to US$ 134 billion, or a 20% share.

Estimates based on available data for the respective regions point to an increase of US$ 3 billion to US$ 22 billion for Africa and a rise of US$ 1 billion to US$ 26 billion for the Middle East, representing 3% and 4% of the world total respectively.

Inbound leaders

In terms of reported tourist arrivals (49 million in 2005), the USA ranks third in the world, behind France and Spain, but in terms of international tourism receipts it ranks first (with US$ 82 billion). In the Americas, the USA is followed in terms of arrivals by Mexico (22 million), in seventh place worldwide, and in terms of receipts by Canada (US$ 14 billion), in 12th place worldwide. The most important destinations in South America in terms of arrivals are Brazil (with 5 million arrivals), Argentina (4 million) and Chile (2 million), while in the Caribbean, the Dominican Republic and Puerto Rico with nearly 4 million arrivals each, followed by Cuba, with 2 million, led the league table.

Outbound leaders

The USA ranked third behind Germany and United Kingdom among the world's outbound tourism markets in 2005 – its tourists spent US$ 63.5 billion abroad, following Germans' (US$ 77.4 billion) and Brittan's' (US$ 66.5). Other countries from the Americas in the top 50 were Canada in 9th place (spending US$ 21.1 billion), Mexico in 13rd place (US$ 13.3 billion), Brazil in 31st place (US$ 4.7 billion) and Argentina in 35th place (US$ 4 billion).

I.2   Overall Performance

In both 2004 and 2005, international tourist arrivals in countries of the Americas increased slightly faster than the world average. This was a welcome improvement after the declines experienced in 2001, 2002 and 2003. In both years, Central and South America performed better than North America and the Caribbean.

The improved performance can broadly be attributed to the strength of the world economy. Global GDP has been growing at its fastest in over 20 years. With the removal of geopolitical and economic constraints, a growing number of countries are becoming significant tourism-generating markets. At the same time, the cost of travelling has been falling in real terms, due especially, but not solely to the emergence of no-frills/low-cost airline services. The internet is making those falling prices and travel options more transparent.

Within the Americas, increased prosperity and greater social and economic integration has been coupled with relative isolation from the political troubles and natural disasters, which have afflicted tourism across the world. For US citizens – regionally by far the most important market – worried by the risks of travelling further afield in a hostile world, this has been no small consideration. However, many tourist resorts around the Caribbean and the Gulf of Mexico were seriously damaged by hurricanes in 2004 and 2005. Hurricane Katrina devastated New Orleans at the end of August 2005, Hurricane Rita struck the Turks and Caicos Islands and Texas at the end of September, and Hurricane Wilma struck the Caribbean coast of Mexico and Central America in October.

A broad range of factors are sustaining the increases in inbound and outbound travel in Latin American countries. These include increased income from growing oil prices (notably for Venezuela, Mexico and Ecuador), increased minerals and agricultural commodities prices (notably for Argentina, Brazil, Chile and Peru), the strength of the national currencies associated with these prices, an all-round improvement in macro-economic conditions (including higher rates of GDP growth and lower rates of inflation in a region formerly chronically afflicted by runaway prices), and higher rates of migration (and not just to the USA). The benefits of financial stability to investment in tourism and day-to-day operations can scarcely be understated.

International tourist arrivals

Arrivals in the Americas increased by 11% in 2004 and 6% in 2005 to a new all-time peak of 133 million, overtaking the 128 million peak value of 2000. These arrivals represented 17% of the world total (down from 19% in 2000 and 21% in 1990). However, as mentioned above, arrivals in Central and South America grew substantially faster than those in North America and the Caribbean.

Americas 2005:   International Tourist Arrivals (ITA): 133 million
International Tourism Receipts (ITR): US$ 145 billion

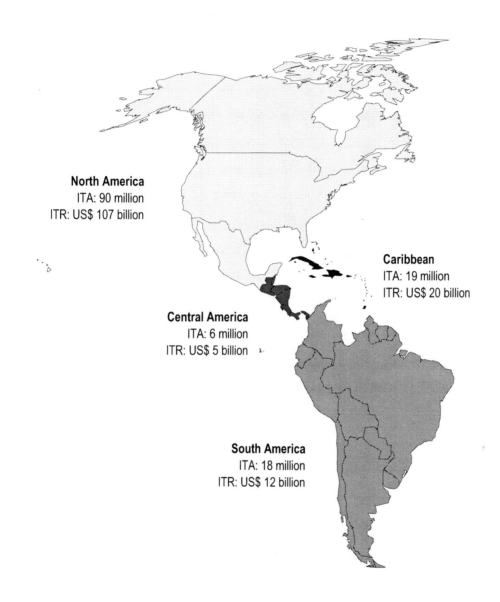

North America
ITA: 90 million
ITR: US$ 107 billion

Caribbean
ITA: 19 million
ITR: US$ 20 billion

Central America
ITA: 6 million
ITR: US$ 5 billion

South America
ITA: 18 million
ITR: US$ 12 billion

North America

In 2005, North America received nearly 90 million tourists, or over 68% of total arrivals in the Americas. The subregion reported growth of less than 5%, compared with 11% in 2004 – but much of the increase of 2004 can be attributed to the recovery after three years of decline. The low US dollar conversion rate continued to attract visitors from Europe, Asia and Australia, and from elsewhere in the Americas, to the USA (which reported a 7% increase in arrivals in 2005). Conversely, the very high exchange rate of the Canadian dollar was largely responsible for a 2% decline in arrivals in Canada. Day trips from the USA (which are of course not included in the Canadian count of tourist arrivals) have been falling for several years. Arrivals in Mexico were up 11% in 2004 and 6% in 2005, reflecting the increased social and economic integration with the USA and neighbouring countries.

The Caribbean

The Caribbean received 14% of total arrivals in the continent – although this does not include the important and growing same-day visitor market generated by cruise ships. Severe weather conditions in 2004 and 2005 affected tourism in several islands like Grenada, the Cayman Islands, Haiti and Jamaica and, partly as a result, the subregion's performance was weaker than in the rest of the Americas. The Caribbean nonetheless posted increases in arrivals of 6% in 2004 and 4% in 2005, sustained by the strength of the US economy and favourable exchange rates against the euro and pound sterling, encouraging visitors from the major European source markets.

The three most important tourism destinations in the subregion all reported healthy increases in arrivals for the second year running: Puerto Rico (+4%), the Dominican Republic (+7%) and Cuba (+12%). Several of the smaller destinations recorded double-digit increases – including Anguilla, Haiti, St Vincent and the Grenadines and the Turks and Caicos Islands.

Central America

Central America received only 5% of all tourists to the Americas, but arrivals have been growing rapidly – they were up 13% in both 2004 and 2005, to 6 million. This growth is being shared by most of the countries in the region – in 2004 and 2005 only Honduras and Belize failed to report double-digit increases.

South America

The South American subregion has also recorded two years of exceptionally rapid growth: arrivals increased by 17% in 2004 and 12% in 2005, to over 18 million. The subregion now represents 14% of total arrivals in the Americas, up from 12% in 2000 and 8% in 1990. Many countries in the subregion recorded double-digit increases (ranging up to the 45% for Venezuela) in both 2004 and 2005.

Generating markets

The Americas benefits from having the third greatest tourism source market in the world, the USA. US tourists travel mostly within the region, especially to neighbouring countries. Moreover intraregional travel, i.e. arrivals from markets within the Americas account for 73% of all arrivals in the region. The weakness of the US market has tended to obscure the remarkable growth of travel between other countries within the region – not just between neighbouring countries, but between countries in different subregions of the Americas. But the recovery of the large US market was also a major factor in the growth of tourism in the Americas in 2004 and 2005.

Arrivals from Europe – the principal long-haul source for most American destinations – were generally strong in 2004 and 2005. In particular, the decline of the US dollar against the sterling pound, the euro and other European currencies in 2004 made the USA a more price-competitive destination. Elsewhere in the Americas, individual countries reported very large increases in arrivals from individual European countries, no doubt reflecting the marketing efforts of their tourism organizations and of individual operators.

World Tourism Organization ©

Many countries also reported large increases in arrivals from Asia and the Pacific. Growing commercial relations between Asian and American countries boosting, not just business travel, but the leisure travel that follows from familiarity. In some cases historical relationships, such as those between Canada and North-East Asia, and between India and the Caribbean, are being rebuilt. An increasing number of countries have been granted Approved Destination Status (ADS) by China, and arrivals from China are rising rapidly, but perhaps not as rapidly as had been expected for. Some destinations were also disappointed by arrivals from Japan in 2005, but this may also have stemmed from exaggerated expectations, following the large increases reported in 2004.

International tourism receipts

International tourism receipts in the Americas, like arrivals, turned up in 2004 after three years of decline, and continued to rise in 2005. In local currencies, constant prices, they rose by 12% in 2004 and 4% in 2005 to US$ 145 billion – over 21% of the world total.

As was the case with arrivals, receipts were up in 2005 much more strongly in Central and South America than in North America and the Caribbean, in US dollar terms. However, because of the appreciation of the currencies of the major commodities producers of South America, receipts in local currency real terms were up only 1.7% in South America – much less than the 4% recorded for North America and the 11% recorded for Central America, and only slightly above than the Caribbean's 1.6%.

I.3 Main Factors Influencing Tourism in 2005

Economic trends

The world economy has been growing faster than at any time in nearly a quarter of a century. Gross domestic product (GDP) worldwide increased in real terms by just under 5% in 2005, almost as fast as in 2004. In the Americas, GDP growth slackened more sharply, from 4.4% to 4%, due to significant slowdowns in the regions' largest economies, including the USA, Canada, Mexico and Brazil. However, many of the smaller economies in the region continued to grow rapidly, and the increase in oil and other commodities prices shifted purchasing power in favour of the countries concerned – shifts which are of course not reflected in GDP at constant prices.

Exchange rates

The shift in the purchasing power of the US dollar seems to have been a significant influence on the choice of destinations in 2004 and 2005. The US dollar fell particularly heavily against the euro in 2004, and although it recovered a little over the course of 2005, the average exchange rate over the year as a whole was the same as in 2004. However, the US dollar continued to fall against the currencies of many of the world's major commodities producers, especially, in the Americas, against the Canadian dollar, the Brazilian real and the Chilean peso. It also drifted down against several other American currencies, in real if not always in nominal terms. On the other hand, the Argentine peso remained stable against the US dollar at a very low rate.

Oil prices

In general, the rise in international oil prices has not yet had a significant effect on tourism demand. In a very competitive environment, airlines have been reluctant to pass on increased fuel prices in ticket prices and surcharges, and to the extent that they have done so, the effect on demand seems to have been limited. In more particular circumstances, the effects have been felt.

On the other hand, car-based tours from the USA into Canada, which may involve long-distance travel in both countries, are reported to have been affected – highlighting the common perception that high energy prices have greater impact on land-based travel than on air transport. But if the increases in oil prices are sustained, airlines can be expected to raise prices, especially if underlying demand remains strong.

Interest rates

Another factor which does not seem to have had a significant effect on tourism demand, but which may yet do so, is the increase in interest rates. These have been at historically extremely low levels, but are now generally rising around the world. This may have a particularly strong effect on disposable incomes and willingness to spend in markets, where consumers are particularly heavily indebted.

Travel formalities

Working against a longer-term trend, worldwide, for visa requirements and travel formalities to become easier and more routine, the USA – which is involved in well over a third of all international travel in the Americas – has tightened up on its security precautions since 2001. Travellers from many countries are finding it more difficult to obtain visas, and the process has become lengthier and more onerous. These difficulties, as well as delays at immigration posts, have been widely reported.

There has also been some confusion resulting from media reports about the planned US Western Hemisphere Travel Initiative, under which all travellers (including US citizens) entering or leaving the USA from Canada and countries in the Caribbean – and who have hitherto been exempt – will need passports or equivalent travel documents. The requirements are not due to come into force until December 2006, but this has not always been made clear and has impacted 2005 travel.

In 2004 several Central American countries standardized their entry procedures at their land borders (El Salvador, Guatemala, Honduras and Nicaragua). Mexico introduced a digital visa system for visitors from Central and South America entering through the Southern border of the country.

Airline services

The transformation and growth of airline services are having major effects on tourism development in individual destinations. Traditional flag carriers and the major carriers in North America continue to struggle (five of the seven largest US carriers operated under Chapter 11 proceedings for at least part of 2005). This is more than counterbalanced by the increase in low-cost services – but the transition is not often smooth. Shortages of capacity were reported in some areas and on some routes in 2005. Notable progress has been made in liberalizing airways in Latin America, with a consequent wave of new low-cost airline services.

Ocean cruising

One sector that was negatively affected by 2005's hurricanes, notably Katrina and Rita, was the cruise business. Prior to Katrina, the industry was confidently predicting a wealthy growth of cruise passengers worldwide. But the decision by the US Government to charter three ships from Carnival Corporation for the period October 2005 to March 2006, to house emergency services personnel following the hurricane, meant a drop in capacity of 7,000 berths, or over 2 million for the six-month period.

Nevertheless, cruising continues to gain in popularity, especially as it is perceived to be a safe option in troubled times. And some parts of the Americas, including Mexico, Bermuda and a number of Caribbean islands, have seen strong growth from the sector and are expecting a good 2006. Disembarkations in some other Caribbean destinations have been affected by hurricanes and repairs to docking facilities, but there have been large increases in embarkations on both the Atlantic and Pacific coasts of North America. Services on both the Atlantic and Pacific coasts of South America are also increasing.

II

Quantitative Analysis of Tourism Performance

II   Quantitative Analysis of Tourism Performance

II.1   Tourism Trends in the Region

II.1.1   Inbound Tourism

For tourism in the Americas, as for tourism worldwide, 2005 was the second year of recovery after the three dismal years of 2001 to 2003. Arrivals throughout the region rose by 6% in 2005, after an 11% increase in 2004, to 133 million. However, as the graph below suggests, these increases have not yet brought arrivals back to the levels implied by their long-term trend. This suggests that, given favourable conditions, the Americas can look forward to several more years of rapid growth – i.e. of growth above the long-term trend rate.

Such has been the experience of the last few years. The tourism industry (and its customers) has come to expect catastrophes, and 2005 was no exception. If the Indian Ocean tsunami of 26 December 2004 was the most appalling disaster, the focus in the Americas was on the hurricane season. If 2004 had already been a negative one, affecting many destinations in the Caribbean. 2005 was worse. Among the many tropical storms of the year, Hurricane Dennis struck Grenada, Haiti and the Cayman Islands – all of which had been hit in 2004 – and other islands in July.

At the end of August Katrina devastated New Orleans and its neighbours, effectively wiping out, for the time being, the local tourism industry. Then, at the end of September, Hurricane Rita struck Texas, and in October Wilma struck the Caribbean coasts of Mexico and Central America.

However devastating such disasters have been for local business, the tourism industry in general has shown a remarkable ability to shrug them off.

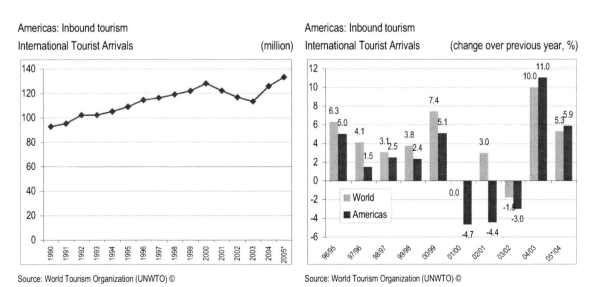

Americas: Inbound tourism
International Tourist Arrivals (million)

Americas: Inbound tourism
International Tourist Arrivals (change over previous year, %)

Source: World Tourism Organization (UNWTO) ©

Source: World Tourism Organization (UNWTO) ©

International tourist arrivals

International tourist arrivals in the Americas reached 133 million in 2005. The rates of growth in 2004 and 2005 – +11% and +6% respectively – were similar to the rates of growth in arrivals worldwide (+10% and +5%). However, in the longer term, arrivals in the Americas have not been growing as fast as those in other regions and the Americas' share of world arrivals fell from 21% in 1990 to under 17% in 2005.

World and regions: Inbound tourism
International Tourist Arrivals   (change 05*/04, %)

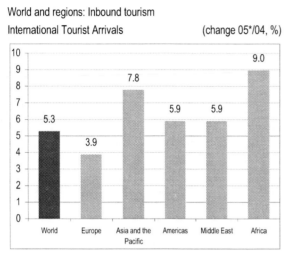

Source: World Tourism Organization (UNWTO) ©

Americas: Inbound tourism
International Tourist Arrivals   (share in world total, %)

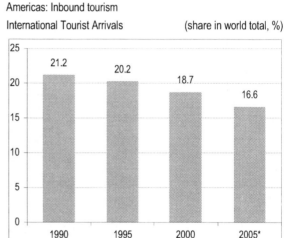

Source: World Tourism Organization (UNWTO) ©

Americas and subregions: Inbound tourism
International Tourist Arrivals, 2005*   (share, %)

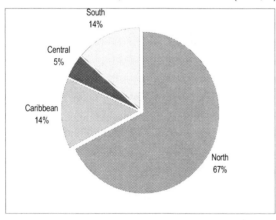
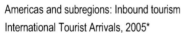

Source: World Tourism Organization (UNWTO) ©

Americas and subregions: Inbound tourism
International Tourist Arrivals   (change 05*/04, %)

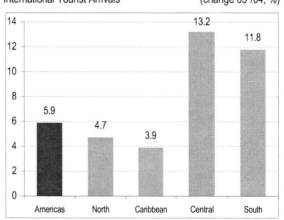

Source: World Tourism Organization (UNWTO) ©

North America – the USA, Canada and Mexico – accounts for two thirds of international tourist arrivals in the Americas. However, its share of American arrivals has been diminishing over the years. Arrivals in the subregion grew by only 2.5% a year between 1990 and 2000 and, in 2005, had still not recovered to their 2000 peak level.

By contrast, arrivals in South America grew by 7% a year between 1990 and 2000 and in 2005 were 19% higher than they had been in 2000. Those in Central America grew even faster, by over 8% a year from 1990 to 2000 and, more remarkably – given the slack growth or declines elsewhere – just as fast in 2000-2005. In 2005, they were 47% higher than they had been in 2000. Growth in the Caribbean has been more moderate, but still outpaced that in North America. Arrivals were up 4% a year in the period 1990-2000, and in 2005 they were 10% higher than they had been in 2000.

World Tourism Organization ©

International Tourist Arrivals by (Sub)region

	International Tourist Arrivals								Market share (%)		Growth rate (%)		Average annual growth (%)	
								(million)						
	1990	1995	2000	2001	2002	2003	2004	2005*	2000	2005*	04/03	05*/04	90-00	00-05*
World	**438.4**	**538.5**	**684.7**	**684.4**	**704.7**	**692.2**	**761.4**	**801.6**	**100**	**100**	**10.0**	**5.3**	**4.6**	**3.2**
Americas	*92.8*	*109.0*	*128.2*	*122.2*	*116.8*	*113.3*	*125.8*	*133.2*	*18.7*	*16.6*	*11.0*	*5.9*	*3.3*	*0.8*
North America	71.7	80.7	91.5	86.4	83.3	77.4	85.8	89.9	13.4	11.2	10.9	4.7	2.5	-0.4
Caribbean	11.4	14.0	17.1	16.8	16.0	17.1	18.1	18.8	2.5	2.3	5.9	3.9	4.1	1.9
Central America	1.9	2.6	4.3	4.4	4.7	4.9	5.6	6.3	0.6	0.8	13.4	13.2	8.4	7.7
South America	7.7	11.7	15.3	14.6	12.8	13.9	16.3	18.2	2.2	2.3	17.3	11.8	7.0	3.6

Source: World Tourism Organization (UNWTO) ©   (Data as collected by UNWTO for TMT 2006 Edition)

International tourism receipts

In 2005, receipts from international tourism in the Americas reached nearly US$ 145 billion, which represented 21% of the world total. In local currency terms, at constant prices, they increased by 4% (after a 12% growth in 2004).

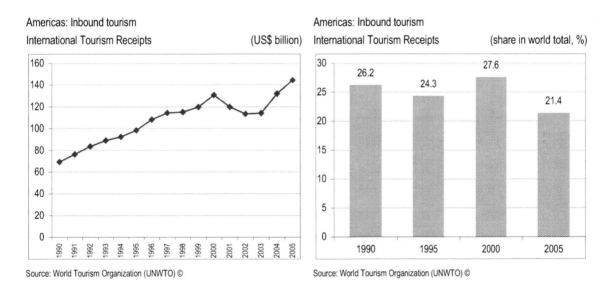

Americas: Inbound tourism
International Tourism Receipts (US$ billion)

Americas: Inbound tourism
International Tourism Receipts (share in world total, %)

Source: World Tourism Organization (UNWTO) ©   Source: World Tourism Organization (UNWTO) ©

North America accounts for an even larger share of receipts – 74% of the total for the Americas – than it does of arrivals (67%). Central and South America have smaller shares of receipts than of arrivals, but the Caribbean has a 14% share of both receipts and arrivals. North, Central and South America all saw substantial growth in receipts in 2004 and 2005, but the growth in receipts in the Caribbean was much more modest.

Receipts per arrival in the Americas were an estimated US$ 1,085 in 2005, the highest in the world. The average for North America (US$ 1,190) was slightly above the regional average, whereas Central and South America (US$ 740 and US$ 680 respectively) lagged behind the other subregions. The Caribbean matches the regional average, but the figures for individual destinations vary widely. Several Caribbean islands with upmarket tourism offers generate very high receipts per arrival.

Americas and subregions: Inbound tourism
International Tourism Receipts, 2005   (share, %)

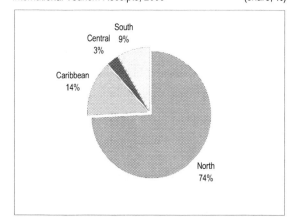

Source: World Tourism Organization (UNWTO) ©

Americas and subregions: Inbound tourism
Receipts per Arrival, 2005   (US$)

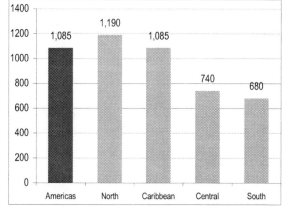

Source: World Tourism Organization (UNWTO) ©

International Tourism Receipts, Americas

	International Tourism Receipts (billion)							Change current prices (%)				Change constant prices (%)			
	1990	1995	2000	2002	2003	2004	2005*	02/01	03/02	04/03	05*/04	02/01	03/02	04/03	05*/04
Local currencies								-4.0	1.2	15.2	7.9	-6.3	-2.1	11.6	3.8
US$	69.2	98.4	130.8	113.4	114.1	132.0	144.5	-5.3	0.6	15.7	9.5	-6.8	-1.7	12.7	5.9
Euro	54.3	75.3	141.6	120.0	100.9	106.1	116.2	-10.3	-15.9	5.2	9.5	-12.3	-17.6	3.0	7.1

Source: World Tourism Organization (UNWTO) ©   (Data as collected in UNWTO database November 2006)

International Tourism Receipts by (Sub)region

	Change Local currencies, constant prices (%)					US$ (billion)		Receipts per arrival 2005*	euro (billion)		Receipts per arrival 2005*	Market share (%) 2005*
	01/00	02/01	03/02	04/03	05*/04	2004	2005*		2004	2005*		
World	-1.9	-0.5	-1.4	9.8	3.1	629.0	675.7	845	505.7	543.1	680	100
Americas	*-10.3*	*-6.3*	*-2.1*	*11.6*	*3.8*	*132.0*	*144.5*	*1,085*	*106.1*	*116.2*	*870*	*21.4*
North America	-12.8	-6.7	-4.7	12.9	4.2	98.2	107.1	1,190	79.0	86.1	955	15.8
Caribbean	-3.7	-2.6	5.5	5.0	1.6	19.3	20.4	1,085	15.5	16.4	875	3.0
Central America	-7.4	3.4	13.2	12.1	10.9	4.0	4.6	740	3.2	3.7	595	0.7
South America	3.6	-12.0	5.2	12.9	1.7	10.6	12.4	680	8.5	10.0	545	1.8

Source: World Tourism Organization (UNWTO) ©   (Data as collected in UNWTO database November 2006)

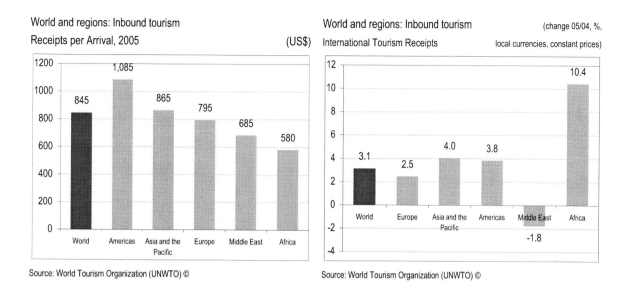

World and regions: Inbound tourism
Receipts per Arrival, 2005   (US$)

Source: World Tourism Organization (UNWTO) ©

World and regions: Inbound tourism   (change 05/04, %,
International Tourism Receipts   local currencies, constant prices)

Source: World Tourism Organization (UNWTO) ©

Inbound tourism by region of origin

International tourist arrivals from within the region – 97 million in 2005 – accounted for 73% of the total count. Arrivals from other regions totalled 32 million (a 24% share). The pattern in the Americas is therefore similar to that in the world overall, with arrivals from within the region greatly outnumbering those from further afield.

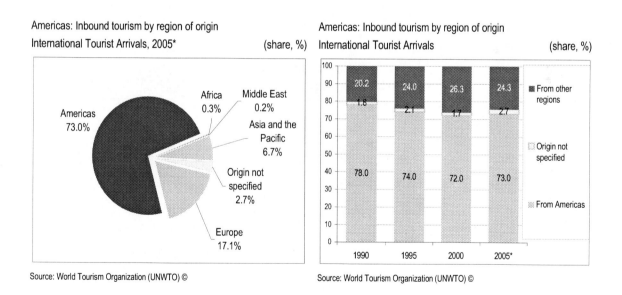

Americas: Inbound tourism by region of origin
International Tourist Arrivals, 2005*   (share, %)

Source: World Tourism Organization (UNWTO) ©

Americas: Inbound tourism by region of origin
International Tourist Arrivals   (share, %)

Source: World Tourism Organization (UNWTO) ©

The period 1995-2000 saw a trend towards a faster rise in interregional tourism (+5% a year) than in intraregional tourism (+3%). This trend was reversed in 2001, however, with very large declines in arrivals from Europe, Africa, Asia and the Pacific, and especially from the Middle East after the events of 11 September 2001 and the Afghan and Iraq wars. Contributing factors included the strength of the US dollar and the increased difficulty – perceived and real – of obtaining entry to the USA, both of which discouraged travellers to the region's principal destination.

The SARS epidemic caused a further decline in arrivals from Asia and the Pacific in 2003. However, with a relaxation of security concerns, a weaker US dollar and greater consumer confidence in economic prosperity, there were large increases in arrivals from Europe, Asia and the Pacific and Africa in 2004 and 2005 and from the Middle East in 2005. In 2005, arrivals from Europe and Africa were finally back up to their levels of 2000, but those from Asia and the Pacific were still well down on 2000 values as so were those from the Middle East.

Americas
Inbound Tourism by Region of Origin (including estimates for countries with missing data)

	International Tourist Arrivals (1000)					Market share (%)			Change (%)			Average annual growth (%)	
	1990	1995	2000	2004	2005*	1990	2000	2005*	03/02	04/03	05*/04	'95-'00	'00-'05*
Americas	**92,804**	**109,028**	**128,193**	**125,792**	**133,198**	**100**	**100**	**100**	**-3.0**	**11.0**	**5.9**	**3.3**	**0.8**
From:													
Americas	72,409	80,629	92,300	92,601	97,192	78.0	72.0	73.0	-3.5	9.8	5.0	2.7	1.0
Other regions	18,713	26,114	33,669	30,073	32,381	20.2	26.3	24.3	-1.3	12.0	7.7	5.2	-0.8
Africa	220	265	416	389	417	0.2	0.3	0.3	1.7	7.5	7.1	9.4	0.1
Asia and the Pacific	6,115	8,897	10,113	8,290	8,913	6.6	7.9	6.7	-12.0	19.3	7.5	2.6	-2.5
Europe	12,216	16,738	22,829	21,198	22,842	13.2	17.8	17.1	3.2	9.4	7.8	6.4	0.0
Middle East	163	214	311	196	209	0.2	0.2	0.2	-11.1	21.8	6.6	7.8	-7.6
Origin not specified	1,681	2,285	2,225	3,119	3,625	1.8	1.7	2.7					

Source: World Tourism Organization (UNWTO) ©   (Data as collected by UNWTO for TMT 2006 Edition)

World and regions: Inbound tourism by region of origin
International Tourist Arrivals, 2005*   (share, %)

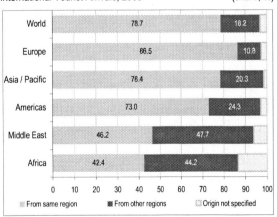

Source: World Tourism Organization (UNWTO) ©

World regions: Inbound tourism by region of origin
International Tourist Arrivals, 2005*   (million)

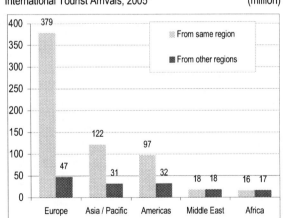

Source: World Tourism Organization (UNWTO) ©

Americas: Inbound tourism by region of origin
International Tourist Arrivals, 2005*   (million)

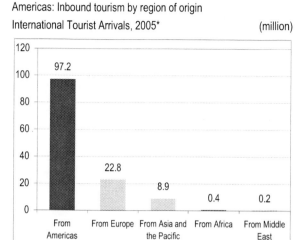

Source: World Tourism Organization (UNWTO) ©

Americas: Inbound tourism by region of origin
International Tourist Arrivals   (change 2005/2004, %)

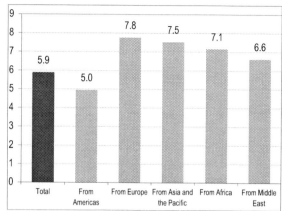

Source: World Tourism Organization (UNWTO) ©

Within the Americas, interregional arrivals are rather more important for South America (28%) and much less important for Central America (11%) than for North America and for the Caribbean (24% each). Europe continues to be, by far, the largest generating region for the Americas, accounting for 17% of total arrivals and 73% of interregional arrivals. It accounts for 24% of total arrivals in the Caribbean and for 24% in South America. Well over 90% of visitors from Asia and the Pacific and from the Middle East go to North America. About three quarters of those from Africa go to North America, but over a fifth go to South America.

Americas and subregions: Inbound tourism by region of origin
International Tourist Arrivals, 2005*   (share, %)

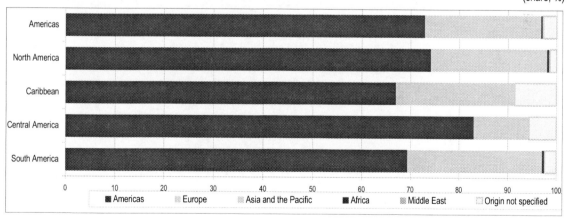

Source: World Tourism Organization (UNWTO) ©

Americas

Inbound Tourism by Region of Origin (including estimates for countries with missing data), 2005*

		Americas				
		Total	North	Caribbean	Central	South
		International Tourist Arrivals (000)				
Total		**133,198**	**89,891**	**18,802**	**6,288**	**18,217**
from:	Americas	97,192	66,736	12,600	5,224	12,632
	Other regions	32,381	21,930	4,590	710	5,152
	Europe	22,842	13,099	4,499	609	4,634
	Asia and the Pacific	8,913	8,321	77	96	419
	Africa	417	314	11	3	89
	Middle East	209	196	2	1	10
	Origin not specified	3,625	1,225	1,613	354	433
		% destination broken down by origin				
Total		100	100	100	100	100
from:	Americas	73.0	74.2	67.0	83.1	69.3
	Other regions	24.3	24.4	24.4	11.3	28.3
	Europe	17.1	14.6	23.9	9.7	25.4
	Asia and the Pacific	6.7	9.3	0.4	1.5	2.3
	Africa	0.3	0.3	0.1	0.1	0.5
	Middle East	0.2	0.2	0.0	0.0	0.1
	Origin not specified	2.7	1.4	8.6	5.6	2.4
		% origin broken down by destination				
Total		100	**67.5**	**14.1**	**4.7**	**13.7**
from:	Americas	100	68.7	13.0	5.4	13.0
	Other regions	100	67.7	14.2	2.2	15.9
	Europe	100	57.3	19.7	2.7	20.3
	Asia and the Pacific	100	93.4	0.9	1.1	4.7
	Africa	100	75.3	2.6	0.8	21.3
	Middle East	100	93.8	0.9	0.5	4.8
	Origin not specified	100	33.8	44.5	9.8	11.9

Source: World Tourism Organization (UNWTO) ©   (Data as collected by UNWTO for TMT 2006 Edition)

Inbound tourism by means of transport

In 2005, 55% of international tourists arrived in American countries by air, compared with 40% by land and 5% by water. In the most important subregion, North America, 51% arrived by air, 48% by land and only 1% by water. The figures for Central America are very similar. In South America, rather more arrived by air (57%) and water (7%) and rather fewer by land (36%). In the Caribbean islands, the breakdown was air (75%) and water (25%).

The longer-term trend is for a preference for air over land transport. Between 1990 and 2000, air travel increased its share of arrivals in the Americas by ten percentage points. However, in 2001-02, the decline in long-haul arrivals and the economic recession temporarily reversed the trend, disguising the quite dramatic impacts of the growth in low-cost airline services, the declining use of coach or bus transport for travel between the USA and Canada and the USA and Mexico, and the tighter security controls in force at US border posts.

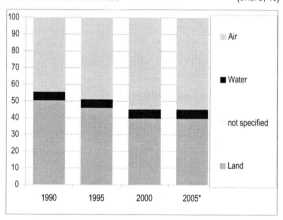

Americas: Inbound tourism by mode of transport
International Tourist Arrivals (share, %)

Source: World Tourism Organization (UNWTO) ©

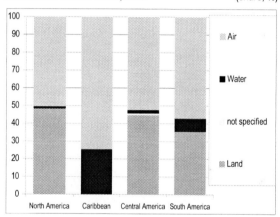

Americas and subregions: Inbound tourism by mode of transport
International Tourist Arrivals, 2005* (share, %)

Source: World Tourism Organization (UNWTO) ©

Americas

Arrivals by mode of transport (including estimates for countries with missing data)

| | International Tourist Arrivals | | | | | | Share | | | Change | | Average annual growth (%) | |
| | | | | | | (million) | | (%) | | | (%) | | |
	1990	1995	2000	2003	2004	2005*	1990	2000	2005*	04/03	05*/04	90-00	00-05*
Total	92.8	109.0	128.2	113.3	125.8	133.2	100	100	100	11.0	5.9	3.3	0.8
Air	41.4	53.3	70.4	60.0	67.4	73.1	44.6	54.9	54.9	12.3	8.4	5.5	0.7
Land	46.4	50.0	50.8	46.5	50.9	52.7	50.0	39.6	39.6	9.5	3.6	0.9	0.7
Water	4.9	5.6	6.9	6.8	7.4	7.4	5.2	5.4	5.5	9.8	-0.6	3.6	1.3
Not specified	0.2	0.0	0.1	0.0	0.1	0.1	0.2	0.1	0.0				

Source: World Tourism Organization (UNWTO) © (Data as collected by UNWTO for TMT 2006 Edition)

The growth in air travel resumed in 2003-05. Latin America in particular has seen a very large increase in the availability of low-cost airline services, but also an improvement in road access. Many Caribbean destinations are constrained by a lack of low-cost airline services, perhaps because the potential traffic does not justify the frequencies required for the conventional model of such services.

Arrivals by mode of transport (including estimates for countries with missing data), 2005*

	Total	Air	Land	Water	Not specified
International Tourist Arrivals (million)					
Americas	133.2	73.1	52.7	7.4	0.1
North America	89.9	45.4	43.4	1.1	0.0
Caribbean	18.8	14.0	0.0	4.8	0.0
Central America	6.3	3.3	2.8	0.1	0.1
South America	18.2	10.4	6.5	1.3	0.0
%					
Americas	100	54.9	39.6	5.5	0.0
North America	100	50.5	48.3	1.3	0.0
Caribbean	100	74.6	0.0	25.4	0.0
Central America	100	52.4	44.8	1.9	0.9
South America	100	57.1	35.5	7.4	0.0

Source: World Tourism Organization (UNWTO) ©   (Data as collected by UNWTO for TMT 2006 Edition)

Inbound tourism by purpose of visit

Care must be taken in interpreting data on purpose of trip, since it is well known that travellers requiring visas for a particular destination often claim to be travelling for leisure rather than business as the visa requirements are usually less strict. In addition, trips may involve more than one purpose. For instance, business and visits to friends and relatives (VFR) trips often include important leisure components. The pattern is also obscured by the high proportion of trips to North America (41%) whose purpose is not specified.

Leisure, recreation and holidays accounted for 59 million arrivals in 2005 – 44% of the total. It is therefore the main purpose of visit to the Americas, albeit to a lesser extent than in most other regions and subregions of the world, where leisure accounts for more than half of all arrivals. The share of leisure in trips to the Caribbean is as high as 85%.

In second place, with more than 22 million arrivals (17% of the total), comes 'VFR, health, religion and other purposes'. Business travel comes third, with a share of 11%.

The share of leisure trips has tended to increase in recent years. Business travel was particularly badly affected from 2001-2003 and, although it staged a partial recovery in 2004-05, numbers are still lower than they were in 2000.

Americas: Inbound tourism by purpose of visit
International Tourist Arrivals   (share, %)

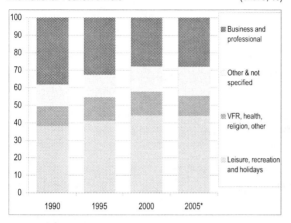

Source: World Tourism Organization (UNWTO) ©

Americas and subregions: Inbound tourism by purpose of visit
International Tourist Arrivals, 2005*   (share, %)

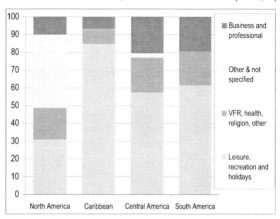

Source: World Tourism Organization (UNWTO) ©

Americas

Arrivals by purpose of visit (including estimates for countries with missing data)

	International Tourist Arrivals						Share			Change		Average annual growth (%)	
						(million)		(%)			(%)		
	1990	1995	2000	2003	2004	2005*	1990	2000	2005*	04/03	05*/04	90-00	00-05*
Total	92.8	109.0	128.2	113.3	125.8	133.2	100	100	100	11.0	5.9	3.3	0.8
Leisure, recreation and holidays	35.5	44.8	56.8	49.9	55.0	58.6	38.3	44.3	44.0	10.1	6.7	4.8	0.6
Business and professional	10.3	14.6	17.3	13.0	15.1	15.1	11.2	13.5	11.4	15.9	0.5	5.3	-2.6
VFR, health, religion, other	11.5	14.2	18.5	18.6	20.7	22.2	12.4	14.5	16.7	10.9	7.4	4.9	3.7
Not specified	35.4	35.4	35.6	31.7	35.1	37.2	38.1	27.8	27.9				

Source: World Tourism Organization (UNWTO) ©   (Data as collected by UNWTO for TMT 2006 Edition)

Arrivals by purpose of visit (including estimates for countries with missing data), 2005*

	Total	Leisure, recreation and holidays	Business and professional	VFR, health, religion, other	Not specified
	International Tourist Arrivals (million)				
Americas	133.2	58.6	15.1	22.2	37.2
North America	89.9	27.9	9.0	15.9	37.1
Caribbean	18.8	15.9	1.3	1.6	0.0
Central America	6.3	3.6	1.3	1.2	0.2
South America	18.2	11.2	3.5	3.5	0.0
	%				
Americas	100	44.0	11.4	16.7	27.9
North America	100	31.0	10.1	17.7	41.2
Caribbean	100	84.8	6.8	8.4	0.0
Central America	100	57.4	20.5	19.7	2.5
South America	100	61.4	19.4	19.2	0.0

Source: World Tourism Organization (UNWTO) ©   (Data as collected by UNWTO for TMT 2006 Edition)

II.1.2 Outbound Tourism

Outbound tourism by (sub) region of destination

In 2005, the Americas generated 136 million international tourist arrivals worldwide, 17% of the world total. Outbound tourism in 2001 to 2003 had declined owing to the combined effects of social and political instability, the sluggish economy, the consequences of the war in Iraq and other factors, but it increased by 12% in 2004 and by 5% in 2005.

The lion's share of the international tourism generated by the Americas remains within the region (72%) and is distributed as follows: North America 49%, the Caribbean and South America 9% each and Central America 4%. Intraregional flows grew by 10% in 2004 and 5% in 2005. Outbound tourism to other regions was up much more, by 19% in 2004 and 6% in 2005. Arrivals from the Americas in Asia and the Pacific were up 28% and 11% in the two years, those in the Middle East by 22% and 9%, in Africa by 21% and 11%, and in Europe by 16% and 4%.

World and regions: Outbound tourism by region of destination
International Tourist Arrivals, 2005* (share, %)

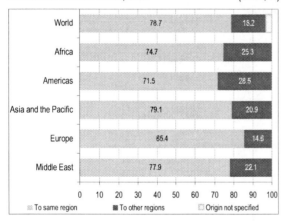

Source: World Tourism Organization (UNWTO) ©

World regions: Outbound tourism by region of destination
International Tourist Arrivals, 2005* (million)

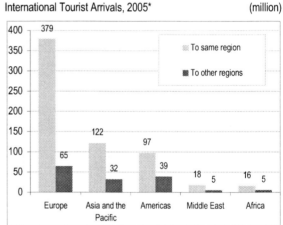

Source: World Tourism Organization (UNWTO) ©

Americas: Outbound tourism by region of destination
International Tourist Arrivals, 2005* (share, %)

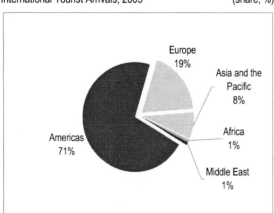

Source: World Tourism Organization (UNWTO) ©

Americas: Outbound tourism by region of destination
International Tourist Arrivals (share, %)

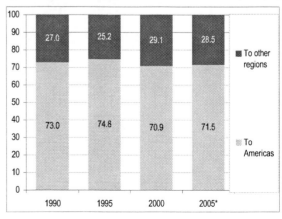

Source: World Tourism Organization (UNWTO) ©

Americas: Outbound tourism by region of destination
International Tourist Arrivals, 2005* (million)

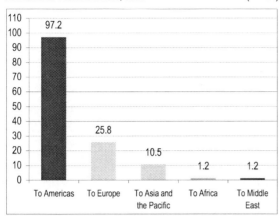

Source: World Tourism Organization (UNWTO) ©

Americas: Outbound tourism by region of destination
International Tourist Arrivals (change, %)

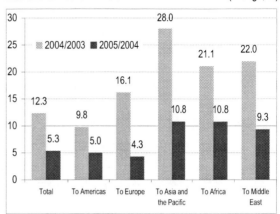

Source: World Tourism Organization (UNWTO) ©

Americas

Outbound Tourism by (sub)region of destination (including estimates for countries with missing data)

	International Tourist Arrivals (1000)					Market share (%)			Growth rate (%)		Average annual growth (%)	
	1990	1995	2000	2004	2005*	1990	2000	2005*	04/03	05*/04	90-00	00-05*
Total	99,238	107,740	130,274	129,007	135,899	100	100	100	12.3	5.3	2.8	0.8
To:												
Americas	*72,409*	*80,629*	*92,300*	*92,601*	*97,192*	*73.0*	*70.9*	*71.5*	*9.8*	*5.0*	*2.5*	*1.0*
North America	56,650	60,008	65,911	64,420	66,736	57.1	50.6	49.1	9.0	3.6	1.5	0.2
Caribbean	8,018	9,137	11,009	12,073	12,600	8.1	8.5	9.3	6.9	4.4	3.2	2.7
Central America	1,677	2,137	3,676	4,752	5,224	1.7	2.8	3.8	14.7	9.9	8.2	7.3
South America	6,064	9,347	11,704	11,356	12,632	6.1	9.0	9.3	15.6	11.2	6.8	1.5
Interregional	*26,829*	*27,110*	*37,974*	*36,406*	*38,707*	*27.0*	*29.1*	*28.5*	*19.3*	*6.3*	*3.5*	*0.4*
Europe	21,364	19,947	27,786	24,756	25,815	21.5	21.3	19.0	16.1	4.3	2.7	-1.5
Northern Europe	5,109	5,265	6,969	6,393	6,337	5.1	5.3	4.7	8.8	-0.9	3.2	-1.9
Western Europe	10,426	8,484	12,453	9,581	9,846	10.5	9.6	7.2	9.1	2.8	1.8	-4.6
Central/Eastern Europe	701	990	1,334	1,837	1,967	0.7	1.0	1.4	21.7	7.1	6.6	8.1
Southern Europe	5,128	5,208	7,030	6,944	7,665	5.2	5.4	5.6	34.8	10.4	3.2	1.7
Asia and the Pacific	4,700	5,986	8,290	9,458	10,478	4.7	6.4	7.7	28.0	10.8	5.8	4.8
North-East Asia	2,403	3,020	4,086	4,839	5,413	2.4	3.1	4.0	39.3	11.9	5.5	5.8
South-East Asia	1,258	1,670	2,412	2,619	2,891	1.3	1.9	2.1	22.1	10.4	6.7	3.7
Oceania	773	886	1,149	1,094	1,117	0.8	0.9	0.8	4.4	2.0	4.0	-0.6
South Asia	266	410	643	906	1,058	0.3	0.5	0.8	25.8	16.7	9.2	10.5
Africa	481	648	1,027	1,121	1,241	0.5	0.8	0.9	21.1	10.8	7.9	3.9
North Africa	137	148	217	190	204	0.1	0.2	0.2	39.4	7.6	4.7	-1.2
West Africa	64	105	139	202	228	0.1	0.1	0.2	17.0	13.0	8.1	10.4
Central Africa	25	32	43	58	63	0.0	0.0	0.0	49.9	7.8	5.5	7.9
East Africa	173	184	332	340	376	0.2	0.3	0.3	25.0	10.7	6.7	2.5
Southern Africa	82	179	296	331	370	0.1	0.2	0.3	8.0	11.8	13.6	4.6
Middle East	284	529	871	1,072	1,172	0.3	0.7	0.9	22.0	9.3	11.9	6.1

Source: World Tourism Organization (UNWTO) © (Data as collected by UNWTO for TMT 2006 Edition)

Europe received 26 million arrivals from the Americas in 2005 – i.e. two thirds of all interregional arrivals from the Americas. Western Europe still receives 38% of American arrivals, but the shares of Southern Europe and (from a much smaller base) Central and Eastern Europe have been growing rapidly.

Asia and the Pacific received 10.5 million arrivals – roughly a quarter of interregional flows from the Americas. Of these, North-East Asia – i.e. largely China, Japan, the Republic of Korea, Hong Kong (China) and Taiwan (province of China) – received the lion's share (52%). South-East Asia received 28%, South Asia 10% and Oceania (whose share has been falling) 11%.

Africa and the Middle East received much smaller numbers – a little more than 1 million arrivals each from the Americas.

International tourism expenditure

International tourism expenditure (including that attributed to same-day visitors) by residents of the Americas amounted to US$ 115 billion – 17% of the world total, compared with Europe's 52%, Asia and the Pacific's 21%, and Africa 1.6% and the Middle East's 3.4%.

Among the world's top 50 spenders on international tourism, the USA ranked second to Germany, Canada ranked 8th, Mexico 22nd, Brazil 27th and Argentina 45th. The three countries of North America – all major generating markets – accounted for 14% of worldwide spending and 83% of spending by the Americas. South America accounted for 11%, the Caribbean for 4% and Central America for 2% of spending by the Americas.

Expenditure, in US dollar terms, was up by 9% in 2005, building on the 15% growth achieved in 2004 after the setbacks of 2001 and 2002 and a marginal increase in 2003. Expenditure exceeded the 2000 total in nominal terms in 2004 and in real terms in 2005.

The fastest growth in 2005 was achieved by Central America (+31%) and South America (+25%), with notably large increases recorded by Brazil (+64%) and, on much smaller values by Guatemala (+93%) and Guyana (+33%). Spending from the Caribbean rose by only 3%, but within the subregion there are countries showing both large increases (e.g. Trinidad and Tobago, Montserrat, Grenada and St Maarten) and large declines (e.g. Haiti, Curaçao and Jamaica). Spending from Canada was up 15% – assisted by the strong Canadian currency – Mexico was up 9%, and the USA only 5%, hampered by a weak, if no longer declining, currency.

World and regions: Outbound tourism
International Tourism Expenditure, 2005*   (share, %)

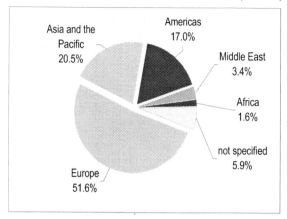

Source: World Tourism Organization (UNWTO) ©

World and regions: Outbound tourism
International Tourism Expenditure, 2005*   (US$ per capita)

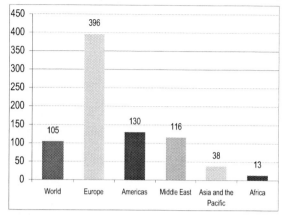

Source: World Tourism Organization (UNWTO) ©

Americas: Outbound tourism
International Tourism Expenditure, 2005*   (US$ billion)

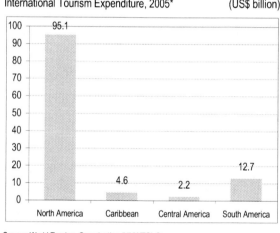

Source: World Tourism Organization (UNWTO) ©

Americas: Outbound tourism
International Tourism Expenditure, 2005*   (US$ per capita)

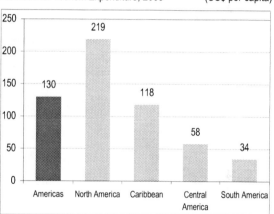

Source: World Tourism Organization (UNWTO) ©

The America's spending per capita on tourism abroad was US$ 130, compared with a world average of US$ 105 and US$ 396 for Europeans. This average masks very wide variations: US$ 560 for Canadians, US$ 234 for US residents, US$ 72 for Mexicans, US$ 118 for the Caribbean, US$ 58 for Central Americans and just US$ 34 for South Americans. There are, of course, very large variations within the Caribbean, ranging from US$ 3,656 for Bermuda and US$ 3,043 for the Aruba to US$ 39 for the Dominican Republic and just US$ 7 for Haiti.

International Tourism Expenditure by Generating Country

	International Tourism Expenditure (US$, million)						Market share in the region (%)			Change (%)		Population (million)	per capita[1]
	1990	1995	2000	2003	2004	2005*	1990	2000	2005*	04/03	05*/04	2005	US$
Americas	*62,376*	*72,982*	*99,957*	*91,638*	*104,986*	*114,703*	*100*	*100*	*100*	*14.6*	*9.3*	*884*	*130*
North America	**53,799**	**58,347**	**82,642**	**77,064**	**88,656**	**95,145**	**86.3**	**82.7**	**82.9**	**15.0**	**7.3**	**435**	**219**
Canada	10,931	10,260	12,438	13,366	15,947	18,370	17.5	12.4	16.0	19.3	15.2	32.8	560
Mexico	5,519	3,171	5,499	6,253	6,959	7,600	8.8	5.5	6.6	11.3	9.2	106.2	72
United States	37,349	44,916	64,705	57,444	65,750	69,175	59.9	64.7	60.3	14.5	5.2	295.7	234
Caribbean	**2,341**	**2,907**	**3,740**	**4,193**	**4,470**	**4,593**	**3.8**	**3.7**	**4.0**	**6.6**	**2.8**	**39**	**118**
Anguilla	4	6	9	9	9	10	0.0	0.0	0.0	0.0	11.1	0.01	755
Antigua,Barb	18	23	31	35	37	40	0.0	0.0	0.0	5.7	8.1	0.07	582
Aruba	40	73	147	189	218	218	0.1	0.1	0.2	15.7	-0.2	0.07	3,043
Bahamas	196	213	261	305	316	344	0.3	0.3	0.3	3.6	9.1	0.30	1,141
Barbados	47	71	94	105	108	108	0.1	0.1	0.1	2.9	-0.2	0.28	387
Bermuda	119	..	..	226	217	239	0.2		0.2	-4.0	10.1	0.07	3,656
Bonaire	..	..	3	3	6	5		0.0	0.0	131.1	-8.7		
Br.Virgin Is	..	40	..	..	..	..						0.02	
Curaçao	82	..	124	176	192	167	0.1	0.1	0.1	8.8	-12.8		
Dominica	4	6	9	9	9	10	0.0	0.0	0.0	0.0	11.1	0.07	145
Dominican Rp	144	173	309	272	310	352	0.2	0.3	0.3	14.0	13.5	9.05	39
Grenada	5	5	8	8	9	11	0.0	0.0	0.0	12.5	22.2	0.09	123
Haiti	37	35	18	42	72	54	0.1	0.0	0.0	71.4	-25.0	8.12	7
Jamaica	114	148	209	252	286	249	0.2	0.2	0.2	13.5	-12.8	2.74	91
Montserrat	2	4	2	2	2	3	0.0	0.0	0.0	0.0	50.0	0.01	321
Puerto Rico	630	833	931	985	1,085	1,142	1.0	0.9	1.0	10.1	5.3	3.91	292
Saint Lucia	17	25	33	36	37	40	0.0	0.0	0.0	2.8	8.1	0.17	241
St.Kitts-Nev	4	5	9	8	10	11	0.0	0.0	0.0	25.0	10.0	0.04	282
St.Maarten	..	59	127	144	88	104		0.1	0.1	-39.0	18.3		
St.Vincent,Grenadines	4	7	9	13	14	14	0.0	0.0	0.0	7.7	0.0	0.12	119
Trinidad Tbg	122	69	147	107	96	222	0.2	0.1	0.2	-10.3	131.3	1.08	206
Turks,Caicos	..	153	..	..	..	..						0.02	
Central America	**468**	**775**	**1,259**	**1,431**	**1,711**	**2,236**	**0.7**	**1.3**	**1.9**	**19.6**	**30.7**	**39**	**58**
Belize	7	21	41	44	41	42	0.0	0.0	0.0	-6.8	1.2	0.3	148
Costa Rica	148	323	485	352	404	468	0.2	0.5	0.4	14.8	15.8	4.0	117
El Salvador	61	72	165	230	302	347	0.1	0.2	0.3	31.7	14.7	6.7	52
Guatemala	100	141	182	312	391	756	0.2	0.2	0.7	25.3	93.2	12.0	63
Honduras	38	57	120	211	244	262	0.1	0.1	0.2	16.0	7.3	7.2	37
Nicaragua	15	40	78	75	89	91	0.0	0.1	0.1	19.1	1.8	5.5	17
Panama	99	121	188	208	239	271	0.2	0.2	0.2	15.0	13.5	3.1	86
South America	**5,768**	**10,952**	**12,317**	**8,950**	**10,149**	**12,728**	**9.2**	**12.3**	**11.1**	**13.4**	**25.4**	**371**	**34**
Argentina	1,505	3,278	4,425	2,511	2,604	2,790	2.4	4.4	2.4	3.7	7.1	39.5	71
Bolivia	68	58	77	139	164	186	0.1	0.1	0.2	18.7	13.4	8.9	21
Brazil	1,582	3,391	3,894	2,261	2,871	4,720	2.5	3.9	4.1	27.0	64.4	186.1	25
Chile	426	703	620	850	977	1,051	0.7	0.6	0.9	14.9	7.5	16.0	66
Colombia	454	878	1,060	1,062	1,108	1,127	0.7	1.1	1.0	4.3	1.7	43.0	26
Ecuador	175	235	299	354	391	429	0.3	0.3	0.4	10.3	9.6	13.4	32
Guyana	..	21	69	26	30	40		0.1	0.0	15.4	33.3	0.8	52
Paraguay	103	133	81	67	71	79	0.2	0.1	0.1	5.7	11.0	6.3	12
Peru	295	297	423	641	643	752	0.5	0.4	0.7	0.3	16.9	27.9	27
Suriname	12	3	23	6	14	17	0.0	0.0	0.0	133.3	21.4	0.4	39
Uruguay	111	236	281	169	194	252	0.2	0.3	0.2	14.7	30.0	3.4	74
Venezuela	1,023	1,714	1,058	859	1,077	1,281	1.6	1.1	1.1	25.4	18.9	25.4	50

Source: World Tourism Organization (UNWTO) ©

(Data as collected by UNWTO for TMT 2006 Edition)

[1] Last year with data available

World Tourism Organization ©

Trips Abroad

Data on outbound trips should be treated with caution, as figures for many countries are not available, and it is often not clear, whether the reported figures refer strictly to tourists (overnight visitors) or to visitors in general (including same-day visitors). For this reason, it is not feasible to present world and (sub)regional aggregates. Furthermore, it is important to note that the number of trips is not equal to the number of arrivals, as a single trip can produce arrivals in several destinations.

The Americas' leading generator of outbound tourism is the USA, which reported 63.5 million trips abroad in 2005, making it the world's third largest generating market after Germany and the United Kingdom. Canada reported an 8% increase in outbound trips to 21 million, and Mexico a 7% increase to 13 million. Other countries in the Americas reporting more than 1 million outbound trips were Brazil (4.7 million), Argentina (4.0 million), Chile (2.7 million), Peru (1.8 million), Colombia (1.6 million), Puerto Rico (1.4 million), El Salvador (1.4 million) and Venezuela (1.1 million). The largest reported increases in 2005, in percentage terms, were those for Venezuela (31%) and Brazil (26%). Many other countries reporting double-digit increases in 2005 such as Guatemala, El Salvador, Costa Rica, the Dominican Republic, Chile, Peru, Panama, Paraguay and Uruguay.

Outbound Tourism, trips abroad (trips can either refer to overnight visits only, or also include same-day visits)

	1990	1995	2000	2003	2004	(1000) 2005*	per 100 popu- lation[1]	Change (%) 04/03	Change (%) 05*/04	Average (%) '90-'00	Average (%) '00-'05*
Americas											
North America											
Canada	20,415	18,206	19,182	17,739	19,545	21,101	64	10.2	8.0	-0.6	1.9
Mexico	7,357	8,450	11,079	11,044	12,494	13,305	13	13.1	6.5	4.2	3.7
United States	44,623	51,285	61,327	56,250	61,809	63,503	21	9.9	2.7	3.2	0.7
Caribbean											
Antigua,Barb	..	386	..	..	..	..					
Bermuda	102	..	..	141	156	161	246	10.6	3.2		
Br.Virgin Is	..	79	..	..	..	..					
Cuba	12	72	139	113	115	..	1	1.8		27.8	
Dominican Rp	..	168	360	321	368	419	5	14.6	13.9		3.1
Martinique	..	..	..	..	..	..					
Puerto Rico	996	1,237	1,259	1,272	1,361	1,410	36	7.0	3.6	2.4	2.3
Trinidad Tbg	254	261	..	..	..	..					
Central America											
Costa Rica	191	273	381	373	425	487	12	13.9	14.6	7.1	5.0
El Salvador	525	348	923	940	1,218	1,397	21	29.6	14.7	5.8	8.6
Guatemala	289	333	488	658	854	982	8	29.8	15.0	5.4	15.0
Honduras	196	149	277	277	295	300	4	6.5	1.7	3.5	1.6
Nicaragua	173	255	486	562	701	740	14	24.7	5.6	10.9	8.8
Panama	151	185	216	227	256	285	9	12.8	11.3	3.6	5.7
South America											
Argentina	2,398	3,815	4,953	3,088	3,904	4,002	10	26.4	2.5	7.5	-4.2
Bolivia	242	249	201	305	331	312	4	8.5	-5.7	-1.8	9.2
Brazil	1,188	2,600	3,228	3,225	3,738	4,696	3	15.9	25.6	10.5	7.8
Chile	768	1,070	1,830	2,100	2,343	2,651	17	11.6	13.1	9.1	7.7
Colombia	781	1,057	1,235	1,177	1,405	1,553	4	19.4	10.5	4.7	4.7
Ecuador	181	271	520	613	603	661	5	-1.6	9.6	11.1	4.9
Paraguay	..	427	175	153	170	188	3	11.1	10.6		1.4
Peru	329	508	730	1,392	1,635	1,841	7	17.5	12.6	8.3	20.3
Suriname	89	..	..	..	..	..					
Uruguay	..	..	667	495	569	658	19	14.9	15.6		-0.3
Venezuela	309	534	954	832	816	1,067	4	-1.9	30.8	11.9	2.3

Source: World Tourism Organization (UNWTO) ©   (Data as collected by UNWTO for TMT 2006 Edition)

[1] values correspond to most recent year with data available

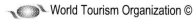

II.2 Tourism Trends by Subregion

II.2.1. North America

International tourist arrivals

After declining in 2001, 2002 and 2003, tourist arrivals in North America picked up in 2004 and continued to rise, more moderately, in 2005. They increased by 11% in 2004 and 5% in 2005, to 90 million. However, they were still 2% short of their 2000 peak, and their share of total arrivals in the Americas (68%) continued to slip.

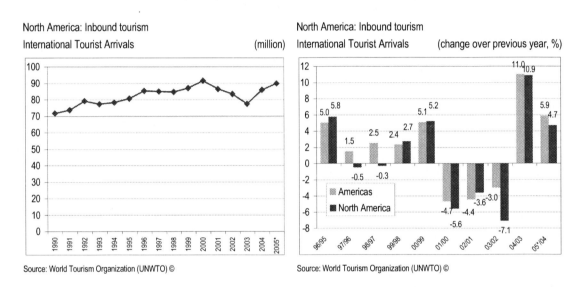

North America: Inbound tourism
International Tourist Arrivals (million)

North America: Inbound tourism
International Tourist Arrivals (change over previous year, %)

Source: World Tourism Organization (UNWTO) ©   Source: World Tourism Organization (UNWTO) ©

The USA, which had suffered the heaviest declines in 2001 to 2003, saw increases in arrivals of 12% in 2004 and 7% in 2005 to 49 million – 37% of the total for the Americas. The low US dollar conversion rate and the recovery in travellers' confidence continued to attract visitors from Europe, Asia and the Pacific and from elsewhere in the Americas. However, visitors were also discouraged by reports – and in many countries the reality – of difficulties and delays in obtaining visas for entry into the USA and of delays at border control points.

Canada had seen a 9% recovery in arrivals in 2004, after the damage caused by local outbreaks of SARS in 2003, but they slipped back by 2% in 2005, to 19 million. Arrivals from the USA (which account for three quarters of the total) were down 4% in 2005. The principal problem was the very high exchange rate of the Canadian dollar, but contributing factors included the uncertainties about passport requirements mentioned above, border delays, higher fuel prices – and particularly their effect on car-based touring – and shortages of airline capacity on some routes.

Same-day visitors to Canada – which are of course not included in the figures shown above – have been in rapid decline for many years. Since 2000 they have fallen by 40%, from 26.6 million to 15.7 million (and that includes a 12% decline in 2005 alone).

The decline in same-day and overnight visitors to Canada from the USA has tended to obscure excellent results from many other markets, in the Americas and further afield. In 2004 and 2005 there were large increases in arrivals from all Canada's other leading sources – including the UK, Japan, France, Germany, Australia, Mexico and Brazil – and from many less important ones.

In spite of the closer relations with neighbouring countries and prosperity resulting from the formation of the North American Free Trade Area (NAFTA), arrivals in Mexico lagged behind the regional average in 1990-2000, but they were relatively modestly affected by the downturn in 2001 to 2003. After increases of 11% in 2004 and 6% in 2005, arrivals in 2005 (22 million) surpassed finally the 2000 peak and by 6%.

International Tourist Arrivals by Country of Destination

	Series	International Tourist Arrivals (1000)						Market share in the region (%)			Change (%)		Average annual growth (%)	
		1990	1995	2000	2003	2004	2005*	1990	2000	2005*	04/03	05*/04	90-00	00-05*
North America		**71,744**	**80,664**	**91,506**	**77,418**	**85,849**	**89,891**	**77.3**	**71.4**	**67.5**	**10.9**	**4.7**	**2.5**	**-0.4**
Canada	TF	15,209	16,932	19,627	17,534	19,145	18,771	16.4	15.3	14.1	9.2	-2.0	2.6	-0.9
Mexico	TF	17,172	20,241	20,641	18,665	20,618	21,915	18.5	16.1	16.5	10.5	6.3	1.9	1.2
United States	TF	39,363	43,491	51,238	41,218	46,086	49,206	42.4	40.0	36.9	11.8	6.8	2.7	-0.8

Source: World Tourism Organization (UNWTO) ©   (Data as collected by UNWTO for TMT 2006 Edition)

International tourism receipts

International tourism receipts in North America reached US$ 107 billion in 2005, making it the world's third largest subregional earner, after Western and Southern and Mediterranean Europe. They grew by 17% in 2004 and by 9% in 2005 in US dollar terms, or by 13% and 4% in local currencies at constant prices.

The USA – the world's leading destination in terms of receipts – earned US$ 82 billion in 2005, 10% more than in 2004 in current terms and below 1% of the peak earnings in 2000. This represented 57% of receipts in the Americas and 12% of worldwide receipts. In Canada, ranked 12th in the world, international tourism receipts rose by 6% (in contrast to the 2% decline in arrivals) to US$ 13.6 billion. In Mexico, ranked third in the Americas, receipts rose by 9% to US$ 11.8 billion.

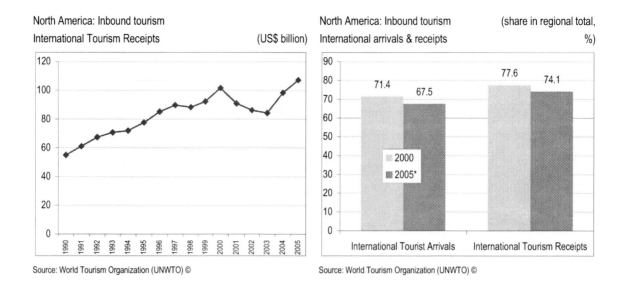

North America: Inbound tourism
International Tourism Receipts (US$ billion)

Source: World Tourism Organization (UNWTO) ©

North America: Inbound tourism (share in regional total, %)
International arrivals & receipts

Source: World Tourism Organization (UNWTO) ©

The USA continues to receive far more per tourist (US$ 1,660) than Canada (US$ 725) or Mexico (US$ 540). This is probably related to the large numbers of short-stay cross-border visitors from the USA into Canada, and from the USA and countries in Central America into Mexico.

International Tourism Receipts by Country of Destination

	International Tourism Receipts (US$, million)						Market share in the region (%)			Change (%)		Receipts per arrival[1]	Receipts per capita[1]
	1990	1995	2000	2003	2004	2005*	1990	2000	2005*	04/03	05*/04		US$
North America	**54,872**	**77,491**	**101,472**	**84,256**	**98,213**	**107,067**	**79.3**	**77.6**	**74.1**	**16.6**	**9.0**	**1,190**	**246**
Canada	6,339	7,917	10,778	10,546	12,871	13,584	9.2	8.2	9.4	22.0	5.5	725	414
Mexico	5,526	6,179	8,294	9,362	10,796	11,803	8.0	6.3	8.2	15.3	9.3	540	111
United States	43,007	63,395	82,400	64,348	74,547	81,680	62.2	63.0	56.5	15.8	9.6	1,660	276

Source: World Tourism Organization (UNWTO) © (Data as collected by UNWTO for TMT 2006 Edition)

[1] Last year with data available

II.2.2. Caribbean

International tourist arrivals

Some destinations in the Caribbean were badly affected by the severe hurricane seasons in 2004 and 2005, and some benefited from diversions from other destinations. The performance of individual destinations therefore varied widely. More generally, arrivals had been relatively little affected by the downturn in 2001 and had recovered relatively early, in 2003. In 2004, they were already 6% higher than they had been in 2000. This helps to explain the relatively modest overall increases in Caribbean arrivals in 2004 (6%) and 2005 (4%). The total reached 19 million in 2005. The Caribbean's share of arrivals in the Americas has risen from 12% in 1990 to 13% in 2000 and 14% in 2005.

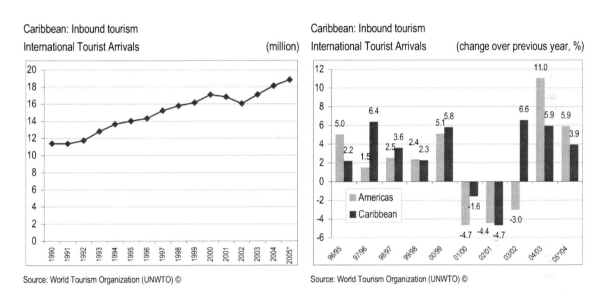

Caribbean: Inbound tourism
International Tourist Arrivals (million)

Caribbean: Inbound tourism
International Tourist Arrivals (change over previous year, %)

Source: World Tourism Organization (UNWTO) ©

Source: World Tourism Organization (UNWTO) ©

Three of the four largest countries in the subregion are also the three most important tourism destinations, and all three achieved strong results in 2004 and 2005. Arrivals in Puerto Rico were up 9% and 4% in the two years respectively, to 3.7 million. Arrivals in Cuba were up 9% and 12%, to 2.3 million. The strong convertible peso and the US embargo discouraged travellers from the USA, but arrivals from elsewhere in the Americas and from Europe increased. Arrivals in the Dominican Republic rose by 5% in 2004 and 7% in 2005 (to 3.7 million) as the political and economic environment improved. Tourism is playing a leading role in the country's economic revival, with considerable foreign direct investment in the sector. But, tourism in the other half of the island, Haiti, remains on a much smaller scale. Arrivals fell by 29% in 2004 and rose by 16% in 2005, but remain much lower than they were in 1990.

Tourist arrivals in the Bahamas have been more or less stable since 1990, at around 1.6 million. They were up 3% in 2005. In the neighbouring Turks and Caicos Islands, however, numbers have quadrupled since 1990 – they were up 6% in 2004 and 16% in 2005, to 200,000. Conversely, arrivals in the Cayman Islands fell by 11% in 2004 and by 35% in 2005 (the islands were hit by hurricanes in both 2004 and 2005).

The only other destination in the Caribbean with more than 1 million arrivals a year is Jamaica, where arrivals were up 5% in both 2004 and 2005.

Martinique, which also receives nearly half a million tourists a year, achieved a modest 3% increase in arrivals in 2005. Most of the smaller islands in the group also saw modest increases or small declines, but Grenada – one of the destinations hit by hurricanes in both 2004 and 2005 – suffered a 27% decline in 2005, after a 6% decline in 2004. Further south, Trinidad and Tobago – another of the 0.5 million a year destinations – achieved relatively strong increases of 8% in 2004 and 5% in 2005.

Many of the much smaller islands achieved large increases in arrivals in 2004, and 2005 was a year of consolidation. However, St Maarten, saw a decline of 1.5% after an 11% increase in 2004.

International Tourist Arrivals by Country of Destination

	Series	International Tourist Arrivals (1000)						Market share in the region (%)			Change (%)		Average annual growth (%)	
		1990	1995	2000	2003	2004	2005*	1990	2000	2005*	04/03	05*/04	90-00	00-05*
Caribbean		**11,392**	**14,023**	**17,086**	**17,080**	**18,095**	**18,802**	**12.3**	**13.3**	**14.1**	**5.9**	**3.9**	**4.1**	**1.9**
Anguilla	TF	31	39	44	47	54	62	0.0	0.0	0.0	15.1	15.0	3.6	7.1
Antigua,Barb	TF	206	220	207	224	245	245	0.2	0.2	0.2	9.6	0.0	0.0	3.5
Aruba	TF	433	619	721	642	728	733	0.5	0.6	0.5	13.4	0.6	5.2	0.3
Bahamas	TF	1,562	1,598	1,544	1,510	1,561	1,608	1.7	1.2	1.2	3.4	3.0	-0.1	0.8
Barbados	TF	432	442	545	531	552	548	0.5	0.4	0.4	3.8	-0.7	2.4	0.1
Bermuda	TF	435	387	332	257	272	270	0.5	0.3	0.2	5.9	-0.7	-2.7	-4.1
Bonaire	TF	37	59	51	62	63	63	0.0	0.0	0.0	1.6	-0.9	3.3	4.2
Br.Virgin Is	TF	160	219	272	318	307	337	0.2	0.2	0.3	-3.2	9.7	5.4	4.4
Cayman Islands	TF	253	361	354	294	260	168	0.3	0.3	0.1	-11.4	-35.4	3.4	-13.9
Cuba	TF	327	742	1,741	1,847	2,017	2,261	0.4	1.4	1.7	9.2	12.1	18.2	5.4
Curaçao	TF	219	224	191	221	223	222	0.2	0.1	0.2	0.9	-0.6	-1.4	3.1
Dominica	TF	45	60	70	73	80	79	0.0	0.1	0.1	9.4	-1.0	4.5	2.5
Dominican Rp	TF	1,305	1,776	2,978	3,282	3,450	3,691	1.4	2.3	2.8	5.1	7.0	8.6	4.4
Grenada	TF	76	108	129	142	134	98	0.1	0.1	0.1	-6.0	-26.6	5.4	-5.3
Guadeloupe	TCE	331	640	603	439	456	372	0.4	0.5	0.3	3.9	-18.4	6.2	-9.2
Haiti	TF	144	145	140	136	96	112	0.2	0.1	0.1	-29.1	16.4	-0.3	-4.3
Jamaica	TF	989	1,147	1,323	1,350	1,415	1,479	1.1	1.0	1.1	4.8	4.5	2.9	2.3
Martinique	TF	282	457	526	453	471	484	0.3	0.4	0.4	3.9	2.8	6.4	-1.6
Montserrat	TF	13	18	10	8	10	10	0.0	0.0	0.0	13.7	1.3	-2.3	-1.3
Puerto Rico	TF	2,560	3,131	3,341	3,238	3,541	3,686	2.8	2.6	2.8	9.3	4.1	2.7	2.0
Saba	TF	..	10	9	10	11	11		0.0	0.0	7.3	4.1		4.7
Saint Lucia	TF	141	231	270	277	298	318	0.2	0.2	0.2	7.8	6.5	6.7	3.3
St.Eustatius	TF	..	9	9	10	11	10		0.0	0.0	5.8	-6.3		2.6
St.Kitts-Nev	TF	73	79	73	91	118	127	0.1	0.1	0.1	29.7	8.0	0.0	11.7
St.Maarten	TF	545	449	432	428	475	468	0.6	0.3	0.4	11.1	-1.5	-2.3	1.6
St.Vincent,Grenadines	TF	54	60	73	79	87	96	0.1	0.1	0.1	10.4	10.1	3.1	5.5
Trinidad Tbg	TF	195	260	399	409	443	463	0.2	0.3	0.3	8.2	4.7	7.4	3.0
Turks,Caicos	TF	49	79	152	164	173	200	0.1	0.1	0.2	5.8	15.6	12.0	5.6
US.Virgin Is	TF	463	454	546	538	544	582	0.5	0.4	0.4	1.1	7.0	1.7	1.3

Source: World Tourism Organization (UNWTO) ©   (Data as collected by UNWTO for TMT 2006 Edition)

World Tourism Organization ©

International tourism receipts

International tourism receipts in the Caribbean totalled US$ 20.4 billion in 2005, an increase of 6% in US dollar terms and 1.6% in local currency real terms over 2004. The largest increase was achieved by Trinidad and Tobago (+33% in US dollar terms). Not far behind, but on much smaller numbers, came Haiti (+26%, making up for large declines in preceding years) and Anguilla (+25%). In all three cases, the increases in receipts were far above the respective increases in arrivals. The Bahamas, the British and US Virgin Islands, Dominican Republic and St Vincent also put in strong performances, in line with their growth in arrivals. But the Cayman Islands and Grenada suffered declines in receipts as heavy as their declines in arrivals.

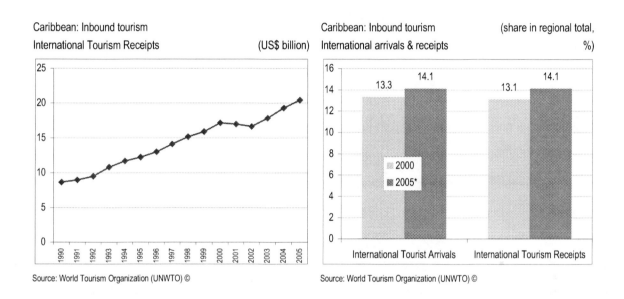

Caribbean: Inbound tourism
International Tourism Receipts (US$ billion)

Caribbean: Inbound tourism (share in regional total, %)
International arrivals & receipts

Source: World Tourism Organization (UNWTO) ©

Source: World Tourism Organization (UNWTO) ©

Receipts per arrival in the Caribbean (US$ 1,085 in 2005) are relatively high – only in Oceania, North America and South Asia are they higher. Many of the smaller islands substantially exceed this average, including Anguilla, Antigua and Barbuda, Aruba, Bahamas, Barbados, Bonaire, Bermuda, Cayman Islands, St Maarten, the Turks and Caicos and the US Virgin Islands.

International Tourism Receipts by Country of Destination

	International Tourism Receipts (US$, million)						Market share in the region (%)			Change (%)		Receipts per arrival[1]	Receipts per capita[1]
	1990	1995	2000	2003	2004	2005*	1990	2000	2005*	04/03	05*/04		US$
Caribbean	**8,639**	**12,236**	**17,154**	**17,842**	**19,292**	**20,415**	**12.5**	**13.1**	**14.1**	**8.1**	**5.8**	**1,085**	**526**
Anguilla	35	50	56	60	69	86	0.1	0.0	0.1	15.3	24.7	1,390	6,512
Antigua,Barb	298	247	291	300	338	327	0.4	0.2	0.2	12.7	-3.3	1,330	4,758
Aruba	350	521	814	859	1,056	1,091	0.5	0.6	0.8	22.9	3.4	1,490	15,245
Bahamas	1,333	1,346	1,734	1,757	1,884	2,072	1.9	1.3	1.4	7.2	9.9	1,290	6,865
Barbados	494	622	723	758	776	776	0.7	0.6	0.5	2.3	0.1	1,420	2,784
Bermuda	490	488	431	348	426	430	0.7	0.3	0.3	22.4	0.9	1,595	6,578
Bonaire	18	37	59	84	84	85	0.0	0.0	0.1	-0.7	1.7	1,360	
Br.Virgin Is	132	211	345	342	393	437	0.2	0.3	0.3	14.9	11.2	1,295	19,302
Cayman Islands	236	394	559	518	519	353	0.3	0.4	0.2	0.2	-32.0	2,105	7,974
Cuba	243	963	1,737	1,846	1,915	1,920	0.4	1.3	1.3	3.7	0.3	850	169
Curaçao	120	175	189	223	222	239	0.2	0.1	0.2	-0.4	7.5	1,075	
Dominica	25	42	48	54	61	56	0.0	0.0	0.0	12.3	-7.2	710	815
Dominican Rp	818	1,571	2,860	3,128	3,152	3,518	1.2	2.2	2.4	0.8	11.6	955	389
Grenada	38	76	93	104	83	71	0.1	0.1	0.0	-19.5	-14.4	725	798
Guadeloupe	197	458	418	..	..	246	0.3	0.3	0.2			660	548
Haiti	46	90	128	93	87	110	0.1	0.1	0.1	-6.5	26.4	980	14
Jamaica	740	1,069	1,333	1,355	1,438	1,545	1.1	1.0	1.1	6.1	7.4	1,045	565
Martinique	240	384	302	247	291	280	0.3	0.2	0.2	17.8	-3.8	580	647
Montserrat	7	17	9	7	9	9	0.0	0.0	0.0	17.1	4.7	925	962
Puerto Rico	1,366	1,828	2,388	2,677	3,024	3,239	2.0	1.8	2.2	13.0	7.1	880	828
Saint Lucia	154	230	281	282	326	356	0.2	0.2	0.2	15.5	9.3	1,120	2,140
St.Kitts-Nev	58	63	58	75	103	107	0.1	0.0	0.1	37.3	4.1	845	2,753
St.Maarten	316	349	511	538	613	619	0.5	0.4	0.4	13.9	1.1	1,325	
St.Vincent,Grenadines	56	53	82	91	96	105	0.1	0.1	0.1	5.5	9.4	1,100	893
Trinidad Tbg	95	77	213	249	341	453	0.1	0.2	0.3	36.9	32.8	980	421
Turks,Caicos	37	53	285	..	..	..	0.1	0.2					
US.Virgin Is	697	822	1,206	1,257	1,356	1,491	1.0	0.9	1.0	7.9	10.0	2,560	13,715

Source: World Tourism Organization (UNWTO) ©   (Data as collected by UNWTO for TMT 2006 Edition)

[1] Last year with data available

II.2.3. Central America

International tourist arrivals

The smallest of the American subregions, in terms of tourism, Central America is also the fastest growing. Arrivals grew by 8% a year between 1990 and 2000 and continued to grow through the recession of 2001 to 2003. They increased by 13% in 2004 and in 2005, to 6 million. Central America's share of total arrivals in the Americas rose from 2% in 1990 to 3% in 2000 and 5% in 2005.

Political stability and faster economic growth are boosting local demand for travel and allowing tourism industries targeting long-haul visitors to develop. The increased economic and social integration within the region is reflected in the large increases in intraregional arrivals reported by most Central American countries in recent years. The treaty for a Central American Free Trade Area, covering Costa Rica, the Dominican Republic, El Salvador, Guatemala, Honduras, Nicaragua and the USA, was signed in 2004, and finally ratified by the US Congress in July 2005. It comes into effect in April 2006.

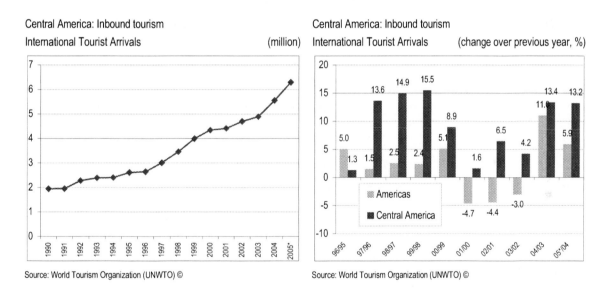

Central America: Inbound tourism
International Tourist Arrivals (million)

Central America: Inbound tourism
International Tourist Arrivals (change over previous year, %)

Source: World Tourism Organization (UNWTO) ©

Source: World Tourism Organization (UNWTO) ©

International Tourist Arrivals by Country of Destination

	Series	International Tourist Arrivals (1000)						Market share in the region (%)			Change (%)		Average annual growth (%)	
		1990	1995	2000	2003	2004	2005*	1990	2000	2005*	04/03	05*/04	90-00	00-05*
Central America		1,945	2,611	4,346	4,900	5,554	6,288	2.1	3.4	4.7	13.4	13.2	8.4	7.7
Belize	TF	197	131	196	221	231	237	0.2	0.2	0.2	4.7	2.5	-0.1	3.8
Costa Rica	TF	435	785	1,088	1,239	1,453	1,679	0.5	0.8	1.3	17.3	15.6	9.6	9.1
El Salvador	TF	194	235	795	857	812	969	0.2	0.6	0.7	-5.3	19.5	15.1	4.0
Guatemala	TF	509	563	826	880	1,182	1,316	0.5	0.6	1.0	34.2	11.4	5.0	9.8
Honduras	TF	290	271	471	611	641	673	0.3	0.4	0.5	5.0	5.0	5.0	7.4
Nicaragua	TF	106	281	486	526	615	712	0.1	0.4	0.5	16.9	15.9	16.4	8.0
Panama	TF	214	345	484	566	621	702	0.2	0.4	0.5	9.8	13.0	8.5	7.7

Source: World Tourism Organization (UNWTO) ©

(Data as collected by UNWTO for TMT 2006 Edition)

In both 2004 and 2005, Costa Rica, El Salvador, Guatemala, Nicaragua and Panama all achieved increases in arrivals of 10% or more (El Salvador managed nearly 20% in 2005). Honduras averaged only 5% a year, but this was after large increases in preceding years. Belize, a relatively isolated and minor destination, and one affected by the hurricanes in 2005, has continued to lag behind.

International tourism receipts

International tourism receipts in Central America totalled US$ 5 billion in 2005 – just 3% of the total for the Americas. This was an increase of 17% in US dollar terms and 11% in local currency real terms over 2004. Almost all the countries in the subregion – including in this case Belize and Honduras – achieved increases of over 10%, and usually well over 10%, in both 2004 and 2005. Only Nicaragua's receipts in 2005 fell short of this threshold, but still at +7%.

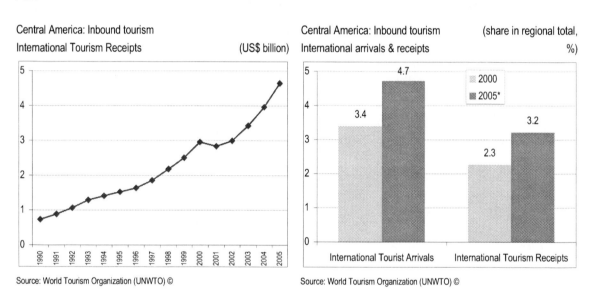

Central America: Inbound tourism
International Tourism Receipts (US$ billion)

Central America: Inbound tourism (share in regional total, %)
International arrivals & receipts

Source: World Tourism Organization (UNWTO) ©

Source: World Tourism Organization (UNWTO) ©

Average receipts per arrival in Central America (US$ 740 in 2005) are lower than those in North America and the Caribbean, but a little higher than those in South America. Within the region, they are higher in Panama (US$ 1,110) and Costa Rica (US$ 935), and lower in El Salvador (US$ 560) and Nicaragua (US$ 290).

International Tourism Receipts by Country of Destination

	International Tourism Receipts (US$, million)						Market share in the region (%)			Change (%)		Receipts per arrival[1]	Receipts per capita[1]
	1990	1995	2000	2003	2004	2005*	1990	2000	2005*	04/03	05*/04		US$
Central America	**735**	**1,523**	**2,958**	**3,421**	**3,965**	**4,645**	**1.1**	**2.3**	**3.2**	**15.9**	**17.2**	**740**	**120**
Belize	44	78	111	117	133	214	0.1	0.1	0.1	13.5	60.7	905	760
Costa Rica	275	681	1,302	1,199	1,359	1,570	0.4	1.0	1.1	13.3	15.6	935	391
El Salvador	18	85	217	383	441	543	0.0	0.2	0.4	15.1	23.2	560	81
Guatemala	185	213	482	621	776	869	0.3	0.4	0.6	25.0	12.0	660	72
Honduras	29	107	260	356	414	464	0.0	0.2	0.3	16.3	12.1	690	65
Nicaragua	12	50	129	160	192	206	0.0	0.1	0.1	19.9	7.4	290	38
Panama	172	309	458	585	651	780	0.2	0.4	0.5	11.3	19.8	1,110	248

Source: World Tourism Organization (UNWTO) ©   (Data as collected by UNWTO for TMT 2006 Edition)

[1] Last year with data available

World Tourism Organization ©

II.2.4. South America

International tourist arrivals

Several countries in South America suffered economic and financial crises in the late 1990s and in 2000 and 2001, and in the subregion as a whole tourism turned down much earlier than it did in the rest of the world, in 1998. Arrivals in 2001 and 2002 were severely affected by the geopolitical situation in North America and the situation in Argentina. In 2003 to 2005, however, with the return of prosperity and with favourable exchange rates, there were large increases in arrivals in the subregion, of 9%, 17% and 12% respectively, to 18 million. South America's share of American arrivals has risen from 8% in 1990 to nearly 14% in 2005, and is now not far short of the Caribbean's.

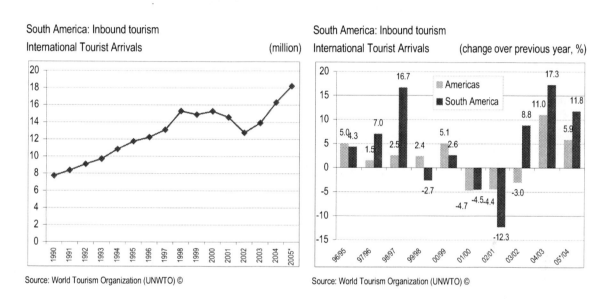

South America: Inbound tourism
International Tourist Arrivals   (million)

South America: Inbound tourism
International Tourist Arrivals   (change over previous year, %)

Source: World Tourism Organization (UNWTO) ©   Source: World Tourism Organization (UNWTO) ©

International Tourist Arrivals by Country of Destination

	Series	International Tourist Arrivals (1000)						Market share in the region (%)			Change (%)		Average annual growth (%)	
		1990	1995	2000	2003	2004	2005*	1990	2000	2005*	04/03	05*/04	90-00	00-05*
South America		**7,722**	**11,731**	**15,255**	**13,896**	**16,295**	**18,217**	**8.3**	**11.9**	**13.7**	**17.3**	**11.8**	**7.0**	**3.6**
Argentina	TF	1,930	2,289	2,909	2,995	3,457	3,823	2.1	2.3	2.9	15.4	10.6	4.2	5.6
Bolivia	TF	254	284	319	420	478	504	0.3	0.2	0.4	13.8	5.4	2.3	9.6
Brazil	TF	1,091	1,991	5,313	4,133	4,794	5,358	1.2	4.1	4.0	16.0	11.8	17.2	0.2
Chile	TF	943	1,540	1,742	1,614	1,785	2,027	1.0	1.4	1.5	10.6	13.6	6.3	3.1
Colombia	TF	813	1,399	557	625	791	933	0.9	0.4	0.7	26.6	18.0	-3.7	10.9
Ecuador	VF	362	440	627	761	819	860	0.4	0.5	0.6	7.6	5.0	5.6	6.5
French Guiana	TF	..	..	..	..	..	95			0.1				
Guyana	TF	64	106	105	101	122	117	0.1	0.1	0.1	20.9	-4.4	5.1	2.1
Paraguay	TF	280	438	289	268	309	341	0.3	0.2	0.3	15.3	10.2	0.3	3.4
Peru	TF	317	479	828	1,070	1,277	1,486	0.3	0.6	1.1	19.4	16.4	10.1	12.4
Suriname	TF	46	43	57	82	138	160	0.0	0.0	0.1	68.1	16.1	2.2	22.9
Uruguay	TF	..	2,022	1,968	1,420	1,756	1,808		1.5	1.4	23.7	2.9		-1.7
Venezuela	TF	525	700	469	337	486	706	0.6	0.4	0.5	44.3	45.2	-1.1	8.5

Source: World Tourism Organization (UNWTO) ©   (Data as collected by UNWTO for TMT 2006 Edition)

The leading destinations in South America are Brazil and Argentina, which together account for half all arrivals in the subregion. Arrivals in Argentina rose by 15% in 2004 and by 11% in 2005 to 4 million, with the help of an extremely favourable exchange rate. Those in Brazil rose just as fast – by 16% in 2004 and 12% in 2005 – to 5 million, but in this case in spite of the appreciation of the real, making the country an more expensive destination.

Chile is the third most important destination in South America, and one which is prosperous and achieving remarkable success in diversifying and upgrading its tourism offer. Arrivals rose by 11% in 2004 and 14% in 2005 to 2 million.

Uruguay is a popular destination for holidaymakers from Argentina and Brazil, which account for 58% and 10% of total arrivals respectively. There were large increases in arrivals from both markets in 2004, but they stabilized in 2005. Overall arrivals in Uruguay increased by 24% in 2004, and by 3% in 2005 to 1.8 million. Paraguay, which depends even more heavily on tourists from Argentina and Brazil, saw arrivals rise by 15% in 2004 and 10% in 2005 to 341,000. Paraguay is also famously a recipient of large numbers of shoppers and day traders from Brazil but, with the opening up of the Brazilian consumer goods market to imports, this traffic is in decline. The recorded number of same-day visitors fell by 12% in 2004 and stagnated in 2005.

Peru has a historical heritage which allows it to attract large numbers of tourists from Europe and North America. It is benefiting from a stable political and security environment and from more effective promotional activities. Arrivals increased by 19% in 2004 and by 16% in 2005 to 1.5 million. With similar attractions, Ecuador has seen more moderate rates of growth, both recently and in the longer term: arrivals increased by 8% in 2004 and by 5% in 2005 to 0.9 million.

Tourism in Colombia and Venezuela has suffered in recent years from some turmoil, but the situation in both countries is improving. Venezuela is benefiting from very high rates of economic growth generated by the increase in international oil prices. Arrivals increased by about 45% in both 2004 and 2005. In Colombia, international arrivals increased by 27% in 2004 and by 18% in 2005, to 900.000.

International tourism receipts

South America's receipts from international tourism rose even more sharply than arrivals in 2004 and 2005, partly because of the appreciation of many of the more important local currencies against the US dollar. They rose by 23% in 2004 and by 18% in 2005 to US$ 12.4 billion – 9% of the total for the Americas. In local currencies at constant prices, the increases were more moderate: 13% in 2004 and 1.7% in 2005.

Among the more important destinations, the largest increases in 2005 were for Venezuela (+30%), Argentina (+22%), Uruguay and Brazil (+20% each). Suriname achieved phenomenal increases in both 2004 and 2005, but from a tiny base.

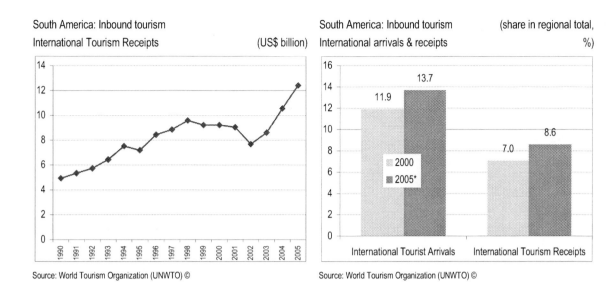

South America: Inbound tourism
International Tourism Receipts   (US$ billion)

South America: Inbound tourism   (share in regional total,
International arrivals & receipts   %)

Source: World Tourism Organization (UNWTO) ©

Source: World Tourism Organization (UNWTO) ©

Average receipts per arrival in South America were only US$ 680 in 2005, the lowest among the American subregions. They were close to this average for the largest destinations – Argentina, Brazil and Chile – higher for Colombia (US$ 1.305), Venezuela (US$ 920) and Peru (US$ 880), but lower for Uruguay (US$ 330), because of its reliance on local holidaymakers and for Bolivia (US$ 475), Guyana (US$ 300), Suriname (US$ 280) and Paraguay (US$ 230).

International Tourism Receipts by Country of Destination

	International Tourism Receipts (US$, million)						Market share in the region (%)			Change (%)		Receipts per arrival[1]	Receipts per capita[1]
	1990	1995	2000	2003	2004	2005*	1990	2000	2005*	04/03	05*/04		US$
South America	**4,946**	**7,189**	**9,216**	**8,597**	**10,553**	**12,397**	**7.1**	**7.0**	**8.6**	**22.8**	**17.5**	**680**	**33**
Argentina	1,131	2,222	2,904	2,006	2,235	2,729	1.6	2.2	1.9	11.4	22.1	715	69
Bolivia	55	55	68	167	192	239	0.1	0.1	0.2	15.1	24.5	475	27
Brazil	1,492	972	1,810	2,479	3,222	3,861	2.2	1.4	2.7	30.0	19.8	720	21
Chile	540	911	819	883	1,095	1,109	0.8	0.6	0.8	24.0	1.3	545	69
Colombia	406	657	1,030	893	1,058	1,218	0.6	0.8	0.8	18.5	15.1	1,305	28
Ecuador	188	255	402	406	462	486	0.3	0.3	0.3	13.8	5.0	565	36
French Guiana	..	..	..	..	..	45			0.0			475	230
Guyana	27	33	75	26	27	35	0.0	0.1	0.0	3.8	29.6	300	46
Paraguay	128	137	73	64	70	78	0.2	0.1	0.1	9.5	11.5	230	12
Peru	217	428	837	963	1,142	1,308	0.3	0.6	0.9	18.6	14.6	880	47
Suriname	1	21	16	4	17	45	0.0	0.0	0.0	325.0	164.7	280	103
Uruguay	238	611	713	345	494	594	0.3	0.5	0.4	43.3	20.3	330	174
Venezuela	496	849	423	331	502	650	0.7	0.3	0.4	51.7	29.5	920	26

Source: World Tourism Organization (UNWTO) ©   (Data as collected by UNWTO for TMT 2006 Edition)

[1] Last year with data available

III

Statistical Trends by Destination Country

III.1   North America

III.1.1   Canada   North America

Promotional: www.canadaTourism.com
Institutional/corporate: www.canadaTourism.com
Research and data: www.canadaTourism.com

Profile

Canada

Americas
North America

Capital	Ottawa
Year of entry in UNWTO	2000
Area (1000 km²)	9,971
Population (2005, million)	32.8
Gross Domestic Product (GDP) (2005, US$ million)	1,132,440
GDP per capita (2005, US$)	35,133
GDP growth (real, %)	

'-> 2004: 3.3;   2005: 2.9;   2006*: 3.1;   2007*: 3.0

	2003	2004	2005*	2004/2003	2005*/2004
International Arrivals					
Visitors (1000)	38,903	38,845	36,160	-0.1	-6.9
Tourists (overnight visitors) (1000)	17,534	19,145	18,771	9.2	-2.0
- per 100 of inhabitants	54	59	57		
Same-day visitors (1000)	21,369	19,750	17,390	-7.6	-11.9
Tourism accommodation					
Number of rooms	363,628	377,771	..	3.9	
Nights spent in collective establishments (1000)	386,166	407,519		5.5	
by non-residents (inbound tourism)	107,698	123,426	125,656	14.6	1.8
by residents (domestic tourism)	278,468	284,093	..	2.0	
Nights spent in hotels and similar establishments (1000)					
by residents (domestic tourism)	53,882	55,312	..	2.7	
Outbound Tourism					
Trips abroad (1000)	17,739	19,545	21,101	10.2	8.0
- per 100 of inhabitants	55	60	64		
Receipts and Expenditure for International Tourism					
International Tourism Receipts (US$ million)	10,546	12,871	13,584	22.0	5.5
- per Tourist Arrival (US$)	601	672	724	11.8	7.6
- per Visitor Arrival (US$)	271	331	376	22.2	13.4
- per capita (US$)	327	396	414		
International Fare Receipts (US$ million)	1,634	2,106	2,240	28.9	6.4
International Tourism Expenditure (US$ million)	13,366	15,947	18,370	19.3	15.2
- per trip (US$)	754	816	871	8.3	6.7
- per capita (US$)	415	491	560		
International Fare Expenditure (US$ million)	2,972	3,743	4,720	25.9	26.1
Δ International Tourism Balance (US$ million)	-2,820	-3,076	-4,786		
Δ International Fare Balance (US$ million)	-1,338	-1,637	-2,480		

Source: World Tourism Organization (UNWTO)   (Data as collected by UNWTO for TMT 2006 Edition)

See annex for methodological notes and reference of external sources used.

International Tourism by Origin

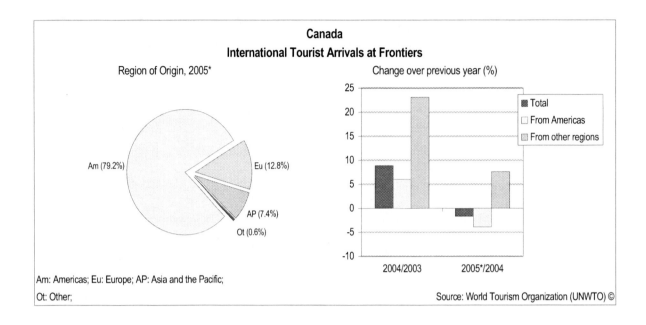

Canada
International Tourist Arrivals at Frontiers

Region of Origin, 2005*

Am (79.2%)
Eu (12.8%)
AP (7.4%)
Ot (0.6%)

Change over previous year (%)

Total
From Americas
From other regions

2004/2003   2005*/2004

Am: Americas; Eu: Europe; AP: Asia and the Pacific;
Ot: Other;

Source: World Tourism Organization (UNWTO) ©

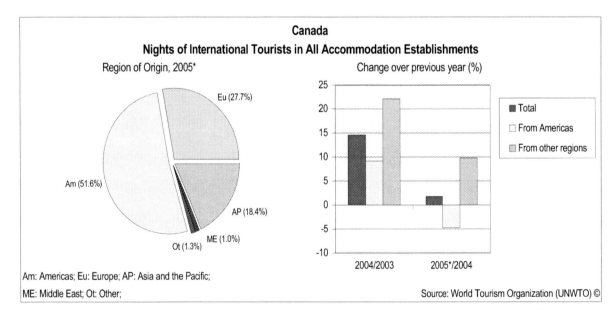

Canada
Nights of International Tourists in All Accommodation Establishments

Region of Origin, 2005*

Eu (27.7%)
Am (51.6%)
AP (18.4%)
ME (1.0%)
Ot (1.3%)

Change over previous year (%)

Total
From Americas
From other regions

2004/2003   2005*/2004

Am: Americas; Eu: Europe; AP: Asia and the Pacific;
ME: Middle East; Ot: Other;

Source: World Tourism Organization (UNWTO) ©

World Tourism Organization ©

Canada
International Tourist Arrivals at Frontiers (by residence)

	1995	2000	2003	2004	2005* (thousand)	Market share (%) 2000	2005*	Growth rate (%) 04/03	05*/04	Average per year (%) 2000-2005*
Total	**16,932**	**19,627**	**17,534**	**19,145**	**18,771**	**100**	**100**	**9.2**	**-2.0**	**-0.9**
From Americas	*13,294*	*15,605*	*14,589*	*15,518*	*14,867*	*79.5*	*79.2*	*6.4*	*-4.2*	*-1.0*
United States	13,005	15,189	14,232	15,088	14,391	77.4	76.7	6.0	-4.6	-1.1
Mexico	63	143	142	173	189	0.7	1.0	21.9	9.3	5.8
Brazil	41	51	31	50	61	0.3	0.3	60.1	22.6	3.5
Trinidad Tbg	14	21	18	21	22	0.1	0.1	16.7	7.5	1.0
Jamaica	18	18	16	21	20	0.1	0.1	31.7	-2.6	2.9
Bermuda	14	21	23	24	24	0.1	0.1	3.6	-0.9	3.0
St.Pierre,Miquelon	..	13	14	16	16	0.1	0.1	8.2	0.6	3.4
Argentina	21	22	10	12	14	0.1	0.1	24.0	17.7	-8.7
Colombia	..	10	8	8	11	0.1	0.1	10.3	33.3	1.9
Venezuela	14	13	6	9	12	0.1	0.1	43.0	29.7	-1.6
Barbados	9	10	8	10	10	0.1	0.1	24.3	-0.4	0.7
Other intraregional	96	93	80	86	96	0.5	0.5	8.3	11.8	0.6
From other regions	*3,638*	*4,023*	*2,946*	*3,627*	*3,903*	*20.5*	*20.8*	*23.1*	*7.6*	*-0.6*
United Kingdom	641	879	708	825	906	4.5	4.8	16.5	9.9	0.6
Japan	589	508	262	414	424	2.6	2.3	57.9	2.4	-3.5
France	430	404	277	332	356	2.1	1.9	20.0	7.4	-2.5
Germany	421	387	260	300	324	2.0	1.7	15.2	8.2	-3.5
Australia	142	175	152	180	202	0.9	1.1	18.2	12.3	3.0
Korea, Republic of	113	134	139	170	180	0.7	1.0	22.6	5.9	6.1
China	..	73	76	102	117	0.4	0.6	33.2	15.3	9.8
Netherlands	100	128	104	117	119	0.7	0.6	12.1	1.6	-1.5
Hong Kong (China)	217	142	92	115	111	0.7	0.6	26.0	-3.5	-4.7
Taiwan (pr. of China)	98	164	68	107	98	0.8	0.5	56.3	-7.9	-9.7
Switzerland	101	103	82	91	97	0.5	0.5	10.5	5.9	-1.4
India	..	52	57	68	78	0.3	0.4	19.8	14.0	8.4
Italy	99	109	57	82	91	0.6	0.5	43.9	9.8	-3.6
Israel	68	76	58	67	80	0.4	0.4	15.3	19.4	1.1
All South Asia	69	..	..	..	..					
Spain	32	39	30	40	47	0.2	0.3	34.7	17.3	3.8
Ireland	18	31	30	38	43	0.2	0.2	24.8	13.0	6.4
Philippines	25	31	32	36	43	0.2	0.2	14.0	17.0	6.5
Belgium	..	51	37	43	43	0.3	0.2	16.9	0.1	-3.2
Belgium/Luxembourg	43	..	..	..	..					
New Zealand	37	36	29	36	39	0.2	0.2	22.9	7.6	1.5
Austria	33	30	25	30	32	0.2	0.2	21.1	5.4	1.1
All Middle East	32	..	..	..	..					
Sweden	28	37	26	30	32	0.2	0.2	15.5	7.4	-2.6
Denmark	21	27	22	24	26	0.1	0.1	9.4	8.0	-0.9
Other interregional	283	405	320	378	414	2.1	2.2	18.0	9.6	0.4

Source: World Tourism Organization (UNWTO) ©   (Data as collected by UNWTO for TMT 2006 Edition)

Canada

Nights of International Tourists in All Accommodation Establishments (by residence)

	1995	2000	2003	2004	2005* (thousand)	Market share (%) 2000	Market share (%) 2005*	Growth rate (%) 04/03	Growth rate (%) 05*/04	Average per year (%) 2000-2005*
Total	**91,983**	**119,381**	**107,698**	**123,426**	**125,656**	**100**	**100**	**14.6**	**1.8**	**1.0**
From Americas	*52,629*	*64,135*	*62,294*	*67,985*	*64,785*	*53.7*	*51.6*	*9.1*	*-4.7*	*0.2*
United States	49,078	58,447	56,723	60,738	57,331	49.0	45.6	7.1	-5.6	-0.4
Mexico	618	1,788	2,101	2,886	3,149	1.5	2.5	37.4	9.1	12.0
Brazil	368	1,009	570	1,049	929	0.8	0.7	84.1	-11.4	-1.6
Trinidad Tbg	382	209	392	372	441	0.2	0.4	-5.3	18.7	16.1
Colombia	..	129	127	247	340	0.1	0.3	94.2	37.6	21.3
Jamaica	289	310	351	281	297	0.3	0.2	-19.9	5.7	-0.8
Argentina	265	369	111	152	237	0.3	0.2	37.4	55.8	-8.4
Bermuda	150	214	317	301	208	0.2	0.2	-5.0	-31.1	-0.6
Venezuela	141	140	123	121	169	0.1	0.1	-1.9	39.7	3.9
St.Pierre,Miquelon	..	61	85	202	157	0.1	0.1	136.2	-22.0	20.9
Greenland	..	2	1	3	2	0.0	0.0	200.0	-11.1	3.7
Other Caribbean	664	943	846	962	774	0.8	0.6	13.7	-19.5	-3.9
Other South America	..	299	353	437	552	0.3	0.4	23.8	26.3	13.0
Other Americas	673	216	195	235	199	0.2	0.2	20.9	-15.5	-1.7
From other regions	*39,354*	*55,246*	*45,404*	*55,441*	*60,871*	*46.3*	*48.4*	*22.1*	*9.8*	*2.0*
United Kingdom	7,327	10,261	8,961	10,221	11,882	8.6	9.5	14.1	16.3	3.0
France	5,230	6,052	4,181	4,891	5,836	5.1	4.6	17.0	19.3	-0.7
Germany	5,089	5,770	3,942	4,588	4,900	4.8	3.9	16.4	6.8	-3.2
Japan	3,487	4,628	2,994	4,742	4,750	3.9	3.8	58.4	0.2	0.5
Korea, Republic of	738	3,507	3,341	3,897	4,466	2.9	3.6	16.6	14.6	5.0
China	..	1,561	2,329	3,114	3,723	1.3	3.0	33.7	19.6	19.0
Australia	1,381	2,099	1,765	2,447	2,447	1.8	1.9	38.6	0.0	3.1
Hong Kong (China)	2,454	1,894	1,623	2,168	2,162	1.6	1.7	33.6	-0.3	2.7
All South Asia	608	1,398	1,297	1,432	1,771	1.2	1.4	10.4	23.7	4.9
Switzerland	1,246	1,851	1,605	1,505	1,684	1.6	1.3	-6.3	11.9	-1.9
Netherlands	1,292	1,767	1,499	1,830	1,580	1.5	1.3	22.0	-13.6	-2.2
Taiwan (pr. of China)	1,643	2,043	1,079	1,308	1,536	1.7	1.2	21.2	17.4	-5.6
All Middle East	411	679	897	1,183	1,285	0.6	1.0	31.9	8.6	13.6
Italy	1,265	1,609	727	1,136	1,061	1.3	0.8	56.3	-6.6	-8.0
Israel	623	917	682	735	929	0.8	0.7	7.8	26.4	0.3
Philippines	232	500	687	745	875	0.4	0.7	8.5	17.5	11.9
Bulgaria	159	349	365	466	680	0.3	0.5	27.7	46.0	14.3
Spain	328	502	422	661	661	0.4	0.5	56.7	0.0	5.7
Commonwealth Indep. States	384	470	430	547	597	0.4	0.5	27.2	9.2	4.9
Poland	496	311	553	575	597	0.3	0.5	4.0	3.7	13.9
Ireland	244	461	444	408	510	0.4	0.4	-8.1	24.9	2.0
Austria	395	452	318	504	477	0.4	0.4	58.2	-5.3	1.1
Sweden	267	448	252	383	474	0.4	0.4	52.1	23.8	1.1
Belgium/Luxembourg	516	711	498	566	464	0.6	0.4	13.7	-18.1	-8.2
New Zealand	345	396	494	428	449	0.3	0.4	-13.5	5.0	2.5
Other interregional	3,194	4,610	4,020	4,964	5,077	3.9	4.0	23.5	2.3	1.9

Source: World Tourism Organization (UNWTO) ©   (Data as collected by UNWTO for TMT 2006 Edition)

World Tourism Organization ©

III.1.2   Mexico   **North America**

Promotional: www.visitmexico.gob.mx
Institutional/corporate: www.sectur.gob.mx
Research and data: www.datatur.sectur.gob.mx

Profile

Mexico

Capital	Mexico City
Year of entry in UNWTO	1975
Area (1000 km²)	1,958
Population (2005, million)	106
Gross Domestic Product (GDP) (2005, US$ million)	768,437
GDP per capita (2005, US$)	7,298

Americas
North America

GDP growth (real, %)
'-> 2004: 4.2;   2005: 3.0;   2006*: 4.0;   2007*: 3.5

	2003	2004	2005*	2004/2003	2005*/2004
International Arrivals					
Visitors (1000)	92,330	99,250	103,146	7.5	3.9
Tourists (overnight visitors) (1000)	18,665	20,618	21,915	10.5	6.3
- per 100 of inhabitants	18	20	21		
Same-day visitors (1000)	68,690	72,139	74,524	5.0	3.3
Cruise passengers (1000)	4,974	6,493	6,707	30.5	3.3
Tourism accommodation					
Number of rooms	496,292	515,904	535,639	4.0	3.8
Nights spent in hotels and similar establishments (1000)	84,726	94,582	98,230	11.6	3.9
by non-residents (inbound tourism)	26,011	30,227	33,623	16.2	11.2
by residents (domestic tourism)	58,715	64,355	64,607	9.6	0.4
Outbound Tourism					
Trips abroad (1000)	11,044	12,494	13,305	13.1	6.5
- per 100 of inhabitants	11	12	13		
Receipts and Expenditure for International Tourism					
International Tourism Receipts (US$ million)	9,362	10,796	11,803	15.3	9.3
- per Tourist Arrival (US$)	502	524	539	4.4	2.9
- per Visitor Arrival (US$)	101	109	114	7.3	5.2
- per capita (US$)	90	103	111		
International Fare Receipts (US$ million)	696	813	998	16.8	22.8
International Tourism Expenditure (US$ million)	6,253	6,959	7,600	11.3	9.2
- per trip (US$)	566	557	571	-1.6	2.6
- per capita (US$)	60	66	72		
International Fare Expenditure (US$ million)	999	1,075	1,351	7.6	25.7
Δ International Tourism Balance (US$ million)	3,108	3,837	4,203		
Δ International Fare Balance (US$ million)	-303	-262	-353		

Source: World Tourism Organization (UNWTO)   (Data as collected by UNWTO for TMT 2006 Edition)

See annex for methodological notes and reference of external sources used.

International Tourism by Origin

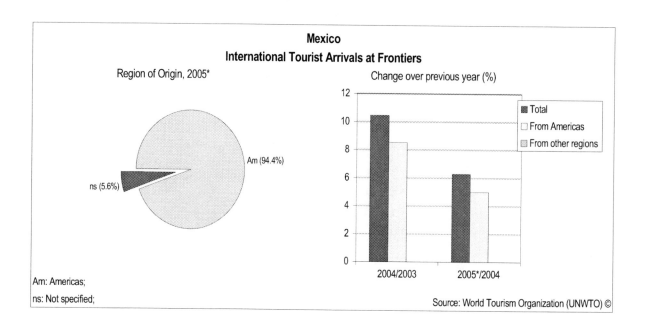

Mexico
International Tourist Arrivals at Frontiers

Region of Origin, 2005*

Change over previous year (%)

Am: Americas;
ns: Not specified;

Source: World Tourism Organization (UNWTO) ©

Mexico
International Tourist Arrivals at Frontiers (by residence)

	1995	2000	2003	2004	2005* (thousand)	Market share (%) 2000	2005*	Growth rate (%) 04/03	05*/04	Average per year (%) 2000-2005*
Total	**20,241**	**20,641**	**18,665**	**20,618**	**21,915**	**100**	**100**	**10.5**	**6.3**	**1.2**
From Americas	*19,862*	*19,950*	*18,155*	*19,706*	*20,691*	*96.7*	*94.4*	*8.5*	*5.0*	*0.7*
United States	19,221	19,285	17,566	19,370	20,325	93.4	92.7	10.3	4.9	1.1
Canada	197	477	292	336	366	2.3	1.7	15.0	9.0	-5.2
Other Americas	445	187	297	..	..	0.9				
From other regions	*339*	*401*	*443*	*..*	*..*	*1.9*				
All Europe	339	401	443	..	..	1.9				
Other World/Not specified	*40*	*291*	*67*	*912*	*1,224*	*1.4*	*5.6*	*1267.4*	*34.1*	*33.3*

Source: World Tourism Organization (UNWTO) ©

(Data as collected by UNWTO for TMT 2006 Edition)

III.1.3   United States   North America

Promotional: http://seeamerica.org ; www.visitusa.org.uk/
Institutional/corporate: www.tinet.ita.doc.gov
Research and data: www.tinet.ita.doc.gov

Profile

United States

Americas
North America

Capital	Washington D.C.
Area (1000 km²)	9,629
Population (2005, million)	296
Gross Domestic Product (GDP) (2005, US$ million)	12,455,830
GDP per capita (2005, US$)	42,000
GDP growth (real, %)	

'-> 2004: 3.9;   2005: 3.2;   2006*: 3.4;   2007*: 2.9

	2003	2004	2005*	2004/2003	2005*/2004
International Arrivals					
Tourists (overnight visitors) (1000)	41,218	46,086	49,206	11.8	6.8
- per 100 of inhabitants	14	16	17		
Tourism accommodation					
Number of rooms	4,415,696	4,411,908	4,402,466	-0.1	-0.2
Outbound Tourism					
Trips abroad (1000)	56,250	61,809	63,503	9.9	2.7
- per 100 of inhabitants	19	21	21		
Receipts and Expenditure for International Tourism					
International Tourism Receipts (US$ million)	64,348	74,547	81,680	15.8	9.6
- per Tourist Arrival (US$)	1,561	1,618	1,660	3.6	2.6
- per capita (US$)	222	254	276		
International Fare Receipts (US$ million)	15,693	18,851	20,931	20.1	11.0
International Tourism Expenditure (US$ million)	57,444	65,750	69,175	14.5	5.2
- per trip (US$)	1,021	1,064	1,089	4.2	2.4
- per capita (US$)	198	224	234		
International Fare Expenditure (US$ million)	20,957	23,723	26,006	13.2	9.6
Δ International Tourism Balance (US$ million)	6,904	8,797	12,505		
Δ International Fare Balance (US$ million)	-5,264	-4,872	-5,075		

Source: World Tourism Organization (UNWTO)   (Data as collected by UNWTO for TMT 2006 Edition)
See annex for methodological notes and reference of external sources used.

International Tourism by Origin

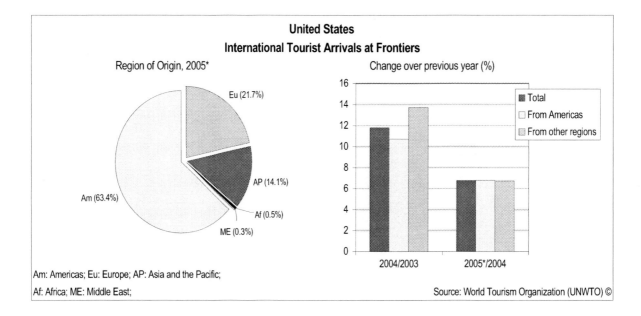

United States
International Tourist Arrivals at Frontiers

Region of Origin, 2005*

- Eu (21.7%)
- AP (14.1%)
- Af (0.5%)
- ME (0.3%)
- Am (63.4%)

Change over previous year (%)

Legend:
- Total
- From Americas
- From other regions

(x-axis: 2004/2003, 2005*/2004)

Am: Americas; Eu: Europe; AP: Asia and the Pacific;
Af: Africa; ME: Middle East;

Source: World Tourism Organization (UNWTO) ©

United States

International Tourist Arrivals at Frontiers (by residence)

	1995	2000	2003	2004	2005* (thousand)	Market share (%) 2000	Market share (%) 2005*	Growth rate (%) 04/03	Growth rate (%) 05*/04	Average per year (%) 2000-2005*
Total	**43,490**	**51,219**	**41,218**	**46,086**	**49,206**	**100**	**100**	**11.8**	**6.8**	**-0.8**
From Americas	*26,853*	*30,338*	*26,368*	*29,196*	*31,178*	*59.2*	*63.4*	*10.7*	*6.8*	*0.5*
Canada	14,662	14,648	12,666	13,857	14,862	28.6	30.2	9.4	7.3	0.3
Mexico	8,189	10,596	10,526	11,907	12,665	20.7	25.7	13.1	6.4	3.6
Brazil	838	737	349	385	485	1.4	1.0	10.3	26.2	-8.0
Venezuela	511	577	284	330	340	1.1	0.7	16.1	3.0	-10.0
Colombia	233	417	280	295	325	0.8	0.7	5.4	10.2	-4.8
Bahamas	281	294	253	266	237	0.6	0.5	4.9	-10.7	-4.2
Dominican Rp	176	197	153	180	221	0.4	0.5	17.7	23.0	2.3
Argentina	382	534	151	168	189	1.0	0.4	11.3	12.6	-18.8
Jamaica	196	243	159	163	175	0.5	0.4	2.2	7.5	-6.3
Guatemala	131	186	152	162	170	0.4	0.3	6.6	5.0	-1.7
El Salvador	82	185	177	181	164	0.4	0.3	2.2	-9.2	-2.3
Peru	127	192	154	151	152	0.4	0.3	-1.9	0.3	-4.6
Ecuador	98	130	120	133	143	0.3	0.3	11.1	7.5	1.9
Costa Rica	118	176	113	127	134	0.3	0.3	12.6	5.3	-5.3
Trinidad Tbg	82	138	112	121	128	0.3	0.3	8.4	6.0	-1.4
Chile	152	192	95	101	102	0.4	0.2	6.1	0.4	-12.0
Honduras	51	91	82	86	90	0.2	0.2	4.1	4.9	-0.2
Other intraregional	543	806	541	582	595	1.6	1.2	7.7	2.1	-5.9
From other regions	*16,637*	*20,880*	*14,850*	*16,890*	*18,027*	*40.8*	*36.6*	*13.7*	*6.7*	*-2.9*
United Kingdom	2,888	4,703	3,936	4,303	4,345	9.2	8.8	9.3	1.0	-1.6
Japan	4,598	5,061	3,170	3,748	3,884	9.9	7.9	18.2	3.6	-5.2
Germany	1,848	1,786	1,180	1,320	1,416	3.5	2.9	11.8	7.2	-4.5
France	922	1,087	689	775	879	2.1	1.8	12.5	13.3	-4.2
Korea, Republic of	592	662	618	627	705	1.3	1.4	1.5	12.5	1.3
Australia	424	540	406	520	582	1.1	1.2	28.2	11.9	1.5
Italy	525	612	409	471	546	1.2	1.1	15.2	15.9	-2.3
Netherlands	408	553	374	425	449	1.1	0.9	13.7	5.6	-4.1
Spain	302	361	284	333	386	0.7	0.8	17.4	15.7	1.3
Ireland	149	286	254	345	383	0.6	0.8	35.7	11.1	6.1
India	123	274	272	309	345	0.5	0.7	13.5	11.7	4.7
Taiwan (pr. of China)	413	457	239	298	319	0.9	0.6	24.6	7.1	-7.0
Sweden	219	322	211	254	291	0.6	0.6	20.3	14.3	-2.0
Israel	216	325	249	275	284	0.6	0.6	10.6	3.2	-2.7
China	167	249	157	203	270	0.5	0.5	28.7	33.4	1.6
Switzerland	397	395	230	243	257	0.8	0.5	5.7	5.6	-8.3
Belgium	206	250	151	176	192	0.5	0.4	16.5	8.9	-5.2
Denmark	108	149	125	151	175	0.3	0.4	20.3	15.7	3.2
Philippines	110	168	134	144	154	0.3	0.3	7.2	6.8	-1.8
New Zealand	142	172	107	127	140	0.3	0.3	18.8	9.7	-4.1
Norway	103	148	113	130	139	0.3	0.3	15.2	6.6	-1.2
Hong Kong (China)	220	203	114	123	135	0.4	0.3	8.1	9.5	-7.8
Poland	48	116	108	123	134	0.2	0.3	14.0	9.3	2.9
Austria	173	176	100	113	118	0.3	0.2	13.0	4.2	-7.7
Singapore	103	136	88	107	116	0.3	0.2	21.7	8.8	-3.2
Other interregional	1,232	1,687	1,131	1,248	1,386	3.3	2.8	10.3	11.1	-3.9

Source: World Tourism Organization (UNWTO) ©   (Data as collected by UNWTO for TMT 2006 Edition)

III.2 Caribbean

III.2.1 Anguilla   Caribbean

Promotional: www.anguilla-vacation.com/ ; http://go-anguilla.com/ ; www.ahta.ai

Profile

Anguilla	Capital	The Valley
	Population (2005, 1000)	13

Americas
Caribbean

	2003	2004	2005*	2004/2003	2005*/2004
International Arrivals					
Visitors (1000)	109	121	143	11.0	18.2
Tourists (overnight visitors) (1000)	47	54	62	15.1	15.0
- per 100 of inhabitants	368	415	468		
Same-day visitors (1000)	62	67	81	8.1	20.9
Tourism accommodation					
Number of rooms	759	756	746	-0.4	-1.3
Nights spent in collective establishments (1000)					
by non-residents (inbound tourism)	399	410	502	2.8	22.4
Receipts and Expenditure for International Tourism					
International Tourism Receipts (US$ million)	60	69	86	15.3	24.7
- per Tourist Arrival (US$)	1,279	1,282	1,390	0.2	8.4
- per Visitor Arrival (US$)	550	572	603	3.9	5.5
- per capita (US$)	4,710	5,320	6,510		
International Tourism Expenditure (US$ million)	9	9	10		11.1
- per capita (US$)	707	692	754		
Δ International Tourism Balance (US$ million)	51	60	76		

Source: World Tourism Organization (UNWTO)   (Data as collected by UNWTO for TMT 2006 Edition)
See annex for methodological notes and reference of external sources used.

International Tourism by Origin

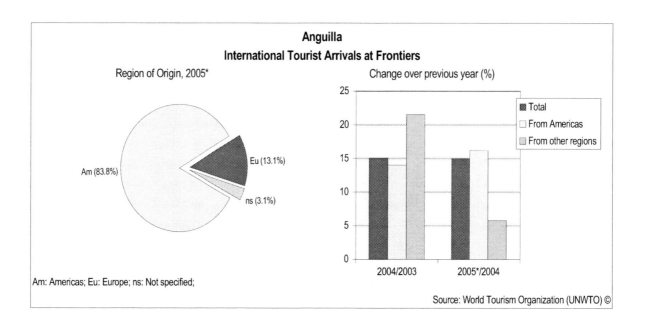

Anguilla
International Tourist Arrivals at Frontiers (by residence)

	1995	2000	2003	2004	2005*	Market share (%) 2000	Market share (%) 2005*	Growth rate (%) 04/03	Growth rate (%) 05*/04	Average per year (%) 2000-2005*
Total	**38,531**	**43,789**	**46,915**	**53,987**	**62,084**	**100**	**100**	**15.1**	**15.0**	**7.2**
From Americas	*35,272*	*33,127*	*39,295*	*44,799*	*52,054*	*75.7*	*83.8*	*14.0*	*16.2*	*9.5*
United States	24,149	24,799	30,644	35,751	41,733	56.6	67.2	16.7	16.7	11.0
All the Caribbean	10,016	6,816	7,362	7,499	8,529	15.6	13.7	1.9	13.7	4.6
Canada	1,107	1,512	1,289	1,549	1,792	3.5	2.9	20.2	15.7	3.5
From other regions	*2,405*	*9,422*	*6,308*	*7,667*	*8,113*	*21.5*	*13.1*	*21.5*	*5.8*	*-2.9*
United Kingdom	2,405	2,786	2,962	3,198	3,834	6.4	6.2	8.0	19.9	6.6
Italy	..	3,737	945	1,086	1,199	8.5	1.9	14.9	10.4	-20.3
Germany	..	522	649	1,019	410	1.2	0.7	57.0	-59.8	-4.7
Other Europe	..	2,377	1,752	2,364	2,670	5.4	4.3	34.9	12.9	2.4
Other World/Not specified	*854*	*1,240*	*1,312*	*1,521*	*1,917*	*2.8*	*3.1*	*15.9*	*26.0*	*9.1*

(Data as collected by UNWTO for TMT 2006 Edition)

III.2.2 Antigua and Barbuda Caribbean

Profile

Antigua and Barbuda

Americas
Caribbean

Capital	Saint John's
Area (10 km²)	44
Population (2005, 1000)	69
Gross Domestic Product (GDP) (2005, US$ million)	873
GDP per capita (2005, US$)	10,727
GDP growth (real, %)	
'-> 2004: 5.2; 2005: 5.0; 2006*: 7.1; 2007*: 3.9	

	2003	2004	2005*	2004/2003	2005*/2004
International Arrivals					
Visitors (1000)	623	791	728	27.0	-8.0
Tourists (overnight visitors) (1000)	224	245	239	9.6	-2.7
- per 100 of inhabitants	330	359	347		
Cruise passengers (1000)	384	523	467	36.2	-10.7
Receipts and Expenditure for International Tourism					
International Tourism Receipts (US$ million)	300	338	327	12.7	-3.3
- per Tourist Arrival (US$)	1,339	1,377	1,369	2.8	-0.6
- per Visitor Arrival (US$)	482	427	449	-11.3	5.1
- per capita (US$)	4,418	4,947	4,758		
International Tourism Expenditure (US$ million)	35	37	40	5.7	8.1
- per capita (US$)	515	542	582		
Δ International Tourism Balance (US$ million)	265	301	287		

Source: World Tourism Organization (UNWTO)   (Data as collected by UNWTO for TMT 2006 Edition)

See annex for methodological notes and reference of external sources used.

International Tourism by Origin

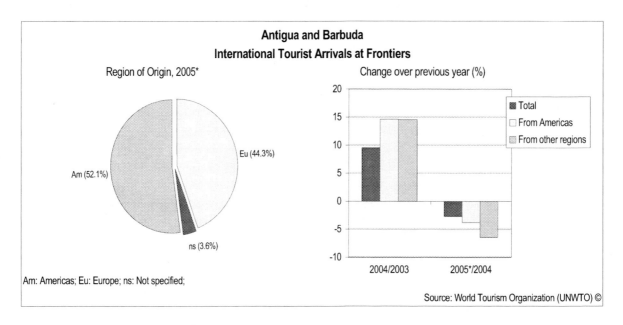

Antigua and Barbuda
International Tourist Arrivals at Frontiers

Region of Origin, 2005*

Am (52.1%)
Eu (44.3%)
ns (3.6%)

Change over previous year (%)

■ Total
□ From Americas
▨ From other regions

2004/2003   2005*/2004

Am: Americas; Eu: Europe; ns: Not specified;

Source: World Tourism Organization (UNWTO) ©

Antigua and Barbuda
International Tourist Arrivals at Frontiers (by residence)

	1995	2000	2003	2004	2005*	Market share (%) 2000	Market share (%) 2005*	Growth rate (%) 04/03	Growth rate (%) 05*/04	Average per year (%) 2000-2005*
Total	**220,000**	**206,871**	**224,032**	**245,456**	**238,804**	**100**	**100**	**9.6**	**-2.7**	**2.9**
From Americas	*123,680*	*107,438*	*112,809*	*129,316*	*124,404*	*51.9*	*52.1*	*14.6*	*-3.8*	*3.0*
United States	66,913	59,012	64,363	70,531	66,644	28.5	27.9	9.6	-5.5	2.5
All the Caribbean	..	34,419	39,843	..	47,319	16.6	19.8			6.6
Canada	12,881	14,007	8,603	9,452	9,571	6.8	4.0	9.9	1.3	-7.3
Trinidad Tbg	3,632	..	..	6,042	..					
Jamaica	3,645	..	..	4,407	..					
Barbados	2,999	..	..	4,129	..					
US.Virgin Is	2,198	..	..	3,304	..					
Guyana	3,576	..	..	3,053	..					
Neth. Antilles	1,065	..	..	1,962	..					
Puerto Rico	1,530	..	..	1,291	..					
Other Caribbean	24,046	..	..	24,405	..					
Other South America	1,195	..	..	740	870		0.4		17.6	
From other regions	*83,799*	*90,049*	*98,665*	*113,033*	*105,735*	*43.5*	*44.3*	*14.6*	*-6.5*	*3.3*
United Kingdom	50,880	74,957	83,447	97,829	90,568	36.2	37.9	17.2	-7.4	3.9
Italy	7,726	..	..	6,116	5,525		2.3		-9.7	
Germany	10,022	..	..	2,344	2,586		1.1		10.3	
France	4,397	..	..	1,177	1,203		0.5		2.2	
Switzerland	5,028	..	..	953	892		0.4		-6.4	
Other Europe	5,746	15,092	15,218	4,614	4,961	7.3	2.1	-69.7	7.5	-19.9
Nationals residing abroad	*8,337*	*..*	*..*	*..*	*..*					
Other World/Not specified	*4,184*	*9,384*	*12,558*	*3,107*	*8,665*	*4.5*	*3.6*	*-75.3*	*178.9*	*-1.6*

Source: World Tourism Organization (UNWTO) ©   (Data as collected by UNWTO for TMT 2006 Edition)
Note: Air arrivals

World Tourism Organization ©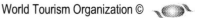

III.2.3   Aruba   Caribbean

Profile

Aruba

Capital	Oranjestad
Year of entry in UNWTO	1987
Area (10 km²)	19
Population (2005, 1000)	72

Americas
Caribbean

	2003	2004	2005*	2004/2003	2005*/2004
International Arrivals					
Visitors (1000)	1,184	1,304	1,286	10.1	-1.4
Tourists (overnight visitors) (1000)	642	728	733	13.4	0.6
- per 100 of inhabitants	906	1,022	1,024		
Cruise passengers (1000)	542	576	553	6.3	-4.0
Tourism accommodation					
Number of rooms	7,731	7,206	7,966	-6.8	10.5
Nights spent in collective establishments (1000)					
by non-residents (inbound tourism)	5,098	5,640	5,695	10.6	1.0
Nights spent in hotels and similar establishments (1000)					
by non-residents (inbound tourism)	4,059	4,615	4,735	13.7	2.6
Receipts and Expenditure for International Tourism					
International Tourism Receipts (US$ million)	859	1,060	1,095	23.4	3.3
- per Tourist Arrival (US$)	1,338	1,455	1,495	8.8	2.7
- per Visitor Arrival (US$)	725	813	852	12.0	4.8
- per capita (US$)	12,124	14,881	15,304		
International Fare Receipts (US$ million)	0	..	..		
International Tourism Expenditure (US$ million)	189	218	218	15.7	-0.2
- per capita (US$)	2,665	3,066	3,044		
International Fare Expenditure (US$ million)	24	30	27	25.0	-10.0
Δ International Tourism Balance (US$ million)	670	841	877		
Δ International Fare Balance (US$ million)	-24	..	..		

Source: World Tourism Organization (UNWTO)   (Data as collected by UNWTO for TMT 2006 Edition)

See annex for methodological notes and reference of external sources used.

International Tourism by Origin

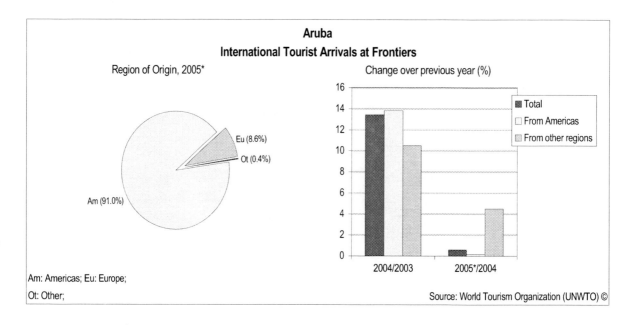

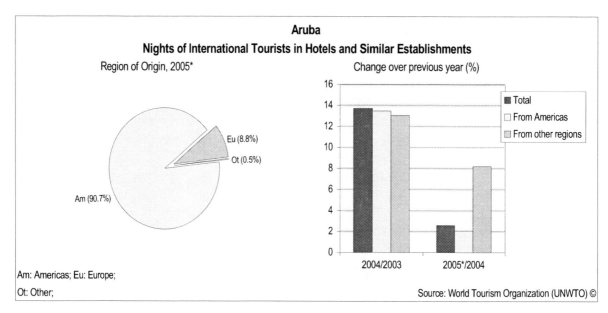

World Tourism Organization ©

Aruba

International Tourist Arrivals at Frontiers (by residence)

	1995	2000	2003	2004	2005*	Market share (%) 2000	2005*	Growth rate (%) 04/03	05*/04	Average per year (%) 2000-2005*
Total	**618,916**	**721,224**	**641,906**	**728,157**	**732,514**	**100**	**100**	**13.4**	**0.6**	**0.3**
From Americas	*564,985*	*670,271*	*584,651*	*665,489*	*666,454*	*92.9*	*91.0*	*13.8*	*0.1*	*-0.1*
United States	344,885	458,132	460,241	531,287	532,352	63.5	72.7	15.4	0.2	3.0
Venezuela	85,640	112,018	54,554	59,218	59,928	15.5	8.2	8.5	1.2	-11.8
Canada	27,169	20,594	17,218	20,560	21,350	2.9	2.9	19.4	3.8	0.7
Neth. Antilles	29,244	23,709	..	..	..	3.3				
Curaçao	..	..	17,061	16,649	15,047		2.1	-2.4	-9.6	
Colombia	26,785	31,367	11,397	10,648	9,863	4.3	1.3	-6.6	-7.4	-20.7
Brazil	29,837	3,309	2,785	4,762	6,067	0.5	0.8	71.0	27.4	12.9
Puerto Rico	..	..	4,225	3,846	3,096		0.4	-9.0	-19.5	
Argentina	8,619	7,371	1,761	2,071	2,569	1.0	0.4	17.6	24.0	-19.0
Suriname	1,251	1,269	1,515	2,084	2,336	0.2	0.3	37.6	12.1	13.0
Dominican Rp	1,293	1,406	921	1,338	1,269	0.2	0.2	45.3	-5.2	-2.0
Trinidad Tbg	587	1,593	2,168	1,487	1,201	0.2	0.2	-31.4	-19.2	-5.5
Mexico	..	..	909	940	1,030		0.1	3.4	9.6	
Peru	2,811	2,510	1,055	1,087	946	0.3	0.1	3.0	-13.0	-17.7
Ecuador	824	699	611	723	679	0.1	0.1	18.3	-6.1	-0.6
Chile	862	1,085	325	416	428	0.2	0.1	28.0	2.9	-17.0
Other Caribbean	2,603	2,363	5,598	5,867	4,970	0.3	0.7	4.8	-15.3	16.0
Other South America	..	..	2,307	2,506	3,323		0.5	8.6	32.6	
Other Americas	2,575	2,846	..	..	..	0.4				
From other regions	*52,156*	*47,278*	*54,873*	*60,639*	*63,372*	*6.6*	*8.7*	*10.5*	*4.5*	*6.0*
Netherlands	33,275	30,575	36,415	38,122	38,667	4.2	5.3	4.7	1.4	4.8
United Kingdom	1,973	3,456	6,722	7,810	7,012	0.5	1.0	16.2	-10.2	15.2
Sweden	..	484	748	1,680	3,472	0.1	0.5	124.6	106.7	48.3
Germany	7,075	3,551	2,905	3,090	3,333	0.5	0.5	6.4	7.9	-1.3
Belgium	..	921	1,536	1,820	1,858	0.1	0.3	18.5	2.1	15.1
Italy	1,904	2,080	1,223	1,319	1,664	0.3	0.2	7.8	26.2	-4.4
Switzerland	1,076	1,128	766	1,153	1,194	0.2	0.2	50.5	3.6	1.1
Spain	..	746	683	724	820	0.1	0.1	6.0	13.3	1.9
Finland	..	120	286	257	664	0.0	0.1	-10.1	158.4	40.8
Austria	..	471	452	609	600	0.1	0.1	34.7	-1.5	5.0
Denmark	..	189	201	204	586	0.0	0.1	1.5	187.3	25.4
Norway	..	629	337	434	575	0.1	0.1	28.8	32.5	-1.8
Scandinavia	442	..	..	..	..					
Japan	274	215	162	211	191	0.0	0.0	30.2	-9.5	-2.3
Russian Federation	..	187	105	159	161	0.0	0.0	51.4	1.3	-2.9
Portugal	..	220	156	158	119	0.0	0.0	1.3	-24.7	-11.6
Other Europe	6,137	2,306	2,176	2,889	2,456	0.3	0.3	32.8	-15.0	1.3
Other World/Not specified	*1,775*	*3,675*	*2,382*	*2,029*	*2,688*	*0.5*	*0.4*	*-14.8*	*32.5*	*-6.1*

Source: World Tourism Organization (UNWTO) ©   (Data as collected by UNWTO for TMT 2006 Edition)

Aruba

Nights of International Tourists in Hotels and Similar Establishments (by residence)

	1995	2000	2003	2004	2005*	Market share (%)		Growth rate (%)		Average per year (%)
						2000	2005*	04/03	05*/04	2000-2005*
Total	**3,725,611**	**4,249,683**	**4,059,145**	**4,615,338**	**4,735,380**	**100**	**100**	**13.7**	**2.6**	**2.2**
From Americas	*3,377,658*	*3,936,726*	*3,708,580*	*4,207,992*	*4,294,975*	*92.6*	*90.7*	*13.5*	*2.1*	*1.8*
United States	2,338,529	3,021,843	3,139,379	3,597,026	3,670,826	71.1	77.5	14.6	2.1	4.0
Venezuela	347,490	461,153	265,222	276,044	273,149	10.9	5.8	4.1	-1.0	-9.9
Canada	226,504	161,922	136,324	162,208	174,295	3.8	3.7	19.0	7.5	1.5
Colombia	119,912	120,026	52,238	51,886	49,610	2.8	1.0	-0.7	-4.4	-16.2
Brazil	172,756	19,717	16,666	29,411	37,514	0.5	0.8	76.5	27.6	13.7
Neth. Antilles	57,283	38,207	40,803	37,474	30,923	0.9	0.7	-8.2	-17.5	-4.1
Argentina	61,679	56,613	14,905	16,733	20,669	1.3	0.4	12.3	23.5	-18.3
Peru	19,679	11,343	4,842	5,918	5,176	0.3	0.1	22.2	-12.5	-14.5
Suriname	2,228	1,830	3,347	3,994	4,240	0.0	0.1	19.3	6.2	18.3
Trinidad Tbg	2,569	4,899	8,899	4,615	4,052	0.1	0.1	-48.1	-12.2	-3.7
Chile	5,169	7,364	2,096	2,755	2,736	0.2	0.1	31.4	-0.7	-18.0
Ecuador	3,369	3,094	1,999	2,184	2,206	0.1	0.0	9.3	1.0	-6.5
Dominican Rp	1,379	2,911	2,193	2,111	1,475	0.1	0.0	-3.7	-30.1	-12.7
Other Caribbean	7,267	14,088	7,446	3,736	2,827	0.3	0.1	-49.8	-24.3	-27.5
Other South America	..	..	..	..	15,277		0.3			
Other Americas	11,845	11,716	12,221	11,897	..	0.3		-2.7		
From other regions	*338,420*	*289,837*	*341,983*	*386,605*	*418,284*	*6.8*	*8.8*	*13.0*	*8.2*	*7.6*
Netherlands	200,987	175,311	186,499	188,713	209,196	4.1	4.4	1.2	10.9	3.6
United Kingdom	12,397	21,561	66,917	83,475	73,969	0.5	1.6	24.7	-11.4	28.0
Sweden	..	..	..	..	30,711		0.6			
Germany	61,229	32,952	26,416	28,913	29,381	0.8	0.6	9.5	1.6	-2.3
Scandinavia	2,676	10,280	11,732	27,430	..	0.2		133.8		
Belgium	..	..	..	..	12,736		0.3			
Italy	11,770	13,293	8,463	9,301	10,019	0.3	0.2	9.9	7.7	-5.5
Switzerland	8,229	9,293	7,474	10,234	9,900	0.2	0.2	36.9	-3.3	1.3
Austria	..	..	..	..	5,784		0.1			
Finland	..	..	..	..	5,507		0.1			
Denmark	..	..	..	..	4,691		0.1			
Spain	..	..	..	..	4,270		0.1			
Norway	..	..	..	..	4,132		0.1			
Portugal	..	..	..	..	743		0.0			
Japan	1,153	832	648	698	719	0.0	0.0	7.7	3.0	-2.9
Russian Federation	..	..	..	..	664		0.0			
Other Europe	39,979	26,315	33,834	37,841	15,862	0.6	0.3	11.8	-58.1	-9.6
Other World/Not specified	*9,533*	*23,120*	*8,582*	*20,741*	*22,121*	*0.5*	*0.5*	*141.7*	*6.7*	*-0.9*

Source: World Tourism Organization (UNWTO) ©　　　　　　　　　　　　(Data as collected by UNWTO for TMT 2006 Edition)

III.2.4   Bahamas   Caribbean

Promotional: www.bahamas.com
Institutional/corporate: www.tourismbahamas.org
Research and data: www.tourismbahamas.org

Profile

Bahamas

Capital	Nassau
Year of entry in UNWTO	2005
Area (100 km²)	139
Population (2005, 1000)	302
Gross Domestic Product (GDP) (2005, US$ million)	5,870
GDP per capita (2005, US$)	18,062

Americas

Caribbean

GDP growth (real, %)

'-> 2004: 1.8;   2005: 2.7;   2006*: 4.0;   2007*: 4.5

	2003	2004	2005*	2004/2003	2005*/2004
International Arrivals					
Visitors (1000)	4,594	5,004	5,036	8.9	0.6
Tourists (overnight visitors) (1000)	1,510	1,561	1,608	3.4	3.0
- per 100 of inhabitants	508	521	533		
Same-day visitors (1000)	114	83	93	-27.2	12.0
Cruise passengers (1000)	2,970	3,360	3,335	13.1	-0.7
Tourism accommodation					
Number of rooms	15,393	15,508	14,800	0.7	-4.6
Nights spent in collective establishments (1000)					
by non-residents (inbound tourism)	8,957	9,898	10,297	10.5	4.0
Receipts and Expenditure for International Tourism					
International Tourism Receipts (US$ million)	1,757	1,884	2,069	7.2	9.8
- per Tourist Arrival (US$)	1,164	1,207	1,287	3.7	6.6
- per Visitor Arrival (US$)	383	377	411	-1.6	9.1
- per capita (US$)	5,908	6,288	6,856		
International Fare Receipts (US$ million)	13	13	10		-24.6
International Tourism Expenditure (US$ million)	305	316	344	3.6	9.0
- per capita (US$)	1,025	1,054	1,141		
International Fare Expenditure (US$ million)	99	153	184	54.5	20.3
Δ International Tourism Balance (US$ million)	1,452	1,568	1,725		
Δ International Fare Balance (US$ million)	-86	-140	-174		

Source: World Tourism Organization (UNWTO)   (Data as collected by UNWTO for TMT 2006 Edition)

See annex for methodological notes and reference of external sources used.

International Tourism by Origin

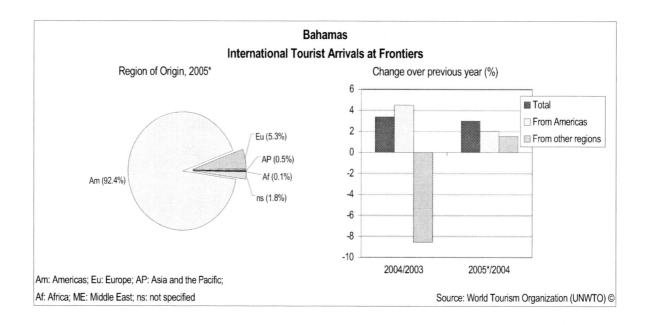

Bahamas
International Tourist Arrivals at Frontiers

Region of Origin, 2005*

Change over previous year (%)

Am (92.4%)
Eu (5.3%)
AP (0.5%)
Af (0.1%)
ns (1.8%)

Total
From Americas
From other regions

Am: Americas; Eu: Europe; AP: Asia and the Pacific;
Af: Africa; ME: Middle East; ns: not specified

Source: World Tourism Organization (UNWTO) ©

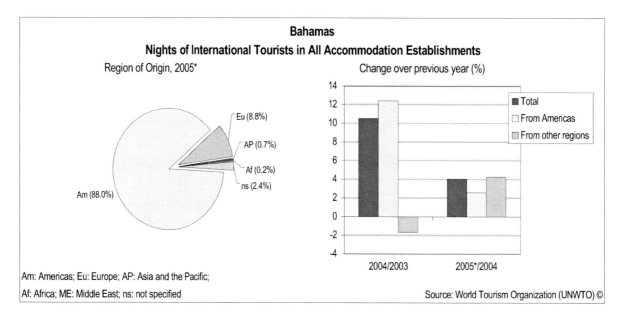

Bahamas
Nights of International Tourists in All Accommodation Establishments

Region of Origin, 2005*

Change over previous year (%)

Am (88.0%)
Eu (8.8%)
AP (0.7%)
Af (0.2%)
ns (2.4%)

Total
From Americas
From other regions

Am: Americas; Eu: Europe; AP: Asia and the Pacific;
Af: Africa; ME: Middle East; ns: not specified

Source: World Tourism Organization (UNWTO) ©

Bahamas
International Tourist Arrivals at Frontiers (by residence)

	1995	2000	2003	2004	2005*	Market share (%) 2000	Market share (%) 2005*	Growth rate (%) 04/03	Growth rate (%) 05*/04	Average per year (%) 2000-2005*
Total	**1,598,135**	**1,543,959**	**1,510,169**	**1,561,312**	**1,608,153**	**100**	**100**	**3.4**	**3.0**	**0.8**
From Americas	*1,432,505*	*1,406,513*	*1,392,578*	*1,455,375*	*1,484,921*	*91.1*	*92.3*	*4.5*	*2.0*	*1.1*
United States	1,328,925	1,294,295	1,305,335	1,360,912	1,380,083	83.8	85.8	4.3	1.4	1.3
Canada	85,600	82,840	63,148	68,462	75,643	5.4	4.7	8.4	10.5	-1.8
Jamaica	..	5,007	5,444	5,835	6,599	0.3	0.4	7.2	13.1	5.7
Mexico	2,440	3,208	3,126	3,094	3,546	0.2	0.2	-1.0	14.6	2.0
Turks,Caicos	..	1,108	1,295	1,920	2,299	0.1	0.1	48.3	19.7	15.7
Brazil	3,065	4,283	1,237	1,487	1,880	0.3	0.1	20.2	26.4	-15.2
Trinidad Tbg	..	1,072	1,328	1,212	1,417	0.1	0.1	-8.7	16.9	5.7
Haiti	..	807	1,243	1,291	1,322	0.1	0.1	3.9	2.4	10.4
Cayman Islands	..	323	923	1,260	1,298	0.0	0.1	36.5	3.0	32.1
Venezuela	..	1,503	1,013	1,077	1,203	0.1	0.1	6.3	11.7	-4.4
Argentina	5,890	3,874	838	926	955	0.3	0.1	10.5	3.1	-24.4
Barbados	..	967	945	939	939	0.1	0.1	-0.6	0.0	-0.6
Bermuda	..	733	784	661	834	0.0	0.1	-15.7	26.2	2.6
Colombia	..	885	547	547	651	0.1	0.0	0.0	19.0	-6.0
Dominican Rp	..	532	344	358	550	0.0	0.0	4.1	53.6	0.7
Peru	..	518	513	405	494	0.0	0.0	-21.1	22.0	-0.9
Costa Rica	..	345	328	395	485	0.0	0.0	20.4	22.8	7.0
Panama	..	365	375	426	480	0.0	0.0	13.6	12.7	5.6
Ecuador	..	317	284	296	440	0.0	0.0	4.2	48.6	6.8
Cuba	..	229	524	546	412	0.0	0.0	4.2	-24.5	12.5
Other intraregional	6,585	3,302	3,004	3,326	3,391	0.2	0.2	10.7	2.0	0.5
From other regions	*135,400*	*123,591*	*102,135*	*93,401*	*94,864*	*8.0*	*5.9*	*-8.6*	*1.6*	*-5.2*
United Kingdom	35,450	47,996	43,249	40,479	44,846	3.1	2.8	-6.4	10.8	-1.3
France	15,865	12,515	20,649	11,408	9,830	0.8	0.6	-44.8	-13.8	-4.7
Italy	17,335	11,245	6,057	8,386	6,775	0.7	0.4	38.5	-19.2	-9.6
Germany	25,100	11,904	7,056	6,630	6,451	0.8	0.4	-6.0	-2.7	-11.5
Switzerland	6,530	5,186	2,947	2,924	3,155	0.3	0.2	-0.8	7.9	-9.5
Australia	1,820	2,075	2,162	2,381	2,597	0.1	0.2	10.1	9.1	4.6
Japan	18,240	11,346	2,391	2,375	2,356	0.7	0.1	-0.7	-0.8	-27.0
Netherlands	2,465	2,320	1,721	1,949	1,682	0.2	0.1	13.2	-13.7	-6.2
Spain	2,495	1,721	1,530	1,428	1,571	0.1	0.1	-6.7	10.0	-1.8
Sweden	1,200	1,394	992	1,219	1,495	0.1	0.1	22.9	22.6	1.4
Ireland	750	1,433	1,407	1,411	1,446	0.1	0.1	0.3	2.5	0.2
Belgium	2,305	1,545	1,288	1,280	1,227	0.1	0.1	-0.6	-4.1	-4.5
South Africa	..	1,215	896	1,032	1,205	0.1	0.1	15.2	16.8	-0.2
Austria	2,835	2,101	1,039	974	1,095	0.1	0.1	-6.3	12.4	-12.2
Denmark	565	578	801	861	888	0.0	0.1	7.5	3.1	9.0
Norway	590	844	839	942	884	0.1	0.1	12.3	-6.2	0.9
New Zealand	..	674	522	642	666	0.0	0.0	23.0	3.7	-0.2
Israel	..	811	545	522	580	0.1	0.0	-4.2	11.1	-6.5
Finland	305	239	330	472	487	0.0	0.0	43.0	3.2	15.3
Greece	505	329	273	312	382	0.0	0.0	14.3	22.4	3.0
Portugal	655	666	736	475	367	0.0	0.0	-35.5	-22.7	-11.2
Other interregional	390	5,454	4,705	5,299	4,879	0.4	0.3	12.6	-7.9	-2.2
Other World/Not specified	*30,230*	*13,855*	*15,456*	*12,536*	*28,368*	*0.9*	*1.8*	*-18.9*	*126.3*	*15.4*

Source: World Tourism Organization (UNWTO) ©   (Data as collected by UNWTO for TMT 2006 Edition)

Bahamas

Nights of International Tourists in All Accommodation Establishments (by residence)

	1995	2000	2003	2004	2005*	Market share (%)		Growth rate (%)		Average per year (%)
						2000	2005*	04/03	05*/04	2000-2005*
Total	9,031,455	9,048,361	8,956,743	9,898,181	10,297,327	100	100	10.5	4.0	2.6
From Americas	*7,588,140*	*7,816,589*	*7,857,967*	*8,831,985*	*9,060,180*	*86.4*	*88.0*	*12.4*	*2.6*	*3.0*
United States	6,787,890	7,005,453	7,172,831	8,012,064	8,176,385	77.4	79.4	11.7	2.1	3.1
Canada	697,135	640,575	518,460	618,772	667,310	7.1	6.5	19.3	7.8	0.8
Jamaica	..	36,939	48,589	57,894	65,602	0.4	0.6	19.2	13.3	12.2
Mexico	14,640	15,733	15,478	19,519	21,854	0.2	0.2	26.1	12.0	6.8
Haiti	..	6,865	9,972	12,215	12,626	0.1	0.1	22.5	3.4	13.0
Turks,Caicos	..	7,792	8,103	11,896	12,507	0.1	0.1	46.8	5.1	9.9
Trinidad Tbg	..	7,381	10,568	11,810	11,283	0.1	0.1	11.8	-4.5	8.9
Brazil	17,090	18,911	6,135	9,207	10,221	0.2	0.1	50.1	11.0	-11.6
Venezuela	..	6,716	6,402	7,115	7,735	0.1	0.1	11.1	8.7	2.9
Barbados	..	5,551	5,344	6,132	6,803	0.1	0.1	14.7	10.9	4.2
Cuba	..	3,323	7,998	9,286	6,546	0.0	0.1	16.1	-29.5	14.5
Bermuda	..	5,036	4,974	4,895	6,374	0.1	0.1	-1.6	30.2	4.8
Cayman Islands	..	3,514	4,473	7,124	6,258	0.0	0.1	59.3	-12.2	12.2
Argentina	32,825	18,807	5,312	5,507	5,650	0.2	0.1	3.7	2.6	-21.4
Colombia	..	3,982	2,894	3,163	4,159	0.0	0.0	9.3	31.5	0.9
Guyana	..	3,301	2,590	2,407	3,779	0.0	0.0	-7.1	57.0	2.7
Other intraregional	38,560	26,710	27,844	32,979	35,088	0.3	0.3	18.4	6.4	5.6
From other regions	*1,201,435*	*1,094,965*	*969,486*	*953,215*	*993,766*	*12.1*	*9.7*	*-1.7*	*4.3*	*-1.9*
United Kingdom	352,940	455,414	428,841	431,220	500,505	5.0	4.9	0.6	16.1	1.9
France	147,215	103,981	170,788	106,087	91,857	1.1	0.9	-37.9	-13.4	-2.4
Germany	267,975	140,125	83,538	84,606	79,487	1.5	0.8	1.3	-6.1	-10.7
Italy	137,960	89,601	47,816	72,429	59,552	1.0	0.6	51.5	-17.8	-7.8
Australia	18,950	24,213	29,964	29,819	32,517	0.3	0.3	-0.5	9.0	6.1
Switzerland	66,250	49,573	30,040	30,453	31,057	0.5	0.3	1.4	2.0	-8.9
South Africa	..	14,120	13,414	15,001	17,593	0.2	0.2	11.8	17.3	4.5
Netherlands	22,425	17,947	16,172	19,064	16,232	0.2	0.2	17.9	-14.9	-2.0
Ireland	..	13,041	12,355	14,065	15,171	0.1	0.1	13.8	7.9	3.1
Sweden	11,000	12,846	10,282	10,273	14,248	0.1	0.1	-0.1	38.7	2.1
Austria	28,325	22,181	10,821	11,357	12,942	0.2	0.1	5.0	14.0	-10.2
Spain	16,805	12,881	14,366	12,112	12,495	0.1	0.1	-15.7	3.2	-0.6
Japan	81,120	47,095	10,567	10,818	12,114	0.5	0.1	2.4	12.0	-23.8
Belgium	21,555	13,915	12,202	11,794	11,027	0.2	0.1	-3.3	-6.5	-4.5
New Zealand	..	10,226	7,169	10,207	9,932	0.1	0.1	42.4	-2.7	-0.6
Denmark	6,990	5,410	6,867	8,040	8,630	0.1	0.1	17.1	7.3	9.8
Norway	5,020	8,627	9,058	7,792	7,161	0.1	0.1	-14.0	-8.1	-3.7
Philippines	..	3,373	3,856	4,534	4,545	0.0	0.0	17.6	0.2	6.1
Finland	2,080	1,442	2,095	5,193	4,154	0.0	0.0	147.9	-20.0	23.6
Poland	..	1,963	3,598	5,756	3,738	0.0	0.0	60.0	-35.1	13.7
Portugal	7,110	5,356	5,711	4,741	3,681	0.1	0.0	-17.0	-22.4	-7.2
Greece	4,310	2,825	2,618	2,590	3,416	0.0	0.0	-1.1	31.9	3.9
Israel	..	5,170	3,773	3,422	3,073	0.1	0.0	-9.3	-10.2	-9.9
India	..	1,543	3,007	2,726	2,817	0.0	0.0	-9.3	3.3	12.8
Russian Federation	..	2,046	1,903	3,143	2,624	0.0	0.0	65.2	-16.5	5.1
Other interregional	3,405	30,051	28,665	35,973	33,198	0.3	0.3	25.5	-7.7	2.0
Other World/Not specified	*241,880*	*136,807*	*129,290*	*112,981*	*243,381*	*1.5*	*2.4*	*-12.6*	*115.4*	*12.2*

Source: World Tourism Organization (UNWTO) ©   (Data as collected by UNWTO for TMT 2006 Edition)

World Tourism Organization ©

III.2.5   Barbados   Caribbean

Promotional: www.barbados.org
Institutional/corporate: www.barmot.gov.bb
Research and data: www.barmot.gov.bb

Profile

Barbados

Americas
Caribbean

Capital					Bridgetown
Area (10 km²)					43
Population (2005, 1000)					279
Gross Domestic Product (GDP) (2005, US$ million)					3,058
GDP per capita (2005, US$)					11,088
GDP growth (real, %)					
'-> 2004: 4.8;	2005: 3.9;	2006*: 4.2;	2007*: 4.9		

	2003	2004	2005*	2004/2003	2005*/2004
International Arrivals					
Visitors (1000)	1,090	1,273	1,111	16.8	-12.7
Tourists (overnight visitors) (1000)	531	552	548	3.8	-0.7
- per 100 of inhabitants	192	199	196		
Cruise passengers (1000)	559	721	563	29.0	-21.9
Tourism accommodation					
Number of rooms	6,210	5,945	6,353	-4.3	6.9
Nights spent in collective establishments (1000)					
by non-residents (inbound tourism)	2,459	2,463	..	0.2	
Receipts and Expenditure for International Tourism					
International Tourism Receipts (US$ million)	758	776	776	2.3	0.1
- per Tourist Arrival (US$)	1,427	1,406	1,418	-1.4	0.8
- per Visitor Arrival (US$)	695	609	699	-12.4	14.7
- per capita (US$)	2,738	2,791	2,784		
International Fare Receipts (US$ million)	9	9	8		-11.1
International Tourism Expenditure (US$ million)	105	108	108	2.9	-0.2
- per capita (US$)	379	389	387		
International Fare Expenditure (US$ million)	49	55	57	12.2	3.6
Δ International Tourism Balance (US$ million)	653	668	668		
Δ International Fare Balance (US$ million)	-40	-46	-49		

Source: World Tourism Organization (UNWTO)   (Data as collected by UNWTO for TMT 2006 Edition)
See annex for methodological notes and reference of external sources used.

International Tourism by Origin

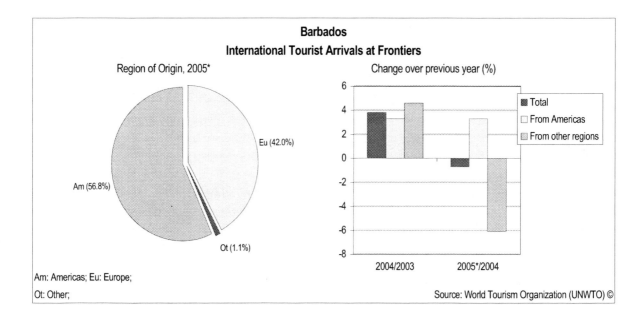

World Tourism Organization ©

Barbados
International Tourist Arrivals at Frontiers (by residence)

	1995	2000	2003	2004	2005*	Market share (%) 2000	Market share (%) 2005*	Growth rate (%) 04/03	Growth rate (%) 05*/04	Average per year (%) 2000-2005*
Total	442,107	544,696	531,211	551,502	547,534	100	100	3.8	-0.7	0.1
From Americas	*237,998*	*278,391*	*291,623*	*301,268*	*311,222*	*51.1*	*56.8*	*3.3*	*3.3*	*2.3*
United States	111,983	112,153	129,326	129,664	131,005	20.6	23.9	0.3	1.0	3.2
Canada	53,373	59,957	49,641	50,032	47,690	11.0	8.7	0.8	-4.7	-4.5
Trinidad Tbg	17,645	23,215	27,530	26,492	30,889	4.3	5.6	-3.8	16.6	5.9
Guyana	8,715	13,516	15,063	16,862	18,698	2.5	3.4	11.9	10.9	6.7
Saint Lucia	8,184	13,540	13,661	14,672	15,592	2.5	2.8	7.4	6.3	2.9
St.Vincent,Grenadines	6,655	9,866	11,800	12,750	13,896	1.8	2.5	8.1	9.0	7.1
Jamaica	4,226	5,972	7,010	7,349	7,969	1.1	1.5	4.8	8.4	5.9
Grenada	3,878	6,699	5,953	7,850	7,896	1.2	1.4	31.9	0.6	3.3
Antigua,Barb	2,981	5,132	6,514	7,337	7,130	0.9	1.3	12.6	-2.8	6.8
Dominica	2,984	4,233	3,907	4,770	5,245	0.8	1.0	22.1	10.0	4.4
St.Kitts-Nev	1,458	2,440	2,479	3,610	4,179	0.4	0.8	45.6	15.8	11.4
Br.Virgin Is	..	2,199	2,288	2,472	2,513	0.4	0.5	8.0	1.7	2.7
Neth. Antilles	610	1,952	1,758	2,209	2,013	0.4	0.4	25.7	-8.9	0.6
Martinique	3,080	2,002	1,068	1,439	1,816	0.4	0.3	34.7	26.2	-1.9
Guadeloupe	692	1,118	982	1,485	1,778	0.2	0.3	51.2	19.7	9.7
Bermuda	1,595	1,426	1,509	1,660	1,595	0.3	0.3	10.0	-3.9	2.3
Venezuela	2,006	2,948	1,823	1,952	1,540	0.5	0.3	7.1	-21.1	-12.2
Bahamas	658	1,176	1,116	1,067	1,173	0.2	0.2	-4.4	9.9	-0.1
Puerto Rico	1,282	1,101	1,187	969	1,019	0.2	0.2	-18.4	5.2	-1.5
Cayman Islands	357	764	820	787	758	0.1	0.1	-4.0	-3.7	-0.2
US.Virgin Is	695	830	697	704	703	0.2	0.1	1.0	-0.1	-3.3
Anguilla	437	997	606	592	664	0.2	0.1	-2.3	12.2	-7.8
Suriname	738	524	528	540	532	0.1	0.1	2.3	-1.5	0.3
Other intraregional	3,766	4,631	4,357	4,004	4,929	0.9	0.9	-8.1	23.1	1.3
From other regions	*197,824*	*265,941*	*239,112*	*250,123*	*234,904*	*48.8*	*42.9*	*4.6*	*-6.1*	*-2.5*
United Kingdom	126,621	226,787	202,564	213,945	201,436	41.6	36.8	5.6	-5.8	-2.3
Germany	28,372	7,850	7,612	6,970	6,995	1.4	1.3	-8.4	0.4	-2.3
Ireland	6,646	4,087	3,915	6,540	4,531	0.8	0.8	67.0	-30.7	2.1
Italy	7,537	4,612	4,912	4,914	3,830	0.8	0.7	0.0	-22.1	-3.6
France	3,270	3,071	2,820	2,272	2,343	0.6	0.4	-19.4	3.1	-5.3
Netherlands	8,825	2,406	1,557	2,209	1,603	0.4	0.3	41.9	-27.4	-7.8
Switzerland	4,329	1,912	1,409	1,438	1,434	0.4	0.3	2.1	-0.3	-5.6
Belgium/Luxembourg	1,265	..	..	..	..					
Denmark	707	628	1,456	991	1,230	0.1	0.2	-31.9	24.1	14.4
Sweden	3,708	4,066	1,413	1,352	1,124	0.7	0.2	-4.3	-16.9	-22.7
Australia	2,004	1,089	2,752	1,178	1,037	0.2	0.2	-57.2	-12.0	-1.0
Spain	500	599	608	674	760	0.1	0.1	10.9	12.8	4.9
Belgium	..	843	541	621	670	0.2	0.1	14.8	7.9	-4.5
Russian Federation	..	221	644	569	659	0.0	0.1	-11.6	15.8	24.4
India	..	329	373	564	644	0.1	0.1	51.2	14.2	14.4
South Africa	..	328	354	373	644	0.1	0.1	5.4	72.7	14.4
Norway	1,603	2,168	868	635	617	0.4	0.1	-26.8	-2.8	-22.2
Austria	1,885	671	640	586	591	0.1	0.1	-8.4	0.9	-2.5
Other interregional	552	4,274	4,674	4,292	4,756	0.8	0.9	-8.2	10.8	2.2
Other World/Not specified	*6,285*	*364*	*476*	*111*	*1,408*	*0.1*	*0.3*	*-76.7*	*1168.5*	*31.1*

Source: World Tourism Organization (UNWTO) ©   (Data as collected by UNWTO for TMT 2006 Edition)

III.2.6   Bermuda   Caribbean

Profile

Bermuda

Americas
Caribbean

	Capital	Hamilton
	Area (10 km²)	5
	Population (2005, 1000)	65

	2003	2004	2005*	2004/2003	2005*/2004
International Arrivals					
Visitors (1000)	483	478	521	-1.0	9.0
Tourists (overnight visitors) (1000)	257	272	270	5.9	-0.7
- per 100 of inhabitants	398	418	412		
Cruise passengers (1000)	226	206	251	-8.8	21.8
Tourism accommodation					
Number of rooms	3,100	2,921	3,067	-5.8	5.0
Nights spent in collective establishments (1000)					
by non-residents (inbound tourism)	1,598	1,733	1,729	8.4	-0.2
Outbound Tourism					
Trips abroad (1000)	141	156	161	10.6	3.2
- per 100 of inhabitants	219	240	246		
Receipts and Expenditure for International Tourism					
International Tourism Receipts (US$ million)	348	426	430	22.4	0.9
- per Tourist Arrival (US$)	1,356	1,568	1,595	15.6	1.7
- per Visitor Arrival (US$)	720	891	825	23.7	-7.4
- per capita (US$)	5,397	6,560	6,578		
International Tourism Expenditure (US$ million)	226	217	239	-4.0	10.1
- per trip (US$)	1,603	1,391	1,484	-13.2	6.7
- per capita (US$)	3,505	3,342	3,656		
Δ International Tourism Balance (US$ million)	122	209	191		

Source: World Tourism Organization (UNWTO)   (Data as collected by UNWTO for TMT 2006 Edition)
See annex for methodological notes and reference of external sources used.

International Tourism by Origin

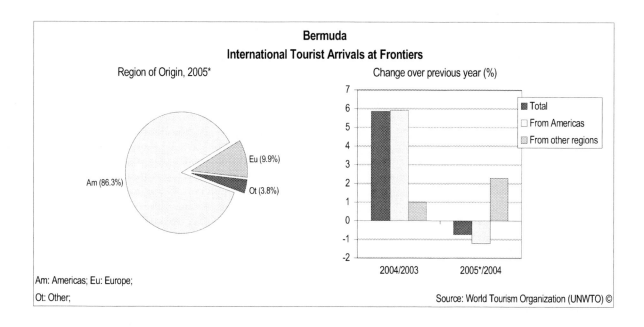

Bermuda
International Tourist Arrivals at Frontiers

Region of Origin, 2005*

Am (86.3%)
Eu (9.9%)
Ot (3.8%)

Change over previous year (%)

- Total
- From Americas
- From other regions

2004/2003   2005*/2004

Am: Americas; Eu: Europe;
Ot: Other;

Source: World Tourism Organization (UNWTO) ©

Bermuda
International Tourist Arrivals at Frontiers (by residence)

	1995	2000	2003	2004	2005*	Market share (%)		Growth rate (%)		Average per year (%)
						2000	2005*	04/03	05*/04	2000-2005*
Total	**387,412**	**332,191**	**256,579**	**271,620**	**269,591**	**100**	**100**	**5.9**	**-0.7**	**-4.1**
From Americas	*348,841*	*287,341*	*222,396*	*235,546*	*232,661*	*86.5*	*86.3*	*5.9*	*-1.2*	*-4.1*
United States	313,375	256,638	197,911	209,054	203,996	77.3	75.7	5.6	-2.4	-4.5
Canada	35,466	30,703	24,485	26,492	28,665	9.2	10.6	8.2	8.2	-1.4
From other regions	*30,646*	*37,044*	*26,441*	*26,707*	*27,317*	*11.2*	*10.1*	*1.0*	*2.3*	*-5.9*
United Kingdom	22,746	29,218	21,667	21,434	22,440	8.8	8.3	-1.1	4.7	-5.1
Germany	3,263	1,695	1,109	1,162	1,051	0.5	0.4	4.8	-9.6	-9.1
France	712	923	730	742	758	0.3	0.3	1.6	2.2	-3.9
Italy	614	1,067	696	559	601	0.3	0.2	-19.7	7.5	-10.8
Switzerland	947	747	411	450	467	0.2	0.2	9.5	3.8	-9.0
Australia	432	482	274	415	412	0.1	0.2	51.5	-0.7	-3.1
Sweden	337	402	220	236	274	0.1	0.1	7.3	16.1	-7.4
Japan	622	644	229	419	227	0.2	0.1	83.0	-45.8	-18.8
Austria	..	165	78	98	97	0.0	0.0	25.6	-1.0	-10.1
Other Europe	973	1,701	1,027	1,192	990	0.5	0.4	16.1	-16.9	-10.3
Other World/Not specified	*7,925*	*7,806*	*7,742*	*9,367*	*9,613*	*2.3*	*3.6*	*21.0*	*2.6*	*4.3*

Source: World Tourism Organization (UNWTO) ©   (Data as collected by UNWTO for TMT 2006 Edition)

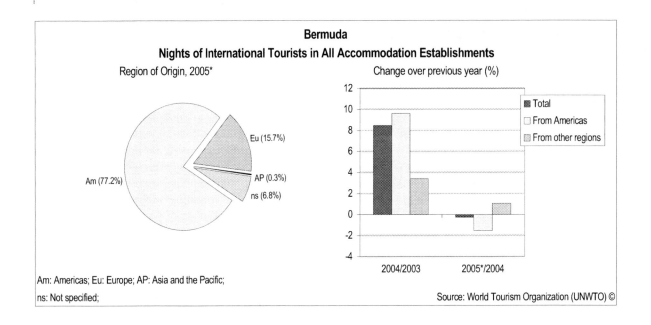

Bermuda

Nights of International Tourists in All Accommodation Establishments

Region of Origin, 2005*

Change over previous year (%)

Am: Americas; Eu: Europe; AP: Asia and the Pacific;

ns: Not specified;

Source: World Tourism Organization (UNWTO) ©

Bermuda

Nights of International Tourists in All Accommodation Establishments (by nationality)

	1995	2000	2003	2004	2005*	Market share (%) 2000	Market share (%) 2005*	Growth rate (%) 04/03	Growth rate (%) 05*/04	Average per year (%) 2000-2005*
Total	**2,420,710**	**1,966,378**	**1,597,677**	**1,733,166**	**1,728,591**	**100**	**100**	**8.5**	**-0.3**	**-2.5**
From Americas	*2,009,813*	*1,546,159*	*1,237,079*	*1,355,968*	*1,335,308*	*78.6*	*77.2*	*9.6*	*-1.5*	*-2.9*
United States	1,720,946	1,305,224	1,024,818	1,094,961	1,063,658	66.4	61.5	6.8	-2.9	-4.0
Canada	288,867	240,935	212,261	261,007	271,650	12.3	15.7	23.0	4.1	2.4
From other regions	*332,881*	*351,086*	*264,237*	*273,273*	*276,214*	*17.9*	*16.0*	*3.4*	*1.1*	*-4.7*
United Kingdom	255,427	285,378	223,812	228,172	233,199	14.5	13.5	1.9	2.2	-4.0
Germany	33,698	15,655	10,412	10,240	9,655	0.8	0.6	-1.7	-5.7	-9.2
Italy	6,419	9,588	6,883	6,248	7,366	0.5	0.4	-9.2	17.9	-5.1
France	5,903	7,870	6,561	5,337	5,716	0.4	0.3	-18.7	7.1	-6.2
Switzerland	8,594	5,288	2,987	3,290	3,493	0.3	0.2	10.1	6.2	-8.0
Australia	4,187	6,752	2,041	3,714	3,222	0.3	0.2	82.0	-13.2	-13.8
Sweden	3,063	2,956	1,976	1,852	2,281	0.2	0.1	-6.3	23.2	-5.1
Japan	3,206	2,861	768	1,938	1,357	0.1	0.1	152.3	-30.0	-13.9
Austria	3,757	1,682	960	1,163	1,309	0.1	0.1	21.1	12.6	-4.9
Other Europe	8,627	13,056	7,837	11,319	8,616	0.7	0.5	44.4	-23.9	-8.0
Other World/Not specified	*78,016*	*69,133*	*96,361*	*103,925*	*117,069*	*3.5*	*6.8*	*7.8*	*12.6*	*11.1*

Source: World Tourism Organization (UNWTO) ©

(Data as collected by UNWTO for TMT 2006 Edition)

World Tourism Organization ©

III.2.7   British Virgin Islands   Caribbean

Profile

British Virgin Islands

Americas
Caribbean

		Road Town
Capital		Road Town
Area (10 km²)		15
Population (2005, 1000)		23

	2003	2004	2005*	2004/2003	2005*/2004
International Arrivals					
Visitors (1000)	658	813	821	23.6	1.0
Tourists (overnight visitors) (1000)	318	307	337	-3.2	9.7
- per 100 of inhabitants	1,462	1,386	1,489		
Same-day visitors (1000)	40	42	34	5.0	-19.0
Cruise passengers (1000)	300	467	449	55.7	-3.9
Tourism accommodation					
Number of rooms	2,661	2,760	2,722	3.7	-1.4
Receipts and Expenditure for International Tourism					
International Tourism Receipts (US$ million)	342	393	437	14.9	11.2
- per Tourist Arrival (US$)	1,076	1,278	1,296	18.8	1.4
- per Visitor Arrival (US$)	520	483	532	-7.0	10.1
- per capita (US$)	15,739	17,713	19,300		

Source: World Tourism Organization (UNWTO)   (Data as collected by UNWTO for TMT 2006 Edition)
See annex for methodological notes and reference of external sources used.

International Tourism by Origin

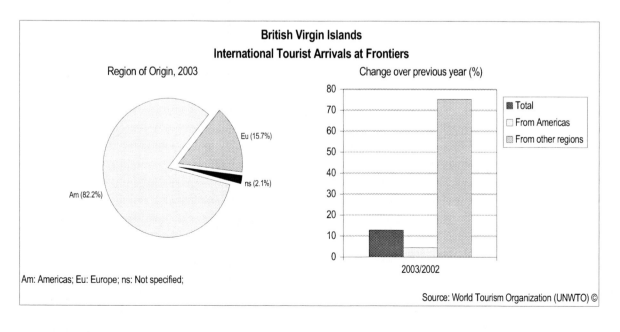

British Virgin Islands
International Tourist Arrivals at Frontiers

Region of Origin, 2003

Eu (15.7%)
ns (2.1%)
Am (82.2%)

Change over previous year (%)

Total
From Americas
From other regions

2003/2002

Am: Americas; Eu: Europe; ns: Not specified;

Source: World Tourism Organization (UNWTO) ©

British Virgin Islands
International Tourist Arrivals at Frontiers (by residence)

	1995	2000	2002	2003	2004	Market share (%)		Growth rate (%)		Average per year (%)
						2000	2004	03/02	04/03	2000-2004
Total	219,481	272,356	281,696	317,758	..	100		12.8		
From Americas	193,757	235,463	250,013	261,201	..	86.5		4.5		
United States	128,234	198,465	209,510	180,443	..	72.9		-13.9		
All the Caribbean	56,485	..	..	..	..					
Puerto Rico	..	13,016	15,378	14,930	..	4.8		-2.9		
Canada	6,566	7,543	6,307	8,961	..	2.8		42.1		
St.Kitts-Nev	..	2,076	2,983	3,411	..	0.8		14.3		
Dominica	..	973	1,456	2,648	..	0.4		81.9		
Jamaica	..	1,036	1,177	2,179	..	0.4		85.1		
St.Vincent,Grenadines	..	1,399	1,584	2,091	..	0.5		32.0		
Trinidad Tbg	..	976	1,499	1,572	..	0.4		4.9		
Antigua,Barb	..	1,009	1,442	1,273	..	0.4		-11.7		
Guyana	..	533	887	1,080	..	0.2		21.8		
Barbados	..	782	940	918	..	0.3		-2.3		
Saint Lucia	..	585	662	905	..	0.2		36.7		
Dominican Rp	..	721	804	837	..	0.3		4.1		
Grenada	..	396	494	621	..	0.1		25.7		
Haiti	..	38	10	73	..	0.0		630.0		
Other Caribbean	..	3,559	3,479	37,644	..	1.3		982.0		
Other Americas	2,472	2,356	1,401	1,615	..	0.9		15.3		
From other regions	21,478	34,122	28,511	49,952	..	12.5		75.2		
United Kingdom	8,272	16,632	14,473	22,053	..	6.1		52.4		
Italy	2,115	2,043	1,998	7,502	..	0.8		275.5		
France	2,500	4,782	3,796	7,497	..	1.8		97.5		
Germany	3,989	3,373	2,463	5,209	..	1.2		111.5		
Spain	1,103	567	489	1,387	..	0.2		183.6		
Netherlands	429	1,169	964	1,094	..	0.4		13.5		
Sweden	402	599	526	508	..	0.2		-3.4		
Other Europe	2,668	4,957	3,802	4,702	..	1.8		23.7		
Other World/Not specified	4,246	2,771	3,172	6,605	..	1.0		108.2		

Source: World Tourism Organization (UNWTO) ©   (Data as collected by UNWTO for TMT 2006 Edition)

World Tourism Organization ©

III.2.8   Cayman Islands   Caribbean

Promotional: www.caymanislands.ky ; www.divecayman.ky
Institutional/corporate: www.statistics.caymanislands.ky ; www.caymanislands.ky/tmp ; www.gov.ky
Research and data: www.statistics.caymanislands.ky ; www.caymanislands.ky/statisitcs

Profile

Cayman Islands

Americas
Caribbean

Capital	George Town
Area (10 km²)	26
Population (2005, 1000)	44

	2003	2004	2005*	2004/2003	2005*/2004
International Arrivals					
Visitors (1000)	2,113	1,953	1,967	-7.6	0.7
Tourists (overnight visitors) (1000)	294	260	168	-11.4	-35.4
- per 100 of inhabitants	700	603	379		
Cruise passengers (1000)	1,819	1,693	1,799	-6.9	6.3
Tourism accommodation					
Number of rooms	5,108	..	2,954		
Receipts and Expenditure for International Tourism					
International Tourism Receipts (US$ million)	518	519	353	0.2	-32.0
- per Tourist Arrival (US$)	1,765	1,997	2,104	13.1	5.4
- per Visitor Arrival (US$)	245	266	179	8.4	-32.5
- per capita (US$)	12,353	12,041	7,974		

Source: World Tourism Organization (UNWTO)   (Data as collected by UNWTO for TMT 2006 Edition)

See annex for methodological notes and reference of external sources used.

International Tourism by Origin

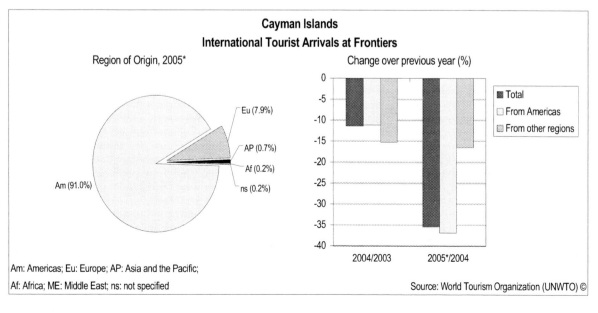

Cayman Islands
International Tourist Arrivals at Frontiers

Region of Origin, 2005*

Change over previous year (%)

- Total
- From Americas
- From other regions

Am (91.0%)
Eu (7.9%)
AP (0.7%)
Af (0.2%)
ns (0.2%)

Am: Americas; Eu: Europe; AP: Asia and the Pacific;
Af: Africa; ME: Middle East; ns: not specified

Source: World Tourism Organization (UNWTO) ©

Cayman Islands
International Tourist Arrivals at Frontiers (by residence)

	1995	2000	2003	2004	2005*	Market share (%) 2000	Market share (%) 2005*	Growth rate (%) 04/03	Growth rate (%) 05*/04	Average per year (%) 2000-2005*
Total	..	**354,087**	**293,513**	**259,929**	**167,802**	**100**	**100**	**-11.4**	**-35.4**	**-13.9**
From Americas	..	*327,479*	*272,381*	*242,012*	*152,735*	*92.5*	*91.0*	*-11.1*	*-36.9*	*-14.1*
United States	..	281,616	232,413	205,206	118,843	79.5	70.8	-11.7	-42.1	-15.8
Jamaica	..	20,323	18,639	18,306	17,005	5.7	10.1	-1.8	-7.1	-3.5
Canada	..	15,003	14,125	12,116	10,480	4.2	6.2	-14.2	-13.5	-6.9
Honduras	..	1,942	1,737	1,255	1,399	0.5	0.8	-27.7	11.5	-6.3
Bahamas	..	604	570	570	556	0.2	0.3	0.0	-2.5	-1.6
Trinidad Tbg	..	608	672	581	554	0.2	0.3	-13.5	-4.6	-1.8
Bermuda	..	444	327	444	422	0.1	0.3	35.8	-5.0	-1.0
Barbados	..	573	511	429	418	0.2	0.2	-16.0	-2.6	-6.1
Costa Rica	..	362	313	296	325	0.1	0.2	-5.4	9.8	-2.1
Cuba	..	762	295	377	317	0.2	0.2	27.8	-15.9	-16.1
Colombia	..	289	319	276	294	0.1	0.2	-13.5	6.5	0.3
Mexico	..	1,387	294	309	291	0.4	0.2	5.1	-5.8	-26.8
Brazil	..	506	296	222	229	0.1	0.1	-25.0	3.2	-14.7
Panama	..	153	129	154	138	0.0	0.1	19.4	-10.4	-2.0
Nicaragua	..	300	195	143	137	0.1	0.1	-26.7	-4.2	-14.5
Turks,Caicos	..	66	74	108	128	0.0	0.1	45.9	18.5	14.2
Dominican Rp	..	193	92	117	122	0.1	0.1	27.2	4.3	-8.8
Guyana	..	105	116	115	117	0.0	0.1	-0.9	1.7	2.2
Belize	..	161	100	80	89	0.0	0.1	-20.0	11.3	-11.2
Venezuela	..	219	147	136	84	0.1	0.1	-7.5	-38.2	-17.4
Puerto Rico	..	64	74	55	74	0.0	0.0	-25.7	34.5	2.9
Other intraregional	..	1,799	943	717	713	0.5	0.4	-24.0	-0.6	-16.9
From other regions	..	*26,393*	*20,914*	*17,723*	*14,796*	*7.5*	*8.8*	*-15.3*	*-16.5*	*-10.9*
United Kingdom	..	15,365	13,372	11,445	9,340	4.3	5.6	-14.4	-18.4	-9.5
Ireland	..	809	743	737	651	0.2	0.4	-0.8	-11.7	-4.3
Germany	..	1,406	750	583	579	0.4	0.3	-22.3	-0.7	-16.3
Italy	..	1,506	842	657	478	0.4	0.3	-22.0	-27.2	-20.5
Australia	..	498	542	513	453	0.1	0.3	-5.4	-11.7	-1.9
Switzerland	..	751	474	362	349	0.2	0.2	-23.6	-3.6	-14.2
France	..	632	530	384	305	0.2	0.2	-27.5	-20.6	-13.6
Netherlands	..	458	468	327	281	0.1	0.2	-30.1	-14.1	-9.3
South Africa	..	310	290	243	235	0.1	0.1	-16.2	-3.3	-5.4
Spain	..	535	304	206	210	0.2	0.1	-32.2	1.9	-17.1
New Zealand	..	194	188	170	177	0.1	0.1	-9.6	4.1	-1.8
Japan	..	604	231	263	169	0.2	0.1	13.9	-35.7	-22.5
Sweden	..	322	221	163	149	0.1	0.1	-26.2	-8.6	-14.3
Austria	..	340	222	193	124	0.1	0.1	-13.1	-35.8	-18.3
Philippines	..	303	65	73	119	0.1	0.1	12.3	63.0	-17.0
Denmark	..	218	153	104	108	0.1	0.1	-32.0	3.8	-13.1
Norway	..	223	119	134	97	0.1	0.1	12.6	-27.6	-15.3
India	..	255	205	150	81	0.1	0.0	-26.8	-46.0	-20.5
Andorra	..	1	158	130	79	0.0	0.0	-17.7	-39.2	139.6
Portugal	..	121	99	57	78	0.0	0.0	-42.4	36.8	-8.4
Other interregional	..	1,542	938	829	734	0.4	0.4	-11.6	-11.5	-13.8
Other World/Not specified	..	*215*	*218*	*194*	*271*	*0.1*	*0.2*	*-11.0*	*39.7*	*4.7*

Source: World Tourism Organization (UNWTO) ©   (Data as collected by UNWTO for TMT 2006 Edition)

World Tourism Organization ©

III.2.9   Cuba   Caribbean

Profile

Cuba

Capital	La Havana
Year of entry in UNWTO	1975
Area (1000 km²)	111
Population (2005, million)	11.3

Americas
Caribbean

	2003	2004	2005*	2004/2003	2005*/2004
International Arrivals					
Visitors (1000)	1,906	2,049	2,319	7.5	13.2
Tourists (overnight visitors) (1000)	1,847	2,017	2,261	9.2	12.1
- per 100 of inhabitants	16	18	20		
Same-day visitors (1000)	59	32	58	-45.8	81.3
Cruise passengers (1000)	20	5	17	-75.0	240.0
Tourism accommodation					
Number of rooms	43,696	45,270	45,644	3.6	0.8
Nights spent in collective establishments (1000)	19,672	20,611	22,335	4.8	8.4
by non-residents (inbound tourism)	12,684	14,190	15,404	11.9	8.6
by residents (domestic tourism)	6,988	6,421	6,931	-8.1	7.9
Nights spent in hotels and similar establishments (1000)	15,093	15,887	17,120	5.3	7.8
by non-residents (inbound tourism)	11,951	13,358	14,572	11.8	9.1
by residents (domestic tourism)	3,142	2,529	2,548	-19.5	0.8
Outbound Tourism					
Trips abroad (1000)	113	115	..	1.8	
- per 100 of inhabitants	1	1	..		
Receipts and Expenditure for International Tourism					
International Tourism Receipts (US$ million)	1,846	1,915	1,920	3.7	0.3
- per Tourist Arrival (US$)	1,000	950	849	-5.0	-10.6
- per Visitor Arrival (US$)	969	935	828	-3.5	-11.4
- per capita (US$)	164	169	169		

Source: World Tourism Organization (UNWTO)   (Data as collected by UNWTO for TMT 2006 Edition)

See annex for methodological notes and reference of external sources used.

International Tourism by Origin

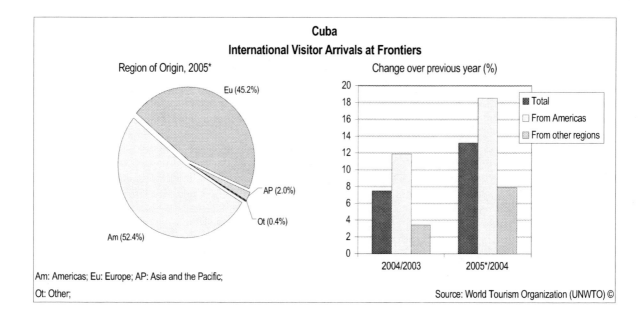

Cuba
International Visitor Arrivals at Frontiers

Region of Origin, 2005*

Eu (45.2%)
AP (2.0%)
Ot (0.4%)
Am (52.4%)

Change over previous year (%)

Total
From Americas
From other regions

2004/2003   2005*/2004

Am: Americas; Eu: Europe; AP: Asia and the Pacific;
Ot: Other;

Source: World Tourism Organization (UNWTO) ©

Cuba

International Visitor Arrivals at Frontiers (by residence)

	1995	2000	2003	2004	2005*	Market share (%)		Growth rate (%)		Average per year (%)
						2000	2005*	04/03	05*/04	2000-2005*
Total	**745,495**	**1,773,986**	**1,905,682**	**2,048,572**	**2,319,334**	**100**	**100**	**7.5**	**13.2**	**5.5**
From Americas	*357,189*	*783,425*	*916,818*	*1,025,756*	*1,215,857*	*44.2*	*52.4*	*11.9*	*18.5*	*9.2*
Canada	143,541	307,725	452,438	563,371	602,377	17.3	26.0	24.5	6.9	14.4
Venezuela	8,621	12,481	15,228	86,258	185,157	0.7	8.0	466.4	114.7	71.5
Mexico	32,069	86,540	88,787	79,752	89,154	4.9	3.8	-10.2	11.8	0.6
United States	20,672	76,898	84,529	49,856	37,233	4.3	1.6	-41.0	-25.3	-13.5
Argentina	32,583	54,185	13,929	23,460	24,922	3.1	1.1	68.4	6.2	-14.4
Chile	13,747	13,718	11,938	14,500	16,744	0.8	0.7	21.5	15.5	4.1
Colombia	21,035	16,388	13,122	13,408	16,175	0.9	0.7	2.2	20.6	-0.3
Brazil	7,825	9,483	8,802	9,216	15,836	0.5	0.7	4.7	71.8	10.8
Guatemala	1,648	5,061	3,860	6,895	8,060	0.3	0.3	78.6	16.9	9.8
Ecuador	3,600	5,501	6,408	6,231	7,014	0.3	0.3	-2.8	12.6	5.0
Honduras	793	2,508	2,263	2,451	6,442	0.1	0.3	8.3	162.8	20.8
Peru	2,922	5,970	5,704	6,072	6,225	0.3	0.3	6.5	2.5	0.8
Panama	2,672	6,185	5,492	4,993	5,763	0.3	0.2	-9.1	15.4	-1.4
Bolivia	868	1,673	1,631	1,862	5,697	0.1	0.2	14.2	206.0	27.8
Bahamas	2,805	6,178	7,280	6,188	5,526	0.3	0.2	-15.0	-10.7	-2.2
Dominican Rp	5,521	6,582	5,872	3,255	4,576	0.4	0.2	-44.6	40.6	-7.0
Costa Rica	3,752	6,147	4,313	6,276	4,557	0.3	0.2	45.5	-27.4	-5.8
Jamaica	2,674	5,945	4,034	3,521	4,118	0.3	0.2	-12.7	17.0	-7.1
Other intraregional	49,841	154,257	181,188	138,191	170,281	8.7	7.3	-23.7	23.2	2.0
From other regions	*387,617*	*990,303*	*988,267*	*1,022,149*	*1,102,917*	*55.8*	*47.6*	*3.4*	*7.9*	*2.2*
United Kingdom	19,614	90,972	120,866	161,189	199,399	5.1	8.6	33.4	23.7	17.0
Spain	89,501	153,197	127,666	146,236	194,103	8.6	8.4	14.5	32.7	4.8
Italy	114,767	175,667	177,627	178,570	169,317	9.9	7.3	0.5	-5.2	-0.7
Germany	57,487	203,403	157,721	143,644	124,527	11.5	5.4	-8.9	-13.3	-9.3
France	34,332	132,089	144,548	119,868	107,518	7.4	4.6	-17.1	-10.3	-4.0
Netherlands	12,648	24,916	29,453	32,983	37,828	1.4	1.6	12.0	14.7	8.7
Portugal	10,585	28,981	28,469	25,608	28,780	1.6	1.2	-10.0	12.4	-0.1
Switzerland	6,011	28,462	24,630	23,106	21,918	1.6	0.9	-6.2	-5.1	-5.1
Belgium	4,369	21,594	24,318	22,007	20,813	1.2	0.9	-9.5	-5.4	-0.7
Russian Federation	8,263	14,429	12,610	17,457	20,711	0.8	0.9	38.4	18.6	7.5
Austria	5,803	21,056	18,739	17,403	16,222	1.2	0.7	-7.1	-6.8	-5.1
Philippines	3,601	6,673	12,718	9,932	13,389	0.4	0.6	-21.9	34.8	14.9
Denmark	1,058	4,165	6,327	7,975	9,163	0.2	0.4	26.0	14.9	17.1
China	1,365	4,940	4,811	7,007	8,700	0.3	0.4	45.6	24.2	12.0
Poland	1,035	5,055	5,562	7,439	8,295	0.3	0.4	33.7	11.5	10.4
Ireland	874	4,049	5,783	6,476	7,492	0.2	0.3	12.0	15.7	13.1
Czech Rep	..	1,800	2,795	4,102	7,425	0.1	0.3	46.8	81.0	32.8
Sweden	1,189	5,950	5,277	6,535	7,184	0.3	0.3	23.8	9.9	3.8
Hungary	272	1,314	3,447	5,113	7,127	0.1	0.3	48.3	39.4	40.2
Norway	725	5,482	6,062	6,076	6,962	0.3	0.3	0.2	14.6	4.9
Ukraine	745	4,137	5,662	6,558	6,706	0.2	0.3	15.8	2.3	10.1
Greece	1,224	6,405	6,420	9,074	6,462	0.4	0.3	41.3	-28.8	0.2
Japan	1,806	9,249	5,317	5,748	6,409	0.5	0.3	8.1	11.5	-7.1
Other interregional	10,343	36,318	51,439	52,043	66,467	2.0	2.9	1.2	27.7	12.8
Other World/Not specified	*689*	*258*	*597*	*667*	*560*	*0.0*	*0.0*	*11.7*	*-16.0*	*16.8*

Source: World Tourism Organization (UNWTO) ©   (Data as collected by UNWTO for TMT 2006 Edition)

III.2.10 Dominica   Caribbean

Promotional: www.dominica.dm

Profile

Dominica

Capital	Roseau
Area (10 km²)	75
Population (2005, 1000)	69
Gross Domestic Product (GDP) (2005, US$ million)	283
GDP per capita (2005, US$)	3,947

Americas
Caribbean

GDP growth (real, %)
'-> 2004: 3.0;   2005: 3.4;   2006*: 3.0;   2007*: 3.0

	2003	2004	2005*	2004/2003	2005*/2004
International Arrivals					
Visitors (1000)	254	466	381	83.5	-18.2
Tourists (overnight visitors) (1000)	73	80	79	9.4	-1.0
- per 100 of inhabitants	105	116	115		
Same-day visitors (1000)	4	3	1	-33.3	-73.1
Cruise passengers (1000)	177	384	301	116.9	-21.6
Tourism accommodation					
Number of rooms	931	791	787	-15.0	-0.5
Receipts and Expenditure for International Tourism					
International Tourism Receipts (US$ million)	54	61	56	12.3	-7.8
- per Tourist Arrival (US$)	738	757	705	2.6	-6.8
- per Visitor Arrival (US$)	213	130	147	-38.8	12.8
- per capita (US$)	775	875	810		
International Tourism Expenditure (US$ million)	9	9	10		11.1
- per capita (US$)	129	130	145		
Δ International Tourism Balance (US$ million)	45	52	46		

Source: World Tourism Organization (UNWTO)   (Data as collected by UNWTO for TMT 2006 Edition)
See annex for methodological notes and reference of external sources used.

World Tourism Organization ©

International Tourism by Origin

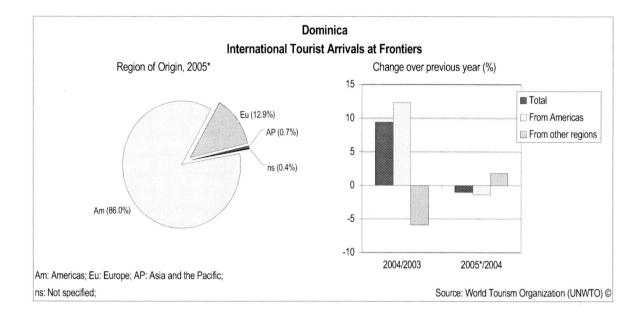

Dominica
International Tourist Arrivals at Frontiers

Region of Origin, 2005*

Eu (12.9%)
AP (0.7%)
ns (0.4%)
Am (86.0%)

Change over previous year (%)

Total
From Americas
From other regions

2004/2003   2005*/2004

Am: Americas; Eu: Europe; AP: Asia and the Pacific;
ns: Not specified;

Source: World Tourism Organization (UNWTO) ©

Dominica
International Tourist Arrivals at Frontiers (by residence)

	1995	2000	2003	2004	2005*	Market share (%) 2000	Market share (%) 2005*	Growth rate (%) 04/03	Growth rate (%) 05*/04	Average per year (%) 2000-2005*
Total	**60,471**	**69,598**	**73,190**	**80,087**	**79,257**	**100**	**100**	**9.4**	**-1.0**	**2.6**
From Americas	*46,676*	*57,383*	*61,536*	*69,115*	*68,164*	*82.4*	*86.0*	*12.3*	*-1.4*	*3.5*
United States	10,923	15,078	15,638	17,574	18,492	21.7	23.3	12.4	5.2	4.2
Guadeloupe	10,810	12,133	11,757	13,515	12,342	17.4	15.6	15.0	-8.7	0.3
Martinique	6,734	6,756	5,938	6,905	6,175	9.7	7.8	16.3	-10.6	-1.8
Haiti	24	..	4,475	7,391	5,808		7.3	65.2	-21.4	
Antigua,Barb	2,754	4,155	5,134	4,978	5,264	6.0	6.6	-3.0	5.7	4.8
US.Virgin Is	3,020	2,821	2,948	3,152	3,345	4.1	4.2	6.9	6.1	3.5
Barbados	1,903	2,284	2,167	2,429	2,298	3.3	2.9	12.1	-5.4	0.1
Saint Lucia	1,484	1,890	2,352	2,471	2,290	2.7	2.9	5.1	-7.3	3.9
St.Maarten	1,775	1,837	1,861	1,987	2,126	2.6	2.7	6.8	7.0	3.0
Canada	1,828	2,176	1,968	1,724	1,977	3.1	2.5	-12.4	14.7	-1.9
Trinidad Tbg	1,343	1,520	1,550	1,510	1,527	2.2	1.9	-2.6	1.1	0.1
Br.Virgin Is	479	968	1,054	1,091	1,244	1.4	1.6	3.5	14.0	5.1
Dominican Rp	38	..	798	485	1,065		1.3	-39.2	119.6	
St.Vincent,Grenadines	414	483	574	492	608	0.7	0.8	-14.3	23.6	4.7
St.Kitts-Nev	502	520	664	617	601	0.7	0.8	-7.1	-2.6	2.9
Jamaica	318	512	481	472	507	0.7	0.6	-1.9	7.4	-0.2
Grenada	350	269	433	366	433	0.4	0.5	-15.5	18.3	10.0
Venezuela	74	132	168	236	337	0.2	0.4	40.5	42.8	20.6
Guyana	205	..	308	358	321		0.4	16.2	-10.3	
Puerto Rico	199	..	312	341	243		0.3	9.3	-28.7	
Cuba	..	..	96	104	222		0.3	8.3	113.5	
Montserrat	510	267	158	204	220	0.4	0.3	29.1	7.8	-3.8
Anguilla	167	..	135	128	107		0.1	-5.2	-16.4	
Curaçao	147	..	92	83	96		0.1	-9.8	15.7	
Bahamas	20	..	70	106	93		0.1	51.4	-12.3	
Other intraregional	655	3,582	405	396	423	5.1	0.5	-2.2	6.8	-34.8
From other regions	*12,994*	*11,574*	*11,258*	*10,595*	*10,787*	*16.6*	*13.6*	*-5.9*	*1.8*	*-1.4*
United Kingdom	4,914	6,140	6,034	6,015	6,117	8.8	7.7	-0.3	1.7	-0.1
France	4,934	2,902	2,532	1,866	1,853	4.2	2.3	-26.3	-0.7	-8.6
Germany	1,255	747	639	751	727	1.1	0.9	17.5	-3.2	-0.5
Netherlands	246	167	200	186	312	0.2	0.4	-7.0	67.7	13.3
China	..	107	182	149	307	0.2	0.4	-18.1	106.0	23.5
Switzerland	433	179	300	272	270	0.3	0.3	-9.3	-0.7	8.6
Sweden	226	282	189	166	170	0.4	0.2	-12.2	2.4	-9.6
Belgium	165	156	189	183	166	0.2	0.2	-3.2	-9.3	1.3
Italy	254	139	177	117	144	0.2	0.2	-33.9	23.1	0.7
Japan	54	133	134	146	125	0.2	0.2	9.0	-14.4	-1.2
Denmark	47	..	62	72	90		0.1	16.1	25.0	
Austria	172	109	100	168	85	0.2	0.1	68.0	-49.4	-4.9
Scandinavia	..	84	..	..	..	0.1				
Australia	..	54	106	65	74	0.1	0.1	-38.7	13.8	6.5
Ireland	16	..	64	62	69		0.1	-3.1	11.3	
Spain	56	53	41	61	51	0.1	0.1	48.8	-16.4	-0.8
Other Europe	184	189	183	241	166	0.3	0.2	31.7	-31.1	-2.6
Other interregional	38	133	126	75	61	0.2	0.1	-40.5	-18.7	-14.4
Other World/Not specified	*801*	*641*	*396*	*377*	*306*	*0.9*	*0.4*	*-4.8*	*-18.8*	*-13.7*

Source: World Tourism Organization (UNWTO) ©   (Data as collected by UNWTO for TMT 2006 Edition)

World Tourism Organization ©

III.2.11 Dominican Republic   Caribbean

Promotional: www.dominicana.com ; www.dominicanrepublic.com
Institutional/corporate: www.dominicana.do
Research and data: www.bancentral.gov.do

Profile

Dominican Republic

Americas
Caribbean

Capital	Santo Domingo
Year of entry in UNWTO	1975
Area (1000 km²)	49
Population (2005, million)	9.1
Gross Domestic Product (GDP) (2005, US$ million)	29,089
GDP per capita (2005, US$)	3,411

GDP growth (real, %)
'-> 2004: 2.0;   2005: 9.3;   2006*: 5.5;   2007*: 5.0

	2003	2004	2005*	2004/2003	2005*/2004
International Arrivals					
Visitors (1000)	3,680	3,906	3,981	6.1	1.9
Tourists (overnight visitors) (1000)	3,282	3,450	3,691	5.1	7.0
- per 100 of inhabitants	37	39	41		
Cruise passengers (1000)	398	456	290	14.6	-36.4
Tourism accommodation					
Number of rooms	56,378	58,932	59,870	4.5	1.6
Nights spent in hotels and similar establishments (1000)					
by non-residents (inbound tourism)	23,920	23,795	28,411	-0.5	19.4
Outbound Tourism					
Trips abroad (1000)	321	368	419	14.6	13.9
- per 100 of inhabitants	4	4	5		
Receipts and Expenditure for International Tourism					
International Tourism Receipts (US$ million)	3,128	3,152	3,508	0.8	11.3
- per Tourist Arrival (US$)	953	914	950	-4.2	4.0
- per Visitor Arrival (US$)	850	807	881	-5.1	9.2
- per capita (US$)	355	352	386		
International Tourism Expenditure (US$ million)	272	310	352	14.0	13.5
- per trip (US$)	847	842	840	-0.6	-0.3
- per capita (US$)	31	35	39		
International Fare Expenditure (US$ million)	136	138	142	1.5	2.9
Δ International Tourism Balance (US$ million)	2,856	2,842	3,156		

Source: World Tourism Organization (UNWTO)   (Data as collected by UNWTO for TMT 2006 Edition)
See annex for methodological notes and reference of external sources used.

International Tourism by Origin

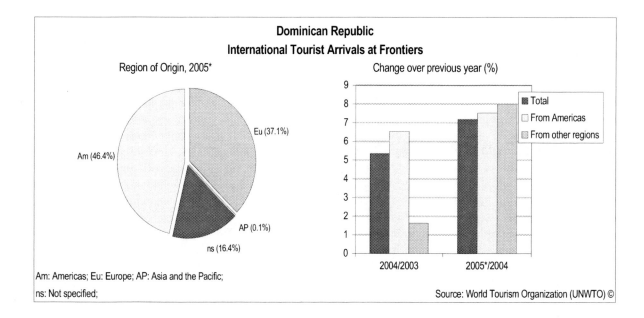

Dominican Republic
International Tourist Arrivals at Frontiers

Region of Origin, 2005*

Am (46.4%)
Eu (37.1%)
AP (0.1%)
ns (16.4%)

Change over previous year (%)

- Total
- From Americas
- From other regions

2004/2003   2005*/2004

Am: Americas; Eu: Europe; AP: Asia and the Pacific;
ns: Not specified;

Source: World Tourism Organization (UNWTO) ©

Dominican Republic
International Tourist Arrivals at Frontiers (by residence)

	1995	2000	2003	2004	2005*	Market share (%) 2000	Market share (%) 2005*	Growth rate (%) 04/03	Growth rate (%) 05*/04	Average per year (%) 2000-2005*
Total	**1,775,873**	**2,972,552**	**3,268,182**	**3,443,205**	**3,690,692**	**100**	**100**	**5.4**	**7.2**	**4.4**
From Americas	..	*1,152,622*	*1,493,912*	*1,591,605*	*1,711,341*	*38.8*	*46.4*	*6.5*	*7.5*	*8.2*
United States	..	580,982	810,833	890,209	986,934	19.5	26.7	9.8	10.9	11.2
Canada	..	249,347	414,296	451,793	429,006	8.4	11.6	9.1	-5.0	11.5
Puerto Rico	..	115,107	130,607	118,848	128,057	3.9	3.5	-9.0	7.7	2.2
Venezuela	..	35,786	23,884	24,562	32,705	1.2	0.9	2.8	33.2	-1.8
Colombia	..	21,761	22,647	20,314	21,739	0.7	0.6	-10.3	7.0	0.0
Chile	..	16,527	16,663	17,313	18,187	0.6	0.5	3.9	5.0	1.9
Mexico	..	12,395	13,060	13,214	17,171	0.4	0.5	1.2	29.9	6.7
Argentina	..	74,164	9,302	7,779	12,349	2.5	0.3	-16.4	58.7	-30.1
Peru	..	9,215	8,510	8,254	9,081	0.3	0.2	-3.0	10.0	-0.3
Haiti	..	768	954	1,835	7,081	0.0	0.2	92.3	285.9	55.9
Brazil	..	3,281	4,768	4,543	6,741	0.1	0.2	-4.7	48.4	15.5
Ecuador	..	2,783	3,823	3,527	5,563	0.1	0.2	-7.7	57.7	14.9
Panama	..	4,693	3,719	3,221	3,580	0.2	0.1	-13.4	11.1	-5.3
Costa Rica	..	3,205	3,633	2,732	3,530	0.1	0.1	-24.8	29.2	2.0
Cuba	..	4,701	2,909	3,006	3,394	0.2	0.1	3.3	12.9	-6.3
Guatemala	..	2,274	3,510	2,368	3,144	0.1	0.1	-32.5	32.8	6.7
El Salvador	..	1,169	1,407	1,344	1,775	0.0	0.0	-4.5	32.1	8.7
St.Maarten	..	1,076	1,360	1,282	1,647	0.0	0.0	-5.7	28.5	8.9
Aruba	..	927	1,523	1,385	1,611	0.0	0.0	-9.1	16.3	11.7
Honduras	..	390	1,004	760	1,497	0.0	0.0	-24.3	97.0	30.9
Other South America	..	4,782	1,665	1,814	1,488	0.2	0.0	8.9	-18.0	-20.8
Other Americas	..	7,289	13,835	11,502	14,225	0.2	0.4	-16.9	23.7	14.3
Other intraregional	..	..	..	..	836		0.0			
From other regions	..	*1,285,429*	*1,250,788*	*1,271,236*	*1,372,774*	*43.2*	*37.2*	*1.6*	*8.0*	*1.3*
France	..	171,315	312,911	295,885	303,720	5.8	8.2	-5.4	2.6	12.1
Spain	..	149,270	202,762	226,653	254,824	5.0	6.9	11.8	12.4	11.3
Germany	..	452,137	243,472	232,956	233,215	15.2	6.3	-4.3	0.1	-12.4
United Kingdom	..	115,102	170,386	196,525	221,697	3.9	6.0	15.3	12.8	14.0
Italy	..	130,698	131,823	121,611	129,926	4.4	3.5	-7.7	6.8	-0.1
Netherlands	..	36,805	35,305	51,243	59,469	1.2	1.6	45.1	16.1	10.1
Belgium	..	38,138	51,024	41,159	43,371	1.3	1.2	-19.3	5.4	2.6
Portugal	..	26,021	34,037	29,184	34,780	0.9	0.9	-14.3	19.2	6.0
Switzerland	..	48,724	41,163	38,855	33,820	1.6	0.9	-5.6	-13.0	-7.0
Austria	..	22,778	10,066	10,471	13,101	0.8	0.4	4.0	25.1	-10.5
Russian Federation	..	..	..	..	11,521		0.3			
Sweden	..	48,802	3,491	8,002	8,825	1.6	0.2	129.2	10.3	-29.0
Finland	..	8,840	1,125	4,216	6,568	0.3	0.2	274.8	55.8	-5.8
Poland	..	..	..	..	4,732		0.1			
Ireland	..	..	..	..	3,907		0.1			
Japan	..	2,628	1,588	1,665	1,520	0.1	0.0	4.8	-8.7	-10.4
Norway	..	..	..	..	1,076		0.0			
Denmark	..	..	..	..	732		0.0			
Other interregional	..	34,171	11,635	12,811	5,970	1.1	0.2	10.1	-53.4	-29.5
Nationals residing abroad	*304,533*	*512,966*	*520,283*	*577,102*	*602,445*	*17.3*	*16.3*	*10.9*	*4.4*	*3.3*
Other World/Not specified	*1,471,340*	*21,535*	*3,199*	*3,262*	*4,132*	*0.7*	*0.1*	*2.0*	*26.7*	*-28.1*

Source: World Tourism Organization (UNWTO) ©   (Data as collected by UNWTO for TMT 2006 Edition)
Note: Air arrivals. Excluding pasangers from Herrera airport

III.2.12 Grenada — Caribbean

Profile

Grenada

Americas
Caribbean

Capital		Saint George's
Area (10 km²)		34
Population (2005, 1000)		90
Gross Domestic Product (GDP) (2005, US$ million)		490
GDP per capita (2005, US$)		4,670
GDP growth (real, %)		
-> 2004: -3.0; 2005: 5.0; 2006*: 6.5; 2007*: 5.0		

	2003	2004	2005*	2004/2003	2005*/2004
International Arrivals					
Visitors (1000)	294	370	380	25.9	2.7
Tourists (overnight visitors) (1000)	142	134	99	-6.0	-26.4
- per 100 of inhabitants	159	150	110		
Same-day visitors (1000)	5	6	6	20.0	
Cruise passengers (1000)	147	230	275	56.5	19.6
Tourism accommodation					
Number of rooms	1,758	1,738	1,470	-1.1	-15.4
Receipts and Expenditure for International Tourism					
International Tourism Receipts (US$ million)	104	83	71	-20.2	-14.5
- per Tourist Arrival (US$)	731	620	720	-15.1	16.2
- per Visitor Arrival (US$)	354	224	187	-36.6	-16.7
- per capita (US$)	1,165	929	793		
International Tourism Expenditure (US$ million)	8	9	11	12.5	22.2
- per capita (US$)	90	101	123		
Δ International Tourism Balance (US$ million)	96	74	60		

Source: World Tourism Organization (UNWTO)   (Data as collected by UNWTO for TMT 2006 Edition)

See annex for methodological notes and reference of external sources used.

World Tourism Organization ©

International Tourism by Origin

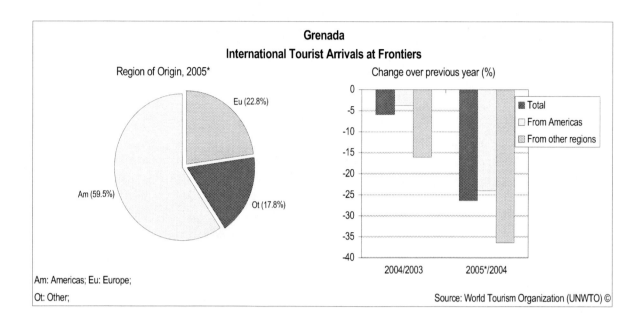

Grenada
International Tourist Arrivals at Frontiers

Region of Origin, 2005*

Eu (22.8%)
Am (59.5%)
Ot (17.8%)

Change over previous year (%)

■ Total
□ From Americas
▨ From other regions

2004/2003   2005*/2004

Am: Americas; Eu: Europe;
Ot: Other;

Source: World Tourism Organization (UNWTO) ©

Grenada
International Tourist Arrivals at Frontiers (by nationality)

	1995	2000	2003	2004	2005*	Market share (%) 2000	2005*	Growth rate (%) 04/03	05*/04	Average per year (%) 2000-2005*
Total	**108,007**	**128,864**	**142,355**	**133,865**	**98,548**	**100**	**100**	**-6.0**	**-26.4**	**-5.2**
From Americas	*51,718*	*62,214*	*80,126*	*77,126*	*58,629*	*48.3*	*59.5*	*-3.7*	*-24.0*	*-1.2*
United States	30,033	32,541	35,191	30,127	25,181	25.3	25.6	-14.4	-16.4	-5.0
Trinidad Tbg	7,097	12,519	19,959	20,228	13,055	9.7	13.2	1.3	-35.5	0.8
Barbados	2,798	4,137	6,040	6,624	4,569	3.2	4.6	9.7	-31.0	2.0
Canada	3,920	4,849	5,599	5,309	4,341	3.8	4.4	-5.2	-18.2	-2.2
Saint Lucia	987	1,362	2,367	2,306	2,202	1.1	2.2	-2.6	-4.5	10.1
St.Vincent,Grenadines	1,165	1,637	2,836	3,010	2,181	1.3	2.2	6.1	-27.5	5.9
Guyana	831	1,235	1,489	1,674	2,164	1.0	2.2	12.4	29.3	11.9
Jamaica	581	1,294	1,365	1,499	1,133	1.0	1.1	9.8	-24.4	-2.6
Venezuela	2,905	381	725	569	586	0.3	0.6	-21.5	3.0	9.0
Dominica	384	341	636	668	529	0.3	0.5	5.0	-20.8	9.2
Antigua,Barb	349	542	746	1,068	485	0.4	0.5	43.2	-54.6	-2.2
St.Kitts-Nev	259	278	293	423	223	0.2	0.2	44.4	-47.3	-4.3
Cuba	..	196	177	177	211	0.2	0.2	0.0	19.2	1.5
St.Maarten	..	1	141	189	130	0.0	0.1	34.0	-31.2	164.7
Mexico	35	51	102	96	95	0.0	0.1	-5.9	-1.0	13.2
Bahamas	24	179	141	155	82	0.1	0.1	9.9	-47.1	-14.5
Brazil	130	107	80	81	77	0.1	0.1	1.3	-4.9	-6.4
Montserrat	54	137	157	115	73	0.1	0.1	-26.8	-36.5	-11.8
Other intraregional	166	427	2,082	2,808	1,312	0.3	1.3	34.9	-53.3	25.2
From other regions	*37,316*	*48,453*	*44,860*	*37,638*	*23,923*	*37.6*	*24.3*	*-16.1*	*-36.4*	*-13.2*
United Kingdom	18,480	32,236	33,286	28,232	15,605	25.0	15.8	-15.2	-44.7	-13.5
Germany	6,342	4,505	3,533	2,701	2,809	3.5	2.9	-23.5	4.0	-9.0
France	1,855	1,874	1,336	1,048	812	1.5	0.8	-21.6	-22.5	-15.4
Italy	2,905	1,208	778	746	545	0.9	0.6	-4.1	-26.9	-14.7
Austria	1,272	1,172	719	613	520	0.9	0.5	-14.7	-15.2	-15.0
Netherlands	1,640	1,186	675	478	394	0.9	0.4	-29.2	-17.6	-19.8
Switzerland	1,804	764	737	529	393	0.6	0.4	-28.2	-25.7	-12.4
Sweden	702	1,008	404	426	239	0.8	0.2	5.4	-43.9	-25.0
Ireland	295	492	341	258	202	0.4	0.2	-24.3	-21.7	-16.3
Norway	346	585	253	187	160	0.5	0.2	-26.1	-14.4	-22.8
Denmark	408	310	301	197	150	0.2	0.2	-34.6	-23.9	-13.5
All Africa	146	..	..	..	..					
Spain	146	125	152	215	137	0.1	0.1	41.4	-36.3	1.9
Nigeria	..	110	154	142	132	0.1	0.1	-7.8	-7.0	3.7
Australia	314	278	378	220	115	0.2	0.1	-41.8	-47.7	-16.2
Belgium	110	199	159	107	97	0.2	0.1	-32.7	-9.3	-13.4
Japan	101	193	194	157	84	0.1	0.1	-19.1	-46.5	-15.3
Former U.S.S.R.	45	88	80	103	79	0.1	0.1	28.8	-23.3	-2.1
South Africa	..	219	180	204	70	0.2	0.1	13.3	-65.7	-20.4
Finland	47	147	69	78	69	0.1	0.1	13.0	-11.5	-14.0
Syrian Arab Republic	..	47	33	34	57	0.0	0.1	3.0	67.6	3.9
Poland	32	41	68	66	52	0.0	0.1	-2.9	-21.2	4.9
Other interregional	326	1,666	1,030	897	1,202	1.3	1.2	-12.9	34.0	-6.3
Nationals residing abroad	*18,145*	*18,068*	*16,715*	*19,076*	*15,907*	*14.0*	*16.1*	*14.1*	*-16.6*	*-2.5*
Other World/Not specified	*828*	*129*	*654*	*25*	*89*	*0.1*	*0.1*	*-96.2*	*256.0*	*-7.2*

Source: World Tourism Organization (UNWTO) ©   (Data as collected by UNWTO for TMT 2006 Edition)

World Tourism Organization ©

III.2.13   Guadeloupe   Caribbean

Profile

Guadeloupe

Americas
Caribbean

Capital	Basse-Terre
Area (10 km²)	171
Population (2005, 1000)	449

	2003	2004	2005*	2004/2003	2005*/2004
International Arrivals					
Visitors (1000)	569	560	445	-1.6	-20.5
Tourists (overnight visitors) (1000)	439	456	372	3.9	-18.4
- per 100 of inhabitants	100	103	83		
Cruise passengers (1000)	130	104	73	-20.0	-29.8
Tourism accommodation					
Number of rooms	7,603	4,416	3,506	-41.9	-20.6
Nights spent in hotels and similar establishments (1000)					
by non-residents (inbound tourism)	1,534	1,736	..	13.2	
Receipts and Expenditure for International Tourism					
International Tourism Receipts (US$ million)	..	..	246		
- per Tourist Arrival (US$)	..	..	661		
- per Visitor Arrival (US$)	..	..	553		
- per capita (US$)	..	..	548		

Source: World Tourism Organization (UNWTO)   (Data as collected by UNWTO for TMT 2006 Edition)

See annex for methodological notes and reference of external sources used.

International Tourism by Origin

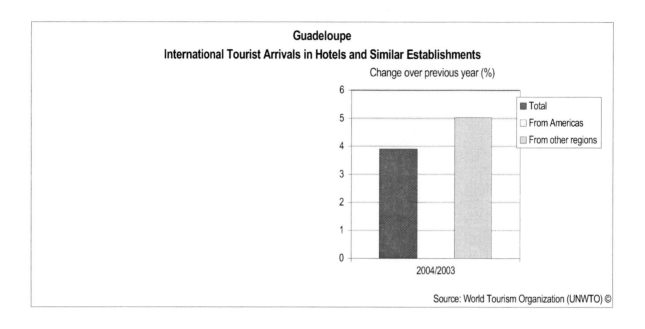

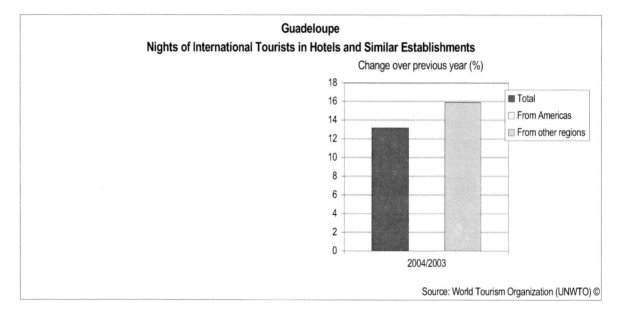

Guadeloupe
International Tourist Arrivals in Hotels and Similar Establishments (by residence)

	1995	2000	2002	2003	2004	Market share (%) 2000	Market share (%) 2004	Growth rate (%) 03/02	Growth rate (%) 04/03	Average per year (%) 2000-2004
Total	152,896	623,134	..	438,819	455,981	100	100		3.9	-7.5
From Americas	11,622	125,871	..	..	..	20.2				
United States	7,826	92,474	..	..	..	14.8				
Canada	2,101	10,431	..	..	..	1.7				
Haiti	..	763	..	..	..	0.1				
All the Caribbean	302	..	..	..	..					
Dominica	..	203	..	..	..	0.0				
Venezuela	144	..	..	..	..					
Cuba	..	39	..	..	..	0.0				
Mexico	28	..	..	..	..					
Other Caribbean	..	7,635	..	..	..	1.2				
Other Americas	1,221	14,326	..	..	..	2.3				
From other regions	140,641	495,385	..	386,737	406,204	79.5	89.1		5.0	-4.8
France	124,885	440,779	..	386,737	406,204	70.7	89.1		5.0	-2.0
Italy	3,485	15,670	..	..	..	2.5				
Switzerland	4,270	9,766	..	..	..	1.6				
Germany	3,525	5,476	..	..	..	0.9				
Benelux	..	5,313	..	..	..	0.9				
United Kingdom/Ireland	..	5,154	..	..	..	0.8				
Spain, Portugal	..	1,952	..	..	..	0.3				
Belgium/Luxembourg	1,659	..	..	..	..					
United Kingdom	561	..	..	..	..					
Netherlands	263	..	..	..	..					
Scandinavia	210	..	..	..	..					
Other Europe	1,783	11,275	..	..	..	1.8				
Other World/Not specified	633	1,878	..	52,082	49,777	0.3	10.9		-4.4	126.9

Source: World Tourism Organization (UNWTO) ©   (Data as collected by UNWTO for TMT 2006 Edition)

Guadeloupe

Nights of International Tourists in Hotels and Similar Establishments (by residence)

	1995	2000	2002	2003	2004	Market share (%) 2000	Market share (%) 2004	Growth rate (%) 03/02	Growth rate (%) 04/03	Average per year (%) 2000-2004
Total	**926,132**	**3,233,487**	..	**1,534,019**	**1,736,232**	**100**	**100**		**13.2**	**-14.4**
From Americas	*66,504*	*753,294*	..	..	..	*23.3*				
United States	41,514	541,525	..	..	..	16.7				
Canada	16,157	84,436	..	..	..	2.6				
Haiti	..	1,913	..	..	..	0.1				
All the Caribbean	862	..	..	..	..					
Venezuela	762	..	..	..	..					
Dominica	..	405	..	..	..	0.0				
Mexico	124	..	..	..	..					
Cuba	..	44	..	..	..	0.0				
Other Caribbean	..	22,448	..	..	..	0.7				
Other Americas	7,085	102,523	..	..	..	3.2				
From other regions	*856,447*	*2,470,230*	..	*1,355,264*	*1,570,857*	*76.4*	*90.5*		*15.9*	*-10.7*
France	743,805	2,120,747	..	1,355,264	1,570,857	65.6	90.5		15.9	-7.2
Italy	20,346	100,398	..	..	..	3.1				
Switzerland	38,941	61,121	..	..	..	1.9				
Germany	27,002	35,817	..	..	..	1.1				
Benelux	..	33,383	..	..	..	1.0				
United Kingdom/Ireland	..	32,925	..	..	..	1.0				
Belgium/Luxembourg	10,541	..	..	..	..					
Spain, Portugal	..	10,055	..	..	..	0.3				
United Kingdom	3,124	..	..	..	..					
Netherlands	1,752	..	..	..	..					
Scandinavia	1,293	..	..	..	..					
Other Europe	9,643	75,784	..	..	..	2.3				
Other World/Not specified	*3,181*	*9,963*	..	*178,755*	*165,375*	*0.3*	*9.5*		*-7.5*	*101.8*

Source: World Tourism Organization (UNWTO) ©   (Data as collected by UNWTO for TMT 2006 Edition)

III.2.14 Haiti   Caribbean

Promotional: www.haititourisme.org ; ww.haiti2004lakay.com
Institutional/corporate: www.haititourisme.org

Profile

Haiti

Capital	Port-au-Prince
Year of entry in UNWTO	1975
Area (1000 km²)	28
Population (2005, million)	8.3
Gross Domestic Product (GDP) (2005, US$ million)	3,983
GDP per capita (2005, US$)	478

Americas

Caribbean

GDP growth (real, %)

'-> 2004: -2.6;   2005: 0.4;   2006*: 2.3;   2007*: 3.6

	2003	2004	2005*	2004/2003	2005*/2004
International Arrivals					
Visitors (1000)	518	385	480	-25.7	24.7
Tourists (overnight visitors) (1000)	136	96	112	-29.1	16.4
- per 100 of inhabitants	2	1	1		
Cruise passengers (1000)	382	289	368	-24.3	27.3
Receipts and Expenditure for International Tourism					
International Tourism Receipts (US$ million)	93	87	110	-6.5	26.4
- per Tourist Arrival (US$)	684	902	980	32.0	8.6
- per Visitor Arrival (US$)	180	226	229	25.9	1.4
- per capita (US$)	12	11	13		
International Tourism Expenditure (US$ million)	42	72	54	71.4	-25.0
- per capita (US$)	5	9	7		
International Fare Expenditure (US$ million)	154	134	119	-13.0	-11.2
Δ International Tourism Balance (US$ million)	51	15	56		

Source: World Tourism Organization (UNWTO)   (Data as collected by UNWTO for TMT 2006 Edition)

See annex for methodological notes and reference of external sources used.

International Tourism by Origin

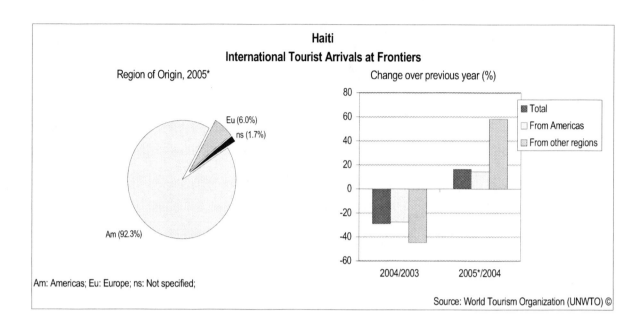

Am: Americas; Eu: Europe; ns: Not specified;

Source: World Tourism Organization (UNWTO) ©

Haiti

International Tourist Arrivals at Frontiers (by residence)

	1995	2000	2003	2004	2005*	Market share (%) 2000	Market share (%) 2005*	Growth rate (%) 04/03	Growth rate (%) 05*/04	Average per year (%) 2000-2005*
Total	**145,369**	**140,492**	**136,031**	**96,439**	**112,267**	**100**	**100**	**-29.1**	**16.4**	**-4.4**
From Americas	*129,266*	*128,048*	*125,214*	*90,615*	*103,595*	*91.1*	*92.3*	*-27.6*	*14.3*	*-4.1*
United States	94,632	92,921	94,515	72,895	77,047	66.1	68.6	-22.9	5.7	-3.7
Canada	13,647	14,752	11,354	8,014	9,986	10.5	8.9	-29.4	24.6	-7.5
Dominican Rp	7,159	7,034	6,586	3,648	5,543	5.0	4.9	-44.6	51.9	-4.7
Jamaica	4,103	3,531	4,548	2,091	3,649	2.5	3.3	-54.0	74.5	0.7
Mexico	255	301	351	237	367	0.2	0.3	-32.5	54.9	4.0
Other Caribbean	5,685	5,486	3,545	1,775	4,147	3.9	3.7	-49.9	133.6	-5.4
Other Americas	3,785	4,023	4,315	1,955	2,856	2.9	2.5	-54.7	46.1	-6.6
From other regions	*14,245*	*10,960*	*7,659*	*4,246*	*6,720*	*7.8*	*6.0*	*-44.6*	*58.3*	*-9.3*
France	7,256	6,420	3,754	1,831	3,349	4.6	3.0	-51.2	82.9	-12.2
Other Europe	6,989	4,540	3,905	2,415	3,371	3.2	3.0	-38.2	39.6	-5.8
Other World/Not specified	*1,858*	*1,484*	*3,158*	*1,578*	*1,952*	*1.1*	*1.7*	*-50.0*	*23.7*	*5.6*

Source: World Tourism Organization (UNWTO) ©   (Data as collected by UNWTO for TMT 2006 Edition)

III.2.15 Jamaica   Caribbean

Promotional: www.visitjamaica.com

Profile

Jamaica

Capital	Kingston
Year of entry in UNWTO	1975
Area (100 km²)	110
Population (2005, million)	2.7
Gross Domestic Product (GDP) (2005, US$ million)	9,731
GDP per capita (2005, US$)	3,657

Americas
Caribbean

GDP growth (real, %)
'-> 2004: 0.9;   2005: 1.4;   2006*: 2.8;   2007*: 3.0

	2003	2004	2005*	2004/2003	2005*/2004
International Arrivals					
Visitors (1000)	2,483	2,515	2,615	1.3	4.0
Tourists (overnight visitors) (1000)	1,350	1,415	1,479	4.8	4.5
- per 100 of inhabitants	50	52	54		
Cruise passengers (1000)	1,133	1,100	1,136	-2.9	3.3
Tourism accommodation					
Number of rooms	20,827	21,322	22,528	2.4	5.7
Nights spent in collective establishments (1000)					
by non-residents (inbound tourism)	12,844	13,134	13,608	2.3	3.6
Nights spent in hotels and similar establishments (1000)					
by non-residents (inbound tourism)	5,687	6,076	6,967	6.8	14.7
Receipts and Expenditure for International Tourism					
International Tourism Receipts (US$ million)	1,355	1,438	1,545	6.1	7.4
- per Tourist Arrival (US$)	1,003	1,016	1,045	1.3	2.8
- per Visitor Arrival (US$)	546	572	591	4.8	3.3
- per capita (US$)	504	530	565		
International Fare Receipts (US$ million)	266	295	238	10.9	-19.3
International Tourism Expenditure (US$ million)	252	287	250	13.5	-12.7
- per capita (US$)	94	106	91		
International Fare Expenditure (US$ million)	17	32	41	88.2	28.1
Δ International Tourism Balance (US$ million)	1,103	1,152	1,295		
Δ International Fare Balance (US$ million)	249	263	197		

Source: World Tourism Organization (UNWTO)   (Data as collected by UNWTO for TMT 2006 Edition)
See annex for methodological notes and reference of external sources used.

International Tourism by Origin

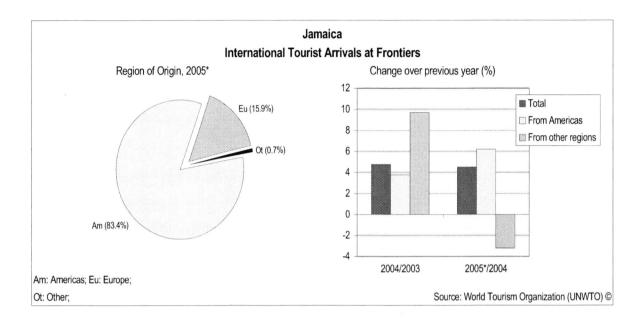

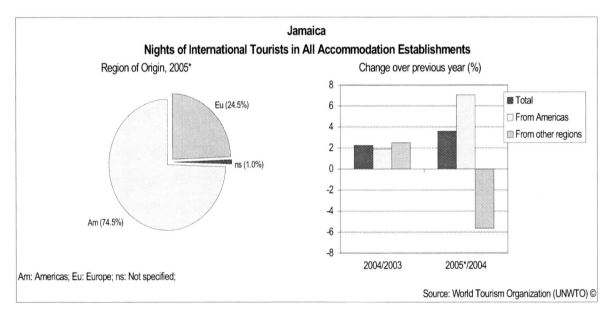

Jamaica
International Tourist Arrivals at Frontiers (by residence)

	1995	2000	2003	2004	2005*	Market share (%) 2000	Market share (%) 2005*	Growth rate (%) 04/03	Growth rate (%) 05*/04	Average per year (%) 2000-2005*
Total	**1,147,001**	**1,322,690**	**1,350,285**	**1,414,786**	**1,478,663**	**100**	**100**	**4.8**	**4.5**	**2.3**
From Americas	*920,391*	*1,108,727*	*1,119,679*	*1,161,840*	*1,233,846*	*83.8*	*83.4*	*3.8*	*6.2*	*2.2*
United States	760,304	942,561	969,699	997,621	1,059,640	71.3	71.7	2.9	6.2	2.4
Canada	108,440	107,492	95,265	105,623	116,862	8.1	7.9	10.9	10.6	1.7
Cayman Islands	8,367	11,148	11,966	15,036	15,822	0.8	1.1	25.7	5.2	7.3
Trinidad Tbg	4,230	6,454	7,308	7,263	7,520	0.5	0.5	-0.6	3.5	3.1
Barbados	2,822	4,889	5,428	5,741	5,320	0.4	0.4	5.8	-7.3	1.7
Bahamas	4,501	6,807	2,946	3,237	2,801	0.5	0.2	9.9	-13.5	-16.3
Bermuda	1,965	2,172	2,442	2,446	2,751	0.2	0.2	0.2	12.5	4.8
Antigua,Barb	1,197	1,860	1,986	2,003	1,946	0.1	0.1	0.9	-2.8	0.9
Guyana	1,218	1,957	1,650	1,771	1,826	0.1	0.1	7.3	3.1	-1.4
Mexico	1,922	2,431	1,892	2,273	1,665	0.2	0.1	20.1	-26.7	-7.3
Saint Lucia	805	1,810	1,920	2,097	1,389	0.1	0.1	9.2	-33.8	-5.2
Dominican Rp	..	778	875	1,210	1,128	0.1	0.1	38.3	-6.8	7.7
Curaçao	..	570	1,422	1,226	1,069	0.0	0.1	-13.8	-12.8	13.4
Brazil	1,955	1,087	735	956	982	0.1	0.1	30.1	2.7	-2.0
Turks,Caicos	391	674	1,021	1,125	977	0.1	0.1	10.2	-13.2	7.7
Panama	1,322	1,335	987	996	939	0.1	0.1	0.9	-5.7	-6.8
Venezuela	899	1,190	761	637	927	0.1	0.1	-16.3	45.5	-4.9
Br.Virgin Is	251	459	620	878	872	0.0	0.1	41.6	-0.7	13.7
St.Kitts-Nev	561	850	822	882	847	0.1	0.1	7.3	-4.0	-0.1
Grenada	328	795	680	633	799	0.1	0.1	-6.9	26.2	0.1
St.Maarten	..	528	732	819	665	0.0	0.0	11.9	-18.8	4.7
Argentina	2,530	1,148	601	495	613	0.1	0.0	-17.6	23.8	-11.8
Other intraregional	16,383	9,732	7,921	6,872	6,486	0.7	0.4	-13.2	-5.6	-7.8
From other regions	*224,254*	*213,882*	*230,547*	*252,918*	*244,781*	*16.2*	*16.6*	*9.7*	*-3.2*	*2.7*
United Kingdom	107,610	135,338	149,714	161,606	152,483	10.2	10.3	7.9	-5.6	2.4
Italy	24,786	14,832	24,303	24,915	24,424	1.1	1.7	2.5	-2.0	10.5
Germany	35,648	25,194	16,290	18,090	19,860	1.9	1.3	11.0	9.8	-4.6
Spain	2,212	1,368	7,042	10,339	6,814	0.1	0.5	46.8	-34.1	37.9
Netherlands	6,676	3,756	3,990	4,180	6,190	0.3	0.4	4.8	48.1	10.5
Belgium	3,001	1,151	2,354	4,174	4,450	0.1	0.3	77.3	6.6	31.1
Japan	23,673	7,779	4,182	4,430	4,304	0.6	0.3	5.9	-2.8	-11.2
France	4,907	3,629	2,597	3,122	3,648	0.3	0.2	20.2	16.8	0.1
Switzerland	4,082	3,349	2,938	4,475	3,352	0.3	0.2	52.3	-25.1	0.0
Austria	2,912	2,606	2,138	2,990	2,998	0.2	0.2	39.9	0.3	2.8
Portugal	..	768	456	823	1,871	0.1	0.1	80.5	127.3	19.5
Australia	..	1,547	2,080	1,488	1,556	0.1	0.1	-28.5	4.6	0.1
Australia, New Zealand	1,521	..	..	..	..					
Russian Federation	..	904	1,133	983	1,333	0.1	0.1	-13.2	35.6	8.1
Sweden	1,287	1,442	1,007	1,138	1,179	0.1	0.1	13.0	3.6	-3.9
Israel	..	985	781	825	948	0.1	0.1	5.6	14.9	-0.8
All Africa	1,132	1,388	1,084	1,139	889	0.1	0.1	5.1	-21.9	-8.5
Poland	..	613	852	682	818	0.0	0.1	-20.0	19.9	5.9
China	..	530	585	532	750	0.0	0.1	-9.1	41.0	7.2
Other interregional	4,807	6,703	7,021	6,987	6,914	0.5	0.5	-0.5	-1.0	0.6
Other World/Not specified	*2,356*	*81*	*59*	*28*	*36*	*0.0*	*0.0*	*-52.5*	*28.6*	*-15.0*

Source: World Tourism Organization (UNWTO) ©   (Data as collected by UNWTO for TMT 2006 Edition)

Jamaica

Nights of International Tourists in All Accommodation Establishments (by residence)

	1995	2000	2003	2004	2005*	Market share (%) 2000	2005*	Growth rate (%) 04/03	05*/04	Average per year (%) 2000-2005*
Total	**11,143,522**	**12,326,858**	**12,843,703**	**13,134,253**	**13,607,597**	**100**	**100**	**2.3**	**3.6**	**2.0**
From Americas	*7,520,613*	*8,939,463*	*9,292,650*	*9,470,028*	*10,138,677*	*72.5*	*74.5*	*1.9*	*7.1*	*2.5*
Canada, USA	7,053,065	8,418,589	8,801,377	8,988,107	9,693,972	68.3	71.2	2.1	7.9	2.9
All the Caribbean	296,034	393,947	390,001	395,979	350,933	3.2	2.6	1.5	-11.4	-2.3
Other Americas	171,514	126,927	101,272	85,942	93,772	1.0	0.7	-15.1	9.1	-5.9
From other regions	*3,431,493*	*3,237,347*	*3,450,220*	*3,536,656*	*3,337,672*	*26.3*	*24.5*	*2.5*	*-5.6*	*0.6*
All Europe	3,431,493	3,237,347	3,450,220	3,536,656	3,337,672	26.3	24.5	2.5	-5.6	0.6
Other World/Not specified	*191,416*	*150,048*	*100,833*	*127,569*	*131,248*	*1.2*	*1.0*	*26.5*	*2.9*	*-2.6*

Source: World Tourism Organization (UNWTO) ©   (Data as collected by UNWTO for TMT 2006 Edition)

World Tourism Organization ©

III.2.16 Martinique   Caribbean

Profile

Martinique

Capital	Fort-de-France
Area (10 km²)	110
Population (2005, 1000)	433

Americas
Caribbean

	2003	2004	2005*	2004/2003	2005*/2004
International Arrivals					
Visitors (1000)	722	630	577	-12.7	-8.4
Tourists (overnight visitors) (1000)	453	471	484	3.9	2.8
- per 100 of inhabitants	106	110	112		
Cruise passengers (1000)	269	159	93	-40.9	-41.5
Tourism accommodation					
Number of rooms	6,766	6,153	6,153	-9.1	
Nights spent in collective establishments (1000)					
by non-residents (inbound tourism)	6,136	6,770	6,496	10.3	-4.0
Nights spent in hotels and similar establishments (1000)					
by non-residents (inbound tourism)	1,693	1,705	1,924	0.7	12.8
Receipts and Expenditure for International Tourism					
International Tourism Receipts (US$ million)	247	291	280	17.8	-3.8
- per Tourist Arrival (US$)	545	618	578	13.4	-6.4
- per Visitor Arrival (US$)	342	462	485	35.0	5.1
- per capita (US$)	580	678	647		

Source: World Tourism Organization (UNWTO)   (Data as collected by UNWTO for TMT 2006 Edition)
See annex for methodological notes and reference of external sources used.

International Tourism by Origin

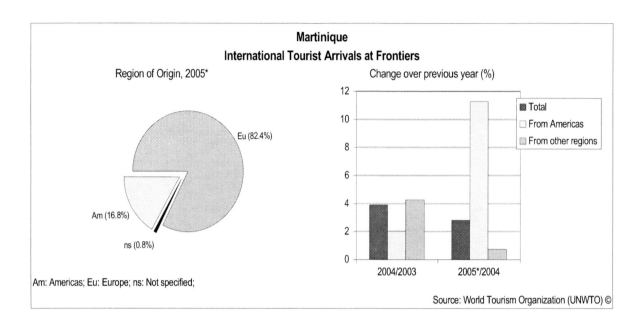

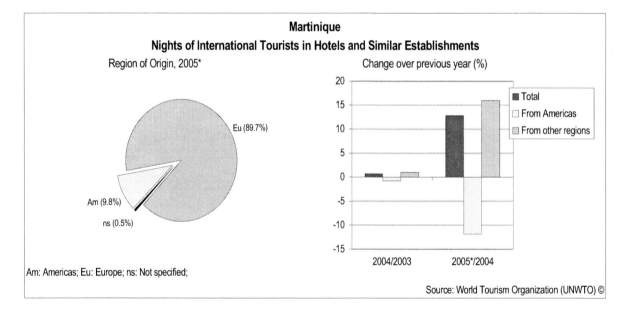

World Tourism Organization ©

Martinique
International Tourist Arrivals at Frontiers (by residence)

	1995	2000	2003	2004	2005*	Market share (%) 2000	Market share (%) 2005*	Growth rate (%) 04/03	Growth rate (%) 05*/04	Average per year (%) 2000-2005*
Total	**457,226**	**526,291**	**453,159**	**470,890**	**484,127**	**100**	**100**	**3.9**	**2.8**	**-1.7**
From Americas	*73,534*	*80,168*	*71,559*	*73,011*	*81,247*	*15.2*	*16.8*	*2.0*	*11.3*	*0.3*
Guadeloupe	26,330	41,102	40,668	40,644	37,030	7.8	7.6	-0.1	-8.9	-2.1
French Guiana	14,305	13,860	10,619	13,407	11,582	2.6	2.4	26.3	-13.6	-3.5
Saint Lucia	..	5,771	5,842	4,603	9,079	1.1	1.9	-21.2	97.2	9.5
United States	14,949	5,074	2,557	3,468	4,984	1.0	1.0	35.6	43.7	-0.4
Venezuela	..	2,817	2,304	2,037	4,771	0.5	1.0	-11.6	134.2	11.1
Canada	6,753	5,425	2,584	3,008	4,569	1.0	0.9	16.4	51.9	-3.4
Dominica	..	1,855	3,033	1,694	3,712	0.4	0.8	-44.1	119.1	14.9
Barbados	..	1,463	1,976	2,399	3,004	0.3	0.6	21.4	25.2	15.5
Other Caribbean	11,197	2,801	1,976	1,751	2,516	0.5	0.5	-11.4	43.7	-2.1
From other regions	*378,663*	*443,046*	*379,922*	*396,138*	*399,083*	*84.2*	*82.4*	*4.3*	*0.7*	*-2.1*
France	342,542	418,536	357,726	373,678	369,705	79.5	76.4	4.5	-1.1	-2.5
Benelux	6,177	6,089	7,831	6,698	8,711	1.2	1.8	-14.5	30.1	7.4
Switzerland	8,741	4,006	2,963	3,857	5,574	0.8	1.2	30.2	44.5	6.8
Italy	3,576	3,541	2,788	2,661	4,506	0.7	0.9	-4.6	69.3	4.9
Germany	10,511	2,504	2,767	3,251	3,998	0.5	0.8	17.5	23.0	9.8
United Kingdom/Ireland	2,637	2,501	1,945	2,220	2,778	0.5	0.6	14.1	25.1	2.1
Scandinavia	1,192	1,829	1,857	1,228	1,967	0.3	0.4	-33.9	60.2	1.5
Other Europe	3,287	4,040	2,045	2,545	1,844	0.8	0.4	24.4	-27.5	-14.5
Other World/Not specified	*5,029*	*3,077*	*1,678*	*1,741*	*3,797*	*0.6*	*0.8*	*3.8*	*118.1*	*4.3*

Source: World Tourism Organization (UNWTO) ©   (Data as collected by UNWTO for TMT 2006 Edition)

Martinique
Nights of International Tourists in Hotels and Similar Establishments (by residence)

	1995	2000	2003	2004	2005*	Market share (%) 2000	Market share (%) 2005*	Growth rate (%) 04/03	Growth rate (%) 05*/04	Average per year (%) 2000-2005*
Total	**2,238,000**	**2,440,576**	**1,693,378**	**1,705,263**	**1,923,949**	**100**	**100**	**0.7**	**12.8**	**-4.6**
From Americas	*269,000*	*286,428*	*215,410*	*213,811*	*188,496*	*11.7*	*9.8*	*-0.7*	*-11.8*	*-8.0*
All the Caribbean	113,000	234,148	198,843	195,142	136,973	9.6	7.1	-1.9	-29.8	-10.2
Canada	31,000	22,823	10,114	10,580	30,062	0.9	1.6	4.6	184.1	5.7
United States	125,000	29,457	6,453	8,089	21,461	1.2	1.1	25.4	165.3	-6.1
From other regions	*1,969,000*	*2,141,628*	*1,472,678*	*1,487,700*	*1,724,949*	*87.8*	*89.7*	*1.0*	*15.9*	*-4.2*
France	1,740,000	2,002,529	1,407,028	1,428,449	1,606,674	82.1	83.5	1.5	12.5	-4.3
Other Europe	229,000	139,099	65,650	59,251	118,275	5.7	6.1	-9.7	99.6	-3.2
Other World/Not specified	*..*	*12,520*	*5,290*	*3,752*	*10,504*	*0.5*	*0.5*	*-29.1*	*180.0*	*-3.5*

Source: World Tourism Organization (UNWTO) ©   (Data as collected by UNWTO for TMT 2006 Edition)

Profile

Montserrat

Americas
Caribbean

Capital	Plymouth
Area (10 km²)	10
Population (2005, 1000)	9

	2003	2004	2005*	2004/2003	2005*/2004
International Arrivals					
Visitors (1000)	14	15	13	5.3	-13.8
Tourists (overnight visitors) (1000)	8	10	10	20.8	-4.4
- per 100 of inhabitants	93	110	104		
Same-day visitors (1000)	5	5	3	-1.9	-33.3
Cruise passengers (1000)	1	0	0	-50.0	-25.0
Receipts and Expenditure for International Tourism					
International Tourism Receipts (US$ million)	7	9	9	22.5	4.7
- per Tourist Arrival (US$)	834	846	927	1.4	9.6
- per Visitor Arrival (US$)	485	564	686	16.4	21.5
- per capita (US$)	778	928	962		
International Tourism Expenditure (US$ million)	2	2	3		50.0
- per capita (US$)	222	216	321		
Δ International Tourism Balance (US$ million)	5	7	6		

Source: World Tourism Organization (UNWTO)　　　　　　　　(Data as collected by UNWTO for TMT 2006 Edition)

See annex for methodological notes and reference of external sources used.

World Tourism Organization ©

International Tourism by Origin

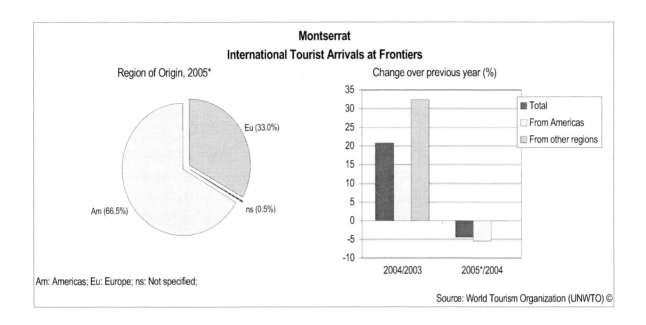

Montserrat
International Tourist Arrivals at Frontiers (by residence)

	1995	2000	2003	2004	2005*	Market share (%) 2000	2005*	Growth rate (%) 04/03	05*/04	Average per year (%) 2000-2005*
Total	**17,675**	**10,337**	**8,390**	**10,138**	**9,690**	**100**	**100**	**20.8**	**-4.4**	**-1.3**
From Americas	*14,250*	*7,231*	*5,932*	*6,822*	*6,448*	*70.0*	*66.5*	*15.0*	*-5.5*	*-2.3*
All the Caribbean	6,099	5,324	4,073	4,385	3,987	51.5	41.1	7.7	-9.1	-5.6
United States	6,836	1,561	1,541	2,084	2,034	15.1	21.0	35.2	-2.4	5.4
Canada	1,284	346	297	334	404	3.3	4.2	12.5	21.0	3.1
Other Americas	31	..	21	19	23		0.2	-9.5	21.1	
From other regions	*2,749*	*2,592*	*2,414*	*3,197*	*3,196*	*25.1*	*33.0*	*32.4*	*0.0*	*4.3*
United Kingdom	2,462	2,592	2,269	3,021	2,968	25.1	30.6	33.1	-1.8	2.7
France	122	..	..	..	..					
Italy	28	..	..	..	..					
Netherlands	18	..	..	..	..					
Germany	1	..	..	..	..					
Spain	1	..	..	..	..					
Sweden	1	..	..	..	..					
Other Europe	116	..	145	176	228		2.4	21.4	29.5	
Other World/Not specified	*676*	*514*	*44*	*119*	*46*	*5.0*	*0.5*	*170.5*	*-61.3*	*-38.3*

Source: World Tourism Organization (UNWTO) ©   (Data as collected by UNWTO for TMT 2006 Edition)

III.2.18 Netherlands Antilles   Caribbean

Profile

Netherlands Antilles

Year of entry in UNWTO	1979
Area (10 km²)	80
Population (2005, 1000)	220
Gross Domestic Product (GDP) (2005, US$ million)	3,204
GDP per capita (2005, US$)	17,270

Americas

Caribbean

GDP growth (real, %)

'-> 2004: 1.0;   2005: 0.7;   2006*: 1.8;   2007*: 2.7

Source: World Tourism Organization (UNWTO)   (Data as collected by UNWTO for TMT 2006 Edition)

See annex for methodological notes and reference of external sources used.

III.2.18.a Bonaire   Caribbean

Profile

Bonaire

Capital   Kralendijk

Americas
Caribbean

	2003	2004	2005*	2004/2003	2005*/2004
International Arrivals					
Visitors (1000)	107	116	103	8.4	-11.2
Tourists (overnight visitors) (1000)	62	63	63	1.6	-0.9
Cruise passengers (1000)	45	53	40	17.8	-24.5
Tourism accommodation					
Number of rooms	1,699	1,175	..	-30.8	
Nights spent in collective establishments (1000)					
by non-residents (inbound tourism)	574	578	587	0.7	1.6
Nights spent in hotels and similar establishments (1000)					
by non-residents (inbound tourism)	415	419	..	1.0	
Receipts and Expenditure for International Tourism					
International Tourism Receipts (US$ million)	84	84	85	-0.7	1.7
- per Tourist Arrival (US$)	1,357	1,326	1,362	-2.3	2.7
- per Visitor Arrival (US$)	788	722	827	-8.4	14.6
International Tourism Expenditure (US$ million)	3	6	5	131.1	-8.7
Δ International Tourism Balance (US$ million)	82	78	80		

Source: World Tourism Organization (UNWTO)   (Data as collected by UNWTO for TMT 2006 Edition)
See annex for methodological notes and reference of external sources used.

Bonaire
Nights of International Tourists in All Accommodation Establishments (by residence)

	1995	2000	2002	2003	2004	Market share (%) 2000	Market share (%) 2004	Growth rate (%) 03/02	Growth rate (%) 04/03	Average per year (%) 2000-2004
Total	**478,681**	**480,567**	**486,055**	**574,102**	**577,997**	**100**	**100**	**18.1**	**0.7**	**4.7**
From Americas	*276,919*	*262,630*	*268,764*	*267,369*	*278,925*	*54.7*	*48.3*	*-0.5*	*4.3*	*1.5*
United States	201,658	208,539	220,827	214,270	226,507	43.4	39.2	-3.0	5.7	2.1
All the Caribbean	22,075	10,802	15,150	16,992	15,571	2.2	2.7	12.2	-8.4	9.6
Canada	9,021	11,588	8,016	9,813	11,521	2.4	2.0	22.4	17.4	-0.1
Other Americas	44,165	31,701	24,771	26,294	25,326	6.6	4.4	6.1	-3.7	-5.5
From other regions	*199,649*	*214,598*	*213,883*	*303,493*	*293,930*	*44.7*	*50.9*	*41.9*	*-3.2*	*8.2*
Netherlands	136,739	159,418	153,814	217,381	212,936	33.2	36.8	41.3	-2.0	7.5
Other Europe	62,910	55,180	60,069	86,112	80,994	11.5	14.0	43.4	-5.9	10.1
Other World/Not specified	*2,113*	*3,339*	*3,408*	*3,240*	*5,142*	*0.7*	*0.9*	*-4.9*	*58.7*	*11.4*

Source: World Tourism Organization (UNWTO) ©   (Data as collected by UNWTO for TMT 2006 Edition)

International Tourism by Origin

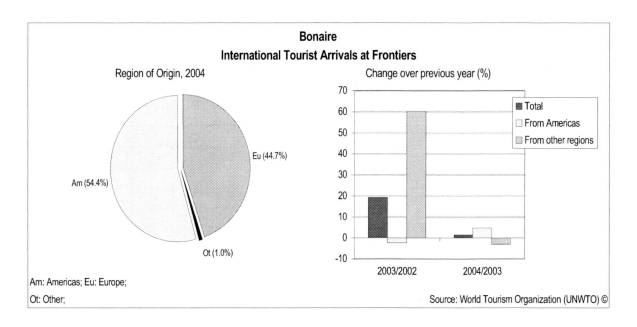

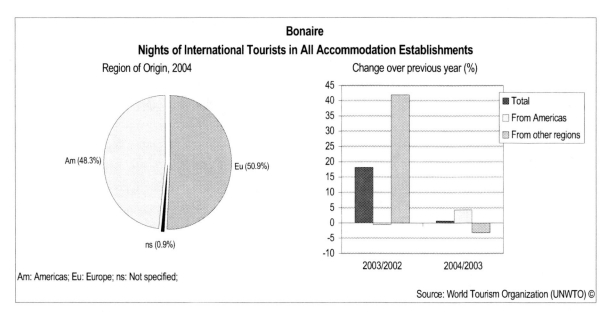

Bonaire
International Tourist Arrivals at Frontiers (by residence)

	1995	2000	2002	2003	2004	Market share (%) 2000	Market share (%) 2004	Growth rate (%) 03/02	Growth rate (%) 04/03	Average per year (%) 2000-2004
Total	**59,410**	**51,269**	**52,085**	**62,179**	**63,156**	**100**	**100**	**19.4**	**1.6**	**5.4**
From Americas	*38,819*	*33,067*	*33,548*	*32,771*	*34,330*	*64.5*	*54.4*	*-2.3*	*4.8*	*0.9*
United States	26,195	25,429	26,499	25,228	26,483	49.6	41.9	-4.8	5.0	1.0
Aruba	4,201	1,515	2,162	2,493	2,790	3.0	4.4	15.3	11.9	16.5
Venezuela	4,851	3,504	2,150	1,725	1,722	6.8	2.7	-19.8	-0.2	-16.3
Canada	958	1,099	593	843	1,068	2.1	1.7	42.2	26.7	-0.7
Peru	23	8	97	655	440	0.0	0.7	575.3	-32.8	172.3
Brazil	886	233	246	234	419	0.5	0.7	-4.9	79.1	15.8
Ecuador	54	28	262	280	351	0.1	0.6	6.9	25.4	88.2
Colombia	571	446	437	235	185	0.9	0.3	-46.2	-21.3	-19.7
Suriname	163	87	175	179	138	0.2	0.2	2.3	-22.9	12.2
Puerto Rico	72	158	212	190	136	0.3	0.2	-10.4	-28.4	-3.7
Dominican Rp	329	203	250	145	122	0.4	0.2	-42.0	-15.9	-12.0
Argentina	200	113	60	36	107	0.2	0.2	-40.0	197.2	-1.4
Jamaica	14	37	66	71	49	0.1	0.1	7.6	-31.0	7.3
Trinidad Tbg	23	50	70	70	47	0.1	0.1	0.0	-32.9	-1.5
Mexico	23	28	31	12	44	0.1	0.1	-61.3	266.7	12.0
US.Virgin Is	29	19	..	31	29	0.0	0.0		-6.5	11.2
Guyana	19	1	..	17	..	0.0				
Panama	24	7	18	18	17	0.0	0.0	0.0	-5.6	24.8
Bahamas	3	4	4	2	15	0.0	0.0	-50.0	650.0	39.2
Curaçao	17	11	..	..	..	0.0				
St.Maarten	12	2	..	..	..	0.0				
Chile	36	22	27	42	11	0.0	0.0	55.6	-73.8	-15.9
Uruguay	12	18	18	13	10	0.0	0.0	-27.8	-23.1	-13.7
Other intraregional	104	45	171	252	147	0.1	0.2	47.4	-41.7	34.4
From other regions	*20,432*	*17,966*	*18,152*	*29,079*	*28,203*	*35.0*	*44.7*	*60.2*	*-3.0*	*11.9*
Netherlands	14,465	13,322	12,814	19,995	19,612	26.0	31.1	56.0	-1.9	10.2
United Kingdom	321	732	1,141	2,305	2,436	1.4	3.9	102.0	5.7	35.1
Germany	2,477	1,841	1,602	2,236	2,052	3.6	3.2	39.6	-8.2	2.7
Switzerland	657	554	570	861	816	1.1	1.3	51.1	-5.2	10.2
Belgium	588	450	429	663	675	0.9	1.1	54.5	1.8	10.7
Sweden	111	96	122	460	572	0.2	0.9	277.0	24.3	56.2
Italy	383	267	287	475	413	0.5	0.7	65.5	-13.1	11.5
France	741	225	231	292	304	0.4	0.5	26.4	4.1	7.8
Austria	252	219	210	353	191	0.4	0.3	68.1	-45.9	-3.4
Norway	41	46	63	292	188	0.1	0.3	363.5	-35.6	42.2
Finland	5	6	122	157	153	0.0	0.2	28.7	-2.5	124.7
Spain	70	70	128	179	114	0.1	0.2	39.8	-36.3	13.0
Denmark	48	31	87	119	111	0.1	0.2	36.8	-6.7	37.6
Portugal	94	18	79	50	32	0.0	0.1	-36.7	-36.0	15.5
Japan	51	16	..	..	..	0.0				
Greece	10	3	18	24	17	0.0	0.0	33.3	-29.2	54.3
Luxembourg	15	19	14	22	7	0.0	0.0	57.1	-68.2	-22.1
Other Europe	103	51	235	596	510	0.1	0.8	153.6	-14.4	77.8
Other World/Not specified	*159*	*236*	*385*	*329*	*623*	*0.5*	*1.0*	*-14.5*	*89.4*	*27.5*

Source: World Tourism Organization (UNWTO) ©   (Data as collected by UNWTO for TMT 2006 Edition)

III.2.18.b Curaçao   Caribbean

Profile

Curaçao

Capital   Willemstad

Americas
Caribbean

	2003	2004	2005*	2004/2003	2005*/2004
International Arrivals					
Visitors (1000)	508	452	510	-11.0	12.8
Tourists (overnight visitors) (1000)	221	223	222	0.9	-0.6
Same-day visitors (1000)	7	10	12	42.9	20.0
Cruise passengers (1000)	279	219	276	-21.5	26.0
Tourism accommodation					
Number of rooms	3,474	3,557	3,647	2.4	2.5
Nights spent in collective establishments (1000)					
by non-residents (inbound tourism)	1,919	1,920	1,960	0.1	2.1
Nights spent in hotels and similar establishments (1000)					
by non-residents (inbound tourism)	754	782	842	3.7	7.7
Receipts and Expenditure for International Tourism					
International Tourism Receipts (US$ million)	223	222	239	-0.4	7.5
- per Tourist Arrival (US$)	1,008	995	1,076	-1.3	8.2
- per Visitor Arrival (US$)	439	492	469	12.0	-4.7
International Tourism Expenditure (US$ million)	176	192	167	8.8	-12.8
Δ International Tourism Balance (US$ million)	47	31	72		

Source: World Tourism Organization (UNWTO)   (Data as collected by UNWTO for TMT 2006 Edition)
See annex for methodological notes and reference of external sources used.

World Tourism Organization ©

International Tourism by Origin

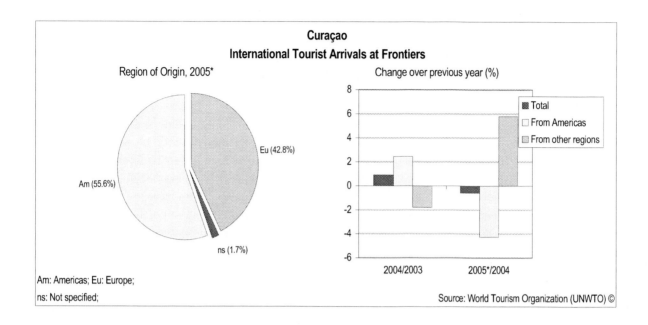

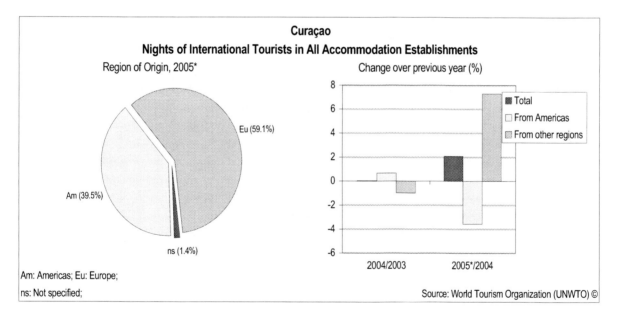

Curaçao
International Tourist Arrivals at Frontiers (by residence)

	1995	2000	2003	2004	2005*	Market share (%) 2000	Market share (%) 2005*	Growth rate (%) 04/03	Growth rate (%) 05*/04	Average per year (%) 2000-2005*
Total	**223,788**	**191,246**	**221,395**	**223,439**	**222,099**	**100**	**100**	**0.9**	**-0.6**	**3.0**
From Americas	*125,137*	*121,421*	*125,794*	*128,873*	*123,391*	*63.5*	*55.6*	*2.4*	*-4.3*	*0.3*
United States	33,198	29,338	40,019	43,105	45,568	15.3	20.5	7.7	5.7	9.2
Venezuela	30,908	35,098	25,099	27,639	24,259	18.4	10.9	10.1	-12.2	-7.1
Aruba	12,695	11,100	12,561	13,102	10,709	5.8	4.8	4.3	-18.3	-0.7
Jamaica	9,081	4,070	7,119	7,473	7,816	2.1	3.5	5.0	4.6	13.9
Canada	3,561	2,682	3,786	4,101	5,224	1.4	2.4	8.3	27.4	14.3
Trinidad Tbg	1,903	4,825	6,895	6,246	4,889	2.5	2.2	-9.4	-21.7	0.3
Dominican Rp	926	6,567	7,009	6,435	4,639	3.4	2.1	-8.2	-27.9	-6.7
Suriname	..	3,806	3,990	4,352	4,051	2.0	1.8	9.1	-6.9	1.3
Colombia	7,423	8,901	5,241	3,004	3,480	4.7	1.6	-42.7	15.8	-17.1
Ecuador	..	771	682	1,514	2,409	0.4	1.1	122.0	59.1	25.6
Haiti	7,687	5,686	4,836	2,924	1,832	3.0	0.8	-39.5	-37.3	-20.3
Brazil	6,977	797	749	1,029	1,460	0.4	0.7	37.4	41.9	12.9
Puerto Rico	985	1,833	1,127	1,188	963	1.0	0.4	5.4	-18.9	-12.1
Guyana	..	1,000	1,059	796	737	0.5	0.3	-24.8	-7.4	-5.9
Barbados	..	491	490	421	546	0.3	0.2	-14.1	29.7	2.1
Argentina	1,456	645	461	448	437	0.3	0.2	-2.8	-2.5	-7.5
Other Caribbean	8,337	1,757	2,245	2,360	1,990	0.9	0.9	5.1	-15.7	2.5
Other South America	..	2,054	2,426	2,736	2,382	1.1	1.1	12.8	-12.9	3.0
From other regions	*82,036*	*65,476*	*91,384*	*89,752*	*94,957*	*34.2*	*42.8*	*-1.8*	*5.8*	*7.7*
Netherlands	66,746	51,917	75,999	73,798	77,879	27.1	35.1	-2.9	5.5	8.4
Germany	7,830	3,541	2,975	3,471	4,073	1.9	1.8	16.7	17.3	2.8
United Kingdom	1,727	1,843	2,775	3,190	2,642	1.0	1.2	15.0	-17.2	7.5
Belgium	2,762	1,592	1,626	2,102	2,435	0.8	1.1	29.3	15.8	8.9
Sweden	..	500	675	871	1,361	0.3	0.6	29.0	56.3	22.2
Italy	1,209	943	1,025	772	654	0.5	0.3	-24.7	-15.3	-7.1
Switzerland	1,099	914	769	662	630	0.5	0.3	-13.9	-4.8	-7.2
Spain	..	486	938	649	608	0.3	0.3	-30.8	-6.3	4.6
Denmark	..	190	398	336	382	0.1	0.2	-15.6	13.7	15.0
Norway	..	373	314	318	336	0.2	0.2	1.3	5.7	-2.1
Portugal	..	423	454	301	262	0.2	0.1	-33.7	-13.0	-9.1
Austria	663	355	224	268	242	0.2	0.1	19.6	-9.7	-7.4
Other Europe	..	2,399	3,212	3,014	3,453	1.3	1.6	-6.2	14.6	7.6
Other World/Not specified	*16,615*	*4,349*	*4,217*	*4,814*	*3,751*	*2.3*	*1.7*	*14.2*	*-22.1*	*-2.9*

Source: World Tourism Organization (UNWTO) ©   (Data as collected by UNWTO for TMT 2006 Edition)

Curaçao

Nights of International Tourists in All Accommodation Establishments (by residence)

	1995	2000	2003	2004	2005*	Market share (%)		Growth rate (%)		Average per year (%)
						2000	2005*	04/03	05*/04	2000-2005*
Total	1,961,140	1,556,664	1,919,036	1,919,656	1,959,760	100	100	0.0	2.1	4.7
From Americas	*795,216*	*729,541*	*796,780*	*802,096*	*773,570*	*46.9*	*39.5*	*0.7*	*-3.6*	*1.2*
United States	203,873	184,774	255,666	285,117	299,094	11.9	15.3	11.5	4.9	10.1
Venezuela	146,687	154,645	121,315	135,342	110,470	9.9	5.6	11.6	-18.4	-6.5
Colombia	57,329	108,721	92,366	65,628	67,421	7.0	3.4	-28.9	2.7	-9.1
Dominican Rp	79,857	67,338	72,442	68,043	52,436	4.3	2.7	-6.1	-22.9	-4.9
Aruba	65,951	50,021	54,460	54,411	49,892	3.2	2.5	-0.1	-8.3	-0.1
Canada	26,659	20,598	29,782	33,589	42,545	1.3	2.2	12.8	26.7	15.6
Jamaica	32,877	17,125	32,452	30,671	33,857	1.1	1.7	-5.5	10.4	14.6
Suriname	44,348	..	..	..	29,897		1.5			
Trinidad Tbg	7,508	12,436	16,636	17,134	15,993	0.8	0.8	3.0	-6.7	5.2
Haiti	43,163	41,123	40,753	24,019	14,922	2.6	0.8	-41.1	-37.9	-18.4
Ecuador	6,166	..	..	..	10,199		0.5			
Brazil	26,286	3,709	4,095	5,106	7,669	0.2	0.4	24.7	50.2	15.6
Puerto Rico	5,503	6,507	5,000	5,029	4,275	0.4	0.2	0.6	-15.0	-8.1
Panama	3,751	..	..	..	..					
Costa Rica	3,198	..	..	..	..					
Peru	3,027	..	..	..	..					
St.Vincent,Grenadines	2,993	..	..	..	..					
Guyana	7,062	..	..	..	2,913		0.1			
Argentina	7,096	3,453	2,651	2,493	2,819	0.2	0.1	-6.0	13.1	-4.0
Barbados	691	..	..	..	1,993		0.1			
Chile	1,469	..	..	..	..					
Antigua,Barb	935	..	..	..	..					
Paraguay	626	..	..	..	..					
Bahamas	463	..	..	..	..					
Mexico	408	..	..	..	..					
Other intraregional	17,290	59,091	69,162	75,514	27,175	3.8	1.4	9.2	-64.0	-14.4
From other regions	*1,160,202*	*798,414*	*1,090,004*	*1,079,342*	*1,157,790*	*51.3*	*59.1*	*-1.0*	*7.3*	*7.7*
Netherlands	955,747	681,069	946,203	920,886	986,591	43.8	50.3	-2.7	7.1	7.7
Germany	91,250	37,467	33,169	41,634	50,179	2.4	2.6	25.5	20.5	6.0
United Kingdom	13,242	15,463	26,115	32,317	28,013	1.0	1.4	23.7	-13.3	12.6
Belgium	26,797	16,587	16,024	22,374	26,088	1.1	1.3	39.6	16.6	9.5
Sweden	930	..	..	..	12,257		0.6			
Finland	114	..	..	..	7,473		0.4			
Spain	1,027	..	..	..	6,082		0.3			
Switzerland	8,195	7,578	6,974	6,067	5,627	0.5	0.3	-13.0	-7.3	-5.8
Denmark	4,012	..	..	..	4,522		0.2			
Italy	7,523	7,244	7,548	5,919	4,460	0.5	0.2	-21.6	-24.6	-9.2
Norway	283	..	..	..	3,160		0.2			
Portugal	8,453	..	..	..	2,321		0.1			
Austria	5,299	2,926	1,832	3,067	2,313	0.2	0.1	67.4	-24.6	-4.6
France	1,948	..	..	..	..					
Japan	829	..	..	..	..					
Other Europe	33,738	30,080	52,139	47,078	18,704	1.9	1.0	-9.7	-60.3	-9.1
Other interregional	815	..	..	..	..					
Other World/Not specified	*5,722*	*28,709*	*32,252*	*38,218*	*28,400*	*1.8*	*1.4*	*18.5*	*-25.7*	*-0.2*

Source: World Tourism Organization (UNWTO) ©   (Data as collected by UNWTO for TMT 2006 Edition)

III.2.18.c Saba   Caribbean

Profile

Saba

Capital   The Bottom

Americas
Caribbean

	2003	2004	2005*	2004/2003	2005*/2004
International Arrivals					
Visitors (1000)	21	23	25	13.2	7.3
Tourists (overnight visitors) (1000)	10	11	11	7.3	4.1
Same-day visitors (1000)	10	12	13	19.6	9.8

Source: World Tourism Organization (UNWTO)   (Data as collected by UNWTO for TMT 2006 Edition)

See annex for methodological notes and reference of external sources used.

World Tourism Organization ©

International Tourism by Origin

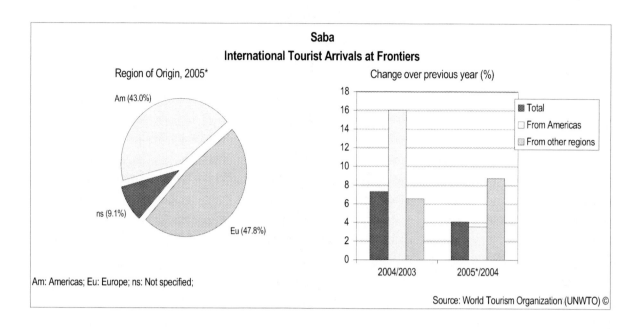

Saba
International Tourist Arrivals at Frontiers

Region of Origin, 2005*

Am (43.0%)
ns (9.1%)
Eu (47.8%)

Change over previous year (%)

■ Total
□ From Americas
▨ From other regions

Am: Americas; Eu: Europe; ns: Not specified;

Source: World Tourism Organization (UNWTO) ©

Saba
International Tourist Arrivals at Frontiers (by residence)

	1995	2000	2003	2004	2005*	Market share (%) 2000	Market share (%) 2005*	Growth rate 04/03	Growth rate (%) 05*/04	Average per year (%) 2000-2005*
Total	**9,983**	**9,120**	**10,260**	**11,012**	**11,462**	**100**	**100**	**7.3**	**4.1**	**4.7**
From Americas	*4,311*	*4,077*	*4,106*	*4,764*	*4,933*	*44.7*	*43.0*	*16.0*	*3.5*	*3.9*
United States	3,930	3,740	3,656	4,172	4,288	41.0	37.4	14.1	2.8	2.8
Canada	260	337	450	592	645	3.7	5.6	31.6	9.0	13.9
Dominican Rp	121	..	..	..	..					
From other regions	*4,540*	*3,768*	*4,732*	*5,043*	*5,484*	*41.3*	*47.8*	*6.6*	*8.7*	*7.8*
All Europe	..	..	..	..	5,484		47.8			
Netherlands	3,234	2,618	3,245	3,320	..	28.7		2.3		
France	785	434	551	753	..	4.8		36.7		
United Kingdom	521	414	591	555	..	4.5		-6.1		
Germany	..	302	278	..	..	3.3				
Italy	..	..	67	..	..					
Other Europe	..	..	..	415	..					
Other World/Not specified	*1,132*	*1,275*	*1,422*	*1,205*	*1,045*	*14.0*	*9.1*	*-15.3*	*-13.3*	*-3.9*

Source: World Tourism Organization (UNWTO) ©   (Data as collected by UNWTO for TMT 2006 Edition)

III.2.18.d Saint Eustatius   Caribbean

Profile

Saint Eustatius

Capital

Oranjestad

Americas
Caribbean

	2003	2004	2005*	2004/2003	2005*/2004
International Arrivals					
Tourists (overnight visitors) (1000)	10	11	10	5.8	-6.3

Source: World Tourism Organization (UNWTO)   (Data as collected by UNWTO for TMT 2006 Edition)
See annex for methodological notes and reference of external sources used.

International Tourism by Origin

Saint Eustatius
International Visitor Arrivals at Frontiers (by residence)

	1995	2000	2002	2003	2004	Market share (%) 2000	Market share (%) 2004	Growth rate (%) 03/02	Growth rate (%) 04/03	Average per year (%) 2000-2004
Total	**20,556**	**19,066**	..	..	..	**100**				
From Americas	*16,261*	*13,941*	..	..	..	*73.1*				
Neth. Antilles	11,727	10,136	..	..	..	53.2				
United States	2,596	2,101	..	..	..	11.0				
Canada	155	155	..	..	..	0.8				
Other Americas	1,783	1,549	..	..	..	8.1				
From other regions	*3,703*	*3,988*	..	..	..	*20.9*				
Netherlands	2,636	2,678	..	..	..	14.0				
Germany	102	225	..	..	..	1.2				
Other Europe	965	1,085	..	..	..	5.7				
Other World/Not specified	*592*	*1,137*	..	..	..	*6.0*				

Source: World Tourism Organization (UNWTO) ©   (Data as collected by UNWTO for TMT 2006 Edition)

III.2.18.e Saint Maarten   Caribbean

Profile

Saint Maarten

Capital   Marigot; Philipsburg

Americas
Caribbean

	2003	2004	2005*	2004/2003	2005*/2004
International Arrivals					
Visitors (1000)	1,600	1,823	1,950	13.9	7.0
Tourists (overnight visitors) (1000)	428	475	462	11.1	-2.6
Cruise passengers (1000)	1,172	1,348	1,488	15.0	10.4
Receipts and Expenditure for International Tourism					
International Tourism Receipts (US$ million)	538	613	619	13.9	1.1
- per Tourist Arrival (US$)	1,258	1,290	1,339	2.5	3.8
- per Visitor Arrival (US$)	336	336	318	0.0	-5.5
International Tourism Expenditure (US$ million)	144	88	104	-39.0	18.3
Δ International Tourism Balance (US$ million)	394	525	515		

Source: World Tourism Organization (UNWTO)   (Data as collected by UNWTO for TMT 2006 Edition)
See annex for methodological notes and reference of external sources used.

International Tourism by Origin

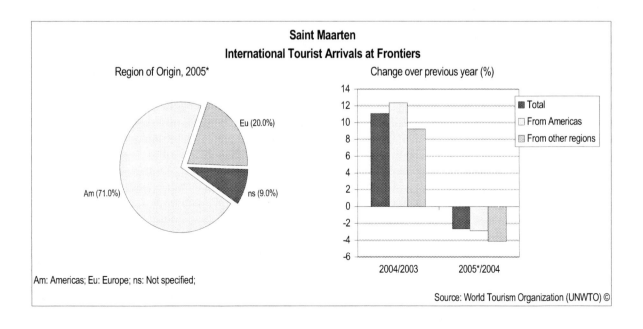

Saint Maarten
International Tourist Arrivals at Frontiers

Region of Origin, 2005*

Eu (20.0%)
Am (71.0%)
ns (9.0%)

Am: Americas; Eu: Europe; ns: Not specified;

Change over previous year (%)

Total
From Americas
From other regions

2004/2003   2005*/2004

Source: World Tourism Organization (UNWTO) ©

Saint Maarten
International Tourist Arrivals at Frontiers (by nationality)

	1995	2000	2003	2004	2005*	Market share (%) 2000	Market share (%) 2005*	Growth rate (%) 04/03	Growth rate (%) 05*/04	Average per year (%) 2000-2005*
Total	**448,614**	**432,292**	**427,587**	**475,032**	**462,492**	**100**	**100**	**11.1**	**-2.6**	**1.4**
From Americas	*305,424*	*271,753*	*301,018*	*338,241*	*328,532*	*62.9*	*71.0*	*12.4*	*-2.9*	*3.9*
United States	197,513	187,786	222,247	251,155	242,159	43.4	52.4	13.0	-3.6	5.2
All the Caribbean	..	..	..	44,907	40,858		8.8		-9.0	
Canada	28,951	28,470	29,545	31,667	35,594	6.6	7.7	7.2	12.4	4.6
St.Kitts-Nev	11,049	7,839	8,997	..	..	1.8				
Antigua,Barb	24,012	3,065	6,382	..	..	0.7				
Dominican Rp	3,673	4,366	4,597	..	..	1.0				
Haiti	2,670	3,765	4,536	..	..	0.9				
Trinidad Tbg	5,323	1,956	2,452	..	..	0.5				
Venezuela	3,732	6,891	2,485	2,756	2,198	1.6	0.5	10.9	-20.2	-20.4
Brazil	1,427	1,082	725	..	..	0.3				
Argentina	1,682	10,413	627	..	..	2.4				
Chile	..	349	163	..	..	0.1				
Other Caribbean	7,767	10,269	12,949	..	..	2.4				
Other South America	17,625	5,502	5,313	..	..	1.3				
Other Americas	..	..	..	7,756	7,723		1.7		-0.4	
From other regions	*107,833*	*121,819*	*88,259*	*96,404*	*92,413*	*28.2*	*20.0*	*9.2*	*-4.1*	*-5.4*
France	96,425	89,803	58,801	..	..	20.8				
Netherlands	11,408	6,828	12,918	15,554	14,755	1.6	3.2	20.4	-5.1	16.7
Italy	..	6,828	4,842	..	..	1.6				
Russian Federation	..	247	191	..	..	0.1				
Other Europe	..	18,113	11,507	80,850	77,658	4.2	16.8	602.6	-3.9	33.8
Nationals residing abroad	*15,157*	*15,235*	*14,742*	*..*	*..*	*3.5*				
Other World/Not specified	*20,200*	*23,485*	*23,568*	*40,387*	*41,547*	*5.4*	*9.0*	*71.4*	*2.9*	*12.1*

Source: World Tourism Organization (UNWTO) ©　　　　　　　　　　　(Data as collected by UNWTO for TMT 2006 Edition)

III.2.19 Puerto Rico   Caribbean

Promotional: www.gotopuertorico.com
Institutional/corporate: www.gotopuertorico.com

Profile

Puerto Rico

Capital	San Juan
Year of entry in UNWTO	2002
Area (100 km²)	90
Population (2005, million)	3.9

Americas
Caribbean

	2003	2004	2005*	2004/2003	2005*/2004
International Arrivals					
Visitors (1000)	4,402	4,889	5,073	11.1	3.8
Tourists (overnight visitors) (1000)	3,238	3,541	3,686	9.3	4.1
- per 100 of inhabitants	84	91	94		
Cruise passengers (1000)	1,164	1,348	1,387	15.8	2.9
Tourism accommodation					
Number of rooms	12,788	12,864	13,459	0.6	4.6
Nights spent in hotels and similar establishments (1000)					
by non-residents (inbound tourism)	2,718	2,835	2,928	4.3	3.3
Outbound Tourism					
Trips abroad (1000)	1,272	1,361	1,410	7.0	3.6
- per 100 of inhabitants	33	35	36		
Receipts and Expenditure for International Tourism					
International Tourism Receipts (US$ million)	2,677	3,024	3,239	13.0	7.1
- per Tourist Arrival (US$)	827	854	879	3.3	2.9
- per Visitor Arrival (US$)	608	619	638	1.7	3.2
- per capita (US$)	690	776	828		
International Tourism Expenditure (US$ million)	985	1,085	1,142	10.1	5.3
- per trip (US$)	775	797	810	2.9	1.6
- per capita (US$)	254	279	292		
International Fare Expenditure (US$ million)	435	499	520	14.7	4.2
Δ International Tourism Balance (US$ million)	1,691	1,939	2,096		

Source: World Tourism Organization (UNWTO)   (Data as collected by UNWTO for TMT 2006 Edition)
See annex for methodological notes and reference of external sources used.

International Tourism by Origin

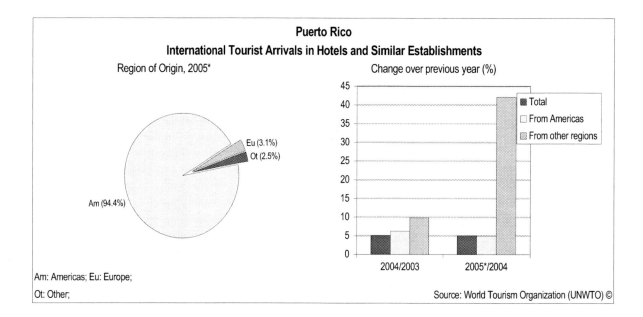

Puerto Rico
International Tourist Arrivals in Hotels and Similar Establishments

Region of Origin, 2005*

Eu (3.1%)
Ot (2.5%)
Am (94.4%)

Change over previous year (%)

- Total
- From Americas
- From other regions

Am: Americas; Eu: Europe;
Ot: Other;

Puerto Rico

International Tourist Arrivals in Hotels and Similar Establishments (by residence)

	1995	2000	2003	2004	2005*	Market share (%)		Growth rate (%)		Average per year (%)
						2000	2005*	04/03	05*/04	2000-2005*
Total	851,382	1,102,912	1,304,610	1,371,003	1,440,008	100	100	5.1	5.0	5.5
From Americas	*730,095*	*989,137*	*1,219,366*	*1,295,431*	*1,359,514*	*89.7*	*94.4*	*6.2*	*4.9*	*6.6*
United States	661,109	900,016	1,131,949	1,198,716	1,251,066	81.6	86.9	5.9	4.4	6.8
Canada	8,451	10,413	12,238	18,783	21,220	0.9	1.5	53.5	13.0	15.3
Mexico	7,840	11,352	12,113	9,940	12,529	1.0	0.9	-17.9	26.0	2.0
Dominican Rp	6,265	5,698	7,631	7,759	9,833	0.5	0.7	1.7	26.7	11.5
US.Virgin Is	15,615	18,187	5,580	6,274	6,765	1.6	0.5	12.4	7.8	-17.9
Venezuela	4,465	3,024	4,568	3,616	4,451	0.3	0.3	-20.8	23.1	8.0
Colombia	2,007	2,280	3,230	3,131	3,377	0.2	0.2	-3.1	7.9	8.2
Argentina	2,351	2,766	2,444	1,736	2,032	0.3	0.1	-29.0	17.1	-6.0
Brazil	1,726	1,120	1,662	1,635	1,873	0.1	0.1	-1.6	14.6	10.8
Costa Rica	697	4,653	1,326	1,297	1,259	0.4	0.1	-2.2	-2.9	-23.0
Panama	609	752	755	784	1,008	0.1	0.1	3.8	28.6	6.0
Chile	454	551	1,525	1,367	912	0.0	0.1	-10.4	-33.3	10.6
Peru	377	599	594	716	884	0.1	0.1	20.5	23.5	8.1
Guatemala	363	213	361	351	401	0.0	0.0	-2.8	14.2	13.5
Ecuador	136	172	341	221	398	0.0	0.0	-35.2	80.1	18.3
El Salvador	143	90	183	176	243	0.0	0.0	-3.8	38.1	22.0
Cuba	29	27	231	239	231	0.0	0.0	3.5	-3.3	53.6
Nicaragua	61	87	113	130	145	0.0	0.0	15.0	11.5	10.8
Uruguay	152	267	243	65	125	0.0	0.0	-73.3	92.3	-14.1
Other intraregional	17,245	26,870	32,279	38,495	40,762	2.4	2.8	19.3	5.9	8.7
From other regions	*29,367*	*29,130*	*31,946*	*35,089*	*49,874*	*2.6*	*3.5*	*9.8*	*42.1*	*11.4*
Spain	5,026	5,412	7,696	7,825	11,001	0.5	0.8	1.7	40.6	15.2
United Kingdom	4,316	4,673	5,703	5,732	5,224	0.4	0.4	0.5	-8.9	2.3
Germany	5,939	4,256	2,858	3,038	4,395	0.4	0.3	6.3	44.7	0.6
Italy	3,113	1,387	1,827	2,358	2,709	0.1	0.2	29.1	14.9	14.3
France	1,832	1,498	1,775	2,009	2,705	0.1	0.2	13.2	34.6	12.5
Australia	..	877	1,493	2,078	2,025	0.1	0.1	39.2	-2.6	18.2
Switzerland	1,195	945	717	1,001	1,170	0.1	0.1	39.6	16.9	4.4
Japan	936	709	697	743	967	0.1	0.1	6.6	30.1	6.4
Netherlands	432	1,541	916	934	774	0.1	0.1	2.0	-17.1	-12.9
Sweden	339	434	640	739	685	0.0	0.0	15.5	-7.3	9.6
Ireland	120	209	171	332	540	0.0	0.0	94.2	62.7	20.9
Finland	94	104	291	238	501	0.0	0.0	-18.2	110.5	36.9
Denmark	140	255	211	416	494	0.0	0.0	97.2	18.8	14.1
Belgium	518	421	486	451	450	0.0	0.0	-7.2	-0.2	1.3
Austria	252	241	546	259	321	0.0	0.0	-52.6	23.9	5.9
All Africa	..	158	669	452	321	0.0	0.0	-32.4	-29.0	15.2
Norway	205	306	225	305	315	0.0	0.0	35.6	3.3	0.6
Portugal	131	191	268	375	302	0.0	0.0	39.9	-19.5	9.6
Philippines	36	176	232	366	289	0.0	0.0	57.8	-21.0	10.4
Israel	..	232	242	285	234	0.0	0.0	17.8	-17.9	0.2
Former U.S.S.R.	10	112	168	191	166	0.0	0.0	13.7	-13.1	8.2
Other interregional	4,733	4,993	4,115	4,962	14,286	0.5	1.0	20.6	187.9	23.4
Nationals residing abroad	*..*	*35,660*	*20,418*	*9,163*	*11,832*	*3.2*	*0.8*	*-55.1*	*29.1*	*-19.8*
Other World/Not specified	*91,920*	*48,985*	*32,880*	*31,320*	*18,788*	*4.4*	*1.3*	*-4.7*	*-40.0*	*-17.4*

Source: World Tourism Organization (UNWTO) ©   (Data as collected by UNWTO for TMT 2006 Edition)

 World Tourism Organization ©

III.2.20 Saint Kitts and Nevis   Caribbean

Promotional: www.stkittsnevis.net ; www.stkitts-nevis.com

Profile

Saint Kitts and Nevis

Americas
Caribbean

Capital	Basseterre
Area (10 km²)	36
Population (2005, 1000)	39
Gross Domestic Product (GDP) (2005, US$ million)	453
GDP per capita (2005, US$)	10,895

GDP growth (real, %)
'-> 2004: 7.1; 2005: 6.7; 2006*: 5.2; 2007*: 4.1

	2003	2004	2005*	2004/2003	2005*/2004
International Arrivals					
Visitors (1000)	244	377	344	54.5	-8.8
Tourists (overnight visitors) (1000)	91	118	127	29.7	8.1
- per 100 of inhabitants	234	303	326		
Same-day visitors (1000)	3	4	3	33.3	-25.0
Cruise passengers (1000)	150	255	214	70.0	-16.1
Tourism accommodation					
Number of rooms	1,611	1,825	..	13.3	
Receipts and Expenditure for International Tourism					
International Tourism Receipts (US$ million)	75	103	107	37.3	4.1
- per Tourist Arrival (US$)	828	876	845	5.9	-3.6
- per Visitor Arrival (US$)	307	273	312	-11.1	14.1
- per capita (US$)	1,935	2,652	2,753		
International Tourism Expenditure (US$ million)	8	10	11	25.0	10.0
- per capita (US$)	206	257	282		
Δ International Tourism Balance (US$ million)	67	93	96		

Source: World Tourism Organization (UNWTO)   (Data as collected by UNWTO for TMT 2006 Edition)

See annex for methodological notes and reference of external sources used.

International Tourism by Origin

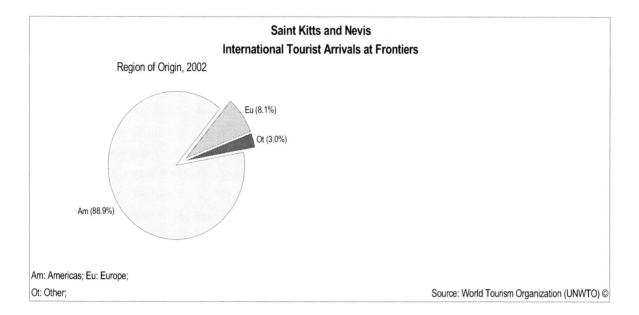

Saint Kitts and Nevis
International Tourist Arrivals at Frontiers

Region of Origin, 2002

Eu (8.1%)

Ot (3.0%)

Am (88.9%)

Am: Americas; Eu: Europe;
Ot: Other;

Source: World Tourism Organization (UNWTO) ©

Saint Kitts and Nevis
International Tourist Arrivals at Frontiers (by residence)

	1995	2000	2002	2003	2004	Market share (%) 2000	Market share (%) 2004	Growth rate (%) 03/02	Growth rate (%) 04/03	Average per year (%) 2000-2004
Total	**78,868**	**73,149**	**67,531**	..	..	**100**				
From Americas	*68,613*	*45,407*	*60,023*	..	..	*62.1*				
All the Caribbean	..	28,513	28,146	..	..	39.0				
United States	36,454	..	27,525	..	..					
US.Virgin Is	6,212	..	..	..	..					
Canada	9,081	..	4,352	..	..					
St.Maarten	2,854	..	..	..	..					
Antigua,Barb	2,769	..	..	..	..					
Anguilla	1,530	..	..	..	..					
Barbados	1,436	..	..	..	..					
Br.Virgin Is	1,357	..	..	..	..					
Puerto Rico	1,118	..	..	..	..					
Montserrat	1,039	..	..	..	..					
Trinidad Tbg	866	..	..	..	..					
Jamaica	613	..	..	..	..					
Guyana	590	..	..	..	..					
St.Vincent,Grenadines	523	..	..	..	..					
Dominica	496	..	..	..	..					
Bermuda	438	..	..	..	..					
Saint Lucia	245	..	..	..	..					
Grenada	134	..	..	..	..					
Guadeloupe	116	..	..	..	..					
Other intraregional	742	16,894	..	..	..	23.1				
From other regions	*9,854*	*15,155*	*5,464*	..	..	*20.7*				
All Europe	..	15,155	..	..	..	20.7				
United Kingdom	6,729	..	5,464	..	..					
Germany	1,601	..	..	..	..					
France	606	..	..	..	..					
Italy	219	..	..	..	..					
Switzerland	153	..	..	..	..					
Netherlands	133	..	..	..	..					
Austria	84	..	..	..	..					
Norway	58	..	..	..	..					
Belgium	49	..	..	..	..					
Spain	47	..	..	..	..					
Sweden	35	..	..	..	..					
Denmark	26	..	..	..	..					
Japan	21	..	..	..	..					
Ireland	15	..	..	..	..					
Other interregional	78	..	..	..	..					
Other World/Not specified	*401*	*12,587*	*2,044*	..	..	*17.2*				

Source: World Tourism Organization (UNWTO) ©   (Data as collected by UNWTO for TMT 2006 Edition)

III.2.21 Saint Lucia   Caribbean

Promotional: www.stlucia.org ; www.stluciajazz.org ; www.inntimatestlucia.org
Institutional/corporate: www.stlucia.org
Research and data: www.stlucia.org

Profile

Saint Lucia

Americas
Caribbean

Capital	Castries
Area (10 km²)	62
Population (2005, 1000)	166
Gross Domestic Product (GDP) (2005, US$ million)	818
GDP per capita (2005, US$)	4,963
GDP growth (real, %)	
'-> 2004: 4.0; 2005: 5.4; 2006*: 6.0; 2007*: 4.0	

	2003	2004	2005*	2004/2003	2005*/2004
International Arrivals					
Visitors (1000)	683	791	720	15.8	-9.0
Tourists (overnight visitors) (1000)	277	298	318	7.8	6.5
- per 100 of inhabitants	171	182	191		
Same-day visitors (1000)	13	11	8	-15.4	-27.3
Cruise passengers (1000)	393	481	394	22.4	-18.1
Tourism accommodation					
Number of rooms	3,749	3,974	4,511	6.0	13.5
Receipts and Expenditure for International Tourism					
International Tourism Receipts (US$ million)	282	326	345	15.6	5.8
- per Tourist Arrival (US$)	1,018	1,092	1,085	7.3	-0.7
- per Visitor Arrival (US$)	413	412	479	-0.2	16.3
- per capita (US$)	1,739	1,985	2,074		
International Tourism Expenditure (US$ million)	36	37	40	2.8	8.1
- per capita (US$)	222	225	241		
Δ International Tourism Balance (US$ million)	246	289	305		

Source: World Tourism Organization (UNWTO)   (Data as collected by UNWTO for TMT 2006 Edition)
See annex for methodological notes and reference of external sources used.

International Tourism by Origin

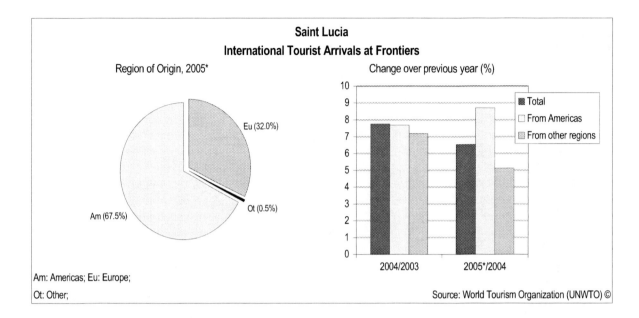

Saint Lucia
International Tourist Arrivals at Frontiers

Region of Origin, 2005*

Eu (32.0%)
Ot (0.5%)
Am (67.5%)

Change over previous year (%)

■ Total
☐ From Americas
▨ From other regions

2004/2003   2005*/2004

Am: Americas; Eu: Europe;
Ot: Other;

Source: World Tourism Organization (UNWTO) ©

World Tourism Organization ©

Saint Lucia
International Tourist Arrivals at Frontiers (by residence)

	1995	2000	2003	2004	2005*	Market share (%) 2000	2005*	Growth rate (%) 04/03	05*/04	Average per year (%) 2000-2005*
Total	**231,259**	**269,850**	**276,948**	**298,431**	**317,939**	**100**	**100**	**7.8**	**6.5**	**3.3**
From Americas	*142,958*	*168,150*	*183,349*	*197,433*	*214,621*	*62.3*	*67.5*	*7.7*	*8.7*	*5.0*
United States	84,377	97,532	98,078	107,089	112,557	36.1	35.4	9.2	5.1	2.9
Barbados	9,394	9,995	14,329	15,186	18,746	3.7	5.9	6.0	23.4	13.4
Canada	11,243	14,968	13,494	15,315	16,506	5.5	5.2	13.5	7.8	2.0
Trinidad Tbg	5,794	8,550	10,639	10,747	13,782	3.2	4.3	1.0	28.2	10.0
Dominica	2,144	2,811	3,700	3,866	4,692	1.0	1.5	4.5	21.4	10.8
St.Vincent,Grenadines	2,932	2,444	3,986	4,072	4,451	0.9	1.4	2.2	9.3	12.7
Grenada	1,262	1,882	3,770	3,494	3,823	0.7	1.2	-7.3	9.4	15.2
Antigua,Barb	1,295	1,194	2,855	3,181	3,188	0.4	1.0	11.4	0.2	21.7
Guyana	..	2,324	2,725	2,857	3,062	0.9	1.0	4.8	7.2	5.7
Jamaica	1,244	2,729	3,495	3,692	2,854	1.0	0.9	5.6	-22.7	0.9
St.Kitts-Nev	519	471	891	933	989	0.2	0.3	4.7	6.0	16.0
US.Virgin Is	1,388	801	1,009	810	797	0.3	0.3	-19.7	-1.6	-0.1
Neth. Antilles	544	659	504	606	566	0.2	0.2	20.2	-6.6	-3.0
Puerto Rico	1,099	579	556	595	416	0.2	0.1	7.0	-30.1	-6.4
Haiti	52	95	201	162	154	0.0	0.0	-19.4	-4.9	10.1
Dominican Rp	85	50	135	122	68	0.0	0.0	-9.6	-44.3	6.3
Other Caribbean	18,321	20,011	21,748	23,919	27,141	7.4	8.5	10.0	13.5	6.3
Other Americas	1,265	1,055	1,234	787	829	0.4	0.3	-36.2	5.3	-4.7
From other regions	*85,802*	*99,372*	*90,566*	*97,075*	*102,050*	*36.8*	*32.1*	*7.2*	*5.1*	*0.5*
United Kingdom	54,557	73,433	75,426	81,370	84,725	27.2	26.6	7.9	4.1	2.9
France	5,448	10,992	6,017	7,682	7,241	4.1	2.3	27.7	-5.7	-8.0
Germany	13,041	7,292	3,582	3,289	3,318	2.7	1.0	-8.2	0.9	-14.6
Italy	2,173	818	697	680	909	0.3	0.3	-2.4	33.7	2.1
Switzerland	3,362	863	566	..	511	0.3	0.2			-10.0
Sweden	1,185	..	394	671	475		0.1	70.3	-29.2	
Spain	204	..	187	310	321		0.1	65.8	3.5	
Austria	3,116	1,121	431	293	315	0.4	0.1	-32.0	7.5	-22.4
Japan	..	503	373	282	260	0.2	0.1	-24.4	-7.8	-12.4
Netherlands	598	412	346	283	256	0.2	0.1	-18.2	-9.5	-9.1
Belgium	..	..	194	156	161		0.1	-19.6	3.2	
Other Europe	2,118	3,938	2,353	2,059	3,558	1.5	1.1	-12.5	72.8	-2.0
Other World/Not specified	*2,499*	*2,328*	*3,033*	*3,923*	*1,268*	*0.9*	*0.4*	*29.3*	*-67.7*	*-11.4*

Source: World Tourism Organization (UNWTO) ©   (Data as collected by UNWTO for TMT 2006 Edition)

III.2.22 Saint Vincent and the Grenadines   Caribbean

Promotional: www.svgtourism.com

Profile

Saint Vincent and the Grenadines

Americas
Caribbean

Capital	Kingstown
Area (10 km²)	39
Population (2005, 1000)	118
Gross Domestic Product (GDP) (2005, US$ million)	421
GDP per capita (2005, US$)	3,950
GDP growth (real, %)	

'-> 2004: 6.8;   2005: 2.2;   2006*: 3.4;   2007*: 3.7

	2003	2004	2005*	2004/2003	2005*/2004
International Arrivals					
Visitors (1000)	242	262	258	8.3	-1.5
Tourists (overnight visitors) (1000)	79	87	96	10.4	10.1
- per 100 of inhabitants	67	74	81		
Same-day visitors (1000)	14	13	9	-7.1	-30.8
Cruise passengers (1000)	149	162	154	8.7	-4.9
Tourism accommodation					
Number of rooms	1,680	1,785	1,692	6.3	-5.2
Receipts and Expenditure for International Tourism					
International Tourism Receipts (US$ million)	91	96	105	5.5	9.4
- per Tourist Arrival (US$)	1,159	1,107	1,099	-4.5	-0.7
- per Visitor Arrival (US$)	376	366	407	-2.6	11.1
- per capita (US$)	779	819	893		
International Tourism Expenditure (US$ million)	13	14	14	7.7	
- per capita (US$)	111	119	119		
Δ International Tourism Balance (US$ million)	78	82	91		

Source: World Tourism Organization (UNWTO)   (Data as collected by UNWTO for TMT 2006 Edition)
See annex for methodological notes and reference of external sources used.

World Tourism Organization ©

International Tourism by Origin

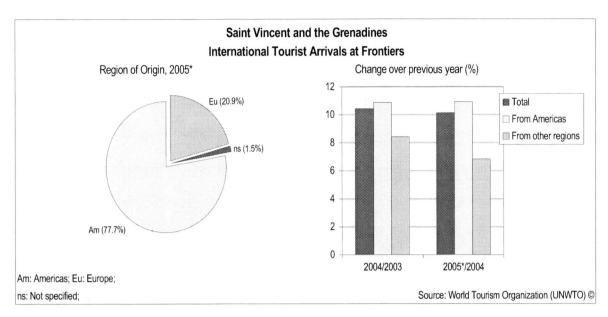

Saint Vincent and the Grenadines
International Tourist Arrivals at Frontiers

Region of Origin, 2005*

Eu (20.9%)
ns (1.5%)
Am (77.7%)

Change over previous year (%)

■ Total
□ From Americas
▨ From other regions

2004/2003   2005*/2004

Am: Americas; Eu: Europe;
ns: Not specified;

Source: World Tourism Organization (UNWTO) ©

Saint Vincent and the Grenadines
International Tourist Arrivals at Frontiers (by residence)

	1995	2000	2003	2004	2005*	Market share (%) 2000	Market share (%) 2005*	Growth rate (%) 04/03	Growth rate (%) 05*/04	Average per year (%) 2000-2005*
Total	**60,206**	**72,895**	**78,535**	**86,722**	**95,506**	**100**	**100**	**10.4**	**10.1**	**5.6**
From Americas	*41,836*	..	*60,315*	*66,871*	*74,173*		*77.7*	*10.9*	*10.9*	
United States	15,762	..	22,194	25,106	27,153		28.4	13.1	8.2	
Barbados	6,560	..	9,906	11,205	12,824		13.4	13.1	14.4	
Trinidad Tbg	4,568	..	9,654	10,194	11,683		12.2	5.6	14.6	
Canada	4,702	..	4,918	5,219	6,187		6.5	6.1	18.5	
Saint Lucia	2,849	..	2,862	3,470	3,450		3.6	21.2	-0.6	
Grenada	1,285	..	2,667	3,175	3,268		3.4	19.0	2.9	
Antigua,Barb	651	..	1,109	1,200	1,357		1.4	8.2	13.1	
Neth. Antilles	324	..	518	538	563		0.6	3.9	4.6	
Other Caribbean	4,815	..	6,060	6,231	6,799		7.1	2.8	9.1	
Other Americas	320	..	427	533	889		0.9	24.8	66.8	
From other regions	*17,551*	..	*17,201*	*18,652*	*19,928*		*20.9*	*8.4*	*6.8*	
United Kingdom	8,518	..	11,547	12,610	13,941		14.6	9.2	10.6	
Italy	1,152	..	1,030	1,249	1,435		1.5	21.3	14.9	
France	3,019	..	1,750	1,765	1,379		1.4	0.9	-21.9	
Germany	2,624	..	815	837	811		0.8	2.7	-3.1	
Switzerland	496	..	468	420	471		0.5	-10.3	12.1	
Sweden	477	..	334	309	393		0.4	-7.5	27.2	
Ireland	..	..	194	132	199		0.2	-32.0	50.8	
Spain	100	..	162	249	188		0.2	53.7	-24.5	
Belgium	..	..	151	181	168		0.2	19.9	-7.2	
Netherlands	95	..	127	180	123		0.1	41.7	-31.7	
Norway	..	..	96	95	95		0.1	-1.0	0.0	
Other Europe	1,070	..	527	625	725		0.8	18.6	16.0	
Other World/Not specified	*819*	*72,895*	*1,019*	*1,199*	*1,405*	*100.0*	*1.5*	*17.7*	*17.2*	*-54.6*

Source: World Tourism Organization (UNWTO) ©   (Data as collected by UNWTO for TMT 2006 Edition)

III.2.23   Trinidad and Tobago   Caribbean

Promotional: www.visittnt.com ; www.filmtnt.com
Institutional/corporate: www.tidco.co.tt
Research and data: www.tidco.co.tt ; www.visittnt.com ; www.investtnt.com

Profile

Trinidad and Tobago

Americas
Caribbean

Capital	Port of Spain
Area (100 km²)	51
Population (2005, million)	1.1
Gross Domestic Product (GDP) (2005, US$ million)	16,252
GDP per capita (2005, US$)	12,625
GDP growth (real, %)	

'-> 2004: 9.1;   2005: 7.9;   2006*: 12.5;   2007*: 6.9

	2003	2004	2005*	2004/2003	2005*/2004
International Arrivals					
Visitors (1000)	465	497	530	6.9	6.6
Tourists (overnight visitors) (1000)	409	443	463	8.2	4.7
- per 100 of inhabitants	37	41	43		
Cruise passengers (1000)	56	54	67	-3.6	24.1
Tourism accommodation					
Number of rooms	5,378	6,007	5,929	11.7	-1.3
Receipts and Expenditure for International Tourism					
International Tourism Receipts (US$ million)	249	341	453	36.9	32.8
- per Tourist Arrival (US$)	609	770	978	26.6	26.9
- per Visitor Arrival (US$)	535	686	855	28.1	24.6
- per capita (US$)	228	315	421		
International Fare Receipts (US$ million)	188	227	208	20.7	-8.4
International Tourism Expenditure (US$ million)	107	96	222	-10.3	131.3
- per capita (US$)	98	89	206		
International Fare Expenditure (US$ million)	36	45	66	25.0	46.7
Δ International Tourism Balance (US$ million)	142	245	231		
Δ International Fare Balance (US$ million)	152	182	142		

Source: World Tourism Organization (UNWTO)   (Data as collected by UNWTO for TMT 2006 Edition)
See annex for methodological notes and reference of external sources used.

International Tourism by Origin

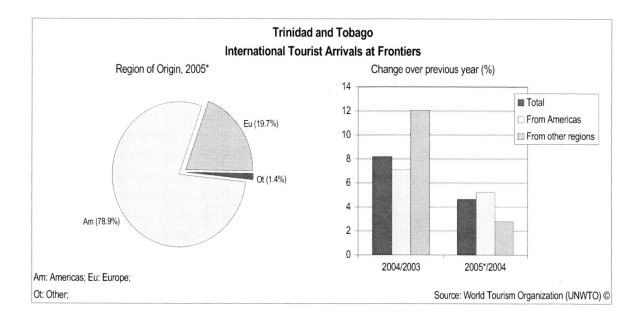

Trinidad and Tobago
International Tourist Arrivals at Frontiers

Region of Origin, 2005*

Change over previous year (%)

Eu (19.7%)

Ot (1.4%)

Am (78.9%)

Total
From Americas
From other regions

Am: Americas; Eu: Europe;
Ot: Other;

Source: World Tourism Organization (UNWTO) ©

Trinidad and Tobago
International Tourist Arrivals at Frontiers (by residence)

	1995	2000	2003	2004	2005*	Market share (%) 2000	Market share (%) 2005*	Growth rate (%) 04/03	Growth rate (%) 05*/04	Average per year (%) 2000-2005*
Total	**259,784**	**398,559**	**409,069**	**442,596**	**463,191**	**100**	**100**	**8.2**	**4.7**	**3.1**
From Americas	*203,802*	*309,122*	*324,175*	*347,181*	*365,311*	*77.6*	*78.9*	*7.1*	*5.2*	*3.4*
United States	92,185	132,578	138,935	159,467	167,985	33.3	36.3	14.8	5.3	4.8
Canada	33,669	47,382	43,036	43,565	47,702	11.9	10.3	1.2	9.5	0.1
Barbados	17,091	31,126	37,320	35,456	35,319	7.8	7.6	-5.0	-0.4	2.6
Guyana	15,339	23,686	22,783	22,328	22,208	5.9	4.8	-2.0	-0.5	-1.3
Grenada	10,379	15,492	19,220	19,575	19,501	3.9	4.2	1.8	-0.4	4.7
St.Vincent,Grenadines	6,025	8,265	11,041	11,747	12,658	2.1	2.7	6.4	7.8	8.9
Venezuela	6,293	11,450	10,273	10,528	10,191	2.9	2.2	2.5	-3.2	-2.3
Saint Lucia	4,457	7,374	7,423	8,192	8,823	1.9	1.9	10.4	7.7	3.7
Jamaica	4,133	6,255	6,186	6,210	7,848	1.6	1.7	0.4	26.4	4.6
Antigua,Barb	2,513	3,249	4,334	4,351	4,692	0.8	1.0	0.4	7.8	7.6
Suriname	833	2,212	2,354	3,547	2,926	0.6	0.6	50.7	-17.5	5.8
US.Virgin Is	1,330	2,610	1,790	1,743	1,840	0.7	0.4	-2.6	5.6	-6.8
St.Kitts-Nev	558	1,199	1,438	1,493	1,779	0.3	0.4	3.8	19.2	8.2
Dominica	921	1,096	1,535	1,564	1,777	0.3	0.4	1.9	13.6	10.1
Colombia	414	777	1,353	1,589	1,717	0.2	0.4	17.4	8.1	17.2
Puerto Rico	1,078	1,797	1,616	1,582	1,576	0.5	0.3	-2.1	-0.4	-2.6
Bahamas	640	927	1,343	1,226	1,560	0.2	0.3	-8.7	27.2	11.0
Br.Virgin Is	490	561	960	1,133	1,342	0.1	0.3	18.0	18.4	19.1
Mexico	340	629	703	967	1,297	0.2	0.3	37.6	34.1	15.6
Brazil	390	749	836	986	1,251	0.2	0.3	17.9	26.9	10.8
Martinique	707	1,452	1,076	900	1,016	0.4	0.2	-16.4	12.9	-6.9
Curaçao	..	..	1,060	885	989		0.2	-16.5	11.8	
Dominican Rp	134	376	574	876	858	0.1	0.2	52.6	-2.1	17.9
Costa Rica	140	330	516	683	836	0.1	0.2	32.4	22.4	20.4
Bermuda	311	620	575	580	813	0.2	0.2	0.9	40.2	5.6
Other intraregional	3,432	6,930	5,895	6,008	6,807	1.7	1.5	1.9	13.3	-0.4
From other regions	*55,733*	*88,639*	*84,859*	*95,086*	*97,739*	*22.2*	*21.1*	*12.1*	*2.8*	*2.0*
United Kingdom	26,332	55,048	57,566	66,090	63,523	13.8	13.7	14.8	-3.9	2.9
Germany	11,660	11,266	7,491	8,178	8,666	2.8	1.9	9.2	6.0	-5.1
Netherlands	1,521	2,618	2,817	3,232	3,966	0.7	0.9	14.7	22.7	8.7
Austria	948	1,009	850	1,318	3,121	0.3	0.7	55.1	136.8	25.3
France	1,652	2,132	2,203	1,942	1,960	0.5	0.4	-11.8	0.9	-1.7
Sweden	2,144	2,107	1,167	1,471	1,720	0.5	0.4	26.0	16.9	-4.0
India	754	818	931	1,188	1,465	0.2	0.3	27.6	23.3	12.4
Switzerland	1,928	1,546	1,180	1,061	1,258	0.4	0.3	-10.1	18.6	-4.0
Ireland	704	1,049	1,103	928	1,233	0.3	0.3	-15.9	32.9	3.3
Norway	909	1,464	1,019	1,100	1,210	0.4	0.3	7.9	10.0	-3.7
Italy	2,438	1,654	1,028	1,048	1,038	0.4	0.2	1.9	-1.0	-8.9
Denmark	575	978	811	931	1,016	0.2	0.2	14.8	9.1	0.8
Australia	1,023	1,469	1,516	870	705	0.4	0.2	-42.6	-19.0	-13.7
China	70	303	377	431	604	0.1	0.1	14.3	40.1	14.8
Spain	310	441	543	539	600	0.1	0.1	-0.7	11.3	6.4
Japan	559	712	599	566	521	0.2	0.1	-5.5	-8.0	-6.1
Other interregional	2,206	4,025	3,658	4,193	5,133	1.0	1.1	14.6	22.4	5.0
Other World/Not specified	*249*	*798*	*35*	*329*	*141*	*0.2*	*0.0*	*840.0*	*-57.1*	*-29.3*

Source: World Tourism Organization (UNWTO) ©   (Data as collected by UNWTO for TMT 2006 Edition)

World Tourism Organization ©

III.2.24 Turks and Caicos Islands   Caribbean

Profile

Turks and Caicos Islands		
	Capital	Cockburn Town
	Area (10 km²)	43
	Population (2005, 1000)	21

Americas
Caribbean

	2003	2004	2005*	2004/2003	2005*/2004
International Arrivals					
Tourists (overnight visitors) (1000)	164	173	200	5.8	15.6
- per 100 of inhabitants	845	867	973		
Tourism accommodation					
Number of rooms	2,473	..	..		

Source: World Tourism Organization (UNWTO)   (Data as collected by UNWTO for TMT 2006 Edition)
See annex for methodological notes and reference of external sources used.

International Tourism by Origin

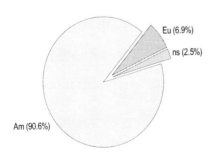

Turks and Caicos Islands
International Tourist Arrivals at Frontiers

Region of Origin, 2002

Eu (6.9%)

ns (2.5%)

Am (90.6%)

Am: Americas; Eu: Europe; AP: Asia and the Pacific;
ns: Not specified;   Source: World Tourism Organization (UNWTO) ©

Turks and Caicos Islands
International Tourist Arrivals at Frontiers (by residence)

	1995	2000	2002	2003	2004	Market share (%) 2000	Market share (%) 2004	Growth rate (%) 03/02	Growth rate (%) 04/03	Average per year (%) 2000-2004
Total	78,957	152,291	154,961	..	..	100				
From Americas	*67,767*	*136,211*	*140,349*	..	..	*89.4*				
United States	54,926	112,511	119,947	..	..	73.9				
Canada	9,073	15,597	14,775	..	..	10.2				
Bahamas	1,602	2,189	1,955	..	..	1.4				
Jamaica	365	1,191	1,482	..	..	0.8				
Haiti	..	1,100	345	..	..	0.7				
Dominican Rp	..	976	266	..	..	0.6				
Cayman Islands	..	245	228	..	..	0.2				
Argentina	..	564	172	..	..	0.4				
Trinidad Tbg	35	158	156	..	..	0.1				
Barbados	126	159	129	..	..	0.1				
Puerto Rico	..	135	101	..	..	0.1				
Bermuda	..	133	92	..	..	0.1				
Brazil	..	147	87	..	..	0.1				
Venezuela	..	77	74	..	..	0.1				
Guyana	13	121	62	..	..	0.1				
Saint Lucia	38	64	42	..	..	0.0				
Antigua,Barb	1	22	27	..	..	0.0				
St.Vincent,Grenadines	7	18	25	..	..	0.0				
Cuba	..	5	24	..	..	0.0				
Belize	189	17	20	..	..	0.0				
Br.Virgin Is	..	51	12	..	..	0.0				
US.Virgin Is	..	22	12	..	..	0.0				
Other intraregional	1,392	709	316	..	..	0.5				
From other regions	*8,494*	*11,942*	*10,669*	..	..	*7.8*				
United Kingdom	2,199	4,766	6,642	..	..	3.1				
France	1,514	1,752	1,569	..	..	1.2				
Italy	1,911	2,188	1,082	..	..	1.4				
Germany	1,586	1,427	357	..	..	0.9				
Switzerland	501	366	320	..	..	0.2				
Sweden	76	123	136	..	..	0.1				
Belgium	235	181	119	..	..	0.1				
Austria	289	365	104	..	..	0.2				
Ireland	..	83	67	..	..	0.1				
Spain	12	104	52	..	..	0.1				
Netherlands	31	71	..	..	..	0.0				
Japan	..	113	35	..	..	0.1				
Norway	57	88	32	..	..	0.1				
Denmark	50	17	21	..	..	0.0				
Portugal	26	49	18	..	..	0.0				
Luxembourg	1	20	10	..	..	0.0				
Greece	6	25	9	..	..	0.0				
Other Europe	..	204	96	..	..	0.1				
Other World/Not specified	*2,696*	*4,138*	*3,943*	..	..	*2.7*				

Source: World Tourism Organization (UNWTO) ©   (Data as collected by UNWTO for TMT 2006 Edition)

III.2.25 United States Virgin Islands   Caribbean

Promotional: www.usvitourism.vi
Institutional/corporate: www.usvitourism.vi
Research and data: www.usviber.org

Profile

United States Virgin Islands	Capital	Charlotte Amalie
	Area (10 km²)	34
	Population (2005, 1000)	109

Americas
Caribbean

	2003	2004	2005*	2004/2003	2005*/2004
International Arrivals					
Visitors (1000)	2,395	2,620	2,605	9.4	-0.6
Tourists (overnight visitors) (1000)	538	544	575	1.1	5.7
- per 100 of inhabitants	494	500	529		
Same-day visitors (1000)	83	111	118	33.7	6.3
Cruise passengers (1000)	1,774	1,965	1,912	10.8	-2.7
Tourism accommodation					
Number of rooms	5,045	4,959	4,762	-1.7	-4.0
Nights spent in collective establishments (1000)					
by non-residents (inbound tourism)	1,052	1,096	1,095	4.2	-0.1
Receipts and Expenditure for International Tourism					
International Tourism Receipts (US$ million)	1,257	1,356	1,493	7.9	10.1
- per Tourist Arrival (US$)	2,336	2,493	2,597	6.7	4.2
- per Visitor Arrival (US$)	525	518	573	-1.4	10.7
- per capita (US$)	11,552	12,466	13,734		

Source: World Tourism Organization (UNWTO)   (Data as collected by UNWTO for TMT 2006 Edition)

See annex for methodological notes and reference of external sources used.

International Tourism by Origin

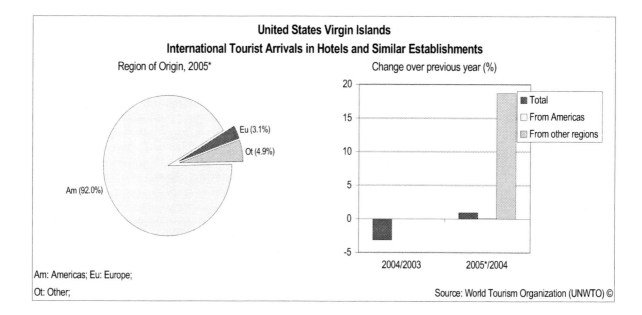

United States Virgin Islands
International Tourist Arrivals in Hotels and Similar Establishments

Region of Origin, 2005*

Change over previous year (%)

Eu (3.1%)
Ot (4.9%)
Am (92.0%)

Total
From Americas
From other regions

2004/2003   2005*/2004

Am: Americas; Eu: Europe;
Ot: Other;

Source: World Tourism Organization (UNWTO) ©

World Tourism Organization ©

United States Virgin Islands

International Tourist Arrivals in Hotels and Similar Establishments (by nationality)

	1995	2000	2003	2004	2005*	Market share (%) 2000	2005*	Growth rate (%) 04/03	05*/04	Average per year (%) 2000-2005*
Total	**363,201**	**607,342**	**623,394**	**603,944**	**609,754**	**100**	**100**	**-3.1**	**1.0**	**0.1**
From Americas	*332,835*	*533,421*	*531,270*	*560,581*	*561,091*	*87.8*	*92.0*	*5.5*	*0.1*	*1.0*
United States	300,214	494,810	496,168	521,264	524,031	81.5	85.9	5.1	0.5	1.2
Puerto Rico	21,385	24,324	23,792	24,717	21,353	4.0	3.5	3.9	-13.6	-2.6
Canada	3,307	4,373	4,822	5,239	5,365	0.7	0.9	8.6	2.4	4.2
Br.Virgin Is	935	3,847	2,926	4,102	4,902	0.6	0.8	40.2	19.5	5.0
Costa Rica	21	51	125	769	754	0.0	0.1	515.2	-2.0	71.4
Jamaica	196	266	147	292	605	0.0	0.1	98.6	107.2	17.9
Barbados	105	388	325	268	523	0.1	0.1	-17.5	95.1	6.2
Brazil	554	334	296	335	360	0.1	0.1	13.2	7.5	1.5
Argentina	2,164	908	171	386	356	0.1	0.1	125.7	-7.8	-17.1
Mexico	171	135	245	394	315	0.0	0.1	60.8	-20.1	18.5
Dominican Rp	30	68	50	114	229	0.0	0.0	128.0	100.9	27.5
Chile	154	140	87	88	171	0.0	0.0	1.1	94.3	4.1
Panama	40	126	104	131	164	0.0	0.0	26.0	25.2	5.4
Trinidad Tbg	76	142	145	248	151	0.0	0.0	71.0	-39.1	1.2
Bahamas	75	299	112	172	144	0.0	0.0	53.6	-16.3	-13.6
Venezuela	214	367	144	233	100	0.1	0.0	61.8	-57.1	-22.9
Peru	81	15	36	76	87	0.0	0.0	111.1	14.5	42.1
Bolivia	4	9	90	25	80	0.0	0.0	-72.2	220.0	54.8
Colombia	72	46	146	61	40	0.0	0.0	-58.2	-34.4	-2.8
Guatemala	10	17	..	5	26	0.0	0.0		420.0	8.9
Uruguay	42	9	10	6	17	0.0	0.0	-40.0	183.3	13.6
Guyana	16	3	21	11	..	0.0		-47.6		
Honduras	1	5	6	11	..	0.0		83.3		
Other intraregional	2,968	2,739	1,302	1,634	1,318	0.5	0.2	25.5	-19.3	-13.6
From other regions	*13,116*	*13,427*	*8,244*	*16,487*	*19,574*	*2.2*	*3.2*	*100.0*	*18.7*	*7.8*
Denmark	4,583	4,281	2,082	8,883	10,391	0.7	1.7	326.7	17.0	19.4
United Kingdom	1,345	3,001	1,744	2,281	1,604	0.5	0.3	30.8	-29.7	-11.8
Greece	31	93	135	223	1,548	0.0	0.3	65.2	594.2	75.5
Italy	1,688	1,283	1,035	1,048	1,129	0.2	0.2	1.3	7.7	-2.5
Germany	1,271	900	748	603	1,099	0.1	0.2	-19.4	82.3	4.1
France	663	731	440	848	535	0.1	0.1	92.7	-36.9	-6.1
Spain	453	264	262	214	499	0.0	0.1	-18.3	133.2	13.6
Switzerland	355	421	428	281	430	0.1	0.1	-34.3	53.0	0.4
Norway	227	375	117	178	247	0.1	0.0	52.1	38.8	-8.0
Japan	550	452	127	159	212	0.1	0.0	25.2	33.3	-14.1
Netherlands	228	127	213	267	192	0.0	0.0	25.4	-28.1	8.6
Sweden	398	307	142	202	192	0.1	0.0	42.3	-5.0	-9.0
Australia	122	187	175	118	168	0.0	0.0	-32.6	42.4	-2.1
All Africa	165	179	134	289	162	0.0	0.0	115.7	-43.9	-2.0
Austria	228	125	69	106	150	0.0	0.0	53.6	41.5	3.7
Taiwan (pr. of China)	51	32	58	71	94	0.0	0.0	22.4	32.4	24.0
Portugal	72	31	30	16	87	0.0	0.0	-46.7	443.8	22.9
Other Europe	554	381	234	575	760	0.1	0.1	145.7	32.2	14.8
Other interregional	132	257	71	125	75	0.0	0.0	76.1	-40.0	-21.8
Other World/Not specified	*17,250*	*60,494*	*83,880*	*26,876*	*29,089*	*10.0*	*4.8*	*-68.0*	*8.2*	*-13.6*

Source: World Tourism Organization (UNWTO) ©   (Data as collected by UNWTO for TMT 2006 Edition)

III.3 Central America

III.3.1 Belize Central America

Profile

Belize

Americas
Central America

Capital		Belmopan
Area (1000 km²)		23
Population (2005, 1000)		281
Gross Domestic Product (GDP) (2005, US$ million)		1,111
GDP per capita (2005, US$)		4,146
GDP growth (real, %)		
'-> 2004: 4.6; 2005: 3.5;	2006*: 5.3;	2007*: 2.6

	2003	2004	2005*	2004/2003	2005*/2004
International Arrivals					
Visitors (1000)	999	1,329	..	33.0	
Tourists (overnight visitors) (1000)	221	231	237	4.7	2.5
- per 100 of inhabitants	82	84	84		
Same-day visitors (1000)	203	247	..	21.7	
Cruise passengers (1000)	575	851	800	48.0	-6.0
Tourism accommodation					
Number of rooms	5,050	5,139	5,593	1.8	8.8
Receipts and Expenditure for International Tourism					
International Tourism Receipts (US$ million)	150	168	204	12.0	21.4
- per Tourist Arrival (US$)	680	728	862	7.0	18.5
- per Visitor Arrival (US$)	150	126	..	-15.8	
- per capita (US$)	560	612	726		
International Tourism Expenditure (US$ million)	46	43	42	-6.5	-2.3
- per capita (US$)	172	157	149		
International Fare Expenditure (US$ million)	4	4	3		-25.0
Δ International Tourism Balance (US$ million)	104	125	162		

Source: World Tourism Organization (UNWTO)   (Data as collected by UNWTO for TMT 2006 Edition)
See annex for methodological notes and reference of external sources used.

International Tourism by Origin

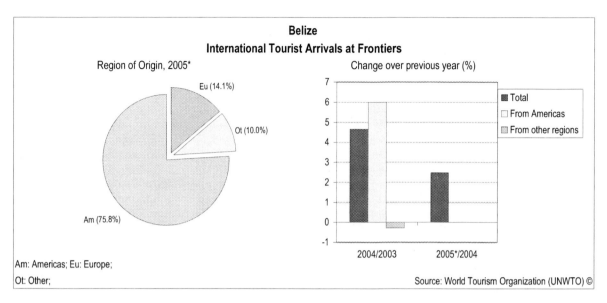

Belize
International Tourist Arrivals at Frontiers

Region of Origin, 2005*

Change over previous year (%)

Eu (14.1%)
Ot (10.0%)
Am (75.8%)

Total
From Americas
From other regions

2004/2003   2005*/2004

Am: Americas; Eu: Europe;
Ot: Other;

Source: World Tourism Organization (UNWTO) ©

Belize
International Tourist Arrivals at Frontiers (by nationality)

	1995	2000	2003	2004	2005*	Market share (%) 2000	Market share (%) 2005*	Growth rate (%) 04/03	Growth rate (%) 05*/04	Average per year (%) 2000-2005*
Total	..	**195,765**	**220,574**	**230,835**	**236,573**	**100**	**100**	**4.7**	**2.5**	**3.9**
From Americas	..	*150,102*	*174,784*	*185,254*	*179,357*	*76.7*	*75.8*	*6.0*	*-3.2*	*3.6*
United States	..	104,717	127,288	137,367	145,977	53.5	61.7	7.9	6.3	6.9
Guatemala	..	17,313	17,632	15,951	13,907	8.8	5.9	-9.5	-12.8	-4.3
Canada	..	9,205	9,831	11,926	13,580	4.7	5.7	21.3	13.9	8.1
Mexico	..	8,688	6,312	6,853	5,893	4.4	2.5	8.6	-14.0	-7.5
Honduras	..	2,789	4,124	3,479	..	1.4		-15.6		
All South America	..	1,703	1,784	1,941	..	0.9		8.8		
Jamaica	..	498	846	735	..	0.3		-13.1		
Other Caribbean	..	1,198	1,209	1,475	..	0.6		22.0		
Other Central America	..	3,991	5,758	5,527	..	2.0		-4.0		
From other regions	..	*31,557*	*37,991*	*37,883*	*33,466*	*16.1*	*14.1*	*-0.3*	*-11.7*	*1.2*
United Kingdom	..	8,007	9,318	9,991	9,989	4.1	4.2	7.2	0.0	4.5
Germany	..	3,757	4,146	4,269	3,966	1.9	1.7	3.0	-7.1	1.1
France	..	1,921	3,115	3,308	3,803	1.0	1.6	6.2	15.0	14.6
Netherlands	..	3,555	4,212	3,585	3,617	1.8	1.5	-14.9	0.9	0.3
Italy	..	2,606	3,847	2,850	3,080	1.3	1.3	-25.9	8.1	3.4
All Asia	..	2,097	2,413	2,729	..	1.1		13.1		
All Oceania	..	1,129	1,341	1,556	..	0.6		16.0		
Spain	..	1,211	1,737	1,401	1,386	0.6	0.6	-19.3	-1.1	2.7
Sweden	..	799	784	836	993	0.4	0.4	6.6	18.8	4.4
Switzerland	..	1,009	1,019	1,028	804	0.5	0.3	0.9	-21.8	-4.4
All Middle East	..	361	370	481	..	0.2		30.0		
All Africa	..	296	337	349	..	0.2		3.6		
Other Europe	..	4,809	5,352	5,500	5,828	2.5	2.5	2.8	6.0	3.9
Nationals residing abroad	..	*14,106*	*7,799*	*7,698*	*7,705*	*7.2*	*3.3*	*-1.3*	*0.1*	*-11.4*
Other World/Not specified	..	..	..	..	*16,045*		*6.8*			

Source: World Tourism Organization (UNWTO) ©   (Data as collected by UNWTO for TMT 2006 Edition)

World Tourism Organization ©

III.3.2　Costa Rica　　　　　Central America

Promotional:　　　　　　　www.costarica.com
Institutional/corporate:　　www.costarica.com ; www.visitecentroamerica.com
Research and data:　　　　www.costarica.com

Profile

Costa Rica

Capital	San José
Year of entry in UNWTO	1995
Area (1000 km²)	51
Population (2005, million)	4.0
Gross Domestic Product (GDP) (2005, US$ million)	19,985
GDP per capita (2005, US$)	4,620

Americas
Central America

GDP growth (real, %)
'-> 2004: 4.1;　　2005: 5.9;　　2006*: 6.5;　　2007*: 4.5

	2003	2004	2005*	2004/2003	2005*/2004
International Arrivals					
Visitors (1000)	1,514	1,771	1,959	17.0	10.6
Tourists (overnight visitors) (1000)	1,239	1,453	1,679	17.3	15.6
- per 100 of inhabitants	32	37	42		
Cruise passengers (1000)	275	318	280	15.6	-11.9
Tourism accommodation					
Number of rooms	35,003	36,299	38,737	3.7	6.7
Outbound Tourism					
Trips abroad (1000)	373	425	487	13.9	14.6
- per 100 of inhabitants	10	11	12		
Receipts and Expenditure for International Tourism					
International Tourism Receipts (US$ million)	1,199	1,358	1,570	13.3	15.6
- per Tourist Arrival (US$)	968	935	935	-3.4	0.0
- per Visitor Arrival (US$)	792	767	801	-3.2	4.5
- per capita (US$)	308	343	391		
International Fare Receipts (US$ million)	131	127	138	-3.1	8.7
International Tourism Expenditure (US$ million)	352	404	479	14.8	18.4
- per trip (US$)	943	951	983	0.8	3.4
- per capita (US$)	90	102	119		
International Fare Expenditure (US$ million)	81	75	86	-7.4	14.7
Δ International Tourism Balance (US$ million)	848	954	1,092		
Δ International Fare Balance (US$ million)	50	52	52		

Source: World Tourism Organization (UNWTO)　　　　(Data as collected by UNWTO for TMT 2006 Edition)
See annex for methodological notes and reference of external sources used.

International Tourism by Origin

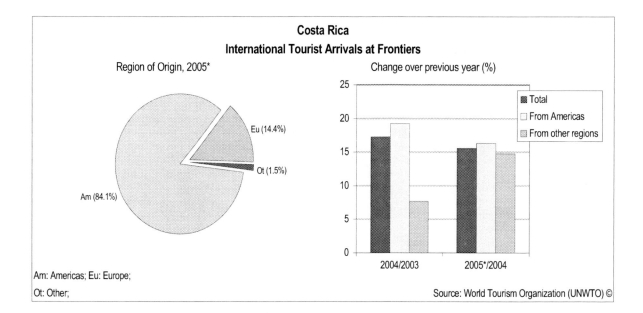

Costa Rica
International Tourist Arrivals at Frontiers

Region of Origin, 2005*

Change over previous year (%)

Eu (14.4%)

Ot (1.5%)

Am (84.1%)

Am: Americas; Eu: Europe;
Ot: Other;

Source: World Tourism Organization (UNWTO) ©

World Tourism Organization ©

Costa Rica
International Tourist Arrivals at Frontiers (by nationality)

	1995	2000	2003	2004	2005*	Market share (%) 2000	Market share (%) 2005*	Growth rate (%) 04/03	Growth rate (%) 05*/04	Average per year (%) 2000-2005*
Total	**784,610**	**1,088,075**	**1,238,692**	**1,452,926**	**1,679,051**	**100**	**100**	**17.3**	**15.6**	**9.1**
From Americas	*633,055*	*907,381*	*1,017,831*	*1,213,784*	*1,411,640*	*83.4*	*84.1*	*19.3*	*16.3*	*9.2*
United States	287,434	429,725	510,751	633,640	758,134	39.5	45.2	24.1	19.6	12.0
Nicaragua	102,557	143,142	163,632	191,398	231,712	13.2	13.8	17.0	21.1	10.1
Canada	41,898	52,696	54,656	74,212	86,906	4.8	5.2	35.8	17.1	10.5
Panama	52,945	54,646	56,490	63,956	72,730	5.0	4.3	13.2	13.7	5.9
Mexico	19,975	33,432	46,113	47,130	50,330	3.1	3.0	2.2	6.8	8.5
El Salvador	22,340	31,149	33,892	38,264	44,873	2.9	2.7	12.9	17.3	7.6
Guatemala	24,305	33,191	35,174	40,166	37,771	3.1	2.2	14.2	-6.0	2.6
Honduras	15,876	24,338	23,004	25,540	27,719	2.2	1.7	11.0	8.5	2.6
Colombia	17,036	40,458	26,645	26,786	27,130	3.7	1.6	0.5	1.3	-7.7
Argentina	7,457	15,823	13,804	14,887	15,622	1.5	0.9	7.8	4.9	-0.3
Venezuela	5,778	10,142	13,635	13,483	14,222	0.9	0.8	-1.1	5.5	7.0
Brazil	4,841	5,560	6,754	7,608	8,607	0.5	0.5	12.6	13.1	9.1
Chile	7,393	7,624	6,700	7,297	7,039	0.7	0.4	8.9	-3.5	-1.6
Peru	5,233	6,883	6,430	6,969	6,319	0.6	0.4	8.4	-9.3	-1.7
Ecuador	8,164	5,435	5,471	5,168	4,825	0.5	0.3	-5.5	-6.6	-2.4
Cuba	2,890	3,570	3,165	3,842	4,395	0.3	0.3	21.4	14.4	4.2
Dominican Rp	2,959	3,906	3,128	3,110	3,674	0.4	0.2	-0.6	18.1	-1.2
Bolivia	..	..	1,759	2,227	2,366		0.1	26.6	6.2	
Uruguay	..	..	2,098	2,139	1,800		0.1	2.0	-15.8	
Trinidad Tbg	242	456	1,146	1,206	981	0.0	0.1	5.2	-18.7	16.6
Jamaica	528	802	663	905	962	0.1	0.1	36.5	6.3	3.7
Other Caribbean	506	716	1,044	1,614	1,593	0.1	0.1	54.6	-1.3	17.3
Other intraregional	2,698	3,687	1,677	2,237	1,930	0.3	0.1	33.4	-13.7	-12.1
From other regions	*148,310*	*173,344*	*215,693*	*232,309*	*266,602*	*15.9*	*15.9*	*7.7*	*14.8*	*9.0*
Spain	19,708	26,877	34,442	42,381	49,218	2.5	2.9	23.1	16.1	12.9
Germany	38,592	26,475	29,151	34,154	38,523	2.4	2.3	17.2	12.8	7.8
United Kingdom	10,697	18,256	23,019	24,158	26,917	1.7	1.6	4.9	11.4	8.1
France	8,215	12,797	23,606	23,467	24,365	1.2	1.5	-0.6	3.8	13.7
Netherlands	11,499	18,994	24,665	21,905	24,173	1.7	1.4	-11.2	10.4	4.9
Italy	19,694	16,736	18,361	19,483	20,726	1.5	1.2	6.1	6.4	4.4
Switzerland	9,266	10,061	10,893	11,604	12,730	0.9	0.8	6.5	9.7	4.8
Israel	2,039	3,911	6,143	6,850	8,862	0.4	0.5	11.5	29.4	17.8
Australia, New Zealand	..	..	..	..	6,586		0.4			
Japan	5,048	5,293	5,883	5,695	6,056	0.5	0.4	-3.2	6.3	2.7
Sweden	2,167	2,998	4,540	5,057	5,947	0.3	0.4	11.4	17.6	14.7
Belgium	1,837	3,900	5,504	5,650	5,602	0.4	0.3	2.7	-0.8	7.5
Austria	3,452	3,366	3,957	4,660	5,212	0.3	0.3	17.8	11.8	9.1
Taiwan (pr. of China)	..	..	2,934	3,315	3,309		0.2	13.0	-0.2	
Korea, Republic of	1,624	2,059	2,471	2,444	3,238	0.2	0.2	-1.1	32.5	9.5
Denmark	2,288	1,808	2,525	2,409	3,115	0.2	0.2	-4.6	29.3	11.5
Norway	1,066	1,898	1,812	1,910	2,253	0.2	0.1	5.4	18.0	3.5
Finland	484	2,165	926	1,056	1,266	0.2	0.1	14.0	19.9	-10.2
Russian Federation	560	1,258	..	..	..	0.1				
Other Asia	1,928	3,093	2,866	3,072	3,295	0.3	0.2	7.2	7.3	1.3
Other Europe	3,092	5,062	8,698	10,328	12,842	0.5	0.8	18.7	24.3	20.5
Other interregional	5,054	6,337	3,297	2,711	2,367	0.6	0.1	-17.8	-12.7	-17.9
Other World/Not specified	*3,245*	*7,350*	*5,168*	*6,833*	*809*	*0.7*	*0.0*	*32.2*	*-88.2*	*-35.7*

Source: World Tourism Organization (UNWTO) ©　　　　　　　(Data as collected by UNWTO for TMT 2006 Edition)

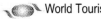

III.3.3   El Salvador   Central America

Promotional: www.elsalvadorturismo.gob.sv
Institutional/corporate: www.sgsica.org

Profile

El Salvador

Capital	San Salvador
Year of entry in UNWTO	1993
Area (1000 km²)	21
Population (2005, million)	6.7
Gross Domestic Product (GDP) (2005, US$ million)	16,974
GDP per capita (2005, US$)	2,468

Americas
Central America

GDP growth (real, %)
'-> 2004: 1.8;   2005: 2.8;   2006*: 3.5;   2007*: 3.5

	2003	2004	2005*	2004/2003	2005*/2004
International Arrivals					
Visitors (1000)	935	1,045	1,333	11.8	27.6
Tourists (overnight visitors) (1000)	857	966	1,154	12.7	19.5
- per 100 of inhabitants	13	15	17		
Same-day visitors (1000)	78	79	179	1.3	126.6
Tourism accommodation					
Number of rooms	4,501	4,766	5,757	5.9	20.8
Nights spent in hotels and similar establishments (1000)					
by non-residents (inbound tourism)	3,430	4,832	6,926	40.9	43.3
Outbound Tourism					
Trips abroad (1000)	940	1,218	1,397	29.6	14.7
- per 100 of inhabitants	15	18	21		
Receipts and Expenditure for International Tourism					
International Tourism Receipts (US$ million)	383	441	543	15.1	23.2
- per Tourist Arrival (US$)	447	456	470	2.1	3.1
- per Visitor Arrival (US$)	410	422	407	2.9	-3.5
- per capita (US$)	59	67	81		
International Fare Receipts (US$ million)	281	295	295	5.0	
International Tourism Expenditure (US$ million)	230	302	347	31.7	14.7
- per trip (US$)	244	248	248	1.6	0.0
- per capita (US$)	35	46	52		
International Fare Expenditure (US$ million)	81	81	83		2.5
Δ International Tourism Balance (US$ million)	154	139	196		
Δ International Fare Balance (US$ million)	200	214	212		

Source: World Tourism Organization (UNWTO)   (Data as collected by UNWTO for TMT 2006 Edition)
See annex for methodological notes and reference of external sources used.

World Tourism Organization ©

International Tourism by Origin

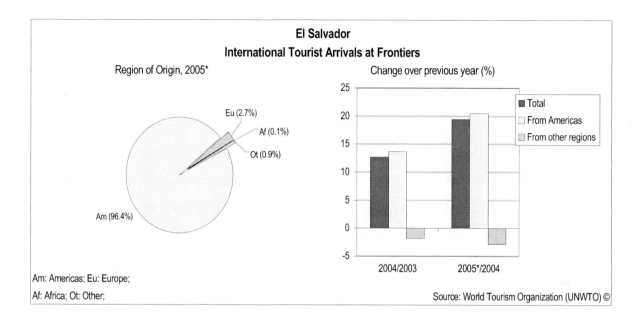

El Salvador
International Tourist Arrivals at Frontiers

Region of Origin, 2005*

Eu (2.7%)
Af (0.1%)
Ot (0.9%)
Am (96.4%)

Change over previous year (%)

- Total
- From Americas
- From other regions

2004/2003   2005*/2004

Am: Americas; Eu: Europe;
Af: Africa; Ot: Other;

Source: World Tourism Organization (UNWTO) ©

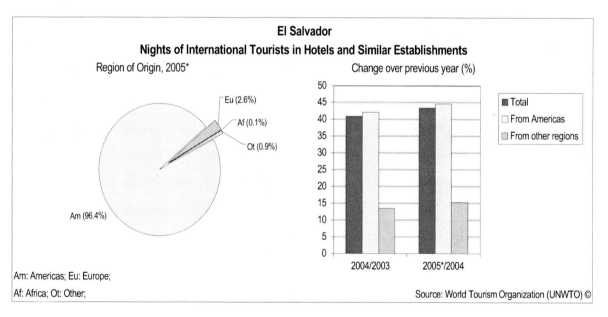

El Salvador
Nights of International Tourists in Hotels and Similar Establishments

Region of Origin, 2005*

Eu (2.6%)
Af (0.1%)
Ot (0.9%)
Am (96.4%)

Change over previous year (%)

- Total
- From Americas
- From other regions

2004/2003   2005*/2004

Am: Americas; Eu: Europe;
Af: Africa; Ot: Other;

Source: World Tourism Organization (UNWTO) ©

El Salvador
International Tourist Arrivals at Frontiers (by nationality)

	1995	2000	2003	2004	2005*	Market share (%) 2000	Market share (%) 2005*	Growth rate (%) 04/03	Growth rate (%) 05*/04	Average per year (%) 2000-2005*
Total	**235,364**	**794,678**	**857,378**	**966,416**	**1,154,386**	**100**	**100**	**12.7**	**19.5**	**7.8**
From Americas	*205,198*	*719,615*	*812,192*	*923,127*	*1,112,319*	*90.6*	*96.4*	*13.7*	*20.5*	*9.1*
Guatemala	33,050	273,543	329,162	326,437	392,235	34.4	34.0	-0.8	20.2	7.5
United States	99,229	142,962	179,712	225,910	236,936	18.0	20.5	25.7	4.9	10.6
Honduras	13,102	151,919	104,598	128,319	203,243	19.1	17.6	22.7	58.4	6.0
Nicaragua	9,521	72,746	108,106	141,627	166,306	9.2	14.4	31.0	17.4	18.0
Costa Rica	12,464	29,046	26,495	29,405	34,744	3.7	3.0	11.0	18.2	3.6
Mexico	11,481	22,427	20,198	22,973	25,069	2.8	2.2	13.7	9.1	2.3
Canada	9,735	11,543	12,660	14,804	16,462	1.5	1.4	16.9	11.2	7.4
Panama	3,800	9,045	8,087	9,073	10,320	1.1	0.9	12.2	13.7	2.7
Colombia	3,641	..	5,091	4,607	5,197		0.5	-9.5	12.8	
Argentina	1,497	..	3,925	3,883	4,374		0.4	-1.1	12.6	
Belize	823	2,451	2,154	2,709	2,965	0.3	0.3	25.8	9.4	3.9
Brazil	930	..	1,725	2,069	2,686		0.2	19.9	29.8	
Chile	1,422	..	2,730	2,669	2,617		0.2	-2.2	-1.9	
Venezuela	1,101	..	1,676	1,867	2,039		0.2	11.4	9.2	
Peru	906	..	1,946	1,864	2,006		0.2	-4.2	7.6	
Dominican Rp	619	..	902	1,112	1,228		0.1	23.3	10.4	
Ecuador	429	..	995	..	..					
Uruguay	285	..	732	..	..					
All South America	..	3,450	..	..	..	0.4				
Bolivia	324	..	393	..	..					
Cuba	235	..	261	290	344		0.0	11.1	18.6	
Paraguay	63	..	218	..	..					
Other intraregional	541	483	426	3,509	3,548	0.1	0.3	723.7	1.1	49.0
From other regions	*30,166*	*30,087*	*44,104*	*43,289*	*42,067*	*3.8*	*3.6*	*-1.8*	*-2.8*	*6.9*
Spain	6,759	9,881	10,019	9,271	9,311	1.2	0.8	-7.5	0.4	-1.2
Germany	4,086	5,734	5,189	4,810	4,624	0.7	0.4	-7.3	-3.9	-4.2
Italy	2,920	3,764	3,940	4,122	3,456	0.5	0.3	4.6	-16.2	-1.7
United Kingdom	2,255	2,993	3,510	3,254	2,725	0.4	0.2	-7.3	-16.3	-1.9
Korea, Republic of	..	..	2,134	2,211	2,403		0.2	3.6	8.7	
Australia	689	..	1,516	2,000	2,296		0.2	31.9	14.8	
Japan	1,789	2,331	2,485	2,315	2,037	0.3	0.2	-6.8	-12.0	-2.7
Sweden	608	..	1,484	1,799	1,866		0.2	21.2	3.7	
Taiwan (pr. of China)	..	..	1,551	1,736	1,780		0.2	11.9	2.5	
Netherlands	1,407	..	..	1,425	1,352		0.1		-5.1	
Switzerland	1,480	..	1,416	1,253	1,091		0.1	-11.5	-12.9	
Belgium	603	..	943	..	..					
Israel	339	681	1,076	906	913	0.1	0.1	-15.8	0.8	6.0
France	2,557	3,959	3,138	1,669	815	0.5	0.1	-46.8	-51.2	-27.1
Denmark	590	..	761	..	..					
Austria	299	..	528	..	..					
Norway	403	..	472	621	522		0.0	31.6	-15.9	
Ireland	190	..	383	..	..					
Finland	249	..	322	..	..					
Other interregional	2,943	744	3,237	5,897	6,876	0.1	0.6	82.2	16.6	56.0
Other World/Not specified	*..*	*44,976*	*1,082*	*..*	*..*	*5.7*				

Source: World Tourism Organization (UNWTO) ©

(Data as collected by UNWTO for TMT 2006 Edition)

World Tourism Organization ©

El Salvador

Nights of International Tourists in Hotels and Similar Establishments (by nationality)

	1995	2000	2003	2004	2005*	Market share (%) 2000	2005*	Growth rate (%) 04/03	05*/04	Average per year (%) 2000-2005*
Total	**128,014**	**3,133,124**	**3,429,512**	**4,832,080**	**6,926,316**	**100**	**100**	**40.9**	**43.3**	**17.2**
From Americas	*113,701*	*2,878,460*	*3,248,768*	*4,615,635*	*6,673,914*	*91.9*	*96.4*	*42.1*	*44.6*	*18.3*
Guatemala	32,760	1,094,172	1,316,648	1,632,185	2,353,410	34.9	34.0	24.0	44.2	16.6
United States	29,973	571,848	718,848	1,129,550	1,421,616	18.3	20.5	57.1	25.9	20.0
Honduras	16,392	607,676	418,392	641,595	1,219,458	19.4	17.6	53.3	90.1	14.9
Nicaragua	6,607	290,984	432,424	708,135	997,836	9.3	14.4	63.8	40.9	27.9
Costa Rica	7,674	116,184	105,980	147,025	208,464	3.7	3.0	38.7	41.8	12.4
Mexico	6,041	89,708	80,792	114,865	150,414	2.9	2.2	42.2	30.9	10.9
All South America	6,926	13,800	78,156	99,265	131,724	0.4	1.9	27.0	32.7	57.0
Canada	1,386	46,172	50,640	74,020	98,772	1.5	1.4	46.2	33.4	16.4
Panama	4,629	36,180	32,348	45,365	61,920	1.2	0.9	40.2	36.5	11.3
Belize	288	9,804	8,616	13,545	17,790	0.3	0.3	57.2	31.3	12.7
All the Caribbean	1,025	1,932	5,924	10,085	12,510	0.1	0.2	70.2	24.0	45.3
From other regions	*14,313*	*74,760*	*180,524*	*204,940*	*236,226*	*2.4*	*3.4*	*13.5*	*15.3*	*25.9*
Spain	2,825	39,524	40,076	46,355	55,866	1.3	0.8	15.7	20.5	7.2
Germany	1,734	22,936	20,756	24,050	27,744	0.7	0.4	15.9	15.4	3.9
All Africa	546	..	1,696	2,910	3,768		0.1	71.6	29.5	
Other Europe	6,410	..	82,600	90,330	99,840		1.4	9.4	10.5	
All East Asia/Pacific	2,798	12,300	35,396	41,295	49,008	0.4	0.7	16.7	18.7	31.8
Other World/Not specified	*..*	*179,904*	*220*	*11,505*	*16,176*	*5.7*	*0.2*	*5129.5*	*40.6*	*-38.2*

Source: World Tourism Organization (UNWTO) ©　　　　　　　　　　　　(Data as collected by UNWTO for TMT 2006 Edition)

III.3.4   Guatemala   Central America

Promotional: www.mayaspirit.com.gt
Institutional/corporate: www.mayaspirit.com.gt
Research and data: www.mayaspirit.com.gt

Profile

Guatemala

Capital	Guatemala
Year of entry in UNWTO	1993
Area (1000 km²)	109
Population (2005, million)	12.2
Gross Domestic Product (GDP) (2005, US$ million)	27,366
GDP per capita (2005, US$)	1,995

Americas

Central America

GDP growth (real, %)

'-> 2004: 2.7;   2005: 3.2;   2006*: 4.1;   2007*: 4.0

	2003	2004	2005*	2004/2003	2005*/2004
International Arrivals					
Tourists (overnight visitors) (1000)	880	1,182	1,316	34.2	11.4
- per 100 of inhabitants	8	10	11		
Tourism accommodation					
Number of rooms	17,519	17,570	19,357	0.3	10.2
Outbound Tourism					
Trips abroad (1000)	658	854	982	29.8	15.0
- per 100 of inhabitants	6	7	8		
Receipts and Expenditure for International Tourism					
International Tourism Receipts (US$ million)	621	776	869	25.0	12.0
- per Tourist Arrival (US$)	706	657	660	-6.9	0.6
- per capita (US$)	53	65	71		
International Fare Receipts (US$ million)	25	30	37	20.0	23.3
International Tourism Expenditure (US$ million)	312	391	756	25.3	93.2
- per trip (US$)	474	458	769	-3.4	68.0
- per capita (US$)	27	33	62		
International Fare Expenditure (US$ million)	61	65	56	6.6	-13.8
Δ International Tourism Balance (US$ million)	309	385	113		
Δ International Fare Balance (US$ million)	-36	-35	-19		

Source: World Tourism Organization (UNWTO)   (Data as collected by UNWTO for TMT 2006 Edition)

See annex for methodological notes and reference of external sources used.

International Tourism by Origin

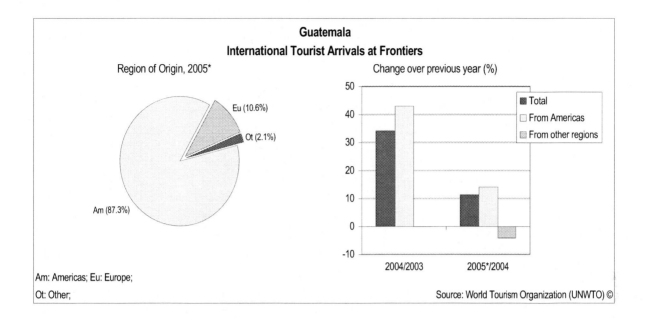

Guatemala
International Tourist Arrivals at Frontiers

Region of Origin, 2005*

Eu (10.6%)
Ot (2.1%)
Am (87.3%)

Change over previous year (%)

- Total
- From Americas
- From other regions

2004/2003   2005*/2004

Am: Americas; Eu: Europe;
Ot: Other;

Source: World Tourism Organization (UNWTO) ©

Guatemala
International Tourist Arrivals at Frontiers (by nationality)

	1995	2000	2003	2004	2005*	Market share (%) 2000	Market share (%) 2005*	Growth rate (%) 04/03	Growth rate (%) 05*/04	Average per year (%) 2000-2005*
Total	**563,478**	**826,240**	**880,223**	**1,181,526**	**1,315,646**	**100**	**100**	**34.2**	**11.4**	**9.8**
From Americas	*446,012*	*688,121*	*703,841*	*1,006,614*	*1,148,318*	*83.3*	*87.3*	*43.0*	*14.1*	*10.8*
El Salvador	122,532	289,970	209,745	411,277	497,430	35.1	37.8	96.1	20.9	11.4
United States	153,139	186,784	209,247	267,126	286,871	22.6	21.8	27.7	7.4	9.0
Honduras	41,202	51,545	64,242	93,975	106,473	6.2	8.1	46.3	13.3	15.6
Mexico	46,323	53,576	70,732	67,502	72,908	6.5	5.5	-4.6	8.0	6.4
Nicaragua	12,449	16,207	29,815	42,876	46,936	2.0	3.6	43.8	9.5	23.7
Costa Rica	15,489	21,851	29,529	31,979	34,693	2.6	2.6	8.3	8.5	9.7
Canada	17,146	15,915	27,048	20,510	24,820	1.9	1.9	-24.2	21.0	9.3
Colombia	7,917	11,619	12,387	10,751	13,211	1.4	1.0	-13.2	22.9	2.6
Belize	3,227	6,374	13,296	13,604	13,112	0.8	1.0	2.3	-3.6	15.5
Panama	5,296	6,651	7,463	8,862	9,733	0.8	0.7	18.7	9.8	7.9
Argentina	3,971	6,346	8,334	8,457	8,952	0.8	0.7	1.5	5.9	7.1
Brazil	2,269	2,857	3,905	4,509	5,485	0.3	0.4	15.5	21.6	13.9
Venezuela	2,056	3,513	2,481	5,466	5,077	0.4	0.4	120.3	-7.1	7.6
Chile	3,347	3,993	3,721	4,674	5,059	0.5	0.4	25.6	8.2	4.8
Cuba	..	2,087	1,765	2,831	4,218	0.3	0.3	60.4	49.0	15.1
Peru	2,167	2,843	3,165	3,281	3,522	0.3	0.3	3.7	7.3	4.4
Ecuador	3,478	1,614	1,970	2,948	2,963	0.2	0.2	49.6	0.5	12.9
Dominican Rp	1,223	1,762	2,026	2,048	2,698	0.2	0.2	1.1	31.7	8.9
Other Caribbean	816	688	762	1,039	908	0.1	0.1	36.4	-12.6	5.7
Other South America	1,706	1,926	2,208	2,899	3,249	0.2	0.2	31.3	12.1	11.0
Other intraregional	259	..	..	..	..					
From other regions	*116,331*	*136,436*	*173,522*	*173,403*	*166,099*	*16.5*	*12.6*	*-0.1*	*-4.2*	*4.0*
Spain	13,706	18,144	24,869	22,824	21,182	2.2	1.6	-8.2	-7.2	3.1
France	12,627	13,965	18,433	20,793	19,219	1.7	1.5	12.8	-7.6	6.6
Germany	21,854	20,045	27,734	21,786	18,258	2.4	1.4	-21.4	-16.2	-1.9
United Kingdom	9,200	10,900	14,776	15,955	16,803	1.3	1.3	8.0	5.3	9.0
Italy	16,927	16,241	17,272	17,708	16,467	2.0	1.3	2.5	-7.0	0.3
Netherlands	6,736	11,402	14,938	15,080	12,061	1.4	0.9	1.0	-20.0	1.1
Korea, Republic of	3,662	6,154	6,631	7,659	9,549	0.7	0.7	15.5	24.7	9.2
Israel	2,266	3,349	4,628	5,549	6,339	0.4	0.5	19.9	14.2	13.6
Australia	1,188	2,775	4,662	4,783	5,547	0.3	0.4	2.6	16.0	14.9
Switzerland	5,920	5,694	7,496	5,733	5,272	0.7	0.4	-23.5	-8.0	-1.5
Belgium	3,149	4,580	6,300	5,712	4,901	0.6	0.4	-9.3	-14.2	1.4
Japan	4,656	4,715	5,104	6,235	4,834	0.6	0.4	22.2	-22.5	0.5
Sweden	..	2,353	2,290	3,327	3,535	0.3	0.3	45.3	6.3	8.5
China	1,798	2,353	4,530	3,059	3,455	0.3	0.3	-32.5	12.9	8.0
Denmark	..	2,520	2,386	2,721	2,989	0.3	0.2	14.0	9.8	3.5
Norway	..	1,773	2,146	2,874	2,658	0.2	0.2	33.9	-7.5	8.4
Austria	..	2,898	2,437	2,679	2,643	0.4	0.2	9.9	-1.3	-1.8
Ireland	..	1,027	1,588	1,379	1,397	0.1	0.1	-13.2	1.3	6.3
All Middle East	364	382	603	365	1,182	0.0	0.1	-39.5	223.8	25.3
Czech Rep	..	367	362	687	927	0.0	0.1	89.8	34.9	20.4
Finland	..	602	1,146	934	908	0.1	0.1	-18.5	-2.8	8.6
Other interregional	12,278	4,197	3,191	5,561	5,973	0.5	0.5	74.3	7.4	7.3
Other World/Not specified	*1,135*	*1,683*	*2,860*	*1,509*	*1,229*	*0.2*	*0.1*	*-47.2*	*-18.6*	*-6.1*

Source: World Tourism Organization (UNWTO) ©   (Data as collected by UNWTO for TMT 2006 Edition)

World Tourism Organization ©

III.3.5   Honduras   Central America

Promotional: www.letsgohonduras.com
Institutional/corporate: www.letsgohonduras.com
Research and data: www.LetsGoHonduras.com

Profile

Honduras

Capital	Tegucigalpa
Year of entry in UNWTO	2001
Area (1000 km²)	112
Population (2005, million)	7.2
Gross Domestic Product (GDP) (2005, US$ million)	8,294
GDP per capita (2005, US$)	1,148

Americas

Central America

GDP growth (real, %)

'-> 2004: 4.6;   2005: 4.2;   2006*: 4.5;   2007*: 4.5

	2003	2004	2005*	2004/2003	2005*/2004
International Arrivals					
Visitors (1000)	887	1,026	1,118	15.6	9.0
Tourists (overnight visitors) (1000)	611	641	673	5.0	5.0
- per 100 of inhabitants	9	9	9		
Same-day visitors (1000)	276	118	168	-57.2	42.4
Cruise passengers (1000)	162	267	277	64.8	3.7
Tourism accommodation					
Number of rooms	18,590	19,519	20,453	5.0	4.8
Outbound Tourism					
Trips abroad (1000)	277	295	300	6.5	1.7
- per 100 of inhabitants	4	4	4		
Receipts and Expenditure for International Tourism					
International Tourism Receipts (US$ million)	350	429	472	22.7	10.0
- per Tourist Arrival (US$)	573	670	702	16.9	4.8
- per Visitor Arrival (US$)	395	419	422	6.1	0.9
- per capita (US$)	51	61	66		
International Fare Receipts (US$ million)	8	6	4	-25.0	-33.3
International Tourism Expenditure (US$ million)	200	227	248	13.5	9.4
- per trip (US$)	722	769	828	6.6	7.6
- per capita (US$)	29	32	35		
International Fare Expenditure (US$ million)	58	63	67	8.6	6.3
Δ International Tourism Balance (US$ million)	150	202	224		
Δ International Fare Balance (US$ million)	-50	-57	-63		

Source: World Tourism Organization (UNWTO)   (Data as collected by UNWTO for TMT 2006 Edition)

See annex for methodological notes and reference of external sources used.

International Tourism by Origin

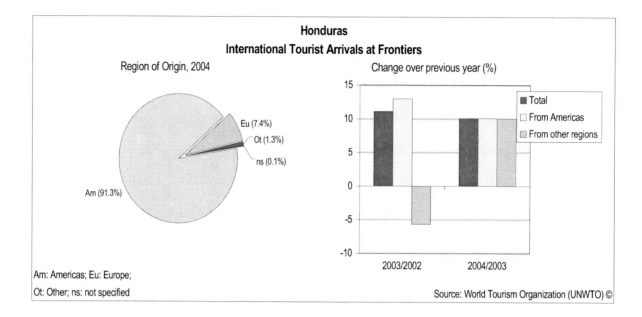

World Tourism Organization ©

Honduras
International Tourist Arrivals at Frontiers (by nationality)

	1995	2000	2003	2004	2005*	Market share (%) 2000	Market share (%) 2005*	Growth rate (%) 04/03	Growth rate (%) 05*/04	Average per year (%) 2000-2005*
Total	**270,549**	**470,727**	**610,535**	**640,981**	**673,035**	**100**	**100**	**5.0**	**5.0**	**7.4**
From Americas	*227,485*	*420,112*	*557,262*	*584,831*	*610,179*	*89.2*	*90.7*	*4.9*	*4.3*	*7.8*
United States	109,693	150,531	161,954	169,692	197,601	32.0	29.4	4.8	16.4	5.6
El Salvador	28,065	79,365	130,547	137,084	159,546	16.9	23.7	5.0	16.4	15.0
Guatemala	18,968	66,924	99,894	104,725	92,612	14.2	13.8	4.8	-11.6	6.7
Nicaragua	25,413	64,350	94,174	98,735	76,646	13.7	11.4	4.8	-22.4	3.6
Costa Rica	9,931	15,755	19,621	20,740	20,855	3.3	3.1	5.7	0.6	5.8
Mexico	7,683	10,902	13,149	13,913	17,212	2.3	2.6	5.8	23.7	9.6
Canada	8,265	8,732	10,324	10,803	11,002	1.9	1.6	4.6	1.8	4.7
Panama	3,710	5,330	7,104	7,516	8,394	1.1	1.2	5.8	11.7	9.5
Colombia	2,494	3,108	3,521	3,723	4,410	0.7	0.7	5.7	18.5	7.2
Argentina	1,671	2,351	2,831	3,000	3,365	0.5	0.5	6.0	12.2	7.4
Belize	1,053	1,595	1,770	1,894	2,717	0.3	0.4	7.0	43.5	11.2
Cayman Islands	..	1,810	1,205	1,272	2,225	0.4	0.3	5.6	74.9	4.2
Chile	1,366	1,451	1,828	1,915	2,134	0.3	0.3	4.8	11.4	8.0
Venezuela	..	1,188	1,460	1,541	2,068	0.3	0.3	5.5	34.2	11.7
Brazil	..	1,077	1,506	1,580	1,916	0.2	0.3	4.9	21.3	12.2
Peru	1,134	1,118	1,260	1,343	1,483	0.2	0.2	6.6	10.4	5.8
Ecuador	1,612	1,084	1,026	1,079	1,320	0.2	0.2	5.2	22.3	4.0
Cuba	645	821	1,065	1,097	1,169	0.2	0.2	3.0	6.6	7.3
Dominican Rp	743	927	1,019	1,076	1,157	0.2	0.2	5.6	7.5	4.5
Bolivia	..	363	557	594	750	0.1	0.1	6.6	26.3	15.6
Uruguay	..	451	468	494	577	0.1	0.1	5.6	16.8	5.1
Other intraregional	5,039	879	979	1,015	1,020	0.2	0.2	3.7	0.5	3.0
From other regions	*41,886*	*50,440*	*52,835*	*55,684*	*62,561*	*10.7*	*9.3*	*5.4*	*12.4*	*4.4*
Italy	3,710	7,245	10,020	10,376	11,975	1.5	1.8	3.6	15.4	10.6
Spain	5,223	6,975	7,335	7,694	8,536	1.5	1.3	4.9	10.9	4.1
Germany	6,877	6,283	5,945	6,293	7,010	1.3	1.0	5.9	11.4	2.2
United Kingdom	4,317	5,372	5,574	5,883	6,878	1.1	1.0	5.5	16.9	5.1
France	2,528	3,497	3,298	3,478	3,903	0.7	0.6	5.5	12.2	2.2
Netherlands	3,109	3,405	3,136	3,294	3,845	0.7	0.6	5.0	16.7	2.5
Japan	2,719	2,157	1,928	2,026	2,282	0.5	0.3	5.1	12.6	1.1
Switzerland	2,368	2,268	1,814	1,926	2,212	0.5	0.3	6.2	14.8	-0.5
Korea, Republic of	1,416	1,485	1,104	889	2,038	0.3	0.3	-19.5	129.2	6.5
Sweden	..	1,448	1,454	1,573	1,627	0.3	0.2	8.2	3.4	2.4
Australia	733	986	1,136	1,222	1,553	0.2	0.2	7.6	27.1	9.5
Belgium	..	1,198	1,108	1,176	1,370	0.3	0.2	6.1	16.5	2.7
China	1,370	1,094	1,055	1,120	1,330	0.2	0.2	6.2	18.8	4.0
Denmark	..	1,137	1,042	1,110	1,249	0.2	0.2	6.5	12.5	1.9
Israel	..	855	839	878	1,105	0.2	0.2	4.6	25.9	5.3
Norway	..	682	724	787	821	0.1	0.1	8.7	4.3	3.8
Austria	..	746	471	499	585	0.2	0.1	5.9	17.2	-4.7
Ireland	..	631	485	517	551	0.1	0.1	6.6	6.6	-2.7
Finland	..	253	372	402	451	0.1	0.1	8.1	12.2	12.3
New Zealand	243	314	285	308	326	0.1	0.0	8.1	5.8	0.8
Other interregional	7,273	2,409	3,710	4,233	2,914	0.5	0.4	14.1	-31.2	3.9
Other World/Not specified	*1,178*	*175*	*438*	*466*	*295*	*0.0*	*0.0*	*6.4*	*-36.7*	*11.0*

Source: World Tourism Organization (UNWTO) ©   (Data as collected by UNWTO for TMT 2006 Edition)

III.3.6   Nicaragua   Central America

Profile

Nicaragua

Capital	Managua
Year of entry in UNWTO	1991
Area (1000 km²)	130
Population (2005, million)	5.5
Gross Domestic Product (GDP) (2005, US$ million)	4,910
GDP per capita (2005, US$)	850

Americas
Central America

GDP growth (real, %)
'-> 2004: 5.1;   2005: 4.0;   2006*: 3.7;   2007*: 4.3

	2003	2004	2005*	2004/2003	2005*/2004
International Arrivals					
Visitors (1000)	646	735	804	13.8	9.4
Tourists (overnight visitors) (1000)	526	615	712	16.9	15.9
- per 100 of inhabitants	10	11	13		
Same-day visitors (1000)	110	113	79	2.7	-30.1
Cruise passengers (1000)	10	7	13	-30.0	85.7
Tourism accommodation					
Number of rooms	4,418	4,753	5,335	7.6	12.2
Nights spent in collective establishments (1000)	653	747	752	14.4	0.7
by non-residents (inbound tourism)	412	527	529	27.9	0.4
by residents (domestic tourism)	241	220	223	-8.7	1.4
Nights spent in hotels and similar establishments (1000)	421	559	570	32.8	2.0
by non-residents (inbound tourism)	319	441	446	38.2	1.1
by residents (domestic tourism)	102	118	124	15.7	5.1
Outbound Tourism					
Trips abroad (1000)	562	701	740	24.7	5.6
- per 100 of inhabitants	11	13	14		
Receipts and Expenditure for International Tourism					
International Tourism Receipts (US$ million)	160	192	207	20.0	7.8
- per Tourist Arrival (US$)	304	312	291	2.6	-7.0
- per Visitor Arrival (US$)	248	261	257	5.5	-1.4
- per capita (US$)	30	36	38		
International Fare Receipts (US$ million)	4	4	4		
International Tourism Expenditure (US$ million)	75	89	90	18.7	1.1
- per trip (US$)	133	127	122	-4.9	-4.2
- per capita (US$)	14	17	16		
International Fare Expenditure (US$ million)	64	65	71	1.6	9.2
Δ International Tourism Balance (US$ million)	85	103	117		
Δ International Fare Balance (US$ million)	-60	-61	-67		

Source: World Tourism Organization (UNWTO)   (Data as collected by UNWTO for TMT 2006 Edition)

See annex for methodological notes and reference of external sources used.

World Tourism Organization ©

International Tourism by Origin

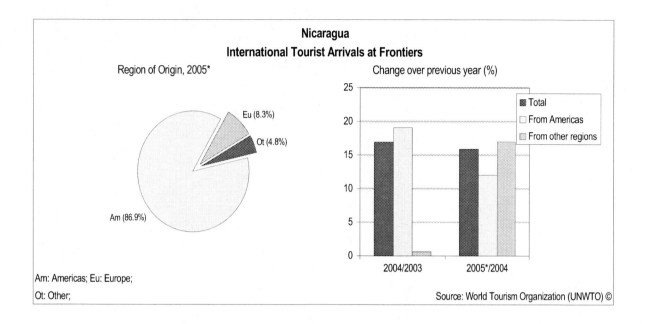

Nicaragua
International Tourist Arrivals at Frontiers

Region of Origin, 2005*

Change over previous year (%)

Eu (8.3%)
Ot (4.8%)
Am (86.9%)

Total
From Americas
From other regions

2004/2003   2005*/2004

Am: Americas; Eu: Europe;
Ot: Other;

Source: World Tourism Organization (UNWTO) ©

Nicaragua

International Tourist Arrivals at Frontiers (by nationality)

	1995	2000	2003	2004	2005*	Market share (%) 2000	Market share (%) 2005*	Growth rate (%) 04/03	Growth rate (%) 05*/04	Average per year (%) 2000-2005*
Total	**281,254**	**485,909**	**525,775**	**614,782**	**712,444**	**100**	**100**	**16.9**	**15.9**	**8.0**
From Americas	*247,452*	*437,062*	*464,176*	*552,846*	*619,305*	*89.9*	*86.9*	*19.1*	*12.0*	*7.2*
United States	43,327	84,399	8,857	131,865	147,331	17.4	20.7	1388.8	11.7	11.8
Honduras	76,201	122,631	107,365	126,916	139,134	25.2	19.5	18.2	9.6	2.6
Costa Rica	41,881	67,189	76,659	99,674	108,598	13.8	15.2	30.0	9.0	10.1
El Salvador	34,458	69,283	73,806	88,103	100,574	14.3	14.1	19.4	14.2	7.7
Guatemala	21,666	36,146	40,132	48,990	58,019	7.4	8.1	22.1	18.4	9.9
Canada	7,741	10,515	13,124	15,586	18,068	2.2	2.5	18.8	15.9	11.4
Panama	6,108	11,608	11,988	13,563	17,591	2.4	2.5	13.1	29.7	8.7
Mexico	4,136	9,406	117,156	10,331	11,550	1.9	1.6	-91.2	11.8	4.2
Argentina	1,164	1,979	2,672	2,735	2,886	0.4	0.4	2.4	5.5	7.8
Colombia	2,000	2,194	2,269	2,692	2,866	0.5	0.4	18.6	6.5	5.5
Venezuela	1,138	1,430	1,816	2,230	2,131	0.3	0.3	22.8	-4.4	8.3
Brazil	772	1,105	1,311	1,430	1,880	0.2	0.3	9.1	31.5	11.2
Bolivia	304	537	591	1,769	1,844	0.1	0.3	199.3	4.2	28.0
Chile	869	1,364	1,407	1,394	1,486	0.3	0.2	-0.9	6.6	1.7
Cuba	1,381	1,572	1,179	1,230	1,175	0.3	0.2	4.3	-4.5	-5.7
Peru	1,697	4,135	1,001	1,120	1,035	0.9	0.1	11.9	-7.6	-24.2
Ecuador	1,351	8,461	767	853	876	1.7	0.1	11.2	2.7	-36.5
Dominican Rp	564	1,880	667	663	628	0.4	0.1	-0.6	-5.3	-19.7
Other intraregional	694	1,228	1,409	1,702	1,633	0.3	0.2	20.8	-4.1	5.9
From other regions	*33,802*	*48,768*	*61,542*	*61,918*	*72,424*	*10.0*	*10.2*	*0.6*	*17.0*	*8.2*
United Kingdom	2,457	3,480	6,600	6,022	10,889	0.7	1.5	-8.8	80.8	25.6
Spain	6,409	8,162	9,039	9,954	9,612	1.7	1.3	10.1	-3.4	3.3
Germany	5,820	5,582	6,886	8,549	9,554	1.1	1.3	24.2	11.8	11.3
Netherlands	2,051	3,227	5,417	4,817	4,819	0.7	0.7	-11.1	0.0	8.4
Italy	2,565	3,919	4,363	4,632	4,377	0.8	0.6	6.2	-5.5	2.2
France	1,576	2,985	3,886	4,126	4,358	0.6	0.6	6.2	5.6	7.9
Switzerland	1,675	2,155	2,371	2,655	2,635	0.4	0.4	12.0	-0.8	4.1
Sweden	1,173	1,662	1,879	2,017	2,400	0.3	0.3	7.3	19.0	7.6
Australia	310	676	1,573	1,740	2,160	0.1	0.3	10.6	24.1	26.2
Philippines	850	2,032	2,074	797	2,034	0.4	0.3	-61.6	155.2	0.0
Korea, Republic of	364	1,110	1,547	1,783	2,016	0.2	0.3	15.3	13.1	12.7
Japan	1,165	1,734	1,908	1,837	1,806	0.4	0.3	-3.7	-1.7	0.8
Denmark	1,265	1,101	1,395	1,612	1,708	0.2	0.2	15.6	6.0	9.2
India	433	432	1,153	304	1,347	0.1	0.2	-73.6	343.1	25.5
Belgium	510	1,085	1,326	1,377	1,320	0.2	0.2	3.8	-4.1	4.0
Taiwan (pr. of China)	..	1,245	905	1,184	1,213	0.3	0.2	30.8	2.4	-0.5
Norway	583	886	995	1,055	1,163	0.2	0.2	6.0	10.2	5.6
Israel	217	535	971	1,171	1,052	0.1	0.1	20.6	-10.2	14.5
Austria	759	688	576	807	1,006	0.1	0.1	40.1	24.7	7.9
Indonesia	10	91	713	41	959	0.0	0.1	-94.2	2239.0	60.2
Ireland	203	399	566	566	719	0.1	0.1	0.0	27.0	12.5
China	1,020	1,805	1,418	438	522	0.4	0.1	-69.1	19.2	-22.0
Finland	326	420	465	543	497	0.1	0.1	16.8	-8.5	3.4
Other interregional	2,061	3,357	3,516	3,891	4,258	0.7	0.6	10.7	9.4	4.9
Nationals residing abroad	*..*	*..*	*..*	*..*	*20,630*		*2.9*			
Other World/Not specified	*..*	*79*	*57*	*18*	*85*	*0.0*	*0.0*	*-68.4*	*372.2*	*1.5*

Source: World Tourism Organization (UNWTO) ©

(Data as collected by UNWTO for TMT 2006 Edition)

World Tourism Organization ©

III.3.7   Panama   Central America

Profile

Panama

Americas
Central America

Capital	Panama City
Year of entry in UNWTO	1996
Area (1000 km²)	76
Population (2005, million)	3.1
Gross Domestic Product (GDP) (2005, US$ million)	15,467
GDP per capita (2005, US$)	4,794
GDP growth (real, %)	
'-> 2004: 7.6; 2005: 6.4; 2006*: 6.5; 2007*: 6.1	

	2003	2004	2005*	2004/2003	2005*/2004
International Arrivals					
Visitors (1000)	897	1,004	1,070	11.9	6.6
Tourists (overnight visitors) (1000)	566	621	702	9.8	13.0
- per 100 of inhabitants	19	20	22		
Same-day visitors (1000)	331	383	368	15.7	-3.9
Cruise passengers (1000)	224	290	255	29.5	-12.1
Tourism accommodation					
Number of rooms	14,488	14,898	15,700	2.8	5.4
Nights spent in hotels and similar establishments (1000)					
by non-residents (inbound tourism)	1,059	1,165	1,453	10.0	24.7
Outbound Tourism					
Trips abroad (1000)	227	256	285	12.8	11.3
- per 100 of inhabitants	7	8	9		
Receipts and Expenditure for International Tourism					
International Tourism Receipts (US$ million)	585	651	780	11.3	19.8
- per Tourist Arrival (US$)	1,034	1,048	1,111	1.4	6.0
- per Visitor Arrival (US$)	652	648	729	-0.6	12.4
- per capita (US$)	192	211	248		
International Fare Receipts (US$ million)	219	252	328	15.1	30.2
International Tourism Expenditure (US$ million)	208	239	271	15.0	13.5
- per trip (US$)	915	933	951	2.0	1.9
- per capita (US$)	68	77	86		
International Fare Expenditure (US$ million)	59	55	114	-6.8	107.5
Δ International Tourism Balance (US$ million)	377	412	509		
Δ International Fare Balance (US$ million)	160	197	214		

Source: World Tourism Organization (UNWTO)   (Data as collected by UNWTO for TMT 2006 Edition)
See annex for methodological notes and reference of external sources used.

International Tourism by Origin

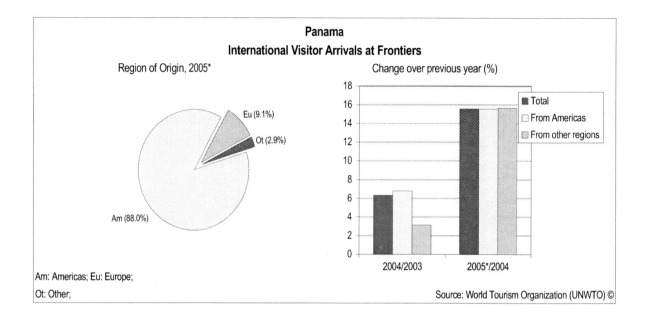

Panama
International Visitor Arrivals at Frontiers

Region of Origin, 2005*

Eu (9.1%)
Ot (2.9%)
Am (88.0%)

Change over previous year (%)

■ Total
☐ From Americas
▨ From other regions

2004/2003   2005*/2004

Am: Americas; Eu: Europe;
Ot: Other;

Source: World Tourism Organization (UNWTO) ©

Panama
International Visitor Arrivals at Frontiers (by residence)

	1995	2000	2003	2004	2005*	Market share (%) 2000	Market share (%) 2005*	Growth rate (%) 04/03	Growth rate (%) 05*/04	Average per year (%) 2000-2005*
Total	**320,824**	**395,551**	**468,686**	**498,415**	**576,050**	**100**	**100**	**6.3**	**15.6**	**7.8**
From Americas	*280,968*	*353,102*	*410,957*	*438,872*	*507,185*	*89.3*	*88.0*	*6.8*	*15.6*	*7.5*
United States	90,818	111,858	128,897	140,062	160,288	28.3	27.8	8.7	14.4	7.5
Colombia	56,581	70,823	90,697	93,510	108,628	17.9	18.9	3.1	16.2	8.9
Mexico	10,008	20,619	23,765	24,532	29,280	5.2	5.1	3.2	19.4	7.3
Ecuador	16,390	14,298	20,252	22,391	25,903	3.6	4.5	10.6	15.7	12.6
Costa Rica	17,273	21,962	20,378	21,459	25,455	5.6	4.4	5.3	18.6	3.0
Canada	5,236	5,872	14,297	16,911	19,660	1.5	3.4	18.3	16.3	27.3
Venezuela	8,598	16,956	14,607	16,249	18,892	4.3	3.3	11.2	16.3	2.2
Guatemala	6,466	10,289	12,121	12,400	14,349	2.6	2.5	2.3	15.7	6.9
Peru	6,233	7,124	10,514	11,058	12,592	1.8	2.2	5.2	13.9	12.1
Argentina	4,283	7,394	8,950	10,108	11,629	1.9	2.0	12.9	15.0	9.5
Brazil	4,111	4,726	7,698	8,256	9,701	1.2	1.7	7.2	17.5	15.5
El Salvador	5,547	5,628	7,624	8,031	9,279	1.4	1.6	5.3	15.5	10.5
Puerto Rico	4,979	5,716	7,526	8,129	8,625	1.4	1.5	8.0	6.1	8.6
Chile	2,727	5,335	6,946	7,406	8,150	1.3	1.4	6.6	10.0	8.8
Dominican Rp	10,583	9,229	6,110	5,923	7,396	2.3	1.3	-3.1	24.9	-4.3
Honduras	3,879	4,785	5,470	6,027	6,584	1.2	1.1	10.2	9.2	6.6
Nicaragua	5,477	5,666	5,341	5,304	6,056	1.4	1.1	-0.7	14.2	1.3
Jamaica	8,988	8,314	4,576	4,629	5,593	2.1	1.0	1.2	20.8	-7.6
Other intraregional	12,791	16,508	15,188	16,487	19,125	4.2	3.3	8.6	16.0	3.0
From other regions	*39,856*	*42,449*	*57,729*	*59,543*	*68,865*	*10.7*	*12.0*	*3.1*	*15.7*	*10.2*
Spain	10,536	8,188	9,196	9,569	10,838	2.1	1.9	4.1	13.3	5.8
France	2,105	2,475	6,766	6,881	7,289	0.6	1.3	1.7	5.9	24.1
Italy	3,326	2,970	4,945	5,198	6,617	0.8	1.1	5.1	27.3	17.4
United Kingdom	2,215	3,288	4,197	4,820	5,828	0.8	1.0	14.8	20.9	12.1
Germany	2,568	3,378	4,091	4,222	4,745	0.9	0.8	3.2	12.4	7.0
Japan	3,605	3,049	3,105	3,150	3,735	0.8	0.6	1.4	18.6	4.1
Israel	1,316	1,906	2,140	2,202	2,561	0.5	0.4	2.9	16.3	6.1
Switzerland	1,190	1,485	1,903	1,999	2,337	0.4	0.4	5.0	16.9	9.5
Netherlands	1,637	1,349	1,782	1,888	1,994	0.3	0.3	5.9	5.6	8.1
Taiwan (pr. of China)	1,952	1,531	1,439	1,352	1,443	0.4	0.3	-6.0	6.7	-1.2
Australia	176	461	842	915	1,073	0.1	0.2	8.7	17.3	18.4
Greece	714	672	599	570	625	0.2	0.1	-4.8	9.6	-1.4
New Zealand	52	141	221	222	254	0.0	0.0	0.5	14.4	12.5
South Africa	32	96	126	134	175	0.0	0.0	6.3	30.6	12.8
Egypt	60	54	52	35	41	0.0	0.0	-32.7	17.1	-5.4
Other Africa	331	222	228	201	215	0.1	0.0	-11.8	7.0	-0.6
Other Asia	4,652	5,936	8,332	8,246	9,555	1.5	1.7	-1.0	15.9	10.0
Other Europe	3,355	5,193	7,736	7,905	9,505	1.3	1.7	2.2	20.2	12.9
Other Oceania	34	55	29	34	35	0.0	0.0	17.2	2.9	-8.6

Source: World Tourism Organization (UNWTO) ©   (Data as collected by UNWTO for TMT 2006 Edition)

Note: Total number of visitors broken down by permanent residence who arrived in Panama at Tocument international airport and Paso Canoa Border Post

III.4   South America

III.4.1   Argentina   South America

Promotional: www.turismo.gov.ar
Institutional/corporate: www.turismo.gov.ar
Research and data: www.turismo.gov.ar/institucionales/estadística

Profile

Argentina

Capital	Buenos Aires
Year of entry in UNWTO	1975
Area (1000 km²)	2,780
Population (2005, million)	39.5
Gross Domestic Product (GDP) (2005, US$ million)	181,549
GDP per capita (2005, US$)	4,799
GDP growth (real, %)	

Americas
South America

'-> 2004: 9.0;   2005: 9.2;   2006*: 8.0;   2007*: 6.0

	2003	2004	2005*	2004/2003	2005*/2004
International Arrivals					
Tourists (overnight visitors) (1000)	2,995	3,457	3,895	15.4	12.7
- per 100 of inhabitants	8	9	10		
Tourism accommodation					
Number of rooms	176,685	182,444	187,425	3.3	2.7
Nights spent in collective establishments (1000)					
by non-residents (inbound tourism)	31,148	36,576	40,668	17.4	11.2
Nights spent in hotels and similar establishments (1000)			38,051		
by non-residents (inbound tourism)	..	..	9,482		
by residents (domestic tourism)	..	..	28,569		
Outbound Tourism					
Trips abroad (1000)	3,088	3,904	4,002	26.4	2.5
- per 100 of inhabitants	8	10	10		
Receipts and Expenditure for International Tourism					
International Tourism Receipts (US$ million)	2,006	2,235	2,753	11.4	23.2
- per Tourist Arrival (US$)	670	647	707	-3.4	9.3
- per capita (US$)	52	57	70		
International Fare Receipts (US$ million)	300	427	488	42.2	14.3
International Tourism Expenditure (US$ million)	2,511	2,604	2,817	3.7	8.2
- per trip (US$)	813	667	704	-18.0	5.5
- per capita (US$)	65	67	71		
International Fare Expenditure (US$ million)	486	600	755	23.3	25.9
Δ International Tourism Balance (US$ million)	-506	-369	-64		
Δ International Fare Balance (US$ million)	-186	-173	-268		

Source: World Tourism Organization (UNWTO)   (Data as collected by UNWTO for TMT 2006 Edition)

See annex for methodological notes and reference of external sources used.

International Tourism by Origin

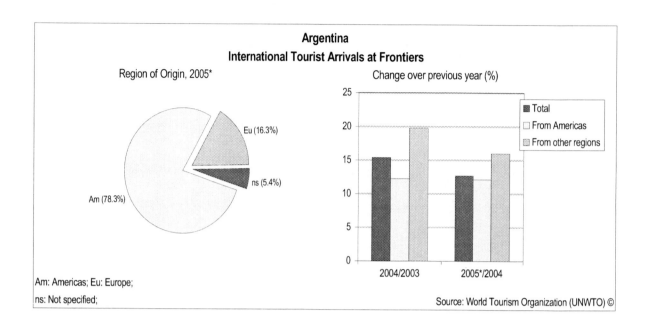

Source: World Tourism Organization (UNWTO) ©

Argentina
International Tourist Arrivals at Frontiers (by nationality)

	1995	2000	2003	2004	2005*	Market share (%)		Growth rate (%)		Average per year (%)
						2000	2005*	04/03	05*/04	2000-2005*
Total	**2,288,694**	**2,909,468**	**2,995,271**	**3,456,526**	**3,895,396**	**100**	**100**	**15.4**	**12.7**	**6.0**
From Americas	*1,988,119*	*2,480,150*	*2,424,735*	*2,721,888*	*3,052,035*	*85.2*	*78.3*	*12.3*	*12.1*	*4.2*
Chile	465,743	571,334	767,758	848,162	978,475	19.6	25.1	10.5	15.4	11.4
Brazil	316,784	451,368	350,298	418,865	453,346	15.5	11.6	19.6	8.2	0.1
Uruguay	387,328	488,037	363,107	370,428	438,153	16.8	11.2	2.0	18.3	-2.1
All North America	178,180	252,384	224,472	302,255	371,407	8.7	9.5	34.7	22.9	8.0
Paraguay	415,945	499,835	429,792	346,266	302,174	17.2	7.8	-19.4	-12.7	-9.6
Bolivia	123,699	95,072	59,678	145,244	151,628	3.3	3.9	143.4	4.4	9.8
Other Americas	100,440	122,120	229,630	290,668	356,852	4.2	9.2	26.6	22.8	23.9
From other regions	*248,348*	*354,050*	*455,998*	*546,184*	*633,536*	*12.2*	*16.3*	*19.8*	*16.0*	*12.3*
All Europe	248,348	354,050	455,998	546,184	633,536	12.2	16.3	19.8	16.0	12.3
Other World/Not specified	*52,227*	*75,268*	*114,538*	*188,454*	*209,825*	*2.6*	*5.4*	*64.5*	*11.3*	*22.8*

Source: World Tourism Organization (UNWTO) ©   (Data as collected by UNWTO for TMT 2006 Edition)

World Tourism Organization ©

III.4.2   Bolivia   South America

Promotional: www.turismobolivia.bo
Institutional/corporate: www.desarrollo.gov.bo
Research and data: www.turismobolivia.bo

Profile

Bolivia

Capital	La Paz
Year of entry in UNWTO	1975
Area (1000 km²)	1,099
Population (2005, million)	8.9
Gross Domestic Product (GDP) (2005, US$ million)	9,358
GDP per capita (2005, US$)	993

Americas
South America

GDP growth (real, %)
'-> 2004: 3.9;   2005: 4.1;   2006*: 4.1;   2007*: 3.9

	2003	2004	2005*	2004/2003	2005*/2004
International Arrivals					
Tourists (overnight visitors) (1000)	420	478	504	13.8	5.4
- per 100 of inhabitants	5	5	6		
Tourism accommodation					
Number of rooms	19,800	20,862	20,949	5.4	0.4
Nights spent in hotels and similar establishments (1000)	2,410	2,553	2,743	5.9	7.4
by non-residents (inbound tourism)	1,006	1,030	1,099	2.4	6.7
by residents (domestic tourism)	1,404	1,523	1,644	8.5	7.9
Outbound Tourism					
Trips abroad (1000)	305	331	312	8.5	-5.7
- per 100 of inhabitants	4	4	4		
Receipts and Expenditure for International Tourism					
International Tourism Receipts (US$ million)	167	192	205	15.1	7.0
- per Tourist Arrival (US$)	396	401	407	1.2	1.5
- per capita (US$)	19	22	23		
International Fare Receipts (US$ million)	74	89	103	19.1	16.0
International Tourism Expenditure (US$ million)	139	192	205	38.4	7.0
- per trip (US$)	454	579	657	27.5	13.5
- per capita (US$)	16	22	23		
International Fare Expenditure (US$ million)	56	65	71	16.2	8.9
Δ International Tourism Balance (US$ million)	28				
Δ International Fare Balance (US$ million)	18	23	32		

Source: World Tourism Organization (UNWTO)   (Data as collected by UNWTO for TMT 2006 Edition)

See annex for methodological notes and reference of external sources used.

International Tourism by Origin

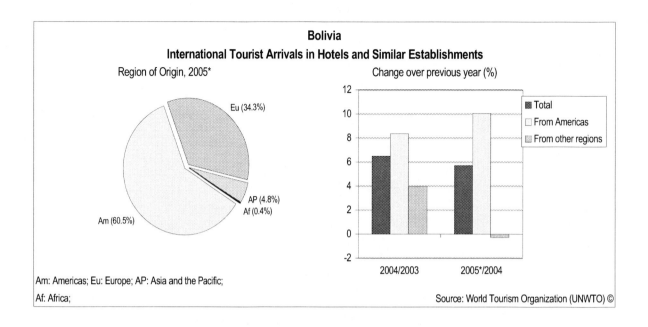

Bolivia

International Tourist Arrivals in Hotels and Similar Establishments

Region of Origin, 2005*

Eu (34.3%)
AP (4.8%)
Af (0.4%)
Am (60.5%)

Change over previous year (%)

Total
From Americas
From other regions

2004/2003   2005*/2004

Am: Americas; Eu: Europe; AP: Asia and the Pacific;
Af: Africa;

Source: World Tourism Organization (UNWTO) ©

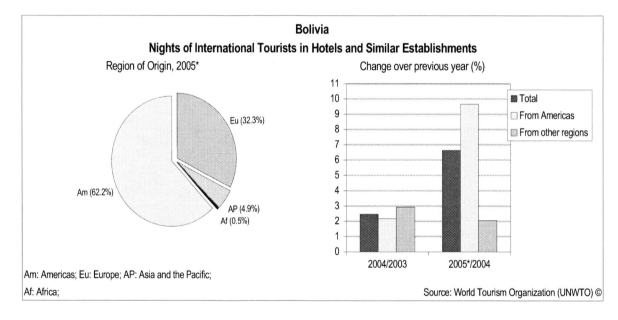

Bolivia

Nights of International Tourists in Hotels and Similar Establishments

Region of Origin, 2005*

Eu (32.3%)
Am (62.2%)
AP (4.9%)
Af (0.5%)

Change over previous year (%)

Total
From Americas
From other regions

2004/2003   2005*/2004

Am: Americas; Eu: Europe; AP: Asia and the Pacific;
Af: Africa;

Source: World Tourism Organization (UNWTO) ©

Bolivia

International Tourist Arrivals in Hotels and Similar Establishments (by nationality)

	1995	2000	2003	2004	2005*	Market share (%) 2000	Market share (%) 2005*	Growth rate (%) 04/03	Growth rate (%) 05*/04	Average per year (%) 2000-2005*
Total	**350,687**	**381,077**	**367,036**	**390,888**	**413,267**	**100**	**100**	**6.5**	**5.7**	**1.6**
From Americas	*211,866*	*219,636*	*209,715*	*227,280*	*250,107*	*57.6*	*60.5*	*8.4*	*10.0*	*2.6*
Peru	56,664	50,162	62,164	68,739	77,380	13.2	18.7	10.6	12.6	9.1
Argentina	35,374	43,818	31,242	36,320	41,610	11.5	10.1	16.3	14.6	-1.0
United States	35,511	44,157	36,801	38,066	37,758	11.6	9.1	3.4	-0.8	-3.1
Brazil	32,533	24,268	23,810	29,745	32,400	6.4	7.8	24.9	8.9	6.0
Chile	23,619	22,431	17,152	14,948	19,234	5.9	4.7	-12.8	28.7	-3.0
Colombia	3,388	5,890	7,503	8,286	8,615	1.5	2.1	10.4	4.0	7.9
Canada	6,150	7,861	7,429	8,120	8,297	2.1	2.0	9.3	2.2	1.1
Mexico	3,446	4,077	5,026	6,016	5,983	1.1	1.4	19.7	-0.5	8.0
Ecuador	2,328	4,580	6,106	4,788	5,315	1.2	1.3	-21.6	11.0	3.0
Paraguay	3,433	2,680	3,498	3,486	3,849	0.7	0.9	-0.3	10.4	7.5
Uruguay	3,421	3,301	2,515	2,591	2,398	0.9	0.6	3.0	-7.4	-6.2
Venezuela	1,853	1,732	1,913	1,944	2,360	0.5	0.6	1.6	21.4	6.4
Other Americas	4,146	4,679	4,556	4,231	4,908	1.2	1.2	-7.1	16.0	1.0
From other regions	*138,821*	*161,441*	*157,321*	*163,608*	*163,160*	*42.4*	*39.5*	*4.0*	*-0.3*	*0.2*
France	16,145	21,047	24,356	24,416	25,167	5.5	6.1	0.2	3.1	3.6
United Kingdom	12,705	18,002	20,434	20,616	20,801	4.7	5.0	0.9	0.9	2.9
Germany	24,982	23,583	19,056	19,804	20,308	6.2	4.9	3.9	2.5	-2.9
Spain	9,917	9,609	10,964	12,140	11,974	2.5	2.9	10.7	-1.4	4.5
Israel	11,466	9,950	12,003	12,149	9,405	2.6	2.3	1.2	-22.6	-1.1
Netherlands	10,253	13,930	10,444	9,764	8,625	3.7	2.1	-6.5	-11.7	-9.1
All Oceania	4,015	7,822	6,125	7,578	8,589	2.1	2.1	23.7	13.3	1.9
Switzerland	9,696	9,689	8,613	8,531	8,519	2.5	2.1	-1.0	-0.1	-2.5
Italy	7,434	7,736	7,631	8,480	8,101	2.0	2.0	11.1	-4.5	0.9
Japan	7,059	7,032	6,379	7,469	7,226	1.8	1.7	17.1	-3.3	0.5
Sweden	2,082	2,825	2,747	3,070	3,084	0.7	0.7	11.8	0.5	1.8
All Africa	733	1,117	1,117	1,278	1,661	0.3	0.4	14.4	30.0	8.3
Other Asia	2,829	3,300	2,787	3,870	4,063	0.9	1.0	38.9	5.0	4.2
Other Europe	19,505	25,799	24,665	24,443	25,637	6.8	6.2	-0.9	4.9	-0.1

Source: World Tourism Organization (UNWTO) ©   (Data as collected by UNWTO for TMT 2006 Edition)

Bolivia

Nights of International Tourists in Hotels and Similar Establishments (by nationality)

	1995	2000	2003	2004	2005*	Market share (%)		Growth rate (%)		Average per year (%)
						2000	2005*	04/03	05*/04	2000-2005*
Total	**975,780**	**990,751**	**1,005,581**	**1,030,479**	**1,099,027**	**100**	**100**	**2.5**	**6.7**	**2.1**
From Americas	*614,234*	*606,560*	*610,409*	*623,735*	*683,919*	*61.2*	*62.2*	*2.2*	*9.6*	*2.4*
Peru	127,791	123,487	139,944	151,483	178,006	12.5	16.2	8.2	17.5	7.6
Argentina	109,012	119,217	107,444	105,751	121,406	12.0	11.0	-1.6	14.8	0.4
United States	106,901	124,298	106,983	111,598	104,246	12.5	9.5	4.3	-6.6	-3.5
Brazil	110,047	70,579	71,951	84,666	91,425	7.1	8.3	17.7	8.0	5.3
Chile	66,034	56,325	50,703	39,783	47,869	5.7	4.4	-21.5	20.3	-3.2
Colombia	11,946	21,005	27,802	29,484	32,685	2.1	3.0	6.0	10.9	9.2
Canada	18,557	20,174	18,599	20,395	21,046	2.0	1.9	9.7	3.2	0.8
Paraguay	11,032	9,078	12,635	13,738	17,138	0.9	1.6	8.7	24.7	13.6
Ecuador	9,340	14,233	25,554	18,686	16,208	1.4	1.5	-26.9	-13.3	2.6
Mexico	10,587	11,911	12,523	15,089	15,526	1.2	1.4	20.5	2.9	5.4
Uruguay	10,013	10,116	9,199	8,392	8,532	1.0	0.8	-8.8	1.7	-3.3
Venezuela	6,433	6,902	9,411	7,155	7,530	0.7	0.7	-24.0	5.2	1.8
Other Americas	16,541	19,235	17,661	17,515	22,302	1.9	2.0	-0.8	27.3	3.0
From other regions	*361,546*	*384,191*	*395,172*	*406,744*	*415,108*	*38.8*	*37.8*	*2.9*	*2.1*	*1.6*
France	35,479	43,848	52,302	51,227	52,622	4.4	4.8	-2.1	2.7	3.7
Germany	62,105	52,028	46,253	45,903	46,955	5.3	4.3	-0.8	2.3	-2.0
United Kingdom	33,869	40,866	45,877	46,951	46,838	4.1	4.3	2.3	-0.2	2.8
Spain	27,314	28,919	33,010	38,192	39,000	2.9	3.5	15.7	2.1	6.2
Israel	32,232	25,535	37,184	38,668	33,484	2.6	3.0	4.0	-13.4	5.6
Netherlands	25,093	29,679	23,952	23,106	22,165	3.0	2.0	-3.5	-4.1	-5.7
Japan	22,920	18,110	22,333	22,519	21,843	1.8	2.0	0.8	-3.0	3.8
Switzerland	23,925	22,758	20,059	20,611	21,270	2.3	1.9	2.8	3.2	-1.3
Italy	19,981	21,865	19,466	20,901	21,208	2.2	1.9	7.4	1.5	-0.6
All Oceania	10,212	17,584	13,735	16,821	19,490	1.8	1.8	22.5	15.9	2.1
Sweden	6,002	7,322	7,201	9,405	9,100	0.7	0.8	30.6	-3.2	4.4
All Africa	2,378	3,269	3,801	4,007	6,013	0.3	0.5	5.4	50.1	13.0
Other Asia	8,544	9,661	8,374	10,912	12,686	1.0	1.2	30.3	16.3	5.6
Other Europe	51,492	62,747	61,625	57,521	62,434	6.3	5.7	-6.7	8.5	-0.1

Source: World Tourism Organization (UNWTO) ©   (Data as collected by UNWTO for TMT 2006 Edition)
Note: Hotel nights in the regional capitals

World Tourism Organization ©

III.4.3   Brazil   South America

Promotional: www.turismo.gov.br
Institutional/corporate: www.turismo.gov.br
Research and data: www.turismo.gov.br

Profile

Brazil

Capital	Brasilia
Year of entry in UNWTO	1975
Area (1000 km²)	8,547
Population (2005, million)	186
Gross Domestic Product (GDP) (2005, US$ million)	795,666
GDP per capita (2005, US$)	4,320

Americas
South America

GDP growth (real, %)
'-> 2004: 4.9;   2005: 2.3;   2006*: 3.6;   2007*: 4.0

	2003	2004	2005*	2004/2003	2005*/2004
International Arrivals					
Tourists (overnight visitors) (1000)	4,133	4,794	5,358	16.0	11.8
- per 100 of inhabitants	2	3	3		
Outbound Tourism					
Trips abroad (1000)	3,225	3,738	4,696	15.9	25.6
- per 100 of inhabitants	2	2	3		
Receipts and Expenditure for International Tourism					
International Tourism Receipts (US$ million)	2,479	3,222	3,861	30.0	19.8
- per Tourist Arrival (US$)	600	672	721	12.1	7.2
- per capita (US$)	14	18	21		
International Fare Receipts (US$ million)	194	167	308	-13.9	84.4
International Tourism Expenditure (US$ million)	2,261	2,871	4,720	27.0	64.4
- per trip (US$)	701	768	1,005	9.6	30.8
- per capita (US$)	12	16	25		
International Fare Expenditure (US$ million)	613	881	1,185	43.7	34.5
Δ International Tourism Balance (US$ million)	218	351	-858		
Δ International Fare Balance (US$ million)	-419	-714	-877		

Source: World Tourism Organization (UNWTO)   (Data as collected by UNWTO for TMT 2006 Edition)
See annex for methodological notes and reference of external sources used.

International Tourism by Origin

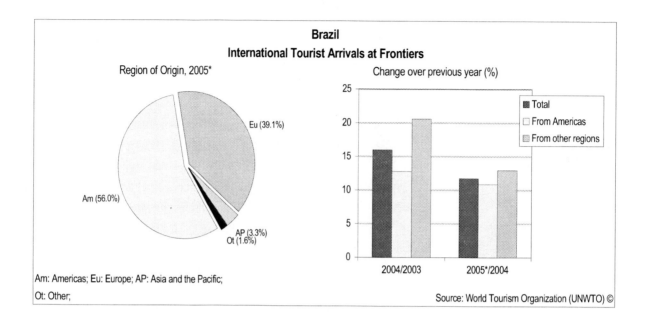

Brazil
International Tourist Arrivals at Frontiers

Region of Origin, 2005*

Eu (39.1%)
Am (56.0%)
AP (3.3%)
Ot (1.6%)

Change over previous year (%)

Total
From Americas
From other regions

2004/2003   2005*/2004

Am: Americas; Eu: Europe; AP: Asia and the Pacific;
Ot: Other;

Source: World Tourism Organization (UNWTO) ©

Brazil
International Tourist Arrivals at Frontiers (by residence)

	1995	2000	2003	2004	2005*	Market share (%) 2000	Market share (%) 2005*	Growth rate (%) 04/03	Growth rate (%) 05*/04	Average per year (%) 2000-2005*
Total	**1,991,416**	**5,313,463**	**4,132,847**	**4,793,703**	**5,358,170**	**100**	**100**	**16.0**	**11.8**	**0.2**
From Americas	*1,374,111*	*3,803,069*	*2,396,832*	*2,703,442*	*2,998,060*	*71.6*	*56.0*	*12.8*	*10.9*	*-4.6*
Argentina	657,942	1,744,004	786,568	922,484	992,299	32.8	18.5	17.3	7.6	-10.7
United States	224,577	648,026	668,668	705,993	793,559	12.2	14.8	5.6	12.4	4.1
Uruguay	200,423	403,896	270,251	309,732	341,647	7.6	6.4	14.6	10.3	-3.3
Paraguay	90,716	371,873	198,170	204,762	249,030	7.0	4.6	3.3	21.6	-7.7
Chile	63,900	172,807	126,591	155,026	169,953	3.3	3.2	22.5	9.6	-0.3
Canada	16,707	54,916	63,183	66,895	75,100	1.0	1.4	5.9	12.3	6.5
Mexico	13,283	41,328	55,556	65,707	73,118	0.8	1.4	18.3	11.3	12.1
Bolivia	20,737	134,640	54,865	60,239	68,670	2.5	1.3	9.8	14.0	-12.6
Peru	14,997	51,627	38,948	56,647	60,251	1.0	1.1	45.4	6.4	3.1
Venezuela	29,490	52,929	39,234	44,257	48,598	1.0	0.9	12.8	9.8	-1.7
Colombia	13,484	50,065	36,283	42,163	47,230	0.9	0.9	16.2	12.0	-1.2
French Guiana	3,435	22,728	12,227	14,244	17,372	0.4	0.3	16.5	22.0	-5.2
Ecuador	4,685	14,573	11,990	13,343	15,149	0.3	0.3	11.3	13.5	0.8
Panama	1,952	4,668	7,217	9,586	10,516	0.1	0.2	32.8	9.7	17.6
Costa Rica	2,563	5,356	4,800	6,741	7,202	0.1	0.1	40.4	6.8	6.1
Puerto Rico	897	2,104	4,188	2,751	3,595	0.0	0.1	-34.3	30.7	11.3
Guyana	4,359	10,322	2,321	3,221	3,248	0.2	0.1	38.8	0.8	-20.6
Suriname	1,894	6,705	2,441	2,899	2,755	0.1	0.1	18.8	-5.0	-16.3
Other Central America	8,070	10,502	13,331	16,752	18,768	0.2	0.4	25.7	12.0	12.3
From other regions	*607,099*	*1,487,793*	*1,730,283*	*2,086,606*	*2,357,416*	*28.0*	*44.0*	*20.6*	*13.0*	*9.6*
Portugal	52,183	147,143	229,594	336,988	357,640	2.8	6.7	46.8	6.1	19.4
Germany	102,106	290,335	283,615	294,989	308,598	5.5	5.8	4.0	4.6	1.2
Italy	84,001	202,903	221,190	276,563	303,878	3.8	5.7	25.0	9.9	8.4
France	55,257	165,117	211,347	224,160	252,099	3.1	4.7	6.1	12.5	8.8
Spain	59,502	110,765	122,641	155,421	172,979	2.1	3.2	26.7	11.3	9.3
United Kingdom	38,520	127,903	138,281	150,336	169,514	2.4	3.2	8.7	12.8	5.8
Netherlands	20,851	42,428	83,999	102,480	109,708	0.8	2.0	22.0	7.1	20.9
Switzerland	33,505	67,947	69,644	83,113	89,789	1.3	1.7	19.3	8.0	5.7
Japan	30,219	40,905	51,387	60,806	68,066	0.8	1.3	18.3	11.9	10.7
Sweden	8,081	24,457	26,939	37,809	45,764	0.5	0.9	40.4	21.0	13.4
South Africa	9,167	13,917	26,963	32,415	36,139	0.3	0.7	20.2	11.5	21.0
Finland	..	..	..	..	33,557		0.6			
Belgium	12,448	20,187	28,237	28,549	32,741	0.4	0.6	1.1	14.7	10.2
Israel	7,569	14,651	20,865	26,095	28,136	0.3	0.5	25.1	7.8	13.9
Norway	4,231	14,820	15,631	23,560	26,812	0.3	0.5	50.7	13.8	12.6
Korea, Republic of	9,547	19,238	19,498	21,353	24,315	0.4	0.5	9.5	13.9	4.8
Austria	12,570	22,868	16,745	21,034	22,558	0.4	0.4	25.6	7.2	-0.3
Australia	6,330	18,388	17,798	18,454	20,949	0.3	0.4	3.7	13.5	2.6
Denmark	6,984	18,593	19,722	15,555	19,672	0.3	0.4	-21.1	26.5	1.1
Poland	..	..	..	..	19,535		0.4			
China	7,749	17,881	10,714	16,305	18,017	0.3	0.3	52.2	10.5	0.2
Hungary	..	..	..	..	16,364		0.3			
Angola	3,795	9,368	8,850	13,679	14,226	0.2	0.3	54.6	4.0	8.7
Other interregional	42,484	97,979	106,623	146,942	166,360	1.8	3.1	37.8	13.2	11.2
Other World/Not specified	*10,206*	*22,601*	*5,732*	*3,655*	*2,694*	*0.4*	*0.1*	*-36.2*	*-26.3*	*-34.6*

Source: World Tourism Organization (UNWTO) ©   (Data as collected by UNWTO for TMT 2006 Edition)

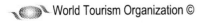 World Tourism Organization ©

III.4.4   Chile   South America

Promotional: www.sernatur.cl
Institutional/corporate: www.sernatur.cl
Research and data: www.sernatur.cl

Profile

Chile

Capital	Santiago de Chile
Year of entry in UNWTO	1975
Area (1000 km²)	757
Population (2005, million)	16.0
Gross Domestic Product (GDP) (2005, US$ million)	115,314
GDP per capita (2005, US$)	7,124

Americas

South America

GDP growth (real, %)

'-> 2004: 6.2;   2005: 6.3;   2006*: 5.2;   2007*: 5.5

	2003	2004	2005*	2004/2003	2005*/2004
International Arrivals					
Tourists (overnight visitors) (1000)	1,614	1,785	2,027	10.6	13.6
- per 100 of inhabitants	10	11	13		
Same-day visitors (1000)	448	856	901	91.1	5.3
Tourism accommodation					
Number of rooms	52,362	53,794	53,335	2.7	-0.9
Nights spent in hotels and similar establishments (1000)	6,826	6,837	8,676	0.2	26.9
by non-residents (inbound tourism)	1,947	2,086	2,877	7.1	37.9
by residents (domestic tourism)	4,879	4,751	5,799	-2.6	22.1
Outbound Tourism					
Trips abroad (1000)	2,100	2,343	2,651	11.6	13.1
- per 100 of inhabitants	13	15	17		
Receipts and Expenditure for International Tourism					
International Tourism Receipts (US$ million)	883	1,150	1,256	30.1	9.3
- per Tourist Arrival (US$)	547	644	620	17.6	-3.8
- per capita (US$)	56	73	79		
International Fare Receipts (US$ million)	427	477	523	11.7	9.6
International Tourism Expenditure (US$ million)	850	977	1,057	14.9	8.2
- per trip (US$)	405	417	399	3.0	-4.4
- per capita (US$)	54	62	66		
International Fare Expenditure (US$ million)	259	273	324	5.4	18.7
Δ International Tourism Balance (US$ million)	33	172	199		
Δ International Fare Balance (US$ million)	168	204	199		

Source: World Tourism Organization (UNWTO)   (Data as collected by UNWTO for TMT 2006 Edition)

See annex for methodological notes and reference of external sources used.

International Tourism by Origin

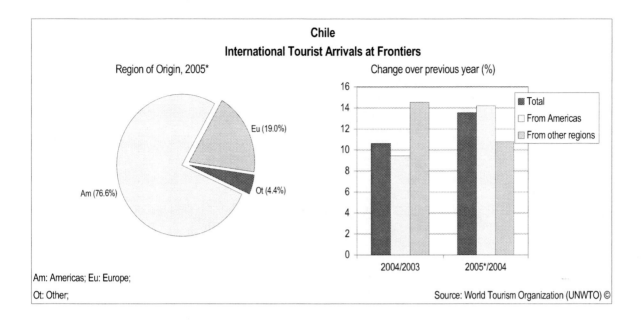

Chile
International Tourist Arrivals at Frontiers

Region of Origin, 2005*

Eu (19.0%)
Am (76.6%)
Ot (4.4%)

Change over previous year (%)

Total
From Americas
From other regions

2004/2003   2005*/2004

Am: Americas; Eu: Europe;
Ot: Other;

Source: World Tourism Organization (UNWTO) ©

Chile

International Tourist Arrivals at Frontiers (by nationality)

	1995	2000	2003	2004	2005*	Market share (%) 2000	2005*	Growth rate (%) 04/03	05*/04	Average per year (%) 2000-2005*
Total	**1,539,593**	**1,742,407**	**1,613,523**	**1,785,024**	**2,027,082**	**100**	**100**	**10.6**	**13.6**	**3.1**
From Americas	*1,345,445*	*1,456,648*	*1,242,956*	*1,360,342*	*1,553,381*	*83.6*	*76.6*	*9.4*	*14.2*	*1.3*
Argentina	788,119	858,709	536,010	576,817	606,567	49.3	29.9	7.6	5.2	-6.7
Peru	182,208	151,863	163,718	186,088	221,384	8.7	10.9	13.7	19.0	7.8
United States	90,695	134,117	147,321	166,321	183,833	7.7	9.1	12.9	10.5	6.5
Bolivia	100,247	110,427	132,312	134,709	177,278	6.3	8.7	1.8	31.6	9.9
Brazil	62,242	72,840	100,341	119,271	167,291	4.2	8.3	18.9	40.3	18.1
Mexico	10,353	19,631	32,088	34,275	36,325	1.1	1.8	6.8	6.0	13.1
Colombia	8,699	15,929	26,724	29,596	33,740	0.9	1.7	10.7	14.0	16.2
Canada	13,771	18,888	21,417	28,118	33,618	1.1	1.7	31.3	19.6	12.2
Uruguay	31,025	22,747	20,227	23,581	24,954	1.3	1.2	16.6	5.8	1.9
Ecuador	8,166	14,325	26,392	23,674	23,755	0.8	1.2	-10.3	0.3	10.6
Paraguay	20,929	14,242	9,590	9,226	13,497	0.8	0.7	-3.8	46.3	-1.1
Venezuela	7,927	9,020	10,540	11,574	13,417	0.5	0.7	9.8	15.9	8.3
Costa Rica	..	2,643	3,141	3,351	3,533	0.2	0.2	6.7	5.4	6.0
Panama	1,178	1,655	2,715	2,949	3,075	0.1	0.2	8.6	4.3	13.2
Guatemala	1,307	1,102	1,670	1,631	2,076	0.1	0.1	-2.3	27.3	13.5
Cuba	..	2,107	1,519	1,669	1,846	0.1	0.1	9.9	10.6	-2.6
Other intraregional	18,579	6,403	7,231	7,492	7,192	0.4	0.4	3.6	-4.0	2.4
From other regions	*192,908*	*283,190*	*369,032*	*422,727*	*468,296*	*16.3*	*23.1*	*14.6*	*10.8*	*10.6*
Germany	33,340	43,936	54,402	58,857	68,225	2.5	3.4	8.2	15.9	9.2
Spain	23,904	36,290	42,841	50,472	60,078	2.1	3.0	17.8	19.0	10.6
France	18,008	32,809	42,644	48,098	53,492	1.9	2.6	12.8	11.2	10.3
United Kingdom	16,019	28,602	50,984	50,286	53,021	1.6	2.6	-1.4	5.4	13.1
Australia	7,810	13,556	23,384	26,703	31,121	0.8	1.5	14.2	16.5	18.1
Italy	14,133	20,041	21,506	25,986	26,060	1.2	1.3	20.8	0.3	5.4
Israel	4,158	9,956	14,871	17,330	18,715	0.6	0.9	16.5	8.0	13.5
Switzerland	8,131	11,647	14,344	16,694	16,659	0.7	0.8	16.4	-0.2	7.4
Netherlands	6,019	10,324	12,544	12,243	13,997	0.6	0.7	-2.4	14.3	6.3
Japan	7,843	11,628	12,409	14,335	13,882	0.7	0.7	15.5	-3.2	3.6
Sweden	7,779	9,600	11,581	11,523	13,113	0.6	0.6	-0.5	13.8	6.4
Belgium	3,878	5,986	7,117	8,448	9,096	0.3	0.4	18.7	7.7	8.7
Austria	3,226	4,919	5,642	6,639	7,359	0.3	0.4	17.7	10.8	8.4
New Zealand	1,468	2,940	5,180	6,459	6,979	0.2	0.3	24.7	8.1	18.9
China	187	2,314	2,857	6,356	6,397	0.1	0.3	122.5	0.6	22.6
Ireland	723	2,154	4,677	4,976	6,260	0.1	0.3	6.4	25.8	23.8
Korea, Republic of	2,114	2,707	4,291	6,181	5,951	0.2	0.3	44.0	-3.7	17.1
Norway	2,544	3,975	4,912	5,335	5,527	0.2	0.3	8.6	3.6	6.8
Philippines	110	958	1,907	5,024	5,356	0.1	0.3	163.5	6.6	41.1
Denmark	2,564	2,963	3,694	4,527	5,349	0.2	0.3	22.6	18.2	12.5
Portugal	1,246	2,013	2,770	3,344	4,085	0.1	0.2	20.7	22.2	15.2
India	896	1,376	1,647	3,148	3,474	0.1	0.2	91.1	10.4	20.3
Finland	1,471	2,136	2,902	3,198	3,018	0.1	0.1	10.2	-5.6	7.2
Poland	221	1,243	2,216	2,787	2,866	0.1	0.1	25.8	2.8	18.2
South Africa	1,275	1,779	2,305	2,730	2,815	0.1	0.1	18.4	3.1	9.6
Other interregional	23,841	17,338	15,405	21,048	25,401	1.0	1.3	36.6	20.7	7.9
Other World/Not specified	*1,240*	*2,569*	*1,535*	*1,955*	*5,405*	*0.1*	*0.3*	*27.4*	*176.5*	*16.0*

Source: World Tourism Organization (UNWTO) ©   (Data as collected by UNWTO for TMT 2006 Edition)

World Tourism Organization ©

III.4.5   Colombia   South America

Promotional: www.turismocolombia.com ; www.mincomercio.gov.co ;
                              www.posadasturisticas.com.co
Institutional/corporate: www.mincomercio.gov.co
Research and data: www.mincomercio.gov.co ; www.banrep.gov.co ; www.aerocivil.gov.co ;
                              www.dane.gov.co ; www.ophotelera.8m.com.

Profile

Colombia

Capital		Bogotá
Year of entry in UNWTO		1975
Area (1000 km²)		1,139
Population (2005, million)		43.0
Gross Domestic Product (GDP) (2005, US$ million)		122,269
GDP per capita (2005, US$)		2,656

Americas
South America

GDP growth (real, %)
'-> 2004: 4.8;   2005: 5.1;   2006*: 4.8;   2007*: 4.0

	2003	2004	2005*	2004/2003	2005*/2004
International Arrivals					
Visitors (1000)	625	791	933	26.6	18.0
- per 100 of inhabitants	1	2	2		
Cruise passengers (1000)	43	49	48	14.0	-2.0
Tourism accommodation					
Number of rooms	60,005	66,576	71,247	11.0	7.0
Outbound Tourism					
Trips abroad (1000)	1,177	1,405	1,553	19.4	10.5
- per 100 of inhabitants	3	3	4		
Receipts and Expenditure for International Tourism					
International Tourism Receipts (US$ million)	893	1,058	1,218	18.5	15.1
- per Visitor Arrival (US$)	1,429	1,338	1,305	-6.4	-2.4
- per capita (US$)	21	25	28		
International Fare Receipts (US$ million)	298	308	352	3.4	14.3
International Tourism Expenditure (US$ million)	1,062	1,108	1,127	4.3	1.7
- per trip (US$)	902	788	725	-12.6	-8.0
- per capita (US$)	25	26	26		
International Fare Expenditure (US$ million)	287	358	435	24.7	21.5
Δ International Tourism Balance (US$ million)	-168	-50	91		
Δ International Fare Balance (US$ million)	11	-50	-83		

Source: World Tourism Organization (UNWTO)   (Data as collected by UNWTO for TMT 2006 Edition)
See annex for methodological notes and reference of external sources used.

International Tourism by Origin

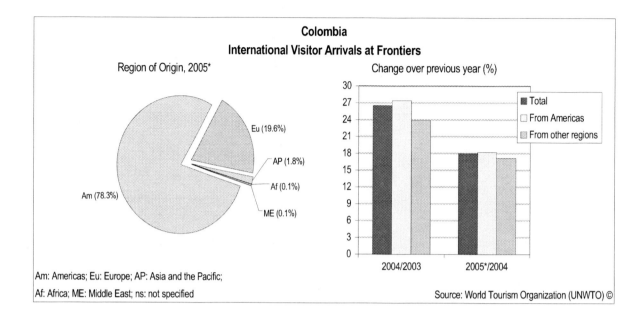

Colombia
International Visitor Arrivals at Frontiers

Region of Origin, 2005*

Eu (19.6%)
AP (1.8%)
Af (0.1%)
Am (78.3%)
ME (0.1%)

Change over previous year (%)

- Total
- From Americas
- From other regions

2004/2003   2005*/2004

Am: Americas; Eu: Europe; AP: Asia and the Pacific;
Af: Africa; ME: Middle East; ns: not specified

Source: World Tourism Organization (UNWTO) ©

Colombia
International Visitor Arrivals at Frontiers (by nationality)

	1995	2000	2003	2004	2005*	Market share (%) 2000	Market share (%) 2005*	Growth rate (%) 04/03	Growth rate (%) 05*/04	Average per year (%) 2000-2005*
Total	**1,398,997**	**557,281**	**624,909**	**790,940**	**933,243**	**100**	**100**	**26.6**	**18.0**	**10.9**
From Americas	*1,232,974*	*413,405*	*485,259*	*618,262*	*730,925*	*74.2*	*78.3*	*27.4*	*18.2*	*12.1*
United States	537,403	137,062	171,906	203,603	235,386	24.6	25.2	18.4	15.6	11.4
Venezuela	163,374	62,195	73,567	92,523	113,674	11.2	12.2	25.8	22.9	12.8
Ecuador	79,849	48,930	64,431	91,682	95,816	8.8	10.3	42.3	4.5	14.4
Peru	41,142	22,049	25,732	36,654	44,490	4.0	4.8	42.4	21.4	15.1
Mexico	35,602	24,046	26,998	34,016	42,580	4.3	4.6	26.0	25.2	12.1
Argentina	32,012	19,354	16,028	23,059	34,025	3.5	3.6	43.9	47.6	11.9
Panama	146,588	13,246	18,764	24,363	28,811	2.4	3.1	29.8	18.3	16.8
Brazil	24,338	14,338	16,938	21,910	27,209	2.6	2.9	29.4	24.2	13.7
Costa Rica	33,600	13,500	18,410	24,478	25,002	2.4	2.7	33.0	2.1	13.1
Canada	20,812	21,626	16,292	20,147	24,471	3.9	2.6	23.7	21.5	2.5
Chile	22,145	13,033	9,858	13,289	19,091	2.3	2.0	34.8	43.7	7.9
Guatemala	10,914	4,283	5,378	5,703	7,174	0.8	0.8	6.0	25.8	10.9
Bolivia	1,469	2,725	3,258	4,771	5,827	0.5	0.6	46.4	22.1	16.4
Dominican Rp	10,061	2,308	2,627	3,051	4,711	0.4	0.5	16.1	54.4	15.3
El Salvador	1,030	2,431	2,339	3,291	4,424	0.4	0.5	40.7	34.4	12.7
Uruguay	..	2,261	2,096	2,902	3,870	0.4	0.4	38.5	33.4	11.3
Cuba	18,658	3,383	2,491	2,820	3,226	0.6	0.3	13.2	14.4	-0.9
Honduras	369	1,993	2,744	2,973	3,134	0.4	0.3	8.3	5.4	9.5
Aruba	38,452	131	1,198	1,852	1,736	0.0	0.2	54.6	-6.3	67.7
Nicaragua	152	1,114	842	1,376	1,627	0.2	0.2	63.4	18.2	7.9
Other intraregional	15,004	3,397	3,362	3,799	4,641	0.6	0.5	13.0	22.2	6.4
From other regions	*166,023*	*143,691*	*139,353*	*172,677*	*202,314*	*25.8*	*21.7*	*23.9*	*17.2*	*7.1*
Spain	63,931	26,430	32,527	45,239	57,064	4.7	6.1	39.1	26.1	16.6
France	34,070	14,975	16,545	20,458	23,060	2.7	2.5	23.7	12.7	9.0
Italy	8,204	17,115	14,899	17,936	19,955	3.1	2.1	20.4	11.3	3.1
Germany	36,694	19,590	14,163	15,881	18,130	3.5	1.9	12.1	14.2	-1.5
United Kingdom	21,758	14,135	12,522	14,645	16,089	2.5	1.7	17.0	9.9	2.6
Netherlands	..	10,407	11,594	13,726	15,721	1.9	1.7	18.4	14.5	8.6
Switzerland	..	5,458	5,226	6,746	7,521	1.0	0.8	29.1	11.5	6.6
Israel	..	3,472	3,717	4,263	5,295	0.6	0.6	14.7	24.2	8.8
Japan	..	5,273	3,665	4,188	4,336	0.9	0.5	14.3	3.5	-3.8
Sweden	..	2,664	2,707	3,041	3,614	0.5	0.4	12.3	18.8	6.3
Australia	..	1,713	1,989	2,586	3,187	0.3	0.3	30.0	23.2	13.2
Belgium	..	1,909	1,850	2,551	2,653	0.3	0.3	37.9	4.0	6.8
Korea, D P Rp	..	62	128	2,232	2,307	0.0	0.2	1643.8	3.4	106.1
Austria	..	1,557	1,441	1,560	1,928	0.3	0.2	8.3	23.6	4.4
Taiwan (pr. of China)	..	109	1,143	1,655	1,927	0.0	0.2	44.8	16.4	77.6
Norway	..	1,288	1,137	1,517	1,724	0.2	0.2	33.4	13.6	6.0
Portugal	..	1,154	1,016	1,385	1,541	0.2	0.2	36.3	11.3	6.0
Russian Federation	..	1,141	932	1,206	1,522	0.2	0.2	29.4	26.2	5.9
Denmark	..	1,013	860	1,146	1,430	0.2	0.2	33.3	24.8	7.1
India	..	922	917	1,161	1,348	0.2	0.1	26.6	16.1	7.9
China	..	1,844	762	864	1,336	0.3	0.1	13.4	54.6	-6.2
Other interregional	1,366	11,460	9,613	8,691	10,626	2.1	1.1	-9.6	22.3	-1.5
Other World/Not specified	*..*	*185*	*297*	*1*	*4*	*0.0*	*0.0*	*-99.7*	*300.0*	*-53.6*

Source: World Tourism Organization (UNWTO) ©   (Data as collected by UNWTO for TMT 2006 Edition)

III.4.6   Ecuador   South America

Profile

Ecuador

Americas
South America

Capital	Quito
Year of entry in UNWTO	1975
Area (1000 km²)	284
Population (2005, million)	13.4
Gross Domestic Product (GDP) (2005, US$ million)	36,489
GDP per capita (2005, US$)	2,761
GDP growth (real, %)	

'-> 2004: 7.9;   2005: 4.7;   2006*: 4.4;   2007*: 3.2

	2003	2004	2005*	2004/2003	2005*/2004
International Arrivals					
Visitors (1000)	761	819	861	7.6	5.1
- per 100 of inhabitants	6	6	6		
Tourism accommodation					
Number of rooms	38,237	38,029	41,342	-0.5	8.7
Outbound Tourism					
Trips abroad (1000)	613	603	661	-1.6	9.6
- per 100 of inhabitants	5	5	5		
Receipts and Expenditure for International Tourism					
International Tourism Receipts (US$ million)	406	462	486	13.8	5.0
- per Visitor Arrival (US$)	534	565	564	5.7	-0.1
- per capita (US$)	31	35	36		
International Fare Receipts (US$ million)	2	2	2		
International Tourism Expenditure (US$ million)	354	391	429	10.3	9.6
- per trip (US$)	578	648	648	12.2	0.0
- per capita (US$)	27	30	32		
International Fare Expenditure (US$ million)	146	186	215	27.4	15.7
Δ International Tourism Balance (US$ million)	52	72	57		
Δ International Fare Balance (US$ million)	-144	-184	-213		

Source: World Tourism Organization (UNWTO)   (Data as collected by UNWTO for TMT 2006 Edition)

See annex for methodological notes and reference of external sources used.

International Tourism by Origin

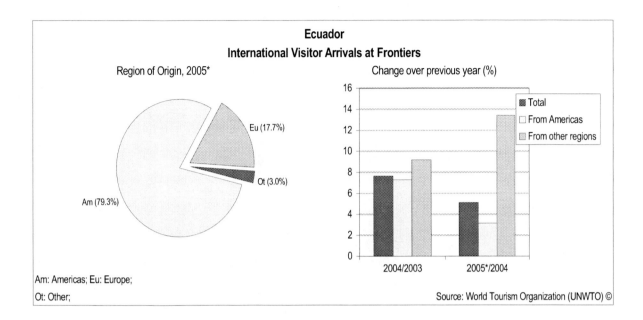

Ecuador
International Visitor Arrivals at Frontiers

Region of Origin, 2005*

Am (79.3%)
Eu (17.7%)
Ot (3.0%)

Change over previous year (%)

Total
From Americas
From other regions

2004/2003   2005*/2004

Am: Americas; Eu: Europe;
Ot: Other;

Source: World Tourism Organization (UNWTO) ©

Ecuador

International Visitor Arrivals at Frontiers (by nationality)

	1995	2000	2003	2004	2005*	Market share (%)		Growth rate (%)		Average per year (%)
						2000	2005*	04/03	05*/04	2000-2005*
Total	**439,523**	**627,090**	**760,776**	**818,927**	**860,784**	**100**	**100**	**7.6**	**5.1**	**6.5**
From Americas	*330,857*	*503,056*	*617,088*	*662,019*	*682,835*	*80.2*	*79.3*	*7.3*	*3.1*	*6.3*
Peru	18,170	90,727	153,520	191,303	209,743	14.5	24.4	24.6	9.6	18.2
United States	95,120	139,333	159,851	182,114	188,942	22.2	21.9	13.9	3.7	6.3
Colombia	149,166	191,501	205,353	179,434	164,123	30.5	19.1	-12.6	-8.5	-3.0
Chile	12,104	15,876	16,656	17,541	18,149	2.5	2.1	5.3	3.5	2.7
Argentina	8,186	11,213	15,395	15,354	16,788	1.8	2.0	-0.3	9.3	8.4
Venezuela	10,815	11,891	14,084	15,544	16,152	1.9	1.9	10.4	3.9	6.3
Canada	7,909	11,428	13,370	15,308	16,142	1.8	1.9	14.5	5.4	7.2
Mexico	5,186	6,680	9,443	10,747	11,808	1.1	1.4	13.8	9.9	12.1
Brazil	6,591	6,879	8,305	10,295	11,792	1.1	1.4	24.0	14.5	11.4
All the Caribbean	2,861	3,405	4,075	5,097	5,589	0.5	0.6	25.1	9.7	10.4
Panama	3,347	3,327	4,495	4,748	5,315	0.5	0.6	5.6	11.9	9.8
Bolivia	2,354	2,556	3,343	4,020	4,614	0.4	0.5	20.3	14.8	12.5
Costa Rica	3,629	2,592	2,753	3,244	4,117	0.4	0.5	17.8	26.9	9.7
Uruguay	1,200	1,415	1,893	2,212	3,977	0.2	0.5	16.9	79.8	23.0
Other Central America	3,205	3,546	3,728	4,087	4,665	0.6	0.5	9.6	14.1	5.6
Other South America	1,011	675	810	965	909	0.1	0.1	19.1	-5.8	6.1
Other Americas	3	12	14	6	10	0.0	0.0	-57.1	66.7	-3.6
From other regions	*108,582*	*124,033*	*143,688*	*156,881*	*177,944*	*19.8*	*20.7*	*9.2*	*13.4*	*7.5*
Spain	10,924	13,175	20,111	26,669	39,702	2.1	4.6	32.6	48.9	24.7
United Kingdom	10,068	16,890	19,554	20,867	21,929	2.7	2.5	6.7	5.1	5.4
Germany	20,073	18,824	18,598	19,451	20,316	3.0	2.4	4.6	4.4	1.5
France	13,144	12,560	13,490	13,336	13,155	2.0	1.5	-1.1	-1.4	0.9
Italy	7,567	8,536	10,395	11,744	12,265	1.4	1.4	13.0	4.4	7.5
Netherlands	5,623	8,377	10,158	8,766	9,785	1.3	1.1	-13.7	11.6	3.2
Switzerland	7,010	7,392	7,590	7,991	8,633	1.2	1.0	5.3	8.0	3.2
Australia	1,641	3,260	3,637	4,654	5,681	0.5	0.7	28.0	22.1	11.7
Japan	4,265	3,873	3,979	4,690	5,576	0.6	0.6	17.9	18.9	7.6
Israel	3,652	4,446	3,335	3,107	3,863	0.7	0.4	-6.8	24.3	-2.8
All Africa	712	1,507	1,720	2,191	2,269	0.2	0.3	27.4	3.6	8.5
New Zealand	663	926	850	1,124	1,171	0.1	0.1	32.2	4.2	4.8
Other Asia	6,687	10,496	9,264	10,643	11,196	1.7	1.3	14.9	5.2	1.3
Other Europe	16,531	13,693	20,906	21,564	22,309	2.2	2.6	3.1	3.5	10.3
Other Oceania	22	78	101	84	94	0.0	0.0	-16.8	11.9	3.8
Other World/Not specified	*84*	*1*	*..*	*27*	*5*	*0.0*	*0.0*		*-81.5*	*38.0*

Source: World Tourism Organization (UNWTO) ©   (Data as collected by UNWTO for TMT 2006 Edition)

III.4.7   French Guiana   South America

Profile

French Guiana

Americas
South America

	Capital	Cayenne
	Area (1000 km²)	90
	Population (2005, 1000)	196

	2003	2004	2005*	2004/2003	2005*/2004
International Arrivals					
Tourists (overnight visitors) (1000)	..	..	95		
- per 100 of inhabitants	..	..	49		
Same-day visitors (1000)	..	..	2		
Tourism accommodation					
Number of rooms	..	..	1,184		
Nights spent in collective establishments (1000)					
by non-residents (inbound tourism)	..	302	391		29.5
Receipts and Expenditure for International Tourism					
International Tourism Receipts (US$ million)	..	..	45		
- per Tourist Arrival (US$)	..	..	474		
- per capita (US$)	..	..	230		

Source: World Tourism Organization (UNWTO)   (Data as collected by UNWTO for TMT 2006 Edition)

See annex for methodological notes and reference of external sources used.

International Tourism by Origin

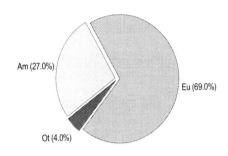

French Guiana
International Tourist Arrivals at Frontiers

Region of Origin, 2002

Am (27.0%)

Eu (69.0%)

Ot (4.0%)

Am: Americas; Eu: Europe;
Ot: Other;

Source: World Tourism Organization (UNWTO) ©

French Guiana
International Tourist Arrivals at Frontiers (by residence)

	1995	2000	2002	2003	2004	Market share (%) 2000	Market share (%) 2004	Growth rate (%) 03/02	Growth rate (%) 04/03	Average per year (%) 2000-2004
Total	..	..	**65,000**	..	..					
From Americas	..	..	*17,550*	..	..					
Martinique	..	..	9,750	..	..					
Guadeloupe	..	..	5,200	..	..					
Other Americas	..	..	2,600	..	..					
From other regions	..	..	*44,850*	..	..					
France	..	..	40,950	..	..					
Other Europe	..	..	3,900	..	..					
Other World/Not specified	..	..	*2,600*	..	..					

Source: World Tourism Organization (UNWTO) ©   (Data as collected by UNWTO for TMT 2006 Edition)

III.4.8   Guyana   South America

Promotional: www.guyana-tourism.com
Research and data: www.guyana-tourism.com

Profile

Guyana

Capital		Georgetown
Area (1000 km²)		215
Population (2005, 1000)		765
Gross Domestic Product (GDP) (2005, US$ million)		786
GDP per capita (2005, US$)		1,039

Americas
South America

GDP growth (real, %)
'-> 2004: 1.6;   2005: -3.0;   2006*: 3.5;   2007*: 4.1

	2003	2004	2005*	2004/2003	2005*/2004
International Arrivals					
Tourists (overnight visitors) (1000)	101	122	117	20.9	-4.4
- per 100 of inhabitants	13	16	15		
Receipts and Expenditure for International Tourism					
International Tourism Receipts (US$ million)	26	27	35	3.8	29.6
- per Tourist Arrival (US$)	258	221	300	-14.1	35.6
- per capita (US$)	34	35	46		
International Fare Receipts (US$ million)	2	2	2		
International Tourism Expenditure (US$ million)	26	30	40	15.4	33.3
- per capita (US$)	34	39	52		
International Fare Expenditure (US$ million)	4	5	5	25.0	
Δ International Tourism Balance (US$ million)		-3	-5		
Δ International Fare Balance (US$ million)	-2	-3	-3		

Source: World Tourism Organization (UNWTO)   (Data as collected by UNWTO for TMT 2006 Edition)
See annex for methodological notes and reference of external sources used.

International Tourism by Origin

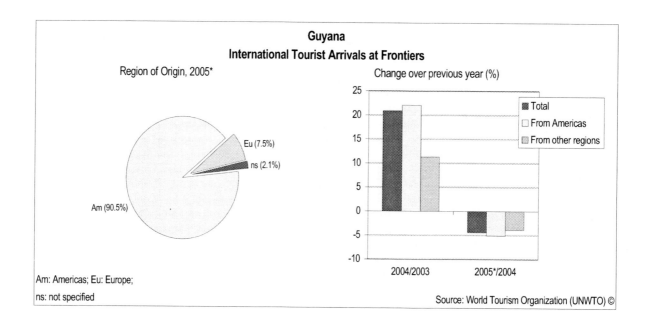

Guyana
International Tourist Arrivals at Frontiers

Region of Origin, 2005*

Eu (7.5%)
ns (2.1%)
Am (90.5%)

Change over previous year (%)

- Total
- From Americas
- From other regions

2004/2003   2005*/2004

Am: Americas; Eu: Europe;
ns: not specified

Source: World Tourism Organization (UNWTO) ©

Guyana
International Tourist Arrivals at Frontiers (by residence)

	1995	2000	2003	2004	2005*	Market share (%) 2000	2005*	Growth rate (%) 04/03	05*/04	Average per year (%) 2000-2005*
Total	**105,848**	**105,042**	**100,911**	**121,989**	**116,596**	**100**	**100**	**20.9**	**-4.4**	**2.1**
From Americas	*97,648*	*96,125*	*91,022*	*111,078*	*105,468*	*91.5*	*90.5*	*22.0*	*-5.1*	*1.9*
United States	38,420	46,177	49,625	64,947	60,071	44.0	51.5	30.9	-7.5	5.4
All the Caribbean	..	29,993	24,779	28,091	26,810	28.6	23.0	13.4	-4.6	-2.2
Suriname	17,880	..	..	..	..					
Canada	16,743	15,948	14,144	15,900	15,876	15.2	13.6	12.4	-0.2	-0.1
Trinidad Tbg	10,606	..	..	..	..					
Barbados	5,599	..	..	..	..					
French Guiana	1,489	..	..	..	..					
Saint Lucia	1,267	..	..	..	..					
Antigua,Barb	950	..	..	..	..					
Jamaica	817	..	..	..	..					
Venezuela	774	..	..	..	..					
Brazil	524	..	..	..	..					
St.Kitts-Nev	465	..	..	..	..					
St.Vincent,Grenadines	360	..	..	..	..					
Grenada	326	..	..	..	..					
Br.Virgin Is	148	..	..	..	..					
Curaçao	141	..	..	..	..					
Dominica	115	..	..	..	..					
Bahamas	109	..	..	..	..					
Other intraregional	915	4,007	2,474	2,140	2,711	3.8	2.3	-13.5	26.7	-7.5
From other regions	*8,200*	*7,229*	*8,136*	*9,056*	*8,704*	*6.9*	*7.5*	*11.3*	*-3.9*	*3.8*
All Europe	..	7,229	8,136	9,056	8,704	6.9	7.5	11.3	-3.9	3.8
United Kingdom	5,213	..	..	..	..					
Netherlands	627	..	..	..	..					
India	302	..	..	..	..					
France	234	..	..	..	..					
Germany	222	..	..	..	..					
China	196	..	..	..	..					
Italy	135	..	..	..	..					
Japan	109	..	..	..	..					
Other interregional	1,162	..	..	..	..					
Other World/Not specified	*..*	*1,688*	*1,753*	*1,855*	*2,424*	*1.6*	*2.1*	*5.8*	*30.7*	*7.5*

Source: World Tourism Organization (UNWTO) ©   (Data as collected by UNWTO for TMT 2006 Edition)

III.4.9   Paraguay   South America

Promotional: www.senatur.gov.py
Institutional/corporate: www.senatur.gov.py

Profile

Paraguay

Americas
South America

Capital	Asunción
Year of entry in UNWTO	1992
Area (1000 km²)	407
Population (2005, million)	6.3
Gross Domestic Product (GDP) (2005, US$ million)	7,468
GDP per capita (2005, US$)	1,288
GDP growth (real, %)	
'-> 2004: 4.1; 2005: 2.9; 2006*: 3.5; 2007*: 4.0	

	2003	2004	2005*	2004/2003	2005*/2004
International Arrivals					
Visitors (1000)	2,859	2,589	2,648	-9.4	2.3
Tourists (overnight visitors) (1000)	268	309	341	15.3	10.2
- per 100 of inhabitants	4	5	5		
Same-day visitors (1000)	2,591	2,280	2,307	-12.0	1.2
Tourism accommodation					
Number of rooms	4,816	4,899	5,058	1.7	3.2
Outbound Tourism					
Trips abroad (1000)	153	170	188	11.1	10.6
- per 100 of inhabitants	3	3	3		
Receipts and Expenditure for International Tourism					
International Tourism Receipts (US$ million)	64	70	82	9.4	17.2
- per Tourist Arrival (US$)	239	226	241	-5.2	6.3
- per Visitor Arrival (US$)	22	27	31	20.8	14.5
- per capita (US$)	11	11	13		
International Fare Receipts (US$ million)	17	17	20		17.6
International Tourism Expenditure (US$ million)	67	71	79	6.0	11.3
- per trip (US$)	438	418	420	-4.6	0.6
- per capita (US$)	11	11	12		
International Fare Expenditure (US$ million)	48	50	50	4.2	
Δ International Tourism Balance (US$ million)	-3	-1	3		
Δ International Fare Balance (US$ million)	-31	-33	-30		

Source: World Tourism Organization (UNWTO)   (Data as collected by UNWTO for TMT 2006 Edition)
See annex for methodological notes and reference of external sources used.

International Tourism by Origin

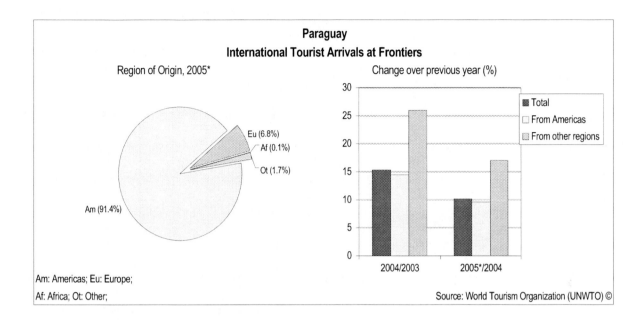

Paraguay
International Tourist Arrivals at Frontiers

Region of Origin, 2005*

Change over previous year (%)

Am: Americas; Eu: Europe;
Af: Africa; Ot: Other;

Source: World Tourism Organization (UNWTO) ©

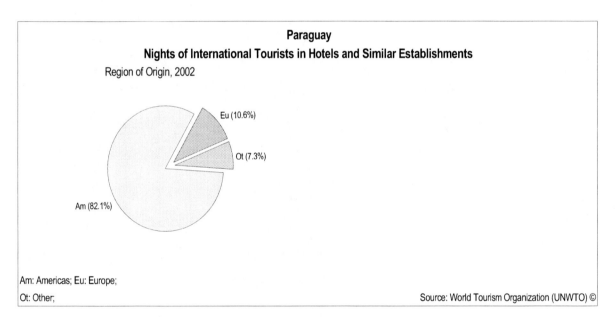

Paraguay
Nights of International Tourists in Hotels and Similar Establishments

Region of Origin, 2002

Am: Americas; Eu: Europe;
Ot: Other;

Source: World Tourism Organization (UNWTO) ©

Paraguay
International Tourist Arrivals at Frontiers (by nationality)

	1995	2000	2003	2004	2005*	Market share (%) 2000	Market share (%) 2005*	Growth rate (%) 04/03	Growth rate (%) 05*/04	Average per year (%) 2000-2005*
Total	**437,653**	**288,515**	**268,175**	**309,287**	**340,845**	**100**	**100**	**15.3**	**10.2**	**3.4**
From Americas	*354,019*	*285,977*	*248,364*	*284,325*	*311,628*	*99.1*	*91.4*	*14.5*	*9.6*	*1.7*
Argentina	138,955	199,220	177,741	197,563	209,130	69.1	61.4	11.2	5.9	1.0
Brazil	93,395	73,283	40,651	48,985	56,036	25.4	16.4	20.5	14.4	-5.2
United States	19,781	3,491	9,210	12,012	13,044	1.2	3.8	30.4	8.6	30.2
Chile	34,642	2,597	6,262	7,282	9,941	0.9	2.9	16.3	36.5	30.8
Uruguay	29,367	4,385	5,775	6,692	9,287	1.5	2.7	15.9	38.8	16.2
Bolivia	..	3,001	2,177	2,825	3,418	1.0	1.0	29.8	21.0	2.6
Peru	..	..	1,749	2,348	2,422		0.7	34.2	3.2	
Colombia	..	..	849	1,446	2,108		0.6	70.3	45.8	
Canada	3,239	..	1,019	1,391	1,787		0.5	36.5	28.5	
Mexico	7,309	..	952	1,137	1,379		0.4	19.4	21.3	
Venezuela	..	..	408	793	822		0.2	94.4	3.7	
All Central America	3,763	..	636	..	..					
Ecuador	..	..	512	496	635		0.2	-3.1	28.0	
Cuba	..	..	..	347	439		0.1		26.5	
All the Caribbean	..	..	419	..	..					
Costa Rica	..	..	..	313	364		0.1		16.3	
Panama	..	..	..	176	213		0.1		21.0	
Guatemala	..	..	..	127	126		0.0		-0.8	
El Salvador	..	..	..	103	120		0.0		16.5	
Other intraregional	23,568	..	4	289	357		0.1	7125.0	23.5	
From other regions	*61,883*	*..*	*19,811*	*24,961*	*29,217*		*8.6*	*26.0*	*17.1*	
Germany	13,435	..	4,826	6,336	7,622		2.2	31.3	20.3	
Spain	9,059	..	3,100	3,618	4,460		1.3	16.7	23.3	
Japan	7,965	..	1,946	2,287	2,836		0.8	17.5	24.0	
Italy	7,265	..	1,565	2,149	2,490		0.7	37.3	15.9	
France	..	..	1,610	2,002	2,341		0.7	24.3	16.9	
Korea, Republic of	..	..	..	1,459	1,685		0.5		15.5	
United Kingdom	..	..	..	1,501	1,393		0.4		-7.2	
Switzerland	..	..	..	1,059	1,129		0.3		6.6	
China	..	..	..	550	598		0.2		8.7	
Austria	..	..	..	398	465		0.1		16.8	
Netherlands	..	..	..	441	425		0.1		-3.6	
Belgium	..	..	..	362	424		0.1		17.1	
Israel	..	..	..	411	399		0.1		-2.9	
Sweden	..	..	..	223	282		0.1		26.5	
Portugal	..	..	..	203	280		0.1		37.9	
Greece	..	..	..	105	232		0.1		121.0	
Norway	..	..	..	137	214		0.1		56.2	
Russian Federation	..	..	..	139	193		0.1		38.8	
Australia	..	..	..	267	169		0.0		-36.7	
India	..	..	..	122	157		0.0		28.7	
Denmark	..	..	..	146	150		0.0		2.7	
Ireland	..	..	..	88	149		0.0		69.3	
Other interregional	24,159	..	6,764	958	1,124		0.3	-85.8	17.3	
Other World/Not specified	*21,751*	*2,538*	*..*	*1*	*..*	*0.9*				

Source: World Tourism Organization (UNWTO) ©   (Data as collected by UNWTO for TMT 2006 Edition)

Paraguay
Nights of International Tourists in Hotels and Similar Establishments (by nationality)

	1995	2000	2002	2003	2004	Market share (%) 2000	2004	Growth rate (%) 03/02	04/03	Average per year (%) 2000-2004
Total	**1,067,436**	**754,888**	**218,750**	..	..	**100**				
From Americas	*854,085*	*618,524*	*179,603*	..	..	*81.9*				
Argentina	277,910	359,432	104,155	..	..	47.6				
Brazil	186,790	118,668	34,390	..	..	15.7				
Chile	138,568	31,032	8,993	..	..	4.1				
United States	98,905	29,052	8,415	..	..	3.8				
Uruguay	58,734	19,268	5,585	..	..	2.6				
Mexico	14,618	3,340	970	..	..	0.4				
Canada	23,898	2,468	713	..	..	0.3				
All Central America	7,526	2,068	595	..	..	0.3				
All the Caribbean	..	..	370	..	..					
Other South America	47,136	53,196	15,417	..	..	7.0				
From other regions	*169,849*	*96,664*	*26,019*	..	..	*12.8*				
Germany	40,305	16,080	4,658	..	..	2.1				
Spain	36,236	13,952	4,040	..	..	1.8				
Italy	29,060	10,460	3,030	..	..	1.4				
Japan	15,930	5,180	1,498	..	..	0.7				
All Africa	..	872	273	..	..	0.1				
Other Asia	10,504	4,448	687	..	..	0.6				
Other Europe	35,890	44,736	11,558	..	..	5.9				
Other East Asia/Pacific	1,924	936	275	..	..	0.1				
Other World/Not specified	*43,502*	*39,700*	*13,128*	..	..	*5.3*				

Source: World Tourism Organization (UNWTO) ©   (Data as collected by UNWTO for TMT 2006 Edition)

III.4.10 Peru — South America

Promotional: www.promperu.gob.pe
Institutional/corporate: www.mincetur.gob.pe
Research and data: www.mincetur.gob.pe

Profile

Peru

Capital	Lima
Year of entry in UNWTO	1975
Area (1000 km²)	1,285
Population (2005, million)	27.9
Gross Domestic Product (GDP) (2005, US$ million)	79,394
GDP per capita (2005, US$)	2,841

Americas
South America

GDP growth (real, %)
'-> 2004: 5.2;   2005: 6.4;   2006*: 6.0;   2007*: 5.0

	2003	2004	2005*	2004/2003	2005*/2004
International Arrivals					
Tourists (overnight visitors) (1000)	1,070	1,277	1,486	19.4	16.4
- per 100 of inhabitants	4	5	5		
Cruise passengers (1000)	4	7	8	75.0	14.3
Tourism accommodation					
Number of rooms	123,932	128,253	132,019	3.5	2.9
Nights spent in hotels and similar establishments (1000)	18,590	19,384	20,785	4.3	7.2
by non-residents (inbound tourism)	3,789	4,409	4,827	16.4	9.5
by residents (domestic tourism)	14,801	14,975	15,958	1.2	6.6
Outbound Tourism					
Trips abroad (1000)	1,392	1,635	1,841	17.5	12.6
- per 100 of inhabitants	5	6	7		
Receipts and Expenditure for International Tourism					
International Tourism Receipts (US$ million)	940	1,142	1,308	21.4	14.6
- per Tourist Arrival (US$)	879	895	880	1.7	-1.6
- per capita (US$)	35	41	47		
International Fare Receipts (US$ million)	60	90	130	50.0	44.4
International Tourism Expenditure (US$ million)	598	643	752	7.5	16.9
- per trip (US$)	430	393	408	-8.5	3.8
- per capita (US$)	22	23	27		
International Fare Expenditure (US$ million)	196	201	220	2.6	9.5
Δ International Tourism Balance (US$ million)	342	499	557		
Δ International Fare Balance (US$ million)	-136	-111	-90		

Source: World Tourism Organization (UNWTO)   (Data as collected by UNWTO for TMT 2006 Edition)
See annex for methodological notes and reference of external sources used.

World Tourism Organization ©

International Tourism by Origin

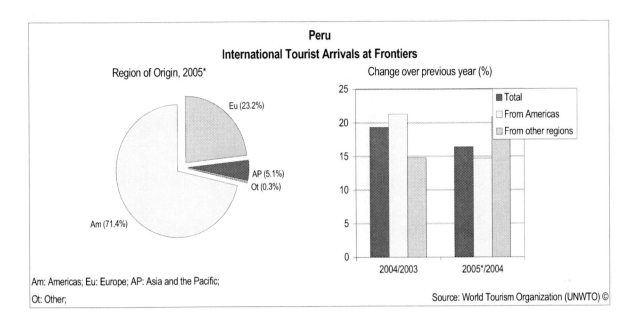

Peru
International Tourist Arrivals at Frontiers

Region of Origin, 2005*

Eu (23.2%)
AP (5.1%)
Ot (0.3%)
Am (71.4%)

Change over previous year (%)

Total
From Americas
From other regions

2004/2003   2005*/2004

Am: Americas; Eu: Europe; AP: Asia and the Pacific;
Ot: Other;

Source: World Tourism Organization (UNWTO) ©

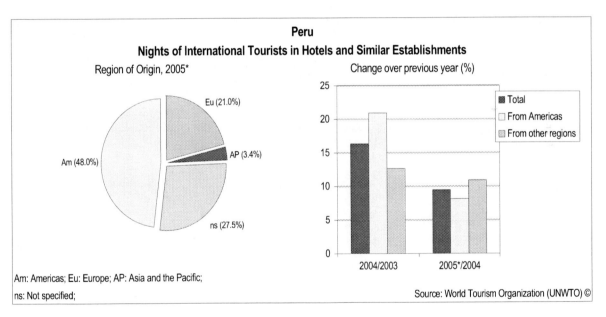

Peru
Nights of International Tourists in Hotels and Similar Establishments

Region of Origin, 2005*

Eu (21.0%)
AP (3.4%)
Am (48.0%)
ns (27.5%)

Change over previous year (%)

Total
From Americas
From other regions

2004/2003   2005*/2004

Am: Americas; Eu: Europe; AP: Asia and the Pacific;
ns: Not specified;

Source: World Tourism Organization (UNWTO) ©

Peru

International Tourist Arrivals at Frontiers (by nationality)

	1995	2000	2003	2004	2005*	Market share (%) 2000	Market share (%) 2005*	Growth rate (%) 04/03	Growth rate (%) 05*/04	Average per year (%) 2000-2005*
Total	**479,231**	**800,491**	**1,069,517**	**1,276,610**	**1,486,005**	**100**	**100**	**19.4**	**16.4**	**13.2**
From Americas	*300,485*	*534,944*	*762,290*	*924,656*	*1,060,708*	*66.8*	*71.4*	*21.3*	*14.7*	*14.7*
Chile	65,771	134,436	249,040	307,432	352,703	16.8	23.7	23.4	14.7	21.3
United States	102,902	186,004	200,800	240,104	291,073	23.2	19.6	19.6	21.2	9.4
Ecuador	9,351	31,920	81,411	111,072	88,215	4.0	5.9	36.4	-20.6	22.5
Bolivia	22,540	35,984	59,337	63,043	71,183	4.5	4.8	6.2	12.9	14.6
Argentina	24,653	36,097	38,039	45,434	53,834	4.5	3.6	19.4	18.5	8.3
Colombia	14,568	24,338	33,782	38,216	48,611	3.0	3.3	13.1	27.2	14.8
Brazil	17,606	20,003	28,211	32,893	43,154	2.5	2.9	16.6	31.2	16.6
Canada	11,479	19,418	21,846	24,385	33,124	2.4	2.2	11.6	35.8	11.3
Mexico	7,391	12,971	16,908	22,858	27,411	1.6	1.8	35.2	19.9	16.1
Venezuela	11,072	15,642	12,939	15,422	20,694	2.0	1.4	19.2	34.2	5.8
Panama	1,863	2,532	2,748	3,670	7,227	0.3	0.5	33.6	96.9	23.3
Uruguay	2,666	3,002	3,209	3,835	5,082	0.4	0.3	19.5	32.5	11.1
Costa Rica	1,711	3,109	3,187	4,455	5,004	0.4	0.3	39.8	12.3	10.0
Guatemala	935	1,251	1,645	1,898	2,216	0.2	0.1	15.4	16.8	12.1
Dominican Rp	781	1,182	1,054	1,229	1,935	0.1	0.1	16.6	57.4	10.4
El Salvador	878	1,332	1,384	1,702	1,868	0.2	0.1	23.0	9.8	7.0
Other intraregional	4,318	5,723	6,750	7,008	7,374	0.7	0.5	3.8	5.2	5.2
From other regions	*178,591*	*260,683*	*305,891*	*351,211*	*424,510*	*32.6*	*28.6*	*14.8*	*20.9*	*10.2*
United Kingdom	16,758	33,353	48,410	50,867	60,452	4.2	4.1	5.1	18.8	12.6
Spain	20,533	24,779	29,853	42,042	58,483	3.1	3.9	40.8	39.1	18.7
France	17,070	33,445	39,736	45,753	53,749	4.2	3.6	15.1	17.5	10.0
Germany	25,168	30,419	33,123	35,033	42,400	3.8	2.9	5.8	21.0	6.9
Japan	17,323	23,071	20,299	27,767	32,991	2.9	2.2	36.8	18.8	7.4
Italy	18,102	18,679	21,679	24,460	27,247	2.3	1.8	12.8	11.4	7.8
Australia	5,226	10,845	13,834	15,995	19,935	1.4	1.3	15.6	24.6	12.9
Netherlands	6,954	14,895	17,594	16,438	17,736	1.9	1.2	-6.6	7.9	3.6
Switzerland	8,655	10,919	12,676	13,798	15,850	1.4	1.1	8.9	14.9	7.7
Israel	4,508	7,069	8,145	9,069	9,799	0.9	0.7	11.3	8.0	6.7
Belgium	3,735	7,600	7,126	8,492	9,079	0.9	0.6	19.2	6.9	3.6
Sweden	2,832	4,677	5,648	5,547	6,775	0.6	0.5	-1.8	22.1	7.7
Korea, Republic of	5,836	3,880	5,029	5,879	6,755	0.5	0.5	16.9	14.9	11.7
Ireland	969	2,020	4,245	5,095	6,643	0.3	0.4	20.0	30.4	26.9
Austria	3,368	4,233	4,111	4,648	6,010	0.5	0.4	13.1	29.3	7.3
China	3,241	3,854	4,316	5,350	5,279	0.5	0.4	24.0	-1.3	6.5
Denmark	2,297	2,976	2,607	2,926	4,117	0.4	0.3	12.2	40.7	6.7
Norway	1,364	2,823	3,524	3,680	4,015	0.4	0.3	4.4	9.1	7.3
Poland	837	1,600	1,971	2,549	3,788	0.2	0.3	29.3	48.6	18.8
New Zealand	1,193	2,316	2,532	2,798	3,604	0.3	0.2	10.5	28.8	9.2
Former Czechoslovakia	715	1,463	1,917	2,023	2,607	0.2	0.2	5.5	28.9	12.2
Portugal	905	1,091	1,139	1,727	2,478	0.1	0.2	51.6	43.5	17.8
Russian Federation	1,962	1,326	1,429	1,978	2,414	0.2	0.2	38.4	22.0	12.7
South Africa	553	1,167	1,560	1,750	2,150	0.1	0.1	12.2	22.9	13.0
Finland	750	1,378	1,607	1,634	2,126	0.2	0.1	1.7	30.1	9.1
Other interregional	7,737	10,805	11,781	13,913	18,028	1.3	1.2	18.1	29.6	10.8
Other World/Not specified	*155*	*4,864*	*1,336*	*743*	*787*	*0.6*	*0.1*	*-44.4*	*5.9*	*-30.5*

Source: World Tourism Organization (UNWTO) ©

(Data as collected by UNWTO for TMT 2006 Edition)

World Tourism Organization ©

Peru

Nights of International Tourists in Hotels and Similar Establishments (by nationality)

	1995	2000	2003	2004	2005*	Market share (%) 2000	Market share (%) 2005*	Growth rate (%) 04/03	Growth rate (%) 05*/04	Average per year (%) 2000-2005*
Total	**1,886,515**	**2,701,893**	**3,789,116**	**4,408,710**	**4,826,896**	**100**	**100**	**16.4**	**9.5**	**12.3**
From Americas	*1,088,772*	*1,330,582*	*1,772,266*	*2,143,094*	*2,318,029*	*49.2*	*48.0*	*20.9*	*8.2*	*11.7*
United States	369,148	642,879	816,879	997,252	1,129,720	23.8	23.4	22.1	13.3	11.9
Brazil	74,738	64,633	115,050	146,889	179,886	2.4	3.7	27.7	22.5	22.7
Argentina	88,453	99,957	177,100	200,718	176,292	3.7	3.7	13.3	-12.2	12.0
Chile	168,195	162,377	147,936	173,259	174,638	6.0	3.6	17.1	0.8	1.5
Canada	108,284	82,814	110,970	137,549	166,382	3.1	3.4	24.0	21.0	15.0
Colombia	76,823	78,217	129,825	143,314	142,124	2.9	2.9	10.4	-0.8	12.7
Mexico	37,021	51,634	86,211	117,693	125,174	1.9	2.6	36.5	6.4	19.4
Ecuador	24,465	44,682	98,737	118,983	108,563	1.7	2.2	20.5	-8.8	19.4
Venezuela	57,826	36,932	45,720	55,263	58,128	1.4	1.2	20.9	5.2	9.5
Bolivia	38,411	31,865	43,838	52,174	57,122	1.2	1.2	19.0	9.5	12.4
Panama	45,408	34,592	..	..	..	1.3				
From other regions	*425,074*	*740,059*	*945,032*	*1,064,635*	*1,181,009*	*27.4*	*24.5*	*12.7*	*10.9*	*9.8*
France	44,991	207,553	287,246	303,079	334,768	7.7	6.9	5.5	10.5	10.0
Spain	113,937	125,735	172,501	222,696	271,324	4.7	5.6	29.1	21.8	16.6
Germany	84,514	175,922	221,013	227,727	241,857	6.5	5.0	3.0	6.2	6.6
Italy	86,368	100,020	133,707	150,785	166,998	3.7	3.5	12.8	10.8	10.8
Japan	95,264	130,829	130,565	160,348	166,062	4.8	3.4	22.8	3.6	4.9
Other World/Not specified	*372,669*	*631,252*	*1,071,818*	*1,200,981*	*1,327,858*	*23.4*	*27.5*	*12.1*	*10.6*	*16.0*

Source: World Tourism Organization (UNWTO) ©   (Data as collected by UNWTO for TMT 2006 Edition)

III.4.11 Suriname — South America

Profile

Suriname

Americas
South America

Capital			Paramaribo
Area (1000 km²)			163
Population (2005, 1000)			460
Gross Domestic Product (GDP) (2005, US$ million)			1,345
GDP per capita (2005, US$)			2,637
GDP growth (real, %)			
'-> 2004: 7.8; 2005: 5.1; 2006*: 4.5; 2007*: 4.4			

	2003	2004	2005*	2004/2003	2005*/2004
International Arrivals					
Visitors (1000)	100	..	..		
Tourists (overnight visitors) (1000)	82	138	160	68.1	16.1
- per 100 of inhabitants	18	30	35		
Cruise passengers (1000)	17	..	..		
Tourism accommodation					
Number of rooms	2,160	4,271	4,575	97.7	7.1
Receipts and Expenditure for International Tourism					
International Tourism Receipts (US$ million)	4	17	45	325.0	164.7
- per Tourist Arrival (US$)	49	123	281	152.9	128.1
- per Visitor Arrival (US$)	40	..	..		
- per capita (US$)	9	37	98		
International Fare Receipts (US$ million)	14	35	51	150.0	45.7
International Tourism Expenditure (US$ million)	6	14	17	133.3	21.4
- per capita (US$)	13	31	37		
International Fare Expenditure (US$ million)	62	71	77	14.5	8.5
Δ International Tourism Balance (US$ million)	-2	3	28		
Δ International Fare Balance (US$ million)	-48	-36	-26		

Source: World Tourism Organization (UNWTO)   (Data as collected by UNWTO for TMT 2006 Edition)
See annex for methodological notes and reference of external sources used.

International Tourism by Origin

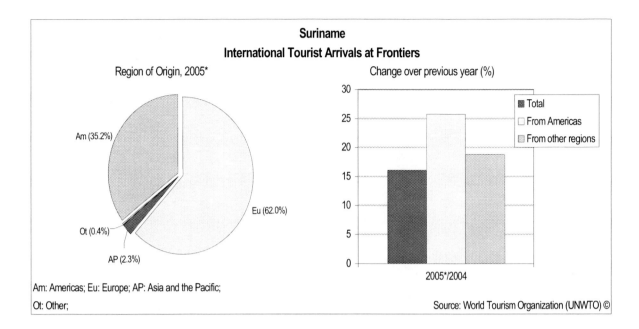

Suriname
International Tourist Arrivals at Frontiers

Region of Origin, 2005*

Am (35.2%)
Ot (0.4%)
AP (2.3%)
Eu (62.0%)

Change over previous year (%)

- Total
- From Americas
- From other regions

2005*/2004

Am: Americas; Eu: Europe; AP: Asia and the Pacific;
Ot: Other;

Source: World Tourism Organization (UNWTO) ©

Suriname
International Tourist Arrivals at Frontiers (by residence)

	1995	2000	2003	2004	2005*	Market share (%) 2000	Market share (%) 2005*	Growth rate (%) 04/03	Growth rate (%) 05*/04	Average per year (%) 2000-2005*
Total	..	..	..	137,808	160,022		100		16.1	
From Americas	..	..	..	*44,802*	*56,338*		*35.2*		*25.7*	
French Guiana	..	..	..	1,840	20,211		12.6		998.4	
Guyana	..	..	..	13,573	13,218		8.3		-2.6	
All the Caribbean	..	..	..	8,621	..					
Brazil	..	..	..	4,260	5,875		3.7		37.9	
United States	..	..	..	4,465	4,699		2.9		5.2	
Trinidad Tbg	..	..	..	..	1,883		1.2			
Haiti	..	..	..	..	1,669		1.0			
Canada	..	..	..	..	1,470		0.9			
Venezuela	..	..	..	..	396		0.2			
Dominican Rp	..	..	..	..	235		0.1			
Colombia	..	..	..	..	181		0.1			
Other Caribbean	..	..	..	..	5,875		3.7			
Other South America	..	..	..	12,043	344		0.2		-97.1	
Other Americas	..	..	..	..	282		0.2			
From other regions	..	..	..	*86,913*	*103,289*		*64.5*		*18.8*	
Netherlands	..	..	..	82,215	93,440		58.4		13.7	
France	..	..	..	..	2,837		1.8			
China	..	..	..	..	2,536		1.6			
Belgium	..	..	..	..	794		0.5			
United Kingdom	..	..	..	..	695		0.4			
Germany	..	..	..	..	499		0.3			
India	..	..	..	..	498		0.3			
All Africa	..	..	..	..	279		0.2			
All Oceania	..	..	..	..	232		0.1			
Indonesia	..	..	..	..	181		0.1			
Japan	..	..	..	..	125		0.1			
Korea, Republic of	..	..	..	..	18		0.0			
Other Asia	..	..	..	..	155		0.1			
Other Europe	..	..	..	4,698	1,000		0.6		-78.7	
Other World/Not specified	..	..	..	*6,093*	*395*		*0.2*		*-93.5*	

Source: World Tourism Organization (UNWTO) ©

(Data as collected by UNWTO for TMT 2006 Edition)

III.4.12 Uruguay — South America

Promotional: www.uruguaynatural.com
Institutional/corporate: www.mintur.gub.uy
Research and data: www.turismo.gub.uy

Profile

Uruguay

Capital	Montevideo
Year of entry in UNWTO	1977
Area (1000 km²)	176
Population (2005, million)	3.4
Gross Domestic Product (GDP) (2005, US$ million)	16,878
GDP per capita (2005, US$)	5,274

Americas
South America

GDP growth (real, %)
-> 2004: 11.8;   2005: 6.6;   2006*: 4.6;   2007*: 4.2

	2003	2004	2005*	2004/2003	2005*/2004
International Arrivals					
Visitors (1000)	1,508	1,871	1,917	24.1	2.5
Tourists (overnight visitors) (1000)	1,420	1,756	1,808	23.7	2.9
- per 100 of inhabitants	42	52	53		
Same-day visitors (1000)	88	115	109	30.7	-5.2
Tourism accommodation					
Number of rooms	18,160	19,151	14,729	5.5	-23.1
Nights spent in collective establishments (1000)					
by non-residents (inbound tourism)	3,531	2,938	2,925	-16.8	-0.4
Nights spent in hotels and similar establishments (1000)					
by non-residents (inbound tourism)	1,903	2,673	2,620	40.5	-2.0
Outbound Tourism					
Trips abroad (1000)	495	569	658	14.9	15.6
- per 100 of inhabitants	15	17	19		
Receipts and Expenditure for International Tourism					
International Tourism Receipts (US$ million)	345	494	594	43.3	20.3
- per Tourist Arrival (US$)	243	281	329	15.8	16.9
- per Visitor Arrival (US$)	229	264	310	15.5	17.4
- per capita (US$)	102	145	174		
International Fare Receipts (US$ million)	74	97	96	31.1	-1.0
International Tourism Expenditure (US$ million)	169	194	194	14.7	
- per trip (US$)	341	340	294	-0.2	-13.5
- per capita (US$)	50	57	57		
International Fare Expenditure (US$ million)	67	73	76	9.0	4.1
Δ International Tourism Balance (US$ million)	176	300	401		
Δ International Fare Balance (US$ million)	7	24	20		

Source: World Tourism Organization (UNWTO)   (Data as collected by UNWTO for TMT 2006 Edition)
See annex for methodological notes and reference of external sources used.

International Tourism by Origin

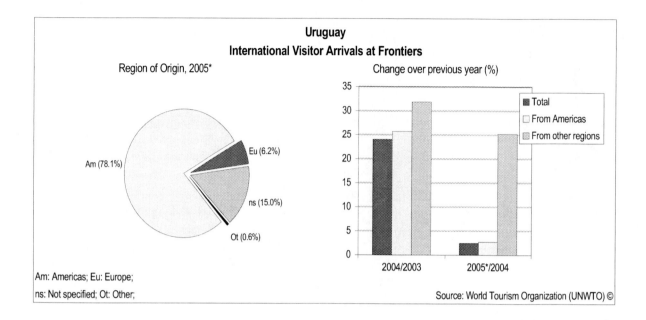

Uruguay
International Visitor Arrivals at Frontiers

Region of Origin, 2005*

Am (78.1%)
Eu (6.2%)
ns (15.0%)
Ot (0.6%)

Change over previous year (%)

- Total
- From Americas
- From other regions

2004/2003   2005*/2004

Am: Americas; Eu: Europe;
ns: Not specified; Ot: Other;

Source: World Tourism Organization (UNWTO) ©

World Tourism Organization ©

Uruguay
International Visitor Arrivals at Frontiers (by nationality)

	1995	2000	2003	2004	2005*	Market share (%) 2000	Market share (%) 2005*	Growth rate (%) 04/03	Growth rate (%) 05*/04	Average per year (%) 2000-2005*
Total	**2,176,930**	**2,235,887**	**1,508,055**	**1,870,858**	**1,917,049**	**100**	**100**	**24.1**	**2.5**	**-3.0**
From Americas	*1,743,468*	*1,758,399*	*1,159,580*	*1,457,944*	*1,497,756*	*78.6*	*78.1*	*25.7*	*2.7*	*-3.2*
Argentina	1,478,036	1,510,386	866,570	1,108,592	1,107,514	67.6	57.8	27.9	-0.1	-6.0
Brazil	178,192	140,905	151,383	187,744	197,672	6.3	10.3	24.0	5.3	7.0
United States	24,474	32,206	35,691	46,372	62,287	1.4	3.2	29.9	34.3	14.1
Chile	25,120	22,080	32,751	38,662	42,154	1.0	2.2	18.0	9.0	13.8
Paraguay	20,827	21,185	17,716	19,227	20,155	0.9	1.1	8.5	4.8	-1.0
Mexico	3,691	6,384	10,567	13,051	17,008	0.3	0.9	23.5	30.3	21.6
Peru	5,739	6,452	10,749	11,346	12,609	0.3	0.7	5.6	11.1	14.3
Canada	2,371	3,019	3,409	5,062	7,335	0.1	0.4	48.5	44.9	19.4
Venezuela	2,271	3,416	3,093	4,390	5,860	0.2	0.3	41.9	33.5	11.4
Bolivia	2,747	1,973	2,442	2,521	2,752	0.1	0.1	3.2	9.2	6.9
Other Americas	..	10,393	25,209	20,977	22,410	0.5	1.2	-16.8	6.8	16.6
From other regions	*91,377*	*91,755*	*79,591*	*104,933*	*131,421*	*4.1*	*6.9*	*31.8*	*25.2*	*7.5*
Spain	23,394	19,237	16,694	23,428	30,214	0.9	1.6	40.3	29.0	9.4
Italy	18,444	10,957	9,607	12,129	15,335	0.5	0.8	26.3	26.4	7.0
Germany	11,164	10,396	9,584	12,724	14,187	0.5	0.7	32.8	11.5	6.4
France	7,355	10,404	9,095	12,211	12,661	0.5	0.7	34.3	3.7	4.0
United Kingdom	5,054	7,725	8,180	10,536	12,623	0.3	0.7	28.8	19.8	10.3
Australia	1,276	1,454	2,063	3,093	4,466	0.1	0.2	49.9	44.4	25.2
Switzerland	3,170	3,105	2,778	3,370	3,747	0.1	0.2	21.3	11.2	3.8
Israel	2,135	2,292	2,325	3,041	3,635	0.1	0.2	30.8	19.5	9.7
Sweden	1,461	1,733	1,699	2,328	3,461	0.1	0.2	37.0	48.7	14.8
Netherlands	1,710	3,244	2,180	2,645	3,416	0.1	0.2	21.3	29.1	1.0
Japan	2,433	2,483	1,847	2,385	2,547	0.1	0.1	29.1	6.8	0.5
Portugal	1,603	1,575	1,456	2,120	2,527	0.1	0.1	45.6	19.2	9.9
Ireland	270	668	1,045	1,621	2,362	0.0	0.1	55.1	45.7	28.7
Belgium	1,129	1,442	1,344	1,761	2,054	0.1	0.1	31.0	16.6	7.3
Austria	1,282	1,195	1,302	1,552	1,844	0.1	0.1	19.2	18.8	9.1
Finland	244	513	761	978	1,537	0.0	0.1	28.5	57.2	24.5
Norway	329	749	956	1,105	1,422	0.0	0.1	15.6	28.7	13.7
Denmark	734	683	813	1,171	1,375	0.0	0.1	44.0	17.4	15.0
New Zealand	316	822	602	958	1,213	0.0	0.1	59.1	26.6	8.1
Greece	708	539	584	1,028	1,117	0.0	0.1	76.0	8.7	15.7
All Middle East	323	201	131	489	182	0.0	0.0	273.3	-62.8	-2.0
Luxembourg	36	34	26	52	75	0.0	0.0	100.0	44.2	17.1
Other North-East Asia	2,853	1,446	986	490	2,160	0.1	0.1	-50.3	340.8	8.4
Other interregional	3,954	8,858	3,533	3,718	7,261	0.4	0.4	5.2	95.3	-3.9
Nationals residing abroad	*336,393*	*362,544*	*264,817*	*301,188*	*284,821*	*16.2*	*14.9*	*13.7*	*-5.4*	*-4.7*
Other World/Not specified	*5,692*	*23,189*	*4,067*	*6,793*	*3,051*	*1.0*	*0.2*	*67.0*	*-55.1*	*-33.3*

Source: World Tourism Organization (UNWTO) ©   (Data as collected by UNWTO for TMT 2006 Edition)

III.4.13 Venezuela   South America

Promotional: www.venezuelaturistica.com
Institutional/corporate: www.turismoparatodos.org.ve
Research and data: www.turismoparatodos.org.ve

Profile

Venezuela

Americas
South America

Capital	Caracas
Year of entry in UNWTO	1975
Area (1000 km²)	912
Population (2005, million)	25.4
Gross Domestic Product (GDP) (2005, US$ million)	132,848
GDP per capita (2005, US$)	5,026
GDP growth (real, %)	

-> 2004: 17.9;   2005: 9.3;   2006*: 7.5;   2007*: 3.7

	2003	2004	2005*	2004/2003	2005*/2004
International Arrivals					
Visitors (1000)	435	618	841	42.1	36.1
Tourists (overnight visitors) (1000)	337	486	706	44.3	45.2
- per 100 of inhabitants	1	2	3		
Same-day visitors (1000)	98	..	..		
Cruise passengers (1000)	..	132	135		2.3
Tourism accommodation					
Number of rooms	82,366	84,607	68,819	2.7	-18.7
Nights spent in collective establishments (1000)					
by non-residents (inbound tourism)	9,819	..	..		
Nights spent in hotels and similar establishments (1000)					
by non-residents (inbound tourism)	4,023	..	..		
Outbound Tourism					
Trips abroad (1000)	832	816	1,067	-1.9	30.8
- per 100 of inhabitants	3	3	4		
Receipts and Expenditure for International Tourism					
International Tourism Receipts (US$ million)	330	481	641	45.9	33.2
- per Tourist Arrival (US$)	979	989	908	1.1	-8.2
- per Visitor Arrival (US$)	758	779	762	2.7	-2.1
- per capita (US$)	13	19	25		
International Fare Receipts (US$ million)	47	54	72	14.9	33.3
International Tourism Expenditure (US$ million)	859	1,076	1,281	25.3	19.1
- per trip (US$)	1,032	1,319	1,201	27.7	-9.0
- per capita (US$)	35	43	50		
International Fare Expenditure (US$ million)	452	527	556	16.6	5.5
Δ International Tourism Balance (US$ million)	-529	-595	-640		
Δ International Fare Balance (US$ million)	-405	-473	-484		

Source: World Tourism Organization (UNWTO)   (Data as collected by UNWTO for TMT 2006 Edition)

See annex for methodological notes and reference of external sources used.

World Tourism Organization ©

International Tourism by Origin

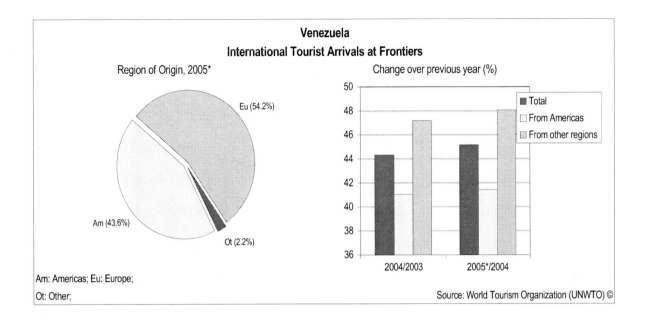

Venezuela
International Tourist Arrivals at Frontiers

Region of Origin, 2005*

Eu (54.2%)
Am (43.6%)
Ot (2.2%)

Change over previous year (%)

- Total
- From Americas
- From other regions

2004/2003   2005*/2004

Am: Americas; Eu: Europe;
Ot: Other;

Source: World Tourism Organization (UNWTO) ©

Venezuela
International Tourist Arrivals at Frontiers (by nationality)

	1995	2000	2003	2004	2005*	Market share (%) 2000	Market share (%) 2005*	Growth rate (%) 04/03	Growth rate (%) 05*/04	Average per year (%) 2000-2005*
Total	**699,837**	**469,047**	**336,974**	**486,401**	**706,103**	**100**	**100**	**44.3**	**45.2**	**8.5**
From Americas	*390,761*	*172,071*	*154,334*	*217,699*	*307,932*	*36.7*	*43.6*	*41.1*	*41.4*	*12.3*
United States	144,255	74,124	66,711	76,202	116,599	15.8	16.5	14.2	53.0	9.5
Canada	60,954	38,045	20,588	31,794	46,533	8.1	6.6	54.4	46.4	4.1
Colombia	25,541	8,902	10,576	32,030	36,294	1.9	5.1	202.9	13.3	32.5
Argentina	19,463	9,538	14,108	18,708	25,862	2.0	3.7	32.6	38.2	22.1
Brazil	45,858	7,984	9,929	13,404	18,667	1.7	2.6	35.0	39.3	18.5
Mexico	7,411	7,569	7,447	10,344	14,568	1.6	2.1	38.9	40.8	14.0
Chile	5,776	4,234	6,345	8,402	11,607	0.9	1.6	32.4	38.1	22.3
Trinidad Tbg	42,415	6,345	4,113	6,120	8,849	1.4	1.3	48.8	44.6	6.9
Peru	7,044	2,577	2,707	3,847	5,324	0.5	0.8	42.1	38.4	15.6
Barbados	4,213	3,201	2,300	3,357	4,821	0.7	0.7	46.0	43.6	8.5
Uruguay	2,604	1,156	1,773	2,518	3,370	0.2	0.5	42.0	33.8	23.9
Costa Rica	2,119	1,691	1,398	1,984	2,825	0.4	0.4	41.9	42.4	10.8
Dominican Rp	6,859	1,339	1,267	1,770	2,501	0.3	0.4	39.7	41.3	13.3
Ecuador	3,504	992	1,222	1,734	2,362	0.2	0.3	41.9	36.2	18.9
Panama	4,663	483	627	890	1,206	0.1	0.2	41.9	35.5	20.1
Cuba	1,428	545	581	827	1,144	0.1	0.2	42.3	38.3	16.0
Grenada	..	665	..	..	..	0.1				
Bolivia	940	589	..	..	..	0.1				
Guyana	1,066	583	..	..	..	0.1				
Other intraregional	4,648	1,509	2,642	3,768	5,400	0.3	0.8	42.6	43.3	29.0
From other regions	*306,861*	*292,421*	*179,439*	*264,129*	*391,110*	*62.3*	*55.4*	*47.2*	*48.1*	*6.0*
Germany	67,102	80,286	42,320	65,733	96,414	17.1	13.7	55.3	46.7	3.7
Netherlands	63,007	71,310	36,039	56,521	83,034	15.2	11.8	56.8	46.9	3.1
United Kingdom	28,012	33,308	19,624	24,399	43,279	7.1	6.1	24.3	77.4	5.4
Italy	36,051	19,681	20,166	27,867	39,176	4.2	5.5	38.2	40.6	14.8
France	23,483	20,417	14,362	21,041	30,629	4.4	4.3	46.5	45.6	8.4
Spain	40,179	14,803	11,389	16,429	23,475	3.2	3.3	44.3	42.9	9.7
Belgium	3,458	15,779	7,660	12,130	17,652	3.4	2.5	58.4	45.5	2.3
Denmark	4,447	10,645	6,325	9,573	13,916	2.3	2.0	51.4	45.4	5.5
Austria	6,779	4,442	3,566	5,071	7,252	0.9	1.0	42.2	43.0	10.3
Switzerland	9,621	4,044	3,588	5,096	7,196	0.9	1.0	42.0	41.2	12.2
Portugal	5,331	3,288	2,967	4,174	5,909	0.7	0.8	40.7	41.6	12.4
Sweden	1,777	2,699	2,149	3,051	4,369	0.6	0.6	42.0	43.2	10.1
Norway	974	3,002	1,977	2,810	4,140	0.6	0.6	42.1	47.3	6.6
Japan	3,565	1,663	1,835	2,511	3,513	0.4	0.5	36.8	39.9	16.1
China	371	474	615	892	1,197	0.1	0.2	45.0	34.2	20.4
Poland	..	1,022	536	758	1,170	0.2	0.2	41.4	54.4	2.7
Israel	2,376	477	551	808	1,092	0.1	0.2	46.6	35.1	18.0
All Africa	799	..	438	640	918		0.1	46.1	43.4	
Australia, New Zealand	..	..	379	542	815		0.1	43.0	50.4	
All Middle East	..	..	371	492	706		0.1	32.6	43.5	
Russian Federation	..	374	271	382	558	0.1	0.1	41.0	46.1	8.3
All South Asia	..	..	270	344	494		0.1	27.4	43.6	
Other interregional	9,529	4,707	2,041	2,865	4,206	1.0	0.6	40.4	46.8	-2.2
Other World/Not specified	*2,215*	*4,555*	*3,201*	*4,573*	*7,061*	*1.0*	*1.0*	*42.9*	*54.4*	*9.2*

Source: World Tourism Organization (UNWTO) ©   (Data as collected by UNWTO for TMT 2006 Edition)

World Tourism Organization ©

Annex

Table of contents

1. International Tourist Arrivals

International Tourist Arrivals, 1950-2005*

	World	Africa	Americas	Asia and the Pacific	Europe	Middle East	World	Africa	Americas	Asia and the Pacific	Europe	Middle East
	International Tourist Arrivals (million)						Change over previous year (%)[1]					
1950	25.3	0.5	7.5	0.2	16.8	0.2						
1960	69.3	0.8	16.7	0.9	50.4	0.6						
1965	112.9	1.4	23.2	2.1	83.7	2.4						
1970	165.8	2.4	42.3	6.2	113.0	1.9						
1975	222.3	4.7	50.0	10.2	153.9	3.5						
1980	277.6	7.2	62.3	23.0	178.0	7.1						
1981	278.2	8.1	62.5	24.9	175.1	7.6	0.2	13.3	0.3	8.0	-1.6	7.3
1982	276.4	7.6	59.7	26.0	174.9	8.3	-0.6	-6.6	-4.5	4.5	-0.1	8.8
1983	281.2	8.2	59.9	26.6	179.0	7.5	1.7	8.4	0.4	2.3	2.4	-9.5
1984	306.2	8.8	67.4	29.5	192.8	7.7	8.9	7.5	12.5	10.8	7.7	2.3
1985	319.5	9.6	65.1	32.9	203.8	8.1	4.3	9.3	-3.4	11.6	5.7	5.6
1986	329.5	9.3	70.9	36.8	205.5	6.9	3.1	-3.1	8.9	12.1	0.9	-14.9
1987	359.0	9.8	76.6	42.1	223.3	7.2	8.9	5.1	8.0	14.3	8.6	4.0
1988	384.1	12.6	83.0	48.7	230.7	9.1	7.0	27.8	8.4	15.8	3.3	26.2
1989	409.0	13.8	86.9	49.4	249.6	9.2	6.5	10.3	4.7	1.4	8.2	1.9
1990	438.4	15.2	92.8	56.2	264.7	9.6	7.2	9.7	6.8	13.7	6.0	4.3
1991	441.3	16.3	95.3	58.0	262.8	8.9	0.6	7.1	2.7	3.3	-0.7	-7.1
1992	478.4	18.2	102.2	65.8	280.9	11.3	8.4	12.0	7.3	13.4	6.9	25.9
1993	494.2	18.8	102.2	72.3	289.5	11.4	3.3	3.2	0.0	10.0	3.0	1.4
1994	518.0	19.1	105.1	80.1	301.5	12.1	4.8	1.8	2.9	10.7	4.2	6.3
1995	538.5	20.1	109.0	82.5	313.2	13.7	3.9	4.9	3.7	3.0	3.9	12.9
1996	572.4	21.8	114.5	90.4	329.9	15.8	6.3	8.7	5.0	9.7	5.3	15.0
1997	596.0	22.8	116.2	89.7	350.6	16.7	4.1	4.5	1.5	-0.8	6.3	5.8
1998	614.3	25.2	119.2	89.4	362.5	18.0	3.1	10.6	2.5	-0.3	3.4	7.9
1999	637.4	26.7	122.0	98.8	368.4	21.5	3.8	6.0	2.4	10.5	1.6	19.5
2000	684.7	27.9	128.2	110.6	393.6	24.5	7.4	4.3	5.1	12.0	6.8	13.7
2001	684.4	28.8	122.2	115.8	393.1	24.5	0.0	3.2	-4.7	4.7	-0.1	0.3
2002	704.7	29.8	116.8	124.9	404.8	28.4	3.0	3.6	-4.4	7.8	3.0	16.0
2003	692.2	31.4	113.3	113.2	404.9	29.5	-1.8	5.3	-3.0	-9.4	0.0	3.7
2004	761.4	34.2	125.8	144.1	421.0	36.2	10.0	9.1	11.0	27.4	4.0	22.7
2005*	801.6	37.3	133.2	155.4	437.4	38.4	5.3	9.0	5.9	7.8	3.9	5.9

Average annual growth (%)						
1950-2000	6.8	8.3	5.8	13.1	6.5	10.1
1950-2005*	6.5	8.1	5.4	12.5	6.1	10.1
1950-1960	10.6	3.7	8.4	14.1	11.6	12.3
1960-1970	9.1	12.4	9.7	21.6	8.4	11.5
1970-1980	5.3	11.5	4.0	13.9	4.6	14.3
1980-1990	4.7	7.8	4.1	9.3	4.0	3.1
1980-1985	2.9	6.2	0.9	7.4	2.7	2.7
1985-1990	6.5	9.5	7.3	11.3	5.4	3.5
1990-2000	4.6	6.3	3.3	7.0	4.0	9.8
1990-1995	4.2	5.7	3.3	8.0	3.4	7.3
1995-2000	4.9	6.8	3.3	6.0	4.7	12.3
2000-2005*	3.2	6.0	0.8	7.0	2.1	9.4

Source: World Tourism Organization (UNWTO) ©ㅤㅤㅤㅤㅤㅤㅤㅤ(Data as collected by UNWTO for TMT 2006 Edition)

[1] Before 1995, data are simple aggregates of country results and are not corrected for changes in series, so changes on previous year might not be in all cases correct.

International Tourist Arrivals by Country of Destination

	Series	International Tourist Arrivals (1000)						Market share in the region (%)			Change (%)		Average annual growth (%)	
		1990	1995	2000	2003	2004	2005*	1990	2000	2005*	04/03	05*/04	90-00	00-05*
Africa		*15,188*	*20,083*	*27,894*	*31,394*	*34,242*	*37,311*	*100*	*100*	*100*	*9.1*	*9.0*	*6.3*	*6.0*
North Africa		**8,398**	**7,271**	**10,240**	**11,094**	**12,769**	**13,911**	**55.3**	**36.7**	**37.3**	**15.1**	**8.9**	**2.0**	**6.3**
Algeria	VF	1,137	520	866	1,166	1,234	1,443	7.5	3.1	3.9	5.8	17.0	-2.7	10.8
Morocco	TF	4,024	2,602	4,278	4,761	5,477	5,843	26.5	15.3	15.7	15.0	6.7	0.6	6.4
Sudan	TF	33	29	38	52	61	246	0.2	0.1	0.7	15.8	305.8	1.4	45.3
Tunisia	TF	3,204	4,120	5,058	5,114	5,998	6,378	21.1	18.1	17.1	17.3	6.3	4.7	4.7
West Africa		**1,352**	**1,913**	**2,434**	**3,062**	**3,452**	**3,585**	**8.9**	**8.7**	**9.6**	**12.7**	**3.9**	**6.1**	**8.1**
Benin	TF	110	138	96	175	174	176	0.7	0.3	0.5	-0.9	1.4	-1.4	12.9
Burkina Faso	THS	74	124	126	163	222	245	0.5	0.5	0.7	36.2	10.1	5.5	14.2
Cape Verde	TF	24	28	115	150	157	198	0.2	0.4	0.5	4.7	26.0	17.0	11.5
Côte d'Ivoire	TF	196	188	..	180	..	..	1.3						
Gambia	TF	100	45	77	89	90	111	0.7	0.3	0.3	1.1	23.2	-2.5	7.5
Ghana	TF	146	286	399	531	584	429	1.0	1.4	1.1	10.0	-26.6	10.6	1.4
Guinea	TF	..	..	33	44	45	45		0.1	0.1	1.5	1.6		6.6
Mali	TF	44	42	86	110	113	143	0.3	0.3	0.4	2.1	26.8	7.0	10.6
Mauritania	TF	..	..	30	..	..	..		0.1					
Niger	TF	21	35	50	55	57	63	0.1	0.2	0.2	3.6	11.3	9.1	4.9
Nigeria	TF	190	656	813	924	962	1,010	1.3	2.9	2.7	4.1	5.0	15.6	4.4
Senegal	THS/TF	246	280	389	495	667	769	1.6	1.4	2.1	34.7	15.3	4.7	14.6
Sierra Leone	TF	98	38	16	38	44	40	0.6	0.1	0.1	14.3	-8.1	-16.6	20.1
Togo	THS	103	53	60	61	83	81	0.7	0.2	0.2	36.5	-2.3	-5.3	6.1
Central Africa		**365**	**357**	**666**	**636**	**728**	**792**	**2.4**	**2.4**	**2.1**	**14.4**	**8.9**	**6.2**	**3.5**
Angola	TF	67	9	51	107	194	210	0.4	0.2	0.6	82.3	8.0	-2.7	32.7
Cameroon	THS	89	100	277	..	190	176	0.6	1.0	0.5		-7.1	12.0	-8.6
Cent.Afr.Rep.	TF	..	26	11	6	8	12		0.0	0.0	43.4	47.1		1.4
Chad	THS	9	19	43	21	26	29	0.1	0.2	0.1	23.5	13.3	16.9	-7.3
Congo	THS	33	37	19	..	..	..	0.2	0.1				-5.4	
Dem.R.Congo	TF	55	35	103	35	30	61	0.4	0.4	0.2	-14.6	103.3	6.5	-9.9
Gabon	TF	109	125	155	222	..	..	0.7	0.6				3.6	
Sao Tome Prn	TF	3	6	7	14	11	11	0.0	0.0	0.0	-21.6	-1.9	9.0	8.1
East Africa		**2,842**	**4,752**	**6,338**	**7,206**	**7,614**	**8,059**	**18.7**	**22.7**	**21.6**	**5.7**	**5.8**	**8.4**	**4.9**
Burundi	TF	109	34	29	74	133	148	0.7	0.1	0.4	79.8	11.4	-12.4	38.6
Comoros	TF	8	23	24	14	18	20	0.1	0.1	0.1	23.7	11.1	11.6	-4.0
Djibouti	TF	33	21	20	23	26	30	0.2	0.1	0.1	13.4	14.8	-4.8	8.5
Eritrea	VF	..	315	70	80	87	83		0.3	0.2	9.1	-4.6		3.5
Ethiopia	TF	79	103	136	180	184	227	0.5	0.5	0.6	2.3	23.5	5.6	10.8
Kenya	TF	814	896	899	927	1,193	1,536	5.4	3.2	4.1	28.7	28.8	1.0	11.3
Madagascar	TF	53	75	160	139	229	277	0.3	0.6	0.7	64.6	21.3	11.7	11.6
Malawi	TF	130	192	228	424	427	438	0.9	0.8	1.2	0.8	2.4	5.8	13.9
Mauritius	TF	292	422	656	702	719	761	1.9	2.4	2.0	2.4	5.9	8.4	3.0
Mozambique	TF	..	..	..	441	470	578			1.5	6.6	23.0		
Reunion	TF	200	304	430	432	430	409	1.3	1.5	1.1	-0.5	-4.9	8.0	-1.0
Rwanda	TF	..	..	104	..	..	..		0.4					
Seychelles	TF	104	121	130	122	121	129	0.7	0.5	0.3	-1.0	6.5	2.3	-0.2
Tanzania	TF	..	285	459	552	566	590		1.6	1.6	2.5	4.2		5.1
Uganda	TF	69	160	193	305	512	468	0.5	0.7	1.3	68.2	-8.7	10.8	19.4
Zambia	TF	141	163	457	413	515	669	0.9	1.6	1.8	24.8	29.9	12.5	7.9
Zimbabwe	VF	636	1,416	1,967	2,256	1,854	1,559	4.2	7.1	4.2	-17.8	-15.9	12.0	-4.5
Southern Africa		**2,231**	**5,790**	**8,215**	**9,396**	**9,679**	**10,964**	**14.7**	**29.5**	**29.4**	**3.0**	**13.3**	**13.9**	**5.9**
Botswana	TF	543	521	1,104	1,406	1,523	1,675	3.6	4.0	4.5	8.3	10.0	7.4	8.7
Lesotho	VF	242	209	302	329	304	304	1.6	1.1	0.8	-7.8	0.0	2.2	0.1
Namibia	TF	..	272	656	695	..	778		2.4	2.1				3.5
South Africa	TF	..	4,488	5,872	6,505	6,678	7,369		21.1	19.7	2.7	10.3		4.6
Swaziland	THS	263	300	281	461	459	839	1.7	1.0	2.2	-0.4	82.8	0.7	24.5

Source: World Tourism Organization (UNWTO) ©

(Data as collected by UNWTO for TMT 2006 Edition)

World Tourism Organization ©

International Tourist Arrivals by Country of Destination

	Series	International Tourist Arrivals (1000)						Market share in the region (%)			Change (%)		Average annual growth (%)	
		1990	1995	2000	2003	2004	2005*	1990	2000	2005*	04/03	05*/04	90-00	00-05*
Americas		*92,804*	*109,028*	*128,193*	*113,293*	*125,792*	*133,198*	*100*	*100*	*100*	*11.0*	*5.9*	*3.3*	*0.8*
North America		**71,744**	**80,664**	**91,506**	**77,418**	**85,849**	**89,891**	**77.3**	**71.4**	**67.5**	**10.9**	**4.7**	**2.5**	**-0.4**
Canada	TF	15,209	16,932	19,627	17,534	19,145	18,771	16.4	15.3	14.1	9.2	-2.0	2.6	-0.9
Mexico	TF	17,172	20,241	20,641	18,665	20,618	21,915	18.5	16.1	16.5	10.5	6.3	1.9	1.2
United States	TF	39,363	43,491	51,238	41,218	46,086	49,206	42.4	40.0	36.9	11.8	6.8	2.7	-0.8
Caribbean		**11,392**	**14,023**	**17,086**	**17,080**	**18,095**	**18,802**	**12.3**	**13.3**	**14.1**	**5.9**	**3.9**	**4.1**	**1.9**
Anguilla	TF	31	39	44	47	54	62	0.0	0.0	0.0	15.1	15.0	3.6	7.1
Antigua,Barb	TF	206	220	207	224	245	245	0.2	0.2	0.2	9.6	0.0	0.0	3.5
Aruba	TF	433	619	721	642	728	733	0.5	0.6	0.5	13.4	0.6	5.2	0.3
Bahamas	TF	1,562	1,598	1,544	1,510	1,561	1,608	1.7	1.2	1.2	3.4	3.0	-0.1	0.8
Barbados	TF	432	442	545	531	552	548	0.5	0.4	0.4	3.8	-0.7	2.4	0.1
Bermuda	TF	435	387	332	257	272	270	0.5	0.3	0.2	5.9	-0.7	-2.7	-4.1
Bonaire	TF	37	59	51	62	63	63	0.0	0.0	0.0	1.6	-0.9	3.3	4.2
Br.Virgin Is	TF	160	219	272	318	307	337	0.2	0.2	0.3	-3.2	9.7	5.4	4.4
Cayman Islands	TF	253	361	354	294	260	168	0.3	0.3	0.1	-11.4	-35.4	3.4	-13.9
Cuba	TF	327	742	1,741	1,847	2,017	2,261	0.4	1.4	1.7	9.2	12.1	18.2	5.4
Curaçao	TF	219	224	191	221	223	222	0.2	0.1	0.2	0.9	-0.6	-1.4	3.1
Dominica	TF	45	60	70	73	80	79	0.0	0.1	0.1	9.4	-1.0	4.5	2.5
Dominican Rp	TF	1,305	1,776	2,978	3,282	3,450	3,691	1.4	2.3	2.8	5.1	7.0	8.6	4.4
Grenada	TF	76	108	129	142	134	98	0.1	0.1	0.1	-6.0	-26.6	5.4	-5.3
Guadeloupe	TCE	331	640	603	439	456	372	0.4	0.5	0.3	3.9	-18.4	6.2	-9.2
Haiti	TF	144	145	140	136	96	112	0.2	0.1	0.1	-29.1	16.4	-0.3	-4.3
Jamaica	TF	989	1,147	1,323	1,350	1,415	1,479	1.1	1.0	1.1	4.8	4.5	2.9	2.3
Martinique	TF	282	457	526	453	471	484	0.3	0.4	0.4	3.9	2.8	6.4	-1.6
Montserrat	TF	13	18	10	8	10	10	0.0	0.0	0.0	13.7	1.3	-2.3	-1.3
Puerto Rico	TF	2,560	3,131	3,341	3,238	3,541	3,686	2.8	2.6	2.8	9.3	4.1	2.7	2.0
Saba	TF	..	10	9	10	11	11		0.0	0.0	7.3	4.1		4.7
Saint Lucia	TF	141	231	270	277	298	318	0.2	0.2	0.2	7.8	6.5	6.7	3.3
St.Eustatius	TF	..	9	9	10	11	10		0.0	0.0	5.8	-6.3		2.6
St.Kitts-Nev	TF	73	79	73	91	118	127	0.1	0.1	0.1	29.7	8.0	0.0	11.7
St.Maarten	TF	545	449	432	428	475	468	0.6	0.3	0.4	11.1	-1.5	-2.3	1.6
St.Vincent,Grenadines	TF	54	60	73	79	87	96	0.1	0.1	0.1	10.4	10.1	3.1	5.5
Trinidad Tbg	TF	195	260	399	409	443	463	0.2	0.3	0.3	8.2	4.7	7.4	3.0
Turks,Caicos	TF	49	79	152	164	173	200	0.1	0.1	0.2	5.8	15.6	12.0	5.6
US.Virgin Is	TF	463	454	546	538	544	582	0.5	0.4	0.4	1.1	7.0	1.7	1.3
Central America		**1,945**	**2,611**	**4,346**	**4,900**	**5,554**	**6,288**	**2.1**	**3.4**	**4.7**	**13.4**	**13.2**	**8.4**	**7.7**
Belize	TF	197	131	196	221	231	237	0.2	0.2	0.2	4.7	2.5	-0.1	3.8
Costa Rica	TF	435	785	1,088	1,239	1,453	1,679	0.5	0.8	1.3	17.3	15.6	9.6	9.1
El Salvador	TF	194	235	795	857	812	969	0.2	0.6	0.7	-5.3	19.5	15.1	4.0
Guatemala	TF	509	563	826	880	1,182	1,316	0.5	0.6	1.0	34.2	11.4	5.0	9.8
Honduras	TF	290	271	471	611	641	673	0.3	0.4	0.5	5.0	5.0	5.0	7.4
Nicaragua	TF	106	281	486	526	615	712	0.1	0.4	0.5	16.9	15.9	16.4	8.0
Panama	TF	214	345	484	566	621	702	0.2	0.4	0.5	9.8	13.0	8.5	7.7
South America		**7,722**	**11,731**	**15,255**	**13,896**	**16,295**	**18,217**	**8.3**	**11.9**	**13.7**	**17.3**	**11.8**	**7.0**	**3.6**
Argentina	TF	1,930	2,289	2,909	2,995	3,457	3,823	2.1	2.3	2.9	15.4	10.6	4.2	5.6
Bolivia	TF	254	284	319	420	478	504	0.3	0.2	0.4	13.8	5.4	2.3	9.6
Brazil	TF	1,091	1,991	5,313	4,133	4,794	5,358	1.2	4.1	4.0	16.0	11.8	17.2	0.2
Chile	TF	943	1,540	1,742	1,614	1,785	2,027	1.0	1.4	1.5	10.6	13.6	6.3	3.1
Colombia	TF	813	1,399	557	625	791	933	0.9	0.4	0.7	26.6	18.0	-3.7	10.9
Ecuador	VF	362	440	627	761	819	860	0.4	0.5	0.6	7.6	5.0	5.6	6.5
French Guiana	TF	..	..	..	..	..	95			0.1				
Guyana	TF	64	106	105	101	122	117	0.1	0.1	0.1	20.9	-4.4	5.1	2.1
Paraguay	TF	280	438	289	268	309	341	0.3	0.2	0.3	15.3	10.2	0.3	3.4
Peru	TF	317	479	828	1,070	1,277	1,486	0.3	0.6	1.1	19.4	16.4	10.1	12.4
Suriname	TF	46	43	57	82	138	160	0.0	0.0	0.1	68.1	16.1	2.2	22.9
Uruguay	TF	..	2,022	1,968	1,420	1,756	1,808		1.5	1.4	23.7	2.9		-1.7
Venezuela	TF	525	700	469	337	486	706	0.6	0.4	0.5	44.3	45.2	-1.1	8.5

(Data as collected by UNWTO for TMT 2006 Edition)

International Tourist Arrivals by Country of Destination

	Series	International Tourist Arrivals (1000)						Market share in the region (%)			Change (%)		Average annual growth (%)	
		1990	1995	2000	2003	2004	2005*	1990	2000	2005*	04/03	05*/04	90-00	00-05*
Asia and the Pacific		*56,165*	*82,451*	*110,573*	*113,166*	*144,150*	*155,353*	*100*	*100*	*100*	*27.4*	*7.8*	*7.0*	*7.0*
North-East Asia		**26,394**	**41,313**	**58,349**	**61,732**	**79,412**	**87,576**	**47.0**	**52.8**	**56.4**	**28.6**	**10.3**	**8.3**	**8.5**
China	TF	10,484	20,034	31,229	32,970	41,761	46,809	18.7	28.2	30.1	26.7	12.1	11.5	8.4
Hong Kong (China)	TF	..	..	8,814	9,676	13,655	14,773		8.0	9.5	41.1	8.2		10.9
Japan	TF	3,236	3,345	4,757	5,212	6,138	6,728	5.8	4.3	4.3	17.8	9.6	3.9	7.2
Korea, D P Rp	*	115	..	..	..	..	..	0.2						
Korea, Republic of	VF	2,959	3,753	5,322	4,754	5,818	6,023	5.3	4.8	3.9	22.4	3.5	6.0	2.5
Macao (China)	TF	2,513	4,202	5,197	6,309	8,324	9,014	4.5	4.7	5.8	31.9	8.3	7.5	11.6
Mongolia	TF	147	108	137	201	301	338	0.3	0.1	0.2	49.4	12.4	-0.7	19.8
Taiwan (pr. of China)	VF	..	2,332	2,624	2,248	2,950	3,378		2.4	2.2	31.2	14.5		5.2
South-East Asia		**21,469**	**28,821**	**36,908**	**35,986**	**47,006**	**49,312**	**38.2**	**33.4**	**31.7**	**30.6**	**4.9**	**5.6**	**6.0**
Brunei Darussalam	VF	377	498	984	..	..	815	0.7	0.9	0.5			10.1	-3.7
Cambodia	TF	17	220	466	701	1,055	1,422	0.0	0.4	0.9	50.5	34.7	39.2	25.0
Indonesia	TF	2,178	4,324	5,064	4,467	5,321	5,002	3.9	4.6	3.2	19.1	-6.0	8.8	-0.2
Lao P.D.R.	TF	14	60	191	196	407	672	0.0	0.2	0.4	107.7	65.1	29.9	28.6
Malaysia	TF	7,446	7,469	10,222	10,577	15,703	16,431	13.3	9.2	10.6	48.5	4.6	3.2	10.0
Myanmar	TF	21	117	208	206	242	232	0.0	0.2	0.1	17.7	-4.0	25.8	2.2
Philippines	TF	1,025	1,760	1,992	1,907	2,291	2,623	1.8	1.8	1.7	20.1	14	6.9	5.7
Singapore	TF	4,842	6,070	6,062	4,703	6,553	7,080	8.6	5.5	4.6	39.3	8.0	2.3	3.2
Thailand	TF	5,299	6,952	9,579	10,082	11,737	11,567	9.4	8.7	7.4	16.4	-1.4	6.1	3.8
Vietnam	VF	250	1,351	2,140	2,429	2,928	3,468	0.4	1.9	2.2	20.6	18.4	24.0	10.1
Oceania		**5,152**	**8,084**	**9,230**	**9,023**	**10,118**	**10,488**	**9.2**	**8.3**	**6.8**	**12.1**	**3.7**	**6.0**	**2.6**
American Samoa	TF	26	34	44	..	..	25	0.0	0.0	0.0			5.4	-11.1
Australia	VF/TF	2,215	3,726	4,530	4,354	4,774	5,020	3.9	4.1	3.2	9.6	5.2	7.4	2.1
Cook Is	TF	34	48	73	78	83	88	0.1	0.1	0.1	6.4	6.1	7.9	3.9
Fiji	TF	279	318	294	431	504	550	0.5	0.3	0.4	17.0	9.1	0.5	13.3
French Polynesia	TF	132	172	252	213	212	208	0.2	0.2	0.1	-0.4	-1.8	6.7	-3.8
Guam	TF	780	1,362	1,287	910	1,160	1,228	1.4	1.2	0.8	27.5	5.8	5.1	-0.9
Kiribati	TF	3	4	5	5	4	3	0.0	0.0	0.0	-26.5	-22.4	4.8	-10.3
Marshall Is	TF	5	6	5	7	9	9	0.0	0.0	0.0	25.2	1.8	0.4	12.0
Micronesia (Fed.St.of)	TF	..	..	21	18	19	19		0.0	0.0	6.0	-1.6		-2.0
N.Mariana Is	TF	426	669	517	452	525	498	0.8	0.5	0.3	16.2	-5.1	2.0	-0.7
New Caledonia	TF	87	86	110	102	100	101	0.2	0.1	0.1	-2.4	1.1	2.4	-1.7
New Zealand	VF	976	1,409	1,787	2,104	2,334	2,366	1.7	1.6	1.5	10.9	1.3	6.2	5.8
Niue	TF	1	2	2	3	3	3	0.0	0.0	0.0	-5.8	9.5	6.6	8.0
Palau	TF	33	53	58	68	95	86	0.1	0.1	0.1	38.9	-9.2	5.8	8.2
Papua New Guinea	TF	41	42	58	56	59	69	0.1	0.1	0.0	4.9	17.3	3.5	3.6
Samoa	TF	48	68	88	92	98	102	0.1	0.1	0.1	6.1	3.7	6.2	3.0
Solomon Is	TF	9	11	5	7	..	9	0.0	0.0	0.0			-5.5	12.6
Tonga	TF	21	29	35	40	41	42	0.0	0.0	0.0	2.7	1.6	5.2	3.6
Tuvalu	TF	1	1	1	1	1	1	0.0	0.0	0.0	-6.3	-15.9	1.0	-0.3
Vanuatu	TF	35	44	58	50	61	62	0.1	0.1	0.0	21.9	1.0	5.2	1.4
South Asia		**3,150**	**4,233**	**6,086**	**6,426**	**7,613**	**7,977**	**5.6**	**5.5**	**5.1**	**18.5**	**4.8**	**6.8**	**5.6**
Bangladesh	TF	115	156	199	245	271	208	0.2	0.2	0.1	10.9	-23.4	5.6	0.9
Bhutan	TF	2	5	8	6	9	14	0.0	0.0	0.0	47.7	47.3	14.3	12.4
India	TF	1,707	2,124	2,649	2,726	3,457	3,919	3.0	2.4	2.5	26.8	13.3	4.5	8.1
Iran	TF	154	489	1,342	1,546	1,659	..	0.3	1.2		7.3		24.2	
Maldives	TF	195	315	467	564	617	395	0.3	0.4	0.3	9.4	-35.9	9.1	-3.3
Nepal	TF	255	363	464	338	385	375	0.5	0.4	0.2	13.9	-2.6	6.2	-4.1
Pakistan	TF	424	378	557	501	648	798	0.8	0.5	0.5	29.4	23.2	2.8	7.5
Sri Lanka	TF	298	403	400	501	566	549	0.5	0.4	0.4	13.1	-3.0	3.0	6.5

Source: World Tourism Organization (UNWTO) ©

(Data as collected by UNWTO for TMT 2006 Edition)

World Tourism Organization ©

International Tourist Arrivals by Country of Destination

	Series	International Tourist Arrivals (1000)						Market share in the region (%)			Change (%)		Average annual growth (%)	
		1990	1995	2000	2003	2004	2005*	1990	2000	2005*	04/03	05*/04	90-00	00-05*
Europe		*264,657*	*313,198*	*393,615*	*404,862*	*421,044*	*437,360*	*100*	*100*	*100*	*4.0*	*3.9*	*4.0*	*2.1*
Northern Europe		**30,634**	**38,259**	**43,770**	**43,886**	**47,564**	**50,902**	**11.6**	**11.1**	**11.6**	**8.4**	**7.0**	**3.6**	**3.1**
Denmark	TCE	..	..	3,535	3,474	3,663	4,562		0.9	1.0	5.4	24.5		5.2
Finland	TF	..	1,779	2,714	2,756	2,840	3,140		0.7	0.7	3.0	10.6		3.0
Iceland	TCE	142	190	634	771	836	871	0.1	0.2	0.2	8.4	4.2	16.1	6.6
Ireland	TF	3,666	4,818	6,646	6,764	6,953	7,334	1.4	1.7	1.7	2.8	5.5	6.1	2.0
Norway	TF	1,955	2,880	3,104	3,269	3,628	3,824	0.7	0.8	0.9	11.0	5.4	4.7	4.3
Sweden	TCE	..	2,309	2,746	2,952	3,003	3,133		0.7	0.7	1.7	4.3		2.7
United Kingdom	TF	17,023	21,719	23,211	22,787	25,677	28,038	6.4	5.9	6.4	12.7	9.2	3.1	3.9
Western Europe		**108,626**	**112,184**	**139,658**	**136,076**	**139,043**	**142,598**	**41.0**	**35.5**	**32.6**	**2.2**	**2.6**	**2.5**	**0.4**
Austria	TCE	19,011	17,173	17,982	19,078	19,373	19,952	7.2	4.6	4.6	1.5	3.0	-0.6	2.1
Belgium	TCE	..	5,560	6,457	6,690	6,710	6,747		1.6	1.5	0.3	0.6		0.9
France	TF	52,497	60,033	77,190	75,048	75,121	75,910	19.8	19.6	17.4	0.1	1.1	3.9	-0.3
Germany	TCE	17,045	14,838	18,992	18,399	20,137	21,500	6.4	4.8	4.9	9.4	6.8	1.1	2.5
Liechtenstein	THS	78	59	62	49	49	50	0.0	0.0	0.0	-1.0	2.6	-2.3	-4.2
Luxembourg	TCE	820	768	852	867	878	913	0.3	0.2	0.2	1.2	4.0	0.4	1.4
Monaco	THS	245	233	300	235	250	286	0.1	0.1	0.1	6.6	14.2	2.0	-1.0
Netherlands	TCE	5,795	6,574	10,003	9,181	9,646	10,012	2.2	2.5	2.3	5.1	3.8	5.6	0.0
Switzerland	TH	7,963	6,946	7,821	6,530	..	7,229	3.0	2.0				-0.2	-1.6
Central/Eastern Europe		**31,490**	**60,035**	**69,431**	**78,134**	**85,927**	**87,050**	**11.9**	**17.6**	**19.9**	**10.0**	**1.3**	**8.2**	**4.6**
Armenia	TCE	..	12	45	206	263	319		0.0	0.1	27.6	21.1		47.9
Azerbaijan	TF	..	93	681	1,014	1,349	1,177		0.2	0.3	33.0	-12.7		11.6
Belarus	TF	..	161	60	64	67	91		0.0	0.0	4.8	34.9		8.6
Bulgaria	TF	..	3,466	2,785	4,048	4,630	4,837		0.7	1.1	14.4	4.5		11.7
Czech Rep	TCE	..	3,381	4,773	5,076	6,061	6,336		1.2	1.4	19.4	4.5		5.8
Estonia	TF	..	530	1,220	1,462	1,750	1,917		0.3	0.4	19.7	9.5		9.5
Former U.S.S.R.	TF	2,286	..	..	..	..	..	0.9						
Georgia	TF	..	85	387	313	368	560		0.1	0.1	17.5	52.1		7.7
Hungary	TF	..	..	..	..	12,212	10,048			2.3		-17.7		
Kazakhstan	TF	..	..	1,471	2,410	3,073	3,143		0.4	0.7	27.5	2.3		16.4
Kyrgyzstan	TF	..	36	59	342	398	315		0.0	0.1	16.4	-20.8		39.8
Latvia	TF	..	539	509	971	1,080	1,116		0.1	0.3	11.2	3.4		17.0
Lithuania	TF	..	650	1,083	1,491	1,800	2,000		0.3	0.5	20.7	11.1		13.1
Poland	TF	..	19,215	17,400	13,720	14,290	15,200		4.4	3.5	4.2	6.4		-2.7
Rep Moldova	TF	..	32	18	21	24	23		0.0	0.0	14.3	-4.2		5.0
Romania	TCE	1,432	766	867	1,105	1,359	1,430	0.5	0.2	0.3	23.0	5.2	-4.9	10.5
Russian Federation	TF	..	..	..	20,443	19,892	19,940			4.6	-2.7	0.2		
Slovakia	TCE	822	903	1,053	1,387	1,401	1,515	0.3	0.3	0.3	1.0	8.1	2.5	7.5
Tajikistan	TF	..	..	4	..	..	..		0.0					
Turkmenistan	TF	..	218	3	8	15	12		0.0	0.0	80.2	-21.5		27.8
Ukraine	TF	..	3,716	6,431	12,514	15,629	..		1.6		24.9			
Uzbekistan	TF	..	92	302	231	262	..		0.1		13.2			
Southern/Mediter. Eu.		**93,907**	**102,720**	**140,756**	**146,766**	**148,510**	**156,809**	**35.5**	**35.8**	**35.9**	**1.2**	**5.6**	**4.1**	**2.2**
Albania	THS	30	40	32	41	42	46	0.0	0.0	0.0	2.4	9.5	0.6	7.5
Andorra	TF	..	..	2,949	3,138	2,791	2,418				-11.0	-13.4		-3.9
Bosnia & Herzg	TCE	..	..	171	165	190	217		0.0	0.0	15.0	14.2		4.9
Croatia	TCE	..	1,485	5,831	7,409	7,912	8,467		1.5	1.9	6.8	7.0		7.7
Cyprus	TF	1,561	2,100	2,686	2,303	2,349	2,470	0.6	0.7	0.6	2.0	5.2	5.6	-1.7
F.Yug.Rp.Macedonia	TCE	..	147	224	158	165	197		0.1	0.0	4.8	19.3		-2.5
Greece	TF	8,873	10,130	13,096	13,969	13,313	14,276	3.4	3.3	3.3	-4.7	7.2	4.0	1.7
Israel	TF	1,063	2,215	2,417	1,063	1,506	1,903	0.4	0.6	0.4	41.6	26.4	8.6	-4.7
Italy	TF	26,679	31,052	41,181	39,604	37,071	36,513	10.1	10.5	8.3	-6.4	-1.5	4.4	-2.4
Malta	TF	872	1,116	1,216	1,118	1,156	1,171	0.3	0.3	0.3	3.4	1.3	3.4	-0.8
Portugal	TF	8,020	9,511	12,097	11,707	10,639	10,612	3.0	3.1	2.4	-9.1	-0.3	4.2	-2.6
San Marino	THS	45	28	43	41	42	50	0.0	0.0	0.0	2.4	19.0	-0.5	3.1
Serbia & Montenegro	TCE	..	228	239	481	580	725		0.1	0.2	20.5	25.0		24.8
Slovenia	TC	..	732	1,090	1,373	1,499	1,555		0.3	0.4	9.2	3.7		7.4
Spain	TF	34,085	34,920	47,898	50,854	52,430	55,916	12.9	12.2	12.8	3.1	6.6	3.5	3.1
Turkey	TF	4,799	7,083	9,586	13,341	16,826	20,273	1.8	2.4	4.6	26.1	20.5	7.2	16.2
Yugoslav SFR	TF	7,880	..	..	..	..	..	3.0						

Source: World Tourism Organization (UNWTO) ©

(Data as collected by UNWTO for TMT 2006 Edition)

World Tourism Organization ©

International Tourist Arrivals by Country of Destination

	Series	International Tourist Arrivals (1000)						Market share in the region (%)			Change (%)		Average annual growth (%)	
		1990	1995	2000	2003	2004	2005*	1990	2000	2005*	04/03	05*/04	90-00	00-05*
Middle East		*9,630*	*13,704*	*24,451*	*29,509*	*36,220*	*38,358*	*100*	*100*	*100*	*22.7*	*5.9*	*9.8*	*9.4*
Bahrain	TF	1,376	1,396	2,420	2,955	3,514	3,914	14.3	9.9	10.2	18.9	11.4	5.8	10.1
Egypt	TF	2,411	2,871	5,116	5,746	7,795	8,244	25.0	20.9	21.5	35.7	5.8	7.8	10.0
Iraq	VF	748	61	78	..	..	..	7.8	0.3				-20.2	
Jordan	TF	572	1,075	1,580	2,353	2,853	2,987	5.9	6.5	7.8	21.2	4.7	10.7	13.6
Kuwait	THS	15	72	78	94	91	..	0.2	0.3		-3.2		17.9	
Lebanon	TF	..	450	742	1,016	1,278	1,140		3.0	3.0	25.9	-10.9		9.0
Libyan Arab Jamahiriya	TF	96	56	174	142	149	..	1.0	0.7		4.9		6.1	
Oman	THS/TF	149	279	571|	1,039	1,195	..	1.5	2.3		15.0		14.4	
Palestine	THS	..	..	310	37	56	88		1.3	0.2	51.4	57.1		-22.3
Qatar	TF	136	309	378	557	732	913	1.4	1.5	2.4	31.5	24.6	10.8	19.3
Saudi Arabia	TF	2,209	3,325|	6,585	7,332	8,599	8,037	22.9	26.9	21.0	17.3	-6.5	11.5	4.1
Syrian Arab Republic	TCE/TF	562	815	1,685	2,085	3,033	3,368	5.8	6.9	8.8	45.5	11.0	11.6	14.9
Untd Arab Emirates	THS	973	2,315	3,907	5,871	..	..	10.1	16.0				14.9	
Yemen	THS	52	61	73	155	274	336	0.5	0.3	0.9	77.0	22.8	3.5	35.7

Source: World Tourism Organization (UNWTO) ©

(Data as collected by UNWTO for TMT 2006 Edition)

| : change of series.

2. International Tourism Receipts

International Tourism Receipts, World

	International Tourism Receipts (billion)						Change current prices (%)				Change constant prices (%)			
	1990	1995	2000	2002	2003	2004	2005*	02/01	03/02	04/03	05*/04	02/01	03/02	04/03	05*/04
Local currencies								1.8	1.0	12.9	6.3	-0.5	-1.4	9.8	3.1
US$	263.9	404.7	474.1	480.1	527.2	629.0	675.7	3.9	9.8	19.3	7.4	2.2	7.3	16.2	3.9
Euro	207.2	309.4	513.3	507.7	466.0	505.7	543.1	-1.6	-8.2	8.5	7.4	-3.8	-10.1	6.3	5.1

Source: World Tourism Organization (UNWTO) ©   (Data as collected in UNWTO database November 2006)

International Tourism Receipts by (Sub)region

	Change Local currencies, constant prices (%)					US$ Receipts (billion)		US$ Receipts per arrival	euro Receipts (billion)		euro Receipts per arrival	Market share (%)
	01/00	02/01	03/02	04/03	05*/04	2004	2005*	2005*	2004	2005*	2005*	2005*
World	-1.9	-0.5	-1.4	9.8	3.1	629.0	675.7	845	505.7	543.1	680	100
Africa	*17.1*	*5.3*	*23.9*	*5.9*	*10.4*	*18.9*	*21.6*	*580*	*15.2*	*17.4*	*465*	*3.2*
North Africa	21.3	-5.6	-2.3	13.4	15.0	6.1	7.0	505	4.9	5.6	405	1.0
West Africa	12.5	1.3	5.4	0.0	20.8	1.4	1.9	530	1.2	1.5	425	0.3
Central Africa	27.2	-2.2	14.1	-3.0	13.9	0.3	0.3	410	0.2	0.3	330	0.0
East Africa	14.5	0.7	8.0	18.2	2.2	3.8	4.1	505	3.1	3.3	405	0.6
Southern Africa	15.0	26.9	75.0	-4.0	8.8	7.3	8.3	760	5.9	6.7	610	1.2
Americas	*-10.3*	*-6.3*	*-2.1*	*11.6*	*3.8*	*132.0*	*144.5*	*1,085*	*106.1*	*116.2*	*870*	*21.4*
North America	-12.8	-6.7	-4.7	12.9	4.2	98.2	107.1	1,190	79.0	86.1	955	15.8
Caribbean	-3.7	-2.6	5.5	5.0	1.6	19.3	20.4	1,085	15.5	16.4	875	3.0
Central America	-7.4	3.4	13.2	12.1	10.9	4.0	4.6	740	3.2	3.7	595	0.7
South America	3.6	-12.0	5.2	12.9	1.7	10.6	12.4	680	8.5	10.0	545	1.8
Asia and the Pacific	*7.3*	*6.6*	*-8.7*	*25.1*	*4.0*	*123.9*	*134.5*	*865*	*99.6*	*108.1*	*695*	*19.9*
North-East Asia	8.7	12.3	-10.7	33.4	7.9	58.6	65.4	745	47.1	52.5	600	9.7
South-East Asia	8.4	-1.0	-16.8	26.1	-0.7	32.8	33.8	685	26.4	27.2	550	5.0
Oceania	3.1	3.7	2.9	7.6	0.9	23.8	25.6	2,445	19.1	20.6	1,965	3.8
South Asia	2.0	9.0	17.8	20.1	4.3	8.6	9.6	1,210	6.9	7.7	970	1.4
Europe	*-1.9*	*-0.9*	*-1.5*	*3.1*	*2.5*	*328.9*	*348.8*	*795*	*264.4*	*280.3*	*640*	*51.6*
Northern Europe	-3.5	2.3	-1.9	6.0	7.7	49.3	53.9	1,060	39.6	43.3	850	8.0
Western Europe	-1.0	-0.5	-3.3	2.0	1.7	117.9	122.5	860	94.8	98.4	690	18.1
Central/Eastern Europe	-4.5	-4.4	-2.6	5.3	0.9	28.9	32.4	375	23.3	26.1	300	4.8
Southern/Mediter. Eu.	-1.5	-1.6	0.6	2.7	1.5	132.8	140.0	895	106.8	112.5	715	20.7
Middle East	*4.8*	*6.0*	*27.5*	*25.3*	*-1.8*	*25.2*	*26.3*	*685*	*20.3*	*21.1*	*550*	*3.9*

Source: World Tourism Organization (UNWTO) ©   (Data as collected in UNWTO database November 2006)

International Tourism Receipts, 1950-2005

	World	Africa	Americas	Asia and the Pacific	Europe	Middle East	World	Africa	Americas	Asia and the Pacific	Europe	Middle East
	International Tourism Receipts (US$, billion)						International Tourism Receipts (euro/ECU, billion)					
1950	2.1	0.1	1.1	0.04	0.9	0.03						
1960	6.9	0.2	2.5	0.2	3.9	0.1						
1965	11.6	0.3	3.4	0.5	7.2	0.3						
1970	17.9	0.5	4.8	1.2	11.0	0.4						
1975	40.7	1.3	10.2	2.5	25.9	0.9	34.1	1.1	8.6	2.1	21.7	0.7
1980	103.4	3.4	24.7	10.3	61.6	3.5	75.4	2.5	18.0	7.5	44.9	2.6
1981	105.0	3.7	27.8	12.1	57.1	4.4	75.4	2.6	19.9	8.7	41.0	3.1
1982	99.0	3.4	25.7	12.2	55.5	2.2	88.7	3.1	23.0	10.9	49.7	2.0
1983	102.2	3.5	26.3	12.8	55.2	4.4	104.3	3.6	26.9	13.0	56.3	4.5
1984	110.7	3.2	32.0	13.7	57.2	4.7	124.4	3.6	35.9	15.3	64.2	5.3
1985	117.4	3.1	33.3	14.5	62.2	4.2	148.8	3.9	42.2	18.4	78.9	5.3
1986	142.8	3.6	38.4	18.8	78.5	3.5	187.2	4.7	50.4	24.6	102.9	4.6
1987	176.0	4.6	43.1	24.8	99.0	4.5	178.8	4.7	43.7	25.2	100.5	4.6
1988	203.5	5.5	51.3	32.4	109.9	4.3	176.3	4.8	44.5	28.0	95.2	3.8
1989	260.9	5.7	60.2	36.1	153.8	5.2	220.7	4.8	51.0	30.5	130.0	4.4
1990	263.9	6.4	69.2	41.1	142.9	4.3	239.5	5.8	62.8	37.3	129.7	3.9
1991	277.5	6.0	76.3	42.9	147.8	4.5	217.9	4.7	59.9	33.7	116.1	3.5
1992	320.4	6.8	83.7	51.0	172.4	6.6	258.6	5.5	67.5	41.1	139.1	5.3
1993	327.0	6.9	89.1	57.0	167.1	6.9	251.9	5.3	68.7	43.9	128.8	5.3
1994	356.2	7.6	92.4	67.3	180.9	8.1	304.2	6.5	78.9	57.4	154.5	6.9
1995	404.7	8.5	98.4	75.9	212.1	9.7	340.2	7.1	82.8	63.8	178.3	8.2
1996	438.3	9.7	108.2	84.8	224.6	11.0	335.1	7.4	82.8	64.9	171.7	8.4
1997	441.8	9.5	114.4	82.2	223.5	12.1	347.9	7.5	90.1	64.7	176.0	9.6
1998	444.1	10.2	115.2	72.1	234.6	12.0	391.6	9.0	101.6	63.6	206.9	10.5
1999	457.3	10.8	119.9	79.0	233.6	14.0	407.9	9.7	106.9	70.4	208.4	12.5
2000	474.1	10.4	130.8	85.2	232.4	15.2	444.9	9.8	122.7	80.0	218.1	14.3
2001	462.2	11.5	119.8	88.0	227.4	15.6	500.4	12.4	129.7	95.3	246.2	16.9
2002	480.1	11.9	113.4	96.3	242.2	16.2	536.0	13.3	126.7	107.5	270.4	18.1
2003	527.2	16.0	114.1	93.5	283.8	19.7	557.5	17.0	120.7	98.9	300.1	20.9
2004	629.0	18.9	132.0	123.9	328.9	25.2	556.0	16.7	116.7	109.5	290.7	22.3
2005	675.7	21.6	144.5	134.5	348.8	26.3	543.2	17.4	116.2	108.1	280.4	21.1

Source: World Tourism Organization (UNWTO) ©   (Data as collected by UNWTO for TMT 2006 Edition)

¹ Receipts data are in current US$ and euro (based on the average annual exchange rate for euro or ECU to US$) and can be strongly influenced by exchange rate fluctuations.

See for tables in euro values pages Annex - 16 to Annex - 20

International Tourism Receipts by Country of Destination

	International Tourism Receipts (US$, million)						Market share in the region (%)			Change (%)		Receipts per arrival[1]	Receipts per capita[1]
	1990	1995	2000	2003	2004	2005*	1990	2000	2005*	04/03	05*/04		US$
Africa	*6,402*	*8,504*	*10,404*	*16,032*	*18,934*	*21,642*	*100*	*100*	*100*	*18.1*	*14.3*	*580*	*27*
North Africa	**2,333**	**2,867**	**3,822**	**4,938**	**6,093**	**7,018**	**36.4**	**36.7**	**32.4**	**23.4**	**15.2**	**505**	**61**
Algeria	105	33	96	112	179	184	1.6	0.9	0.9	59.4	3.1	130	6
Morocco	1,259	1,296	2,039	3,225	3,924	4,621	19.7	19.6	21.4	21.6	17.8	790	141
Sudan	21	8	5	18	21	89	0.3	0.0	0.4	16.7	324.4	365	2
Tunisia	948	1,530	1,682	1,582	1,970	2,124	14.8	16.2	9.8	24.5	7.8	335	211
West Africa	**605**	**541**	**944**	**1,329**	**1,442**	**1,891**	**9.5**	**9.1**	**8.7**	**8.5**	**31.1**	**530**	**7**
Benin	55	85	77	106	119	..	0.9	0.7		12.3		685	16
Burkina Faso	11	..	19	29	45	..	0.2	0.2		55.3		205	3
Cape Verde	6	10	41	87	99	127	0.1	0.4	0.6	13.9	28.5	645	305
Côte d'Ivoire	51	89	49	69	82	83	0.8	0.5	0.4	18.8	1.2	385	5
Gambia	26	28	48	51	58	62	0.4	0.5	0.3	12.5	8.2	560	39
Ghana	81	11	335	414	466	796	1.3	3.2	3.7	12.6	70.8	1,855	36
Guinea	30	1	12	31	30	..	0.5	0.1		-3.2		670	3
Guinea-Bissau	..	..	..	2	1	..				-50.0			1
Mali	47	25	40	128	140	148	0.7	0.4	0.7	9.4	5.7	1,035	13
Mauritania	9	11	..	..	..	..	0.1						
Niger	17	7	23	28	31	34	0.3	0.2	0.2	10.7	9.7	535	3
Nigeria	25	17	101	49	21	18	0.4	1.0	0.1	-57.6	-14.2	20	0
Senegal	167	168	144	209	212	..	2.6	1.4		1.4		320	19
Sierra Leone	19	57	11	60	58	64	0.3	0.1	0.3	-3.3	10.3	1,600	11
Togo	58	13	8	15	19	..	0.9	0.1		26.7		230	4
Central Africa	**98**	**133**	**143**	**261**	**274**	**323**	**1.5**	**1.4**	**1.5**	**5.0**	**18.0**	**410**	**3**
Angola	13	10	18	49	66	88	0.2	0.2	0.4	34.3	34.0	420	7
Cameroon	53	36	57	114	..	..	0.8	0.5					7
Cent.Afr.Rep.	3	4	5	4	4	..	0.0	0.0		0.0		490	1
Chad	8	43	14	..	..	..	0.1	0.1					
Congo	8	14	12	29	22	34	0.1	0.1	0.2	-24.1	54.5		9
Dem.R.Congo	7	..	..	1	1	..	0.1			2.3		30	0
Equatorial Guinea	1	1	5	..	..	..	0.0	0.0					
Gabon	3	18	20	15	10	..	0.0	0.2		-33.3		70	7
Sao Tome Prn	2	..	10	11	13	14	0.0	0.1	0.1	20.8	6.3	1,295	73
East Africa	**1,285**	**2,323**	**2,377**	**3,065**	**3,802**	**4,074**	**20.1**	**22.8**	**18.8**	**24.0**	**7.2**	**505**	**15**
Burundi	4	1	1	1	1	2	0.1	0.0	0.0	71.4	25.0	10	0
Comoros	2	22	15	11	13	14	0.0	0.1	0.1	16.8	12.8	720	21
Djibouti	..	4	..	7	7	7			0.0	-1.8	4.3	235	15
Eritrea	..	58	36	74	73	66		0.3	0.3	-1.4	-9.6	790	14
Ethiopia	25	16	57	114	174	168	0.4	0.5	0.8	52.6	-3.3	740	2
Kenya	443	486	283	347	486	579	6.9	2.7	2.7	39.8	19.2	375	17
Madagascar	40	58	121	44	56	62	0.6	1.2	0.3	27.3	10.7	225	3
Malawi	16	17	25	23	24	24	0.2	0.2	0.1	2.9	-0.1	55	2
Mauritius	244	430	542	696	853	871	3.8	5.2	4.0	22.5	2.2	1,145	708
Mozambique	..	..	74	98	95	130		0.7	0.6	-2.4	36.0	225	7
Reunion	..	283	296	413	448	442		2.8	2.0	8.5	-1.3	1,080	569
Rwanda	10	2	4	26	44	49	0.2	0.0	0.2	69.1	11.4		6
Seychelles	126	129	139	171	172	192	2.0	1.3	0.9	0.3	11.9	1,495	2,366
Tanzania	65	502	377	647	746	824	1.0	3.6	3.8	15.4	10.4	1,395	22
Uganda	10	78	165	184	256	381	0.2	1.6	1.8	39.1	48.8	815	14
Zambia	41	47	111	149	161	164	0.6	1.1	0.8	8.1	1.9	245	15
Zimbabwe	60	145	125	61	194	99	0.9	1.2	0.5	217.5	-48.9	65	8
Southern Africa	**2,081**	**2,640**	**3,118**	**6,439**	**7,323**	**8,336**	**32.5**	**30.0**	**38.5**	**13.7**	**13.8**	**760**	**163**
Botswana	117	162	222	457	549	562	1.8	2.1	2.6	20.2	2.3	335	343
Lesotho	17	27	24	28	34	30	0.3	0.2	0.1	21.4	-11.8	100	15
Namibia	85	278	160	330	403	348	1.3	1.5	1.6	22.1	-13.8	445	171
South Africa	1,832	2,125	2,675	5,523	6,282	7,327	28.6	25.7	33.9	13.7	16.6	995	165
Swaziland	30	48	37	101	54	69	0.5	0.4	0.3	-46.5	27.8	80	61

Source: World Tourism Organization (UNWTO) ©

(Data as collected by UNWTO for TMT 2006 Edition)

International Tourism Receipts by Country of Destination

	International Tourism Receipts (US$, million)						Market share in the region (%)			Change (%)		Receipts per arrival[1]	Receipts per capita[1]
	1990	1995	2000	2003	2004	2005*	1990	2000	2005*	04/03	05*/04		US$
Americas	*69,191*	*98,438*	*130,800*	*114,116*	*132,023*	*144,523*	*100*	*100*	*100*	*15.7*	*9.5*	*1,085*	*164*
North America	**54,872**	**77,491**	**101,472**	**84,256**	**98,213**	**107,067**	**79.3**	**77.6**	**74.1**	**16.6**	**9.0**	**1,190**	**246**
Canada	6,339	7,917	10,778	10,546	12,871	13,584	9.2	8.2	9.4	22.0	5.5	725	414
Mexico	5,526	6,179	8,294	9,362	10,796	11,803	8.0	6.3	8.2	15.3	9.3	540	111
United States	43,007	63,395	82,400	64,348	74,547	81,680	62.2	63.0	56.5	15.8	9.6	1,660	276
Caribbean	**8,639**	**12,236**	**17,154**	**17,842**	**19,292**	**20,415**	**12.5**	**13.1**	**14.1**	**8.1**	**5.8**	**1,085**	**526**
Anguilla	35	50	56	60	69	86	0.1	0.0	0.1	15.3	24.7	1,390	6,512
Antigua,Barb	298	247	291	300	338	327	0.4	0.2	0.2	12.7	-3.3	1,330	4,758
Aruba	350	521	814	859	1,056	1,091	0.5	0.6	0.8	22.9	3.4	1,490	15,245
Bahamas	1,333	1,346	1,734	1,757	1,884	2,072	1.9	1.3	1.4	7.2	9.9	1,290	6,865
Barbados	494	622	723	758	776	776	0.7	0.6	0.5	2.3	0.1	1,420	2,784
Bermuda	490	488	431	348	426	430	0.7	0.3	0.3	22.4	0.9	1,595	6,578
Bonaire	18	37	59	84	84	85	0.0	0.0	0.1	-0.7	1.7	1,360	
Br.Virgin Is	132	211	345	342	393	437	0.2	0.3	0.3	14.9	11.2	1,295	19,302
Cayman Islands	236	394	559	518	519	353	0.3	0.4	0.2	0.2	-32.0	2,105	7,974
Cuba	243	963	1,737	1,846	1,915	1,920	0.4	1.3	1.3	3.7	0.3	850	169
Curaçao	120	175	189	223	222	239	0.2	0.1	0.2	-0.4	7.5	1,075	
Dominica	25	42	48	54	61	56	0.0	0.0	0.0	12.3	-7.2	710	815
Dominican Rp	818	1,571	2,860	3,128	3,152	3,518	1.2	2.2	2.4	0.8	11.6	955	389
Grenada	38	76	93	104	83	71	0.1	0.1	0.0	-19.5	-14.4	725	798
Guadeloupe	197	458	418	..	..	246	0.3	0.3	0.2			660	548
Haiti	46	90	128	93	87	110	0.1	0.1	0.1	-6.5	26.4	980	14
Jamaica	740	1,069	1,333	1,355	1,438	1,545	1.1	1.0	1.1	6.1	7.4	1,045	565
Martinique	240	384	302	247	291	280	0.3	0.2	0.2	17.8	-3.8	580	647
Montserrat	7	17	9	7	9	9	0.0	0.0	0.0	17.1	4.7	925	962
Puerto Rico	1,366	1,828	2,388	2,677	3,024	3,239	2.0	1.8	2.2	13.0	7.1	880	828
Saint Lucia	154	230	281	282	326	356	0.2	0.2	0.2	15.5	9.3	1,120	2,140
St.Kitts-Nev	58	63	58	75	103	107	0.1	0.0	0.1	37.3	4.1	845	2,753
St.Maarten	316	349	511	538	613	619	0.5	0.4	0.4	13.9	1.1	1,325	
St.Vincent,Grenadines	56	53	82	91	96	105	0.1	0.1	0.1	5.5	9.4	1,100	893
Trinidad Tbg	95	77	213	249	341	453	0.1	0.2	0.3	36.9	32.8	980	421
Turks,Caicos	37	53	285	..	..	..	0.1	0.2					
US.Virgin Is	697	822	1,206	1,257	1,356	1,491	1.0	0.9	1.0	7.9	10.0	2,560	13,715
Central America	**735**	**1,523**	**2,958**	**3,421**	**3,965**	**4,645**	**1.1**	**2.3**	**3.2**	**15.9**	**17.2**	**740**	**120**
Belize	44	78	111	117	133	214	0.1	0.1	0.1	13.5	60.7	905	760
Costa Rica	275	681	1,302	1,199	1,359	1,570	0.4	1.0	1.1	13.3	15.6	935	391
El Salvador	18	85	217	383	441	543	0.0	0.2	0.4	15.1	23.2	560	81
Guatemala	185	213	482	621	776	869	0.3	0.4	0.6	25.0	12.0	660	72
Honduras	29	107	260	356	414	464	0.0	0.2	0.3	16.3	12.1	690	65
Nicaragua	12	50	129	160	192	206	0.0	0.1	0.1	19.9	7.4	290	38
Panama	172	309	458	585	651	780	0.2	0.4	0.5	11.3	19.8	1,110	248
South America	**4,946**	**7,189**	**9,216**	**8,597**	**10,553**	**12,397**	**7.1**	**7.0**	**8.6**	**22.8**	**17.5**	**680**	**33**
Argentina	1,131	2,222	2,904	2,006	2,235	2,729	1.6	2.2	1.9	11.4	22.1	715	69
Bolivia	55	55	68	167	192	239	0.1	0.1	0.2	15.1	24.5	475	27
Brazil	1,492	972	1,810	2,479	3,222	3,861	2.2	1.4	2.7	30.0	19.8	720	21
Chile	540	911	819	883	1,095	1,109	0.8	0.6	0.8	24.0	1.3	545	69
Colombia	406	657	1,030	893	1,058	1,218	0.6	0.8	0.8	18.5	15.1	1,305	28
Ecuador	188	255	402	406	462	486	0.3	0.3	0.3	13.8	5.0	565	36
French Guiana	..	..	..	..	..	45			0.0			475	230
Guyana	27	33	75	26	27	35	0.0	0.1	0.0	3.8	29.6	300	46
Paraguay	128	137	73	64	70	78	0.2	0.1	0.1	9.5	11.5	230	12
Peru	217	428	837	963	1,142	1,308	0.3	0.6	0.9	18.6	14.6	880	47
Suriname	1	21	16	4	17	45	0.0	0.0	0.0	325.0	164.7	280	103
Uruguay	238	611	713	345	494	594	0.3	0.5	0.4	43.3	20.3	330	174
Venezuela	496	849	423	331	502	650	0.7	0.3	0.4	51.7	29.5	920	26

Source: World Tourism Organization (UNWTO) ©

(Data as collected by UNWTO for TMT 2006 Edition)

World Tourism Organization ©

International Tourism Receipts by Country of Destination

	International Tourism Receipts (US$, million)						Market share in the region (%)			Change (%)		Receipts per arrival[1]	Receipts per capita[1]
	1990	1995	2000	2003	2004	2005*	1990	2000	2005*	04/03	05*/04		US$
Asia and the Pacific	*41,138*	*75,928*	*85,224*	*93,536*	*123,900*	*134,475*	*100*	*100*	*100*	*32.5*	*8.5*	*865*	*37*
North-East Asia	**17,284**	**31,339**	**39,428**	**42,336**	**58,627**	**65,368**	**42.0**	**46.3**	**48.6**	**38.5**	**11.5**	**745**	**42**
China	2,218	8,730	16,231	17,406	25,739	29,296	5.4	19.0	21.8	47.9	13.8	625	22
Hong Kong (China)	4,682	7,760	5,907	7,137	8,999	10,292	11.4	6.9	7.7	26.1	14.4	695	1,492
Japan	3,578	3,224	3,373	8,817	11,269	6,630	8.7	4.0	4.9	27.8	-41.2	985	52
Korea, D P Rp	29	..	..	..	..	..	0.1						
Korea, Republic of	3,559	5,150	6,834	5,358	6,069	5,806	8.7	8.0	4.3	13.3	-4.3	965	119
Macao (China)	1,473	3,102	3,208	5,155	7,479	7,980	3.6	3.8	5.9	45.1	6.7	885	17,765
Mongolia	5	21	36	143	185	177	0.0	0.0	0.1	29.4	-4.4	525	63
Taiwan (pr. of China)	1,740	3,286	3,738	2,977	4,054	4,977	4.2	4.4	3.7	36.2	22.8	1,475	217
South-East Asia	**14,479**	**27,354**	**26,710**	**25,084**	**32,843**	**33,847**	**35.2**	**31.3**	**25.2**	**30.9**	**3.1**	**685**	**59**
Cambodia	..	53	304	389	604	840		0.4	0.6	55.1	39.2	590	62
Indonesia	2,105	5,229	4,975	4,037	4,798	4,521	5.1	5.8	3.4	18.8	-5.8	905	19
Lao P.D.R.	3	51	114	87	119	147	0.0	0.1	0.1	36.7	23.4	220	24
Malaysia	1,667	3,969	5,011	5,898	8,198	8,543	4.1	5.9	6.4	39.0	4.2	520	357
Myanmar	9	151	162	56	84	..	0.0	0.2		50.0		345	2
Philippines	1,306	1,136	2,156	1,544	2,017	2,265	3.2	2.5	1.7	30.6	12.3	865	26
Singapore	4,937	7,611	5,142	3,781	5,221	5,908	12.0	6.0	4.4	38.1	13.2	835	1,335
Thailand	4,326	8,039	7,468	7,828	10,034	9,591	10.5	8.8	7.1	28.2	-4.4	830	149
Vietnam	85	..	..	1,400	1,700	1,880	0.2			21.4	10.6	540	23
Oceania	**7,321**	**13,831**	**14,289**	**19,386**	**23,802**	**25,622**	**17.8**	**16.8**	**19.1**	**22.8**	**7.6**	**2,445**	**783**
American Samoa	10	..	..	..	..	..	0.0						
Australia	4,246	8,125	9,274	12,349	15,191	16,866	10.3	10.9	12.5	23.0	11.0	3,360	840
Cook Is	16	28	36	69	72	92	0.0	0.0	0.1	4.3	27.8	1,040	4,301
Fiji	202	291	182	340	420	434	0.5	0.2	0.3	23.3	3.3	790	485
French Polynesia	171	326	..	480	523	522	0.4		0.4	8.9	-0.3	2,505	1,928
Guam	936	..	..	..	..	..	2.3						
Kiribati	1	2	3	..	..	..	0.0	0.0					
Marshall Is	..	3	4	..	..	..		0.0					
Micronesia (Fed.St.of)	..	..	15	17	17	17		0.0	0.0	-1.2	3.6	900	158
N.Mariana Is	455	655	..	..	..	..	1.1						
New Caledonia	94	108	111	196	241	253	0.2	0.1	0.2	22.7	5.1	2,515	1,170
New Zealand	1,030	2,318	2,267	3,981	4,790	4,865	2.5	2.7	3.6	20.3	1.6	2,055	1,206
Niue	..	2	..	..	..	1			0.0			430	
Palau	..	..	53	76	97	97		0.1	0.1	28.2	0.3	1,130	4,789
Papua New Guinea	41	25	21	16	18	4	0.1	0.0	0.0	16.1	-80.3	50	1
Samoa	20	35	41	54	70	77	0.0	0.0	0.1	29.6	10.0	755	434
Solomon Is	7	16	4	2	4	2	0.0	0.0	0.0	127.4	-56.2	165	3
Tonga	9	10	7	14	15	11	0.0	0.0	0.0	7.1	-26.7	265	98
Vanuatu	39	45	56	52	64	74	0.1	0.1	0.1	23.1	15.6	1,190	360
South Asia	**2,055**	**3,404**	**4,797**	**6,729**	**8,628**	**9,638**	**5.0**	**5.6**	**7.2**	**28.2**	**11.7**	**1,210**	**6**
Bangladesh	11	25	50	57	67	70	0.0	0.1	0.1	17.2	4.8	335	0
Bhutan	2	5	10	8	12	19	0.0	0.0	0.0	50.0	48.6	1,360	8
India	1,539	2,581	3,460	4,463	6,170	7,524	3.7	4.1	5.6	38.2	21.9	1,920	7
Iran	61	67	467	1,033	1,044	992	0.1	0.5	0.7	1.1	-5.0	630	15
Maldives	89	211	321	402	408	287	0.2	0.4	0.2	1.6	-29.7	725	821
Nepal	64	177	158	200	230	132	0.2	0.2	0.1	15.0	-42.7	350	5
Pakistan	156	110	81	122	179	181	0.4	0.1	0.1	46.7	1.1	225	1
Sri Lanka	132	226	248	441	513	429	0.3	0.3	0.3	16.3	-16.4	780	21

Source: World Tourism Organization (UNWTO) ©

(Data as collected by UNWTO for TMT 2006 Edition)

International Tourism Receipts by Country of Destination

	International Tourism Receipts (US$, million)						Market share in the region (%)			Change (%)		Receipts per arrival[1]	Receipts per capita[1]
	1990	1995	2000	2003	2004	2005*	1990	2000	2005*	04/03	05*/04		US$
Europe	*142,885*	*212,105*	*232,446*	*283,753*	*328,888*	*348,765*	*100*	*100*	*100*	*15.9*	*6.0*	*795*	*396*
Northern Europe	**26,267**	**33,916**	**35,938**	**41,399**	**49,275**	**53,891**	**18.4**	**15.5**	**15.5**	**19.0**	**9.4**	**1,060**	**605**
Denmark	3,645	3,673	3,694	5,265	5,670	4,956	2.6	1.6	1.4	7.7	-12.6	1,085	912
Finland	1,167	1,641	1,411	1,873	2,076	2,186	0.8	0.6	0.6	10.8	5.3	695	419
Iceland	151	186	229	320	372	409	0.1	0.1	0.1	16.2	10.1	470	1,378
Ireland	1,453	2,208	2,633	3,856	4,398	4,744	1.0	1.1	1.4	14.1	7.9	645	1,181
Norway	1,570	2,238	2,050	2,659	3,136	3,495	1.1	0.9	1.0	18.0	11.5	915	761
Sweden	2,906	3,471	4,064	5,297	6,196	7,427	2.0	1.7	2.1	17.0	19.9	2,370	825
United Kingdom	15,375	20,500	21,857	22,656	28,221	30,675	10.8	9.4	8.8	24.6	8.7	1,095	508
Western Europe	**63,114**	**80,776**	**82,774**	**103,183**	**117,870**	**122,459**	**44.2**	**35.6**	**35.1**	**14.2**	**3.9**	**860**	**658**
Austria	13,417	12,927	9,931	13,954	15,582	16,012	9.4	4.3	4.6	11.7	2.8	800	1,956
Belgium	..	4,548	6,592	8,191	9,233	9,868		2.8	2.8	12.7	6.9	1,465	952
Belgium/Luxembourg	3,702	..	..	..	..	..							
France	20,184	27,541	30,757	36,593	40,841	42,276	14.1	13.2	12.1	11.6	3.5	555	697
Germany	14,245	18,001	18,693	23,106	27,668	29,173	10.0	8.0	8.4	19.7	5.4	1,355	354
Luxembourg	..	1,721	1,806	2,994	3,657	3,616		0.8	1.0	22.2	-1.1	3,960	7,716
Netherlands	4,155	6,578	7,217	9,159	10,333	10,475	2.9	3.1	3.0	12.8	1.4	1,045	638
Switzerland	7,411	9,459	7,777	9,186	10,556	11,040	5.2	3.3	3.2	14.9	4.6	1,525	1,474
Central/Eastern Europe	**2,097**	**19,633**	**20,350**	**24,047**	**28,930**	**32,445**	**1.5**	**8.8**	**9.3**	**20.3**	**12.2**	**375**	**85**
Armenia	..	1	38	73	85	141		0.0	0.0	16.4	65.9	445	47
Azerbaijan	228	70	63	58	65	77	0.2	0.0	0.0	12.1	18.5	65	10
Belarus	..	23	93	267	270	253		0.0	0.1	1.1	-6.3	2,785	25
Bulgaria	320	473	1,076	1,693	2,221	2,430	0.2	0.5	0.7	31.2	9.4	500	326
Czech Rep	419	2,880	2,973	3,556	4,172	4,668	0.3	1.3	14.4	17.3	11.9	735	456
Estonia	..	357	508	669	891	951		0.2	0.3	33.2	6.8	495	714
Georgia	..	..	97	147	177	241		0.0	0.1	20.1	36.7	430	52
Hungary	824	2,953	3,757	4,046	4,061	4,271	0.6	1.6	1.2	0.4	5.2	425	427
Kazakhstan	..	122	356	564	718	701		0.2	0.2	27.3	-2.4	225	46
Kyrgyzstan	..	5	15	48	76	73		0.0	0.0	58.3	-3.9	230	14
Latvia	..	20	131	222	267	341		0.1	0.1	20.1	27.8	305	149
Lithuania	..	77	391	638	776	921		0.2	0.3	21.7	18.7	460	256
Poland	358	6,614	5,677	4,069	5,833	6,274	0.3	2.4	1.8	43.4	7.6	415	163
Rep Moldova	..	57	39	58	96	107		0.0	0.0	65.5	11.1	4,635	24
Romania	106	590	359	448	505	1,060	0.1	0.2	0.3	12.7	109.9	740	47
Russian Federation	..	4,312	3,429	4,502	5,225	5,564		1.5	1.6	16.1	6.5	280	39
Slovakia	70	623	433	865	901	1,210	0.0	0.2	0.3	4.2	34.3	800	223
Tajikistan	..	..	..	2	1	2			0.0	-50.0	100.0		0
Ukraine	..	191	394	935	2,560	3,125		0.2	0.9		22.1	165	66
Uzbekistan	..	..	27	24	28	..		0.0		16.7		105	1
Southern/Mediter. Eu.	**51,408**	**77,781**	**93,385**	**115,124**	**132,812**	**139,970**	**36.0**	**40.2**	**40.1**	**15.4**	**5.4**	**895**	**624**
Albania	4	65	389	522	727	860	0.0	0.2	0.2	39.3	18.3	18,705	241
Bosnia & Herzg	..	..	233	376	483	514		0.1	0.1	28.5	6.5	2,365	116
Croatia	..	1,349	2,782	6,304	6,848	7,463		1.2	2.1	8.6	9.0	880	1,660
Cyprus	1,258	1,798	1,941	2,091	2,252	2,331	0.9	0.8	0.7	7.7	3.5	945	2,988
F.Yug.Rp.Macedonia	..	19	38	57	72	84		0.0	0.0	26.6	16.9	425	41
Greece	2,587	4,135	9,219	10,741	12,872	13,731	1.8	4.0	3.9	19.8	6.7	960	1,287
Israel	1,396	2,993	4,088	2,060	2,380	2,853	1.0	1.8	0.8	15.6	19.9	1,500	455
Italy	16,458	28,731	27,493	31,247	35,656	35,398	11.5	11.8	10.1	14.1	-0.7	970	609
Malta	496	654	590	721	773	759	0.3	0.3	0.2	7.2	-1.9	650	1,903
Portugal	3,555	4,831	5,243	6,616	7,707	7,712	2.5	2.3	2.2	16.5	0.1	725	730
Serbia & Montenegro	..	42	30	201	..	..		0.0				420	19
Slovenia	..	1,082	965	1,340	1,630	1,801		0.4	0.5	21.6	10.5	1,160	895
Spain	18,484	25,252	29,968	39,645	45,248	47,970	12.9	12.9	13.8	14.1	6.0	860	1,189
Turkey	3,225	4,957	7,636	13,203	15,888	18,152	2.3	3.3	5.2	20.3	14.2	895	261
Yugoslav SFR	2,774	..	..	..	..	..	1.9						

Source: World Tourism Organization (UNWTO) ©

(Data as collected by UNWTO for TMT 2006 Edition)

World Tourism Organization ©

International Tourism Receipts by Country of Destination

	International Tourism Receipts (US$, million)						Market share in the region (%)			Change (%)		Receipts per arrival[1]	Receipts per capita[1]
	1990	1995	2000	2003	2004	2005*	1990	2000	2005*	04/03	05*/04		US$
Middle East	*4,279*	*9,744*	*15,242*	*19,740*	*25,239*	*26,254*	*100*	*100*	*100*	*27.9*	*4.0*	*685*	*133*
Bahrain	135	247	573	720	864	920	3.2	3.8	3.5	20.0	6.5	235	1,337
Egypt	1,100	2,684	4,345	4,584	6,125	6,851	25.7	28.5	26.1	33.6	11.8	830	88
Iraq	173	18	2	..	..	..	4.1	0.0					
Jordan	512	660	723	1,062	1,330	1,441	12.0	4.7	5.5	25.2	8.3	480	250
Kuwait	132	121	98	117	176	164	3.1	0.6	0.6	50.2	-6.8	1,940	70
Lebanon	..	..	..	6,374	5,411	5,432			20.7	-15.1	0.4	4,765	1,420
Libyan Arab Jamahiriya	6	2	75	205	218	250	0.1	0.5	1.0	6.3	14.7	1,465	43
Oman	69	..	221	385	414	481	1.6	1.5	1.8	7.4	16.4	345	160
Palestine	..	255	283	107	56	..		1.9		-47.7		1,000	15
Qatar	..	..	128	369	498	760		0.8	2.9	35.0	52.8	835	881
Saudi Arabia	..	..	..	3,413	6,486	5,177			19.7	90.0	-20.2	645	196
Syrian Arab Republic	320	1,258	1,082	773	1,800	2,175	7.5	7.1	8.3	132.9	20.8	645	118
Untd Arab Emirates	315	632	1,063	1,439	1,594	2,200	7.4	7.0	8.4	10.8	38.0	245	858
Yemen	20	50	73	139	213	262	0.5	0.5	1.0	53.2	23.0	780	13

Source: World Tourism Organization (UNWTO) ©   (Data as collected by UNWTO for TMT 2006 Edition)

[1] Last year with data available

| : change of series.

See for tables in US$ values pages Annex - 11 to Annex – 15

International Tourism Receipts by Country of Destination

	International Tourism Receipts (euro, million)						Market share in the region (%)			Change (%)		Receipts per arrival[1]	Receipts per capita[1]
	1990	1995	2000	2003	2004	2005*	1990	2000	2005*	04/03	05*/04		euro
Africa	*5,027*	*6,502*	*11,264*	*14,173*	*15,221*	*17,396*	*100*	*100*	*100*	*7.4*	*14.3*	*465*	*22*
North Africa	**1,832**	**2,192**	**4,138**	**4,365**	**4,899**	**5,641**	**36.4**	**36.7**	**32.4**	**12.2**	**15.2**	**405**	**49**
Algeria	82	25	104	99	144	148	1.6	0.9	0.9	44.9	3.1	100	5
Morocco	989	991	2,208	2,851	3,154	3,714	19.7	19.6	21.4	10.6	17.8	635	114
Sudan	16	6	5	16	17	72	0.3	0.0	0.4	6.1	324.3	290	2
Tunisia	744	1,170	1,821	1,399	1,584	1,707	14.8	16.2	9.8	13.2	7.8	270	169
West Africa	**475**	**414**	**1,022**	**1,175**	**1,159**	**1,520**	**9.5**	**9.1**	**8.7**	**-1.3**	**31.1**	**425**	**6**
Benin	43	65	83	94	96	..	0.9	0.7		2.1		550	13
Burkina Faso	9	..	21	26	37	..	0.2	0.2		41.2		165	3
Cape Verde	5	8	44	77	80	102	0.1	0.4	0.6	3.6	28.5	520	245
Côte d'Ivoire	40	68	53	61	66	67	0.8	0.5	0.4	8.1	1.2	340	4
Gambia	20	21	52	45	46	50	0.4	0.5	0.3	2.3	8.2	450	31
Ghana	64	8	363	366	375	640	1.3	3.2	3.7	2.4	70.8	1,495	29
Guinea	24	1	13	27	24	..	0.5	0.1		-12.0		540	3
Guinea-Bissau	..	..	..	2	1	..				-54.5			1
Mali	37	19	43	113	113	119	0.7	0.4	0.7	-0.5	5.7	835	10
Mauritania	7	8	..	..	..	..	0.1						
Niger	13	5	25	25	25	27	0.3	0.2	0.2	0.7	9.7	430	2
Nigeria	20	13	109	44	17	14	0.4	1.0	0.1	-61.4	-14.2	15	0
Senegal	131	128	156	185	170	..	2.6	1.4		-7.8		255	15
Sierra Leone	15	44	12	53	47	51	0.3	0.1	0.3	-12.1	10.3	1,285	9
Togo	46	10	9	13	15	..	0.9	0.1		15.2		185	3
Central Africa	**77**	**102**	**155**	**230**	**220**	**260**	**1.5**	**1.4**	**1.5**	**-4.5**	**18.0**	**330**	**2**
Angola	10	8	19	43	53	71	0.2	0.2	0.4	22.1	34.0	340	6
Cameroon	42	28	62	101	..	..	0.8	0.5					6
Cent.Afr.Rep.	2	3	5	4	3	..	0.0	0.0		-9.1		395	1
Chad	6	33	15	..	..	..	0.1	0.1					
Congo	6	11	13	26	18	27	0.1	0.1	0.2	-31.0	54.5		8
Dem.R.Congo	5	..	..	1	1	..	0.1			-6.9		25	0
Equatorial Guinea	1	1	5	..	..	..	0.0	0.0					
Gabon	2	14	22	13	8	..	0.0	0.2		-39.4		60	6
Sao Tome Prn	2	..	11	9	10	11	0.0	0.1	0.1	9.8	6.2	1,040	58
East Africa	**1,009**	**1,776**	**2,573**	**2,710**	**3,056**	**3,275**	**20.1**	**22.8**	**18.8**	**12.8**	**7.1**	**405**	**12**
Burundi	3	1	1	1	1	1	0.1	0.0	0.0	55.9	25.0	10	0
Comoros	2	17	16	9	10	11	0.0	0.1	0.1	6.2	12.8	580	17
Djibouti	..	3	..	6	5	6			0.0	-10.7	4.3	190	12
Eritrea	..	44	39	65	59	53		0.3	0.3	-10.3	-9.6	635	11
Ethiopia	20	12	62	101	140	135	0.4	0.5	0.8	38.8	-3.3	595	2
Kenya	348	372	306	307	390	465	6.9	2.7	2.7	27.1	19.2	305	14
Madagascar	31	44	131	39	45	50	0.6	1.2	0.3	15.7	10.7	180	3
Malawi	13	13	28	21	19	19	0.2	0.2	0.1	-6.4	-0.1	45	2
Mauritius	192	329	587	615	686	700	3.8	5.2	4.0	11.4	2.2	920	569
Mozambique	..	..	80	86	77	104		0.7	0.6	-11.2	36.0	180	5
Reunion	..	216	320	365	360	355		2.8	2.0	-1.4	-1.3	870	457
Rwanda	8	2	5	23	35	39	0.2	0.0	0.2	53.8	11.3		5
Seychelles	99	99	151	151	138	154	2.0	1.3	0.9	-8.8	11.9	1,200	1,902
Tanzania	51	384	408	572	600	662	1.0	3.6	3.8	4.9	10.4	1,120	18
Uganda	8	60	179	163	206	306	0.2	1.6	1.8	26.5	48.8	655	11
Zambia	32	36	120	132	129	132	0.6	1.1	0.8	-1.7	1.8	195	12
Zimbabwe	47	111	135	54	156	80	0.9	1.2	0.5	188.8	-48.9	50	7
Southern Africa	**1,634**	**2,019**	**3,376**	**5,692**	**5,887**	**6,700**	**32.5**	**30.0**	**38.5**	**3.4**	**13.8**	**610**	**131**
Botswana	92	124	241	404	442	452	1.8	2.1	2.6	9.3	2.3	270	275
Lesotho	13	21	26	25	27	24	0.3	0.2	0.1	10.4	-11.8	80	12
Namibia	67	213	173	292	324	279	1.3	1.5	1.6	11.1	-13.8	360	138
South Africa	1,438	1,625	2,896	4,883	5,050	5,890	28.6	25.7	33.9	3.4	16.6	800	133
Swaziland	24	37	40	89	43	55	0.5	0.4	0.3	-51.4	27.8	65	49

Source: World Tourism Organization (UNWTO) ©

(Data as collected by UNWTO for TMT 2006 Edition)

World Tourism Organization ©

International Tourism Receipts by Country of Destination

	International Tourism Receipts (euro, million)						Market share in the region (%)			Change (%)		Receipts per arrival[1]	Receipts per capita[1]
	1990	1995	2000	2003	2004	2005*	1990	2000	2005*	04/03	05*/04		euro
Americas	*54,335*	*75,258*	*141,618*	*100,880*	*106,136*	*116,167*	*100*	*100*	*100*	*5.2*	*9.5*	*870*	*131*
North America	**43,090**	**59,243**	**109,864**	**74,484**	**78,956**	**86,060**	**79.3**	**77.6**	**74.1**	**6.0**	**9.0**	**955**	**198**
Canada	4,978	6,053	11,669	9,323	10,347	10,918	9.2	8.2	9.4	11.0	5.5	580	333
Mexico	4,339	4,724	8,980	8,276	8,679	9,488	8.0	6.3	8.2	4.9	9.3	435	89
United States	33,773	48,467	89,215	56,885	59,930	65,654	62.2	63.0	56.5	5.4	9.6	1,335	222
Caribbean	**6,784**	**9,354**	**18,573**	**15,773**	**15,509**	**16,409**	**12.5**	**13.1**	**14.1**	**-1.7**	**5.8**	**875**	**423**
Anguilla	27	38	61	53	56	69	0.1	0.0	0.1	4.9	24.7	1,115	5,234
Antigua,Barb	234	189	315	265	272	263	0.4	0.2	0.2	2.5	-3.3	1,070	3,825
Aruba	275	398	881	759	849	877	0.5	0.6	0.8	11.8	3.4	1,195	12,254
Bahamas	1,047	1,029	1,878	1,554	1,515	1,665	1.9	1.3	1.4	-2.5	9.9	1,035	5,518
Barbados	388	476	783	670	623	624	0.7	0.6	0.5	-6.9	0.1	1,140	2,237
Bermuda	385	373	467	308	342	346	0.7	0.3	0.3	11.3	0.9	1,280	5,287
Bonaire	14	28	64	75	67	68	0.0	0.0	0.1	-9.7	1.7	1,095	
Br.Virgin Is	104	161	374	302	316	351	0.2	0.3	0.3	4.5	11.2	1,040	15,515
Cayman Islands	185	301	605	458	417	284	0.3	0.4	0.2	-8.9	-32.0	1,690	6,409
Cuba	191	736	1,881	1,632	1,540	1,543	0.4	1.3	1.3	-5.7	0.2	680	136
Curaçao	94	134	205	197	179	192	0.2	0.1	0.2	-9.4	7.5	865	
Dominica	20	32	52	48	49	45	0.0	0.0	0.0	2.1	-7.2	570	655
Dominican Rp	642	1,201	3,097	2,765	2,534	2,828	1.2	2.2	2.4	-8.4	11.6	765	312
Grenada	30	58	101	92	67	57	0.1	0.1	0.0	-26.8	-14.4	585	642
Guadeloupe	155	350	453	..	..	198	0.3	0.3	0.2			530	441
Haiti	36	69	139	82	70	88	0.1	0.1	0.1	-14.9	26.4	790	11
Jamaica	581	817	1,443	1,198	1,156	1,242	1.1	1.0	1.1	-3.5	7.4	840	454
Martinique	188	294	327	218	234	225	0.3	0.2	0.2	7.1	-3.8	465	520
Montserrat	5	13	10	6	7	7	0.0	0.0	0.0	6.5	4.7	745	773
Puerto Rico	1,073	1,397	2,585	2,366	2,431	2,603	2.0	1.8	2.2	2.7	7.1	705	666
Saint Lucia	121	176	304	249	262	286	0.2	0.2	0.2	5.0	9.3	900	1,720
St.Kitts-Nev	46	48	63	66	83	86	0.1	0.0	0.1	24.9	4.1	680	2,213
St.Maarten	248	267	553	476	493	498	0.5	0.4	0.4	3.6	1.0	1,065	
St.Vincent,Grenadines	44	41	89	80	77	84	0.1	0.1	0.1	-4.1	9.4	885	718
Trinidad Tbg	75	59	231	220	274	364	0.1	0.2	0.3	24.5	32.8	785	339
Turks,Caicos	29	41	309	..	..	..	0.1	0.2					
US.Virgin Is	547	628	1,306	1,111	1,090	1,198	1.0	0.9	1.0	-1.9	9.9	2,060	11,024
Central America	**577**	**1,164**	**3,203**	**3,025**	**3,187**	**3,734**	**1.1**	**2.3**	**3.2**	**5.4**	**17.1**	**595**	**96**
Belize	35	60	120	104	107	172	0.1	0.1	0.1	3.2	60.7	725	611
Costa Rica	216	521	1,410	1,060	1,092	1,262	0.4	1.0	1.1	3.0	15.5	750	314
El Salvador	14	65	235	339	354	436	0.0	0.2	0.4	4.6	23.1	450	65
Guatemala	145	163	522	549	624	698	0.3	0.4	0.6	13.6	12.0	530	58
Honduras	23	82	281	314	332	373	0.0	0.2	0.3	5.7	12.1	555	52
Nicaragua	9	38	139	142	154	166	0.0	0.1	0.1	9.0	7.4	235	30
Panama	135	236	496	517	523	627	0.2	0.4	0.5	1.2	19.8	895	200
South America	**3,884**	**5,496**	**9,978**	**7,599**	**8,484**	**9,964**	**7.1**	**7.0**	**8.6**	**11.6**	**17.5**	**545**	**27**
Argentina	888	1,699	3,144	1,773	1,797	2,193	1.6	2.2	1.9	1.3	22.1	575	55
Bolivia	43	42	74	147	154	192	0.1	0.1	0.2	4.7	24.4	380	22
Brazil	1,172	743	1,960	2,191	2,590	3,104	2.2	1.4	2.7	18.2	19.8	580	17
Chile	424	696	887	781	880	891	0.8	0.6	0.8	12.7	1.3	440	56
Colombia	319	502	1,116	790	851	979	0.6	0.8	0.8	7.7	15.1	1,050	23
Ecuador	148	195	435	359	372	390	0.3	0.3	0.3	3.5	5.0	455	29
French Guiana	..	..	..	..	..	36			0.0			380	185
Guyana	21	25	81	23	22	28	0.0	0.1	0.0	-5.6	29.6	240	37
Paraguay	101	105	79	56	56	62	0.2	0.1	0.1	-0.4	11.5	185	10
Peru	170	327	906	851	918	1,052	0.3	0.6	0.9	7.8	14.5	710	38
Suriname	1	16	17	4	14	36	0.0	0.0	0.0	286.5	164.7	225	83
Uruguay	187	467	772	305	397	478	0.3	0.5	0.4	30.3	20.3	265	140
Venezuela	389	649	458	293	404	522	0.7	0.3	0.4	37.9	29.5	740	21

Source: World Tourism Organization (UNWTO) ©   (Data as collected by UNWTO for TMT 2006 Edition)

International Tourism Receipts by Country of Destination

	International Tourism Receipts (euro, million)						Market share in the region (%)			Change (%)		Receipts per arrival[1]	Receipts per capita[1]
	1990	1995	2000	2003	2004	2005*	1990	2000	2005*	04/03	05*/04	euro	
Asia and the Pacific	*32,305*	*58,048*	*92,272*	*82,687*	*99,606*	*108,090*	*100*	*100*	*100*	*20.5*	*8.5*	*695*	*29*
North-East Asia	**13,573**	**23,959**	**42,688**	**37,426**	**47,132**	**52,543**	**42.0**	**46.3**	**48.6**	**25.9**	**11.5**	**600**	**34**
China	1,742	6,674	17,573	15,387	20,692	23,548	5.4	19.0	21.8	34.5	13.8	505	18
Hong Kong (China)	3,677	5,932	6,395	6,309	7,234	8,273	11.4	6.9	7.7	14.7	14.4	560	1,199
Japan	2,810	2,465	3,652	7,794	9,059	5,329	8.7	4.0	4.9	16.2	-41.2	790	42
Korea, D P Rp	23	..	..	..	..	..	0.1						
Korea, Republic of	2,795	3,937	7,400	4,737	4,879	4,667	8.7	8.0	4.3	3.0	-4.4	775	96
Macao (China)	1,157	2,372	3,474	4,557	6,013	6,414	3.6	3.8	5.9	32.0	6.7	710	14,280
Mongolia	4	16	39	126	149	142	0.0	0.0	0.1	17.6	-4.4	420	51
Taiwan (pr. of China)	1,366	2,512	4,047	2,632	3,259	4,000	4.2	4.4	3.7	23.8	22.7	1,185	175
South-East Asia	**11,370**	**20,912**	**28,919**	**22,175**	**26,403**	**27,206**	**35.2**	**31.3**	**25.2**	**19.1**	**3.0**	**550**	**47**
Cambodia	..	41	329	344	485	675		0.4	0.6	41.1	39.2	475	50
Indonesia	1,653	3,998	5,386	3,569	3,857	3,634	5.1	5.8	3.4	8.1	-5.8	725	15
Lao P.D.R.	2	39	123	77	96	118	0.0	0.1	0.1	24.3	23.4	175	19
Malaysia	1,309	3,034	5,425	5,214	6,590	6,867	4.1	5.9	6.4	26.4	4.2	420	287
Myanmar	7	115	175	50	68	..	0.0	0.2		36.4		280	1
Philippines	1,026	868	2,334	1,365	1,622	1,821	3.2	2.5	1.7	18.8	12.3	695	21
Singapore	3,877	5,819	5,567	3,342	4,197	4,749	12.0	6.0	4.4	25.6	13.2	670	1,073
Thailand	3,397	6,146	8,085	6,920	8,066	7,709	10.5	8.8	7.1	16.6	-4.4	665	120
Vietnam	67	..	..	1,238	1,367	1,511	0.2		1.4	10.4	10.6	435	18
Oceania	**5,749**	**10,574**	**15,471**	**17,137**	**19,135**	**20,595**	**17.8**	**16.8**	**19.1**	**11.7**	**7.6**	**1,965**	**630**
American Samoa	8	..	..	..	..	..	0.0						
Australia	3,334	6,212	10,041	10,917	12,212	13,557	10.3	10.9	12.5	11.9	11.0	2,700	675
Cook Is	13	21	39	61	58	74	0.0	0.0	0.1	-5.1	27.8	835	3,457
Fiji	159	222	197	301	337	349	0.5	0.2	0.3	12.1	3.3	635	390
French Polynesia	134	249	..	424	420	419	0.4		0.4	-0.9	-0.3	2,015	1,550
Guam	735	..	..	..	..	..	2.3						
Kiribati	1	2	3	..	..	..	0.0	0.0					
Marshall Is	..	2	4	..	..	..		0.0					
Micronesia (Fed.St.of)	..	..	16	15	13	14		0.0	0.0	-10.1	3.6	725	127
N.Mariana Is	357	501	..	..	..	..	1.1						
New Caledonia	74	83	120	174	194	204	0.2	0.1	0.2	11.5	5.1	2,020	940
New Zealand	809	1,772	2,454	3,519	3,851	3,911	2.5	2.7	3.6	9.4	1.5	1,655	969
Niue	..	2	..	..	..	1			0.0			345	
Palau	..	..	57	67	78	78		0.1	0.1	16.6	0.3	905	3,849
Papua New Guinea	32	19	23	14	15	3	0.1	0.0	0.0	5.6	-80.3	40	1
Samoa	16	27	44	48	56	62	0.0	0.0	0.1	17.9	10.0	610	349
Solomon Is	5	12	4	1	3	1	0.0	0.0	0.0	106.8	-56.2	130	2
Tonga	7	8	8	12	12	9	0.0	0.0	0.0	-2.6	-26.7	210	79
Vanuatu	31	34	61	46	51	59	0.1	0.1	0.1	11.9	15.6	960	289
South Asia	**1,614**	**2,602**	**5,194**	**5,949**	**6,936**	**7,747**	**5.0**	**5.6**	**7.2**	**16.6**	**11.7**	**970**	**5**
Bangladesh	9	19	54	50	54	56	0.0	0.1	0.1	6.6	4.8	270	0
Bhutan	2	4	11	7	10	15	0.0	0.0	0.0	36.4	48.5	1,095	7
India	1,208	1,973	3,746	3,945	4,960	6,048	3.7	4.1	5.6	25.7	21.9	1,545	6
Iran	48	51	506	913	839	797	0.1	0.5	0.7	-8.1	-5.0	505	12
Maldives	70	161	347	355	328	230	0.2	0.4	0.2	-7.6	-29.7	585	660
Nepal	50	135	171	177	185	106	0.2	0.2	0.1	4.6	-42.7	280	4
Pakistan	123	84	88	108	144	145	0.4	0.1	0.1	33.4	1.1	180	1
Sri Lanka	104	173	269	390	412	345	0.3	0.3	0.3	5.8	-16.4	630	17

Source: World Tourism Organization (UNWTO) ©

(Data as collected by UNWTO for TMT 2006 Edition)

World Tourism Organization ©

International Tourism Receipts by Country of Destination

	International Tourism Receipts (euro, million)						Market share in the region (%)			Change (%)		Receipts per arrival[1]	Receipts per capita[1]
	1990	1995	2000	2003	2004	2005*	1990	2000	2005*	04/03	05*/04		euro
Europe	*112,205*	*162,159*	*251,670*	*250,843*	*264,400*	*280,335*	*100*	*100*	*100*	*5.4*	*6.0*	*640*	*318*
Northern Europe	**20,627**	**25,930**	**38,910**	**36,597**	**39,614**	**43,317**	**18.4**	**15.5**	**15.5**	**8.2**	**9.3**	**850**	**487**
Denmark	2,862	2,808	3,999	4,655	4,559	3,984	2.6	1.6	1.4	-2.1	-12.6	875	733
Finland	916	1,255	1,528	1,656	1,669	1,757	0.8	0.6	0.6	0.8	5.3	560	336
Iceland	119	142	247	283	299	329	0.1	0.1	0.1	5.7	10.0	375	1,108
Ireland	1,141	1,688	2,851	3,409	3,536	3,813	1.0	1.1	1.4	3.7	7.8	520	950
Norway	1,233	1,711	2,220	2,350	2,521	2,809	1.1	0.9	1.0	7.3	11.4	735	612
Sweden	2,282	2,654	4,400	4,682	4,981	5,969	2.0	1.7	2.1	6.4	19.9	1,905	663
United Kingdom	12,074	15,672	23,665	20,028	22,688	24,656	10.8	9.4	8.8	13.3	8.7	880	408
Western Europe	**49,562**	**61,755**	**89,620**	**91,216**	**94,759**	**98,432**	**44.2**	**35.6**	**35.1**	**3.9**	**3.9**	**690**	**529**
Austria	10,536	9,883	10,752	12,336	12,527	12,870	9.4	4.3	4.6	1.5	2.7	645	1,572
Belgium	..	3,477	7,137	7,241	7,423	7,932		2.8	2.8	2.5	6.9	1,175	765
Belgium/Luxembourg	2,907	..	..	..	..	..							
France	15,850	21,056	33,301	32,349	32,833	33,981	14.1	13.2	12.1	1.5	3.5	450	560
Germany	11,187	13,762	20,239	20,426	22,243	23,449	10.0	8.0	8.4	8.9	5.4	1,090	284
Luxembourg	..	1,316	1,956	2,646	2,940	2,906		0.8	1.0	11.1	-1.2	3,185	6,202
Netherlands	3,263	5,029	7,814	8,097	8,307	8,420	2.9	3.1	3.0	2.6	1.4	840	513
Switzerland	5,820	7,232	8,420	8,121	8,486	8,874	5.2	3.3	3.2	4.5	4.6	1,230	1,185
Central/Eastern Europe	**1,647**	**15,010**	**22,032**	**21,258**	**23,257**	**26,079**	**1.5**	**8.8**	**9.3**	**9.4**	**12.1**	**300**	**68**
Armenia	..	1	41	65	68	113		0.0	0.0	5.9	65.9	355	38
Azerbaijan	179	54	68	51	52	62	0.2	0.0	0.0	1.9	18.4	55	8
Belarus	..	18	101	236	217	203		0.0	0.1	-8.0	-6.3	2,240	20
Bulgaria	251	362	1,165	1,496	1,785	1,953	0.2	0.5	0.7	19.3	9.4	405	262
Czech Rep	329	2,202	3,219	3,144	3,354	3,752	0.3	1.3	1.3	6.7	11.9	590	366
Estonia	..	273	550	591	716	764		0.2	0.3	21.1	6.7	400	574
Georgia	..	..	105	130	142	194		0.0	0.1	9.2	36.7	345	41
Hungary	647	2,258	4,067	3,577	3,265	3,433	0.6	1.6	1.2	-8.7	5.1	340	343
Kazakhstan	..	93	386	499	577	563		0.2	0.2	15.7	-2.4	180	37
Kyrgyzstan	..	4	16	42	61	59		0.0	0.0	44.0	-4.0	185	11
Latvia	..	15	142	197	215	274		0.1	0.1	9.2	27.8	245	120
Lithuania	..	59	424	564	624	740		0.2	0.3	10.6	18.6	370	206
Poland	281	5,057	6,147	3,597	4,689	5,043	0.3	2.4	1.8	30.4	7.5	330	131
Rep Moldova	..	44	43	51	77	86		0.0	0.0	50.5	11.0	3,725	19
Romania	83	451	389	396	406	852	0.1	0.2	0.3	2.5	109.9	595	38
Russian Federation	..	3,297	3,713	3,980	4,200	4,472		1.5	1.6	5.6	6.5	225	31
Slovakia	55	476	469	765	724	972	0.0	0.2	0.3	-5.3	34.2	640	179
Tajikistan	..	..	..	2	1	2			0.0	-54.5	100.0		0
Ukraine	..	146	427	827	2,058	2,512		0.2	0.9		22.1	130	53
Uzbekistan	..	..	29	21	23	..		0.0		6.1		85	1
Southern/Mediter. Eu.	**40,369**	**59,465**	**101,108**	**101,771**	**106,771**	**112,507**	**36.0**	**40.2**	**40.1**	**4.9**	**5.4**	**715**	**502**
Albania	3	50	421	461	585	692	0.0	0.2	0.2	26.7	18.3	15,035	194
Bosnia & Herzg	..	..	252	332	388	413		0.1	0.1	16.8	6.4	1,900	93
Croatia	..	1,031	3,012	5,573	5,506	5,999		1.2	2.1	-1.2	9.0	710	1,334
Cyprus	988	1,375	2,102	1,848	1,811	1,874	0.9	0.8	0.7	-2.0	3.5	760	2,402
F.Yug.Rp.Macedonia	..	15	41	50	58	67		0.0	0.0	15.2	16.8	340	33
Greece	2,032	3,161	9,981	9,495	10,348	11,037	1.8	4.0	3.9	9.0	6.7	775	1,035
Israel	1,097	2,288	4,426	1,821	1,914	2,293	1.0	1.8	0.8	5.1	19.8	1,205	365
Italy	12,924	21,965	29,767	27,623	28,665	28,453	11.5	11.8	10.1	3.8	-0.7	780	490
Malta	389	500	639	638	622	610	0.3	0.3	0.2	-2.5	-1.9	520	1,530
Portugal	2,792	3,693	5,677	5,849	6,195	6,199	2.5	2.3	2.2	5.9	0.1	585	587
Serbia & Montenegro	..	32	32	178	..	..		0.0				370	16
Slovenia	..	827	1,045	1,184	1,310	1,447		0.4	0.5	10.6	10.5	930	720
Spain	14,515	19,306	32,446	35,047	36,376	38,558	12.9	12.9	13.8	3.8	6.0	690	956
Turkey	2,533	3,790	8,268	11,672	12,773	14,590	2.3	3.3	5.2	9.4	14.2	720	209
Yugoslav SFR	2,178	..	..	..	..	..	1.9						

(Data as collected by UNWTO for TMT 2006 Edition)

International Tourism Receipts by Country of Destination

	International Tourism Receipts (euro, million)						Market share in the region (%)			Change (%)		Receipts per arrival[1]	Receipts per capita[1]
	1990	1995	2000	2003	2004	2005*	1990	2000	2005*	04/03	05*/04		euro
Middle East	*3,360*	*7,449*	*16,502*	*17,450*	*20,290*	*21,103*	*100*	*100*	*100*	*16.3*	*4.0*	*550*	*107*
Bahrain	106	189	620	636	695	739	3.2	3.8	3.5	9.1	6.5	190	1,074
Egypt	864	2,052	4,704	4,052	4,924	5,506	25.7	28.5	26.1	21.5	11.8	670	71
Iraq	136	14	2	..	..	..	4.1	0.0					
Jordan	402	505	783	939	1,069	1,158	12.0	4.7	5.5	13.9	8.3	390	201
Kuwait	104	93	106	104	142	132	3.1	0.6	0.6	36.6	-6.9	1,560	57
Lebanon	..	..	..	5,635	4,350	4,366			20.7	-22.8	0.4	3,830	1,141
Libyan Arab Jamahiriya	5	2	81	181	175	201	0.1	0.5	1.0	-3.3	14.7	1,175	35
Oman	54	..	239	340	332	387	1.6	1.5	1.8	-2.3	16.3	280	129
Palestine	..	195	306	95	45	..		1.9		-52.4		805	12
Qatar	..	..	138	326	400	611		0.8	2.9	22.8	52.7	670	708
Saudi Arabia	..	..	..	3,017	5,214	4,162			19.7	72.8	-20.2	520	158
Syrian Arab Republic	251	962	1,171	683	1,447	1,748	7.5	7.1	8.3	111.8	20.8	520	95
Untd Arab Emirates	247	483	1,151	1,272	1,281	1,768	7.4	7.0	8.4	0.7	38.0	215	690
Yemen	16	38	79	123	171	211	0.5	0.5	1.0	39.4	23.0	625	10

Source: World Tourism Organization (UNWTO) ©

(Data as collected by UNWTO for TMT 2006 Edition)

[1] Last year with data available

| : change of series.

World Tourism Organization ©

3.   Methodological Notes

3.1   Concepts and Definitions

According to the UNWTO/United Nations *Recommendations on Tourism Statistics*, Tourism comprises *the activities of persons travelling to and staying in places outside their usual environment for not more than one consecutive year for leisure, business and other purposes.*

This concept can be applied to different forms of tourism. Depending upon whether a person is travelling to, from or within a certain country the following forms can be distinguished:
*   **Inbound Tourism**, involving the non-residents received by a destination country from the point of view of that destination;
*   **Outbound Tourism**, involving residents travelling to another country from the point of view of the country of origin;
*   **Domestic tourism**, involving residents of a given country travelling within that country.

All types of travellers engaged in tourism are described as visitors. Visitors can be distinguished as same-day visitors or tourists (overnight visitors).

There are various units of measure to quantify the volume of tourism. An overview is set out below:

Unit of measurement			Comment
Visitors	*Arrivals*	*- at frontiers (VF)*	or at a specific place in case of domestic tourism
Tourists (overnight visitors)	*Arrivals*	*- at frontiers (TF)*	
		- at collective tourism establishments (e.g. hotels and other, such as campings, etc.) (TCE) *- at hotels and similar establishments (THS)*	- excludes tourism in private accommodation; - arrivals are counted in every new accommodation visited
	Nights	*- at collective tourism establishments (e.g. hotels and other) (NCE)* *- at hotels and similar establishments (NHS)*	

Inbound Tourism
Unless otherwise stated, this report concentrates on **International Tourism** as measured from an **Inbound Tourism** perspective, i.e. the tourism received by any given destination country (and in a few cases territories) from non-residents travelling to that destination.

The most common unit of measure used to quantify the volume of International Tourism for statistical purposes is the number of International Tourist Arrivals. For a proper understanding of this unit, two considerations should be taken into account:
*   Data refer exclusively to tourists (overnight visitors): 'a visitor who stays at least one night in a collective or private accommodation in the country visited'. Same-day visitors are not included.
*   Data refer to the number of arrivals and not to the number of persons. The same person who makes several trips to a given country during a given period will be counted as a

new arrival each time, as well as a person who travels through several countries on one trip is counted as a new arrival each time.

Figures on the volume of international tourism presented in the regional and subregional tables, preferably relate to the concept of *international tourist arrivals at frontiers*. However, as not all countries are collecting data according to this concept, another series may be used instead. In the tables, the series are indicated as follows:

TF: International tourist arrivals at frontiers (excluding same-day visitors);
VF: International visitor arrivals at frontiers (including tourists and same-day visitors);
TCE: International tourist arrivals at collective tourism establishments;
THS: International tourist arrivals at hotels and similar establishments.

With respect to the inbound tourism volume, if available, in the profile tables for individual countries in Chapter III, except for data on International Tourist Arrivals, furthermore, data is included on International Visitor Arrivals, Same-day Visitor Arrivals, Cruise passengers (considered as a special category of same-day visitors) and Nights spent in collective establishments and / or in hotels and similar establishments.

Outbound Tourism

Data on outbound tourism volume in this series of reports originate from two different sources and likewise relate to two dissimilar concepts:

- On one hand, many countries are reporting the number of outbound trips of their residents. Data availability and comparability, however, is still limited and it is often not clear whether the reported figures refer only to tourists or to visitors in general.
- On the other hand, data are synthesised from the data on inbound tourism to destination countries (an arrival received in a destination can also be taken as an arrival generated by the generating country). Data on arrivals to destinations broken down by region of origin are taken to estimate and aggregate the number of arrivals originating from each region. The unit of measurement is the number of international tourist arrivals generated by the region of origin concerned. For a proper understanding, it should be borne in mind that these figures do not correspond to the number of trips, as one trip taken might result in various arrivals in destinations.

Domestic Tourism

International comparable data on domestic tourism is unfortunately still rather scarce. If available for a certain country, this series is represented in the profile tables for countries in Chapter III of the regional volumes in the form of the number of nights spent by residents at hotels and similar establishments and / or at all collective tourism establishments.

Accommodation

As a measure for the capacity of accommodation, data is included on the number of rooms or the number of bed places in the country. When expressed in bed places, the number of rooms roughly will be half, as rooms on average count two bed places. The actual capacity of a country might eventually be larger, as some countries exclude hotels below a certain category or less than a certain size.

International Tourism Receipts and Expenditure

International Tourism Receipts are the receipts earned by a destination country from inbound tourism and cover all tourism receipts resulting from expenditure made by visitors from abroad, on for instance lodging, food and drinks, fuel, transport in the country, entertainment, shopping, etc. This concept includes receipts generated by overnight as well as by same-day trips, which can be substantial, as will be the case with countries where a lot of shopping for goods and services takes place by visitors from neighbouring countries. It excludes, however, the receipts related to international transport contracted by residents of other countries (for instance ticket receipts from foreigners travelling with a national company). These receipts are covered in the separate category **International Fare Receipts**, which for most recent years is estimated at about 15-20% of total tourism and fare receipts.

International Tourism Expenditure is the expenditure on tourism outside their country of residence made by visitors (same-day visitors and tourists) from a given country of origin.

Data on receipts and expenditure related to international tourism are generally gathered in the framework of the Balance of Payments under the items 'Services, Travel, Credit and Debit' (International Tourism Receipts and Expenditure) and 'Transportation, Passenger Services, Credit and Debit' (International Fare Receipts and Expenditure). See the *Balance of Payments Statistics Yearbook, Part 2 and Part 3* of the International Monetary Fund (IMF) for details on methodologies, compilation practices and data sources.

The International Tourism Balance and International Fare Balance as included in the profile tables in Chapter III of the regional volumes correspond to the net receipts or expenditure of a given country on respectively international tourism or international fares, i.e. receipts less expenditure.

Further information
More detailed information on concepts, definitions, classifications, indicators, methods of compiling and units of measure can be obtained from:
- the *Basic References on Tourism Statistics* on the UNWTO website under the link <http://www.unwto.org/statistics/index.htm> setting out the main components that make up the System of Tourism Statistics (STS);

or from the following UNWTO publications:
- *Recommendations on tourism statistics* (1994),
- *Technical Manual No. 1: Concepts Definitions, and Classifications for Tourism Statistics* (1995);
- *Technical Manual No. 2: Collection for Tourism Expenditure Statistics* (1995);
- *Technical Manual No. 3: Collection of Domestic Tourism Statistics* (1995);
- *Technical Manual No. 4: Collection and Compilation of Tourism Statistics* (1995);
- *Data Collection & Analysis for Tourism Management, Marketing & Planning* (2000).

3.2   Sources, Data Treatment and Acknowledgement

General
Quantitative tourism-related data in this report is based on a selection of data included in the UNWTO database on World Tourism Statistics. This database contains a variety of series for over 200 countries and territories covering data for most countries from the 1980's on. The database is maintained by the UNWTO Secretariat and is updated on a continuous base.

Except where otherwise indicated, statistical data has been collected by the UNWTO Secretariat from the official institutions of the countries and territories (UNWTO member as well as non-member countries) or from other international bodies, e.g. the Caribbean Tourism Organization (CTO), the International Monetary Fund (IMF), etc.

The data for individual countries corresponding to 2005 are based on full year results, or projections, as communicated to the UNWTO Secretariat by the authorities of the countries and territories or disseminated through news releases, publications or on the Internet. For many countries, 2005 figures are still preliminary and subject to revision.

In the world and (sub)regional aggregates, estimates are included for countries and territories with data still missing based upon data available for a part of the year or the general trend for the region. In particular for the Middle East and Africa, the regional and subregional aggregates should be treated with caution as estimations are based on a relatively small number of countries and territories that supplied data for the entire year. In the tables, provisional figures are marked with an asterisk (*).

UNWTO tourism statistics generally refer to figures for a country as a whole. In the collection of statistics, however, except for independent states, there are also a number of dependencies or territories of special sovereignty included (for instance Hong Kong (China) or French Polynesia). These territories report tourism figures independently and are for the sake of tourism statistics considered as an entity in itself. Because of this, where reference is made to "countries" the term generally should be taken to mean "countries and territories". In a few other cases, dependencies are not separately listed but included in the total for the country they depend upon (for instance Guernsey, Jersey and the Isle of Man in United Kingdom).

In general, UNWTO does not collect data on the level of regions, states, provinces or specific destinations within a country (Hawaii is one of the few exceptions made because of its relevance for Asian outbound travel; in the overview tables, however, Hawaii is included in the United States figure). Most countries will have a further regional breakdown available as well as other series not included in the UNWTO database on World Tourism Statistics. Please refer to national sources for this data.

The regional country groupings are according to the UNWTO regional commissions. See the tables by country in the annex for the countries and territories included in the various regions and subregions.

The World Tourism Organization is aware of the limitations of the available statistical information on tourism. Despite the considerable progress made in recent decades, international tourism statistics are often not uniform, because definitions and methods of data collection tend to differ. Every user of this information should bear in mind that the international comparability of statistical data is still not optimal.

Tourism series in this report
The tourism data series in Chapter II and in the profile tables of countries in Chapter III correspond to the basic indicators included in the UNWTO *Compendium of Tourism Statistics*. Please refer to the latest publication for additional series, methodological references and notes on the series for specific countries.

A number of derived series are included relating tourism volume to the size of the population or tourism receipts and expenditure to tourism volume. In the profile tables in Chapter III, those series are marked with '-'. Ratios are based on simple divisions of the concept in question by the population or of the receipts or expenditure by the corresponding concepts:

$$\text{International Tourist Arrivals per 100 of inhabitants} = \frac{\text{International Tourist Arrivals}}{\text{Population}} * 100$$

Trips abroad per 100 of inhabitants = $\dfrac{\text{Trips abroad}}{\text{Population}} * 100$

International Tourism Receipts per International Tourist Arrival = $\dfrac{\text{International Tourism Receipts}}{\text{International Tourist Arrivals}}$

International Tourism Receipts per International Visitor Arrival = $\dfrac{\text{International Tourism Receipts}}{\text{International Visitor Arrivals}}$

International Tourism Receipts per capita = $\dfrac{\text{International Tourism Receipts}}{\text{Population}}$

International Tourism Expenditure per trip abroad = $\dfrac{\text{International Tourism Expenditure}}{\text{Trips Abroad}}$

International Tourism Expenditure per capita = $\dfrac{\text{International Tourism Expenditure}}{\text{Population}}$

Financial data is generally collected and kept in the UNWTO database in US dollars. In the cases where countries report in local currency, values are transferred by UNWTO into US dollars applying the average exchange rate for the corresponding year. However, part of the tables are also published in euros. These euro values are in general derived from the US dollar values using the corresponding average annual exchange rates for the two currencies. The following exchange rates have been applied:

Exchange rates US$ versus euro (ECU for the years before 1999) annual averages

	€/ECU per US$	Change (%)	US$ per €/ECU	Change (%)
1995	0.76452		1.30801	
1996	0.78756	3.0	1.26975	-2.9
1997	0.88180	12.0	1.13404	-10.7
1998	0.89199	1.2	1.12109	-1.1
1999	0.93828	5.2	1.06578	-4.9
2000	1.08270	15.4	0.92361	-13.3
2001	1.11653	3.1	0.89563	-3.0
2002	1.05756	-5.3	0.94557	5.6
2003	0.88402	-16.4	1.13120	19.6
2004	0.80392	-9.1	1.24390	10.0
2005	0.80379	0.0	1.24410	0.0

Source: Eurostat, European Central Bank (ECB)

As exchange rates fluctuate substantially over time, the evolution of International Tourism Receipts is estimated in (weighted) local currencies. For this, receipts in US dollars are recomputed in local currencies using an exchange rate table provided by IMF. In order to take care of inflation, receipts are calculated in constant prices using country data on inflation from IMF as deflator.

The data in the tables on international tourist or visitor arrivals and nights of international tourists by country of origin included in Chapter III correspond to the series as included in the UNWTO *Yearbook of Tourism Statistics*. Please refer to the latter publication for additional series, metrological references and notes on the series for specific countries.

Series from external sources

Information included, but not referring to tourism indicators, are in general taken from specialised international organizations and not collected by the UNWTO Secretariat from the individual countries and territories. Data are meant as indicators, providing a context for tourism performance and do not necessarily coincide fully with national data. The following series are included:

Population

Data refer to total midyear population as included in the International Database (IDB) of the International Programs Center (IPC) of the Population Division of the U.S. Bureau of the Census, <www.census.gov/ipc/www>. The IDB combines data from country sources (especially censuses and surveys) with IPC's estimates and projections to provide information dating back as far as 1950 and as far ahead as 2050. The IDB can be considered as a practically complete and consistent set of population data covering 227 countries and areas with 1998 populations of 5,000 or more.

Area

Data on the dimension of the area of countries and territories are taken from the Statistical database of the Food and Agriculture Organization of the United Nations (FAO) <www.fao.org> and refer to the total area of the country, including area under inland water bodies for the year 2000. In the case of Belgium and Luxembourg data is taken from national sources.

Economic Indicators

The series on Gross Domestic Product (GDP), Gross Domestic Product per capita and economic growth (annual per cent change of Real Gross Domestic Product) are based on the World Economic Outlook (WEO) of the International Monetary Fund (IMF). See <www.imf.org/external/pubs/ft/weo/weorepts.htm>.

World Tourism Organization ©

4. Sources of Information

A. UNWTO website <www.unwto.org>

The UNWTO has a comprehensive website available with news and information on its programme activities, members, regional activities, publications, special projects, etc. in English, French and Spanish with a growing section in Russian, including:.

- A qualitative and quantitative overview of world tourism and selected statistical country data, available under the *Facts & Figures* link (see Tourism Indicators), including the most updated tourism trends and data in the *UNWTO World Tourism Barometer;*
- An overview of available publications and electronic products with detailed information on each item including contents and sample chapters can be found in the UNWTO Infoshop at <http://pub.unwto.org> or the WTOelibrary at <www.WTOelibrary.org>.

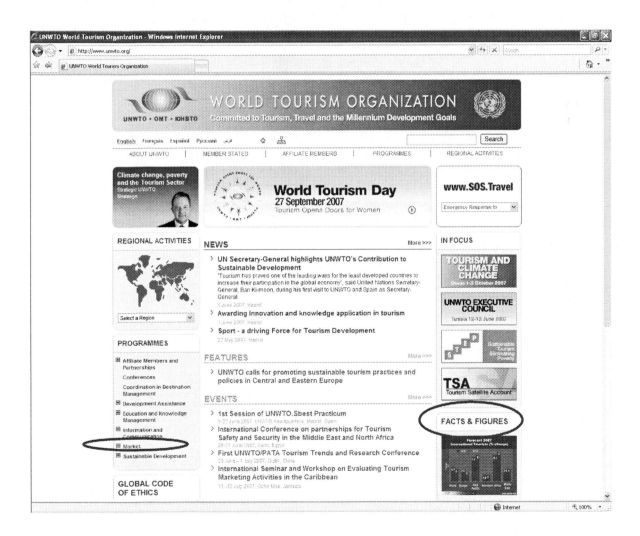

B.   *Related Publications of the World Tourism Organization*

Inbound Tourism

This report is part of the *Tourism Market Trends, 2006 Edition* series consisting of 6 volumes:
- World Overview and Tourism Topics (in English, French and Spanish);
- Africa (in English and French);
- Americas (in English and Spanish);
- Asia and the Pacific (in English);
- Europe (in English and French);
- Middle East (in English).

Excerpts of this series are included in:
- *Tourism Highlights, 2006 Edition* (in English, French, Spanish and Russian). The electronic version can be downloaded free of charge from the Facts & Figures section of the UNWTO website at <http://www.unwto.org/facts/menu.html>.

- *Special report No 23:* Inbound Tourism to the Middle East and North Africa (2003; in English).

Outbound Tourism

- *Tourism Generating Markets: Overview and Country Profiles* (1999; in English, French and Spanish).
- Special Reports on specific markets:
  - No. 4: *Outbound Tourism of Korea* (2001; in English).
  - No. 5: *Outbound Tourism of Australia* (2001; in English).
  - No. 6: *Outbound Tourism of Japan* (2001; in English).
  - No. 7: *Outbound Tourism of Belgium* (2001; in English).
  - No. 8: *Outbound Tourism of Spain* (2001; in English and Spanish).
  - No. 9: *Outbound Tourism of Japan & Korea, Results 2000* (2001; in English).
  - No. 21: *Outbound Tourism of Scandinavia, Market Profile* (2002; in English).
- *Youth Outbound Travel of the Germans, the British & the French* (2002, in English, French and Spanish).
- *Chinese Outbound Tourism* (2003; in English).
- *Outbound Tourism from Saudi Arabia* (2003; in English).

Short-term Indicators

- UNWTO *World Tourism Barometer* (3 times a year since June 2003; in electronic format (PDF) and print, in English, French and Spanish).

The *UNWTO World Tourism Barometer* monitors the short-term evolution of tourism and aims at providing adequate and timely information on the state of the sector. The Barometer is published three times a year (January, June, and October). It contains an overview of short-term tourism data from destination countries and tourism sectors such as air transport, a retrospective and prospective evaluation of tourism performance by the UNWTO Panel of Tourism Experts and selected economic data relevant for tourism.

For more information see the "Facts & Figures" section of the UNWTO website www.unwto.org.

Forecasting

UNWTO's long-term forecast *Tourism 2020 Vision* has been published in a series of 7 reports consisting of one summary volume and six regional volumes (2000, 2001):

- Global Forecasts and Profiles of Market Segments (in English, French and Spanish).
- Africa (in English and French).
- Americas (in English and Spanish).
- East Asia and the Pacific (in English).
- Europe (in English and French).
- Middle East (in English).
- South Asia (in English).

Tourism Products

- Tourism and Sport:
  - *Sport and Tourism. 1st World Conference* (in English, French and Spanish; forthcoming). Excerpts of the presentations and of the results of the World Conference on Sport and Tourism held February 2001 in Barcelona, Spain.
  - *Introductory Report on Sport & Tourism* (2001).
  - *Sport Activities during the outbound holidays of the Germans, the Dutch and the French* (2001, in English, French and Spanish).
  - *Deporte Y Turismo: Destino América Latina* (2003; in Spanish only).
- Ecotourism:
  - *Special report No. 10: The German Ecotourism Market* (2001).
  - *Special report No. 11: The British Ecotourism Market* (2001).
  - *Special report No. 12: The U.S. Ecotourism Market* (2002).
  - *Special report No. 13: The Italian Ecotourism Market* (2002).
  - *Special report No. 14: The Spanish Ecotourism Market* (2002).
  - *Special report No. 15: The Canadian Ecotourism Market* (2002).
  - *Special report No. 16: The French Ecotourism Market* (2002).
- MICE:
  - *MICE Outbound Tourism 2000* (2003; in English).
- Cruises:
  - *Worldwide Cruise Ship Activity* (2003; in English, French and Spanish).
- Cultural Tourism:
  - *City Tourism and Culture: The European Experience* (2005; in English, French and Spanish).

UNWTO Tourism Recovery Committee

- Special report No. 17: *The impact of the attacks in the United States on international tourism: An initial analysis* (included in the Annex of Special report No. 18, not available separately).
- Special report No. 18: *Tourism after 11 September 2001: Analysis, remedial actions and prospects* (2001; in English, French and Spanish).
- Special report No. 19: *Tourism Recovery Committee for the Mediterranean Region* (2002; in English, French and Spanish).
- Special report No. 20: *The impact of the September 11th attacks on tourism: The light at the end of the tunnel* (2002; in English, French and Spanish).
- Special report No. 21: *2002: Climbing Towards Recovery?* (2002; in English).
- Special report No. 22: *Fourth Meeting of the Tourism Recovery Committee - ITB Berlin 2003* (2003; in English).

Basic Statistical Reference

- *Compendium of Tourism Statistics* (2005; tri-lingual edition in English, French and Spanish and table descriptions in Arabic and Russian).
- *Yearbook of Tourism Statistics* (2005; tri-lingual edition in English, French and Spanish).

Statistical Methodology

- *Recommendations on Tourism Statistics* (1994; in English, French, Spanish, Russian, Arabic and Chinese).
- *Technical Manuals* (1995; in English, French, Spanish and Russian):
  - *No. 1: Concepts, Definitions and Classifications for Tourism Statistics.*
  - *No. 2: Collection of Tourism Expenditure Statistics.*
  - *No. 3: Collection of Domestic Tourism Statistics.*
  - *No. 4: Collection and Compilation of Tourism Statistics.*
- *Data Collection and Analysis for Tourism Management, Marketing and Planning* (2000; in English).

See for detailed information on concepts, definitions, classifications, indicators, methods of compiling and units of measure also the *Basic References on Tourism Statistics*, setting out the main components that make up the System of Tourism Statistics (STS), on the UNWTO website at: <http://www.unwto.org/statistics/index.htm>.

See for documentation on the Tourism Satellite Account methodology the UNWTO website at: <http://www.unwto.org/statistics/index.htm>.

Other

- *Tourism in the Age of Alliances, Mergers and Acquisitions* (2002, in English, French and Spanish).
- *Apuntes de la Metodología de la Investigación en Turismo* (2001, in Spanish only).
- *Marketing Papers No.1* (2002).
- *Evaluating NTO Marketing Activities* (2003; in English, French and Spanish).
- Special report No 26 - *The impact of rising oil prices on International Tourism* (2006; in English, French and Spanish).
- Structures and Budgets of National Tourism Organizations, 2004-2005 (2006; in English and Spanish)
- Handbook on Tourism Market Segmentation – Maximizing Marketing Effectiveness (2007, in English)

C. References

International Organizations

- United Nations; <www.un.org>.
- United Nations Development Programme; <www.undp.org>.
- International Monetary Fund (IMF); <www.imf.org>.
- World Bank; <www.worldbank.org>.
- Organisation for Economic Cooperation and Development (OECD); <www.oecd.org>.
- World Trade Organization (WTO); <www.wto.org>.

Country Sources

References for information on the Internet of National Tourism Administrations (NTA), National Tourism Organisations (NTO) and / or web directions for research and data are included in the country contributions of Chapter III of the regional volumes of the *Tourism Market Trends, 2006* series.